Microsoft Dynamics 365 Extensions Cookbook

More than 80 extension recipes to get the most out of Microsoft Dynamics CRM

Rami Mounla

Packt>

BIRMINGHAM - MUMBAI

Microsoft Dynamics 365 Extensions Cookbook

First published: June 2017

Production reference: 1020617

Published by Packt Publishing Ltd.
Livery Place
35 Livery Street
Birmingham
B3 2PB, UK.
ISBN 978-1-78646-417-0

www.packtpub.com

Credits

Author

Rami Mounla

Reviewer

Nicolae Tarla

Commissioning Editor

Aaron Lazar

Acquisition Editor

Shaon Basu

Content Development Editor

Lawrence Veigas

Technical Editors

Pranali Badge

Dhiraj Chandanshive

Copy Editor

Zainab Bootwala

Project Coordinator

Prajakta Naik

Proofreader

Safis Editing

Indexer

Tejal Daruwale Soni

Graphics

Abhinash Sahu

Production Coordinator

Melwyn Dsa

Foreword

We all need recipes! Some we learn from books, some we ask for, and some we accidentally stumble across. Software recipes are no different to culinary ones, in that, they enable us to cook up great things with ease and repeatability. Rami's *Microsoft Dynamics 365 Extensions Cookbook* is no exception!

I have followed Rami's technical community contributions and blog for many years, and so I was really pleased to learn of his well-deserved Microsoft MVP award back in 2015. When we first met, I was immediately struck by his infectious enthusiasm for Microsoft Dynamics CRM and related technologies, along with his commitment to continuously improving the way we deliver solutions on this unique platform.

Naturally, we both share the same passion for the benefits of using Microsoft Dynamics 365 online, along with all of its value-added services. Rami's recent major public sector implementation of Microsoft Dynamics 365 Online is the first of its kind in New Zealand, which clearly shows that the trust in Microsoft's ability to deliver a world class software-as-a-service is ever-growing. This is further evident as an increasing number of organizations are choosing Microsoft Dynamics 365 Online in conjunction with Microsoft Office 365 and Microsoft Azure to build their next generation of business solutions. Microsoft's continued and significant investment in areas such as Machine Learning, Big Data, and IoT (Internet of things) allows them to constantly reinvent the platform to increase the value and productivity that they can bring to their customers.

For me, Microsoft's platform-first approach has always been their market differentiator. Now that the Dynamics product team is being steered by Scott Guthrie (Microsoft executive vice president, Microsoft Cloud and Enterprise), we are increasingly seeing Microsoft Azure services being utilized to bring new features and to rapidly evolve the platform into areas that present exciting new "Digital Transformation" opportunities. For instance, companies that historically would have been purely focused on monitoring of their product sensors, now, with an Azure IoT Hub, can now take advantage of Microsoft Dynamics 365 to provide predictive maintenance to their customers through Microsoft Azure Machine Learning. Furthermore, sales organizations that previously relied on their sales staff to spend valuable time and effort on maintaining account plans can now use Customer Insights and LinkedIn Sales Navigator to increase productivity and drive business growth. These kinds of projects no longer need large teams of data scientists and machine learning researchers, but are available to us mere mortals, enabling our users and customers to do business in a way that was previously cost prohibitive and inaccessible to most.

In this book, Rami offers clear and concise solutions so that you may benefit from his many years' experience with the Microsoft Dynamics CRM and Microsoft Dynamics 365 platform, and get the most out of its powerful features and extensibility points. The recipes are logically organized into categories to make it easy to understand their applicability, each with not only clear and practical steps on how to implement them, but also crucial technical details of how and why they will work. We are certainly lucky to be part of such an active technical community with many great contributors, so I particularly like that for each technique Rami shows you, he also offers you additional resources to grow your understanding and develop your skills further.

It is true that we will rarely encounter an implementation challenge that has not already been solved by someone before us. I am a firm believer in learning from the experience of those people so that we may *stand on the shoulders of giants*! By following Rami's recipes in this book, no matter whether you are using Microsoft Dynamics 365 On-Premises or Dynamics 365 Online, if you are implementing large-scale enterprise solutions or smaller ones, the consistency and quality that the contents of this book will bring to your implementation will not only give you more time to focus on delivering business value, but also make your solutions more supportable and upgradable in the future.

As we see Microsoft continuing to develop their exciting platform, I am confident that by reading this book, you will learn many valuable practical skills from Rami that will accelerate your career into the next chapter of Microsoft Dynamics 365's evolution.

Scott Durow

Solution Architect, Develop 1 Ltd.

Microsoft Business Solutions MVP

Author of the Ribbon Workbench and SparkleXrm

About the Author

Rami Mounla is a Solution Architect with over 15 years of experience in IT. He was introduced to Dynamics CRM 3.0 when it first came out and has built a career around the product since then. Based in Wellington, New Zealand, his focus is on enterprise-scale Dynamics CRM solutions targeted at the public sector and large multinational corporations. Throughout his career, he has worked on some of the largest CRM implementations in New Zealand, both on-premise and in the cloud.

Rami is active in the Dynamics community, a leader of the Wellington Dynamics User Group, a frequent speaker at Microsoft Ignite New Zealand, and a supporter of open source Dynamics 365 extensions. His contributions over the last few years gained him the Microsoft Business Solutions MVP status in 2015, a title that reflects his ambitions.

After being frustrated with frequently reviewing poor-quality CRM implementations, Rami decided to write about best practices and promote quality CRM implementations. The topics and ideas inspired this book on extending Dynamics 365.

I would like to dedicate this book to my patient wife, Amanda, who supported me throughout the journey, despite having a 2-year-old and a newborn to look after. You rock!
To my two boys, Alexander and Riaan, who make every day worth it.
I would also like to thank my Mum and Pup without whom none of this would be possible.
A special mention to my brother Edd who pushed me really hard over the years to strive for excellence and encouraged me to write this book.
Thank you Aung Khaing for answering the tough questions and for the long conversations when I was tossing between ideas. Thank you Abhay Mishra and Mingyao Lin for the good times and for the coffees when I needed them the most.
Nicolae Tarla, thank you for all the constructive feedback and for sharing your years of experience in Dynamics and in book writing.
Scott Durow and the MVP family, thank you for your enthusiasm and for your ever-so-inspiring community work that encouraged me to become an MVP and to keep contributing.
Last but not least, thank you to the team at Packt for turning my dream into reality.

About the Reviewer

Nicolae Tarla is a Microsoft Dynamics 365 Consultant specialized in solution architecture and technical presales. He has worked on various mid-to-enterprise-level Dynamics CRM, Office 365, and SharePoint implementations for both the private and public sectors. He has been delivering Microsoft Dynamics CRM solutions since version 3.0 of the product.

Nicolae has participated as a technical reviewer and author on several books, presented at several events and conferences, and is blogging at `http://www.thecrmwiz.com`.

He was awarded the Business Solutions MVP title for his contributions to the Dynamics CRM Community.

I would like to thank the author for offering me the opportunity to review this book. It was a great experience assisting on this project.
In addition, a big thanks goes to the Dynamics 365 Community for appreciating these efforts, and driving us to give back and share our knowledge.

www.PacktPub.com

For support files and downloads related to your book, please visit www.PacktPub.com.

Did you know that Packt offers eBook versions of every book published, with PDF and ePub files available? You can upgrade to the eBook version at www.PacktPub.comand as a print book customer, you are entitled to a discount on the eBook copy. Get in touch with us at service@packtpub.com for more details.

At www.PacktPub.com, you can also read a collection of free technical articles, sign up for a range of free newsletters and receive exclusive discounts and offers on Packt books and eBooks.

Mapt

https://www.packtpub.com/mapt

Get the most in-demand software skills with Mapt. Mapt gives you full access to all Packt books and video courses, as well as industry-leading tools to help you plan your personal development and advance your career.

Why subscribe?

- Fully searchable across every book published by Packt
- Copy and paste, print, and bookmark content
- On demand and accessible via a web browser

Customer Feedback

Thanks for purchasing this Packt book. At Packt, quality is at the heart of our editorial process. To help us improve, please leave us an honest review on this book's Amazon page at `https://www.amazon.com/dp/1786464179`.

If you'd like to join our team of regular reviewers, you can e-mail us at `customerreviews@packtpub.com`. We award our regular reviewers with free eBooks and videos in exchange for their valuable feedback. Help us be relentless in improving our products!

Table of Contents

Preface

Microsoft Dynamics 365 is a powerful and versatile platform that has been around for more than a decade. With each release, the platform increased in richness and popularity. Being a moving target, it is often difficult to keep up with the features and capabilities introduced in the latest version. This book will help you narrow that knowledge gap in respect to the Dynamics CRM side of the product.

This *Microsoft Dynamics 365 Extensions Cookbook* not only covers classical configuration and customization extension topics, but also new Dynamics 365 features applicable to online Software-as-a-Service (SaaS) cloud ecosystems. Some topics are applicable to older versions of Dynamics CRM, but most cover new patterns, frameworks, and tools that synergise well with the latest version. Unorthodox ideas, design patterns, and best practices are discussed throughout the book, differentiating it from other pieces of work.

With its cookbook format, this book sets out to enable you to harness the power of the Dynamics 365 platform, and caters to your unique circumstances through simple-to-follow step-by-step extension recipes.

Hope you enjoy it.

What this book covers

`Chapter 1`, *No Code Extensions*, starts by covering some of the fundamental entity modeling techniques you could use when configuring your Dynamics 365 instance. This chapter also lightly touches on some of the point-and-click configuration capabilities of the platform, such as workflows, actions, rollup and calculated fields, and others.

`Chapter 2`, *Client-Side Extensions*, delves straight into the client-side development capabilities of the platform. It covers best practice reusability techniques, Web API queries, debugging walkthroughs, and advanced web resource building using frameworks such as AngularJS.

`Chapter 3`, *SDK Enterprise Capabilities*, lets you take a look inside the SDK for some valuable gems. Ranging from tools, to new Dynamics 365 features, to extensions that improve your productivity, this chapter is essential when working on large-scale enterprise solutions.

`Chapter 4`, *Server-Side Extensions*, guides you through the server-side customization's realm. Core to this book, this chapter deals with different ways of setting up your environment to build custom plugins, workflows, and activities. This chapter also walks you through server-side debugging techniques for online as well as on-premises Dynamics 365 implementations.

`Chapter 5`, *External Integration*, gives you a glimpse into different integration patterns. Using out-of-the-box interfaces or third-party tools, this chapter covers a few typical scenarios you might face in real life when integrating from and to Dynamics 365 whilst using different programming languages.

`Chapter 6`, *Enhancing Your Code*, builds on the previously discussed code extensions and introduces best practices and code structures to render your extensions cleaner and more maintainable--an essential practice when building large-scale solutions. Improved code structures further enable different types of unit testing possibilities that are also covered in this chapter. This chapter also briefly touches upon plugin profiling, building read audits, and setting up Cross Origin Resource Sharing with Dynamics 365 online.

`Chapter 7`, *Security*, covers core non-functional capabilities of the platform. With its comprehensive security capabilities, this chapter demonstrates different modeling techniques and features that will enhance your platform's security, such as team structures, field-level security, and encryption, along with their performance implications.

`Chapter 8`, *DevOps*, deals with the topics of source control integration and deployments by discussing solution structuring techniques, patching, automation, and release orchestration integration with third-party tools. This chapter's smaller recipes form the bigger picture for a complete continuous integration pipeline.

`Chapter 9`, *Dynamics 365 Extensions*, takes you beyond Dynamics CRM and covers the latest enhancements introduced with the Dynamics 365 rebranding. Dynamics 365 apps, AppSource, and the common data services with Flow are among the topics discussed in this chapter.

`Appendix A`, *Architectural Views*, is written in a solution architecture document format with different views to cater for different stakeholders. It covers a business view, a logical view, a deployment view, and a collection of non-functional requirement controls.

`Appendix B`, *Dynamics 365*, finishes off this book by talking about the significance of the Dynamics 365 release compared to previous Dynamics CRM releases, and ends the book with a brief conclusion.

What you need for this book

All recipes in this book will require a Microsoft Dynamics 365 instance up and running. Most recipes are targeted at the online version, with a good portion also applicable to on-premises instances.

It is highly recommended that you use a non-production instance to try the recipes. Alternatively, a trial version can be requested from `https://trials.dynamics.com/CustomerEngagement/ChangeSignup/`.

Code customization requires Microsoft Visual Studio to facilitate the development. At the time of writing, the most compatible version is Visual Studio 2015. Some of the recipes will also require the Dynamics 365 SDK.

Some recipes require third-party products and tools that need to be installed. Most offer a free trial or a free edition, as described in their respective recipes.

Who this book is for

This book is aimed at a wide audience. Mainly focused on people looking at extending Dynamics 365, it can also be used by executives and influencers to understand the platform's capabilities and versatility.

New or seasoned developers, administrators, consultants, and power users who want to learn about best practices when extending Dynamics 365 for enterprises will benefit the most from this book. The wide target audience is the reason for the range of different topic complexity covered in this book, ranging from no code configuration to complex coding customization.

A basic understanding of the Dynamics CRM/365 platform, as well as some basic development skills, are recommended, but not necessary.

Sections

In this book, you will find several headings that appear frequently (Getting ready, How to do it, How it works, There's more, and See also).

To give clear instructions on how to complete a recipe, we use these sections as follows.

Getting ready

This section tells you what to expect in the recipe, and describes how to set up any software or any preliminary settings required for the recipe.

How to do it...

This section contains the steps required to follow the recipe.

How it works...

This section usually consists of a detailed explanation of what happened in the previous section.

There's more...

This section consists of additional information about the recipe in order to make the reader more knowledgeable about the recipe.

See also

This section provides helpful links to other useful information for the recipe.

Conventions

In this book, you will find a number of text styles that distinguish between different kinds of information. Here are some examples of these styles and an explanation of their meaning.

Code words in text, database table names, folder names, filenames, file extensions, pathnames, dummy URLs, user input, and Twitter handles are shown as follows: "You will need to have access to a Dynamics 365 instance along with a `System Customizer security` role or higher."

A block of code is set as follows:

```
packtNs.graduateForm = packtNs.graduateForm || {};
packtNs.graduateForm.loadEvent = function(){
  Xrm.Page.getAttribute("packt_supervisor").addOnChange(
  populateWithTodaysDate);
}
```

Any command-line input or output is written as follows:

```
# cp /usr/src/asterisk-addons/configs/cdr_mysql.conf.sample
/etc/asterisk/cdr_mysql.conf
```

New terms and **important words** are shown in bold. Words that you see on the screen, for example, in menus or dialog boxes, appear in the text like this: "Navigate to **Settings** | **Solutions** | **Packt**."

Warnings or important notes appear in a box like this.

Tips and tricks appear like this.

Reader feedback

Feedback from our readers is always welcome. Let us know what you think about this book-what you liked or disliked. Reader feedback is important for us as it helps us develop titles that you will really get the most out of.

To send us general feedback, simply e-mail `feedback@packtpub.com`, and mention the book's title in the subject of your message.

If there is a topic that you have expertise in and you are interested in either writing or contributing to a book, see our author guide at `www.packtpub.com/authors` .

Customer support

Now that you are the proud owner of a Packt book, we have a number of things to help you to get the most from your purchase.

Downloading the example code

You can download the example code files for this book from your account at `http://www.packtpub.com`. If you purchased this book elsewhere, you can visit `http://www.packtpub.com/support`and register to have the files e-mailed directly to you.

You can download the code files by following these steps:

1. Log in or register to our website using your e-mail address and password.
2. Hover the mouse pointer on the **SUPPORT** tab at the top.
3. Click on **Code Downloads & Errata**.
4. Enter the name of the book in the **Search** box.
5. Select the book for which you're looking to download the code files.
6. Choose from the drop-down menu where you purchased this book from.
7. Click on **Code Download**.

You can also download the code files by clicking on the **Code Files** button on the book's webpage at the Packt Publishing website. This page can be accessed by entering the book's name in the **Search** box. Please note that you need to be logged in to your Packt account.

Once the file is downloaded, please make sure that you unzip or extract the folder using the latest version of:

- WinRAR / 7-Zip for Windows
- Zipeg / iZip / UnRarX for Mac
- 7-Zip / PeaZip for Linux

The code bundle for the book is also hosted on GitHub at `https://github.com/PacktPublishing/Microsoft-Dynamics-365-Extensions-Cookbook`. We also have other code bundles from our rich catalog of books and videos available at `https://github.com/PacktPublishing/`. Check them out!

Errata

Although we have taken every care to ensure the accuracy of our content, mistakes do happen. If you find a mistake in one of our books-maybe a mistake in the text or the code-we would be grateful if you could report this to us. By doing so, you can save other readers from frustration and help us improve subsequent versions of this book. If you find any errata, please report them by visiting `http://www.packtpub.com/submit-errata`, selecting your book, clicking on the **Errata Submission Form** link, and entering the details of your errata. Once your errata are verified, your submission will be accepted and the errata will be uploaded to our website or added to any list of existing errata under the Errata section of that title.

To view the previously submitted errata, go to `https://www.packtpub.com/books/content/support`and enter the name of the book in the search field. The required information will appear under the **Errata** section.

Piracy

Piracy of copyrighted material on the Internet is an ongoing problem across all media. At Packt, we take the protection of our copyright and licenses very seriously. If you come across any illegal copies of our works in any form on the Internet, please provide us with the location address or website name immediately so that we can pursue a remedy.

Please contact us at `copyright@packtpub.com` with a link to the suspected pirated material.

We appreciate your help in protecting our authors and our ability to bring you valuable content.

Questions

If you have a problem with any aspect of this book, you can contact us at `questions@packtpub.com`, and we will do our best to address the problem.

1
No Code Extensions

In this chapter, we will cover the following recipes:

- Modeling denormalized entities
- Modeling normalized entities with a common parent
- Modeling independent normalized entities
- Using a Business Rule to show and hide attributes
- Building a configurable e-mail notification workflow
- Building your first action
- Setting up rollup fields
- Setting up calculated fields
- Duplicate detection using alternate keys

Introduction

Commercial off-the-shelf products (**COTS**) are attractive options for enterprise organizations as they are packed with configurable out-of-the-box features that address a good portion of business requirements without writing any code. Dynamics 365 is no exception. Dynamics CRM 365 specifically offers a powerful modularized feature-rich product that can be tailored to suit your organization's needs.

Generally speaking, configurable, no-code extensions are cheaper to implement, easier to maintain, and easier to upgrade, as the product evolves. Modeled correctly, those extensions can greatly enhance the value of your investment. Modeled incorrectly, they can lead to a platform that is locked down to one purpose only.

Using the same analogy as that of the Dynamics 365 suite, you can build your CRM application for general use by loosely coupling your entities, or you can build a specialized application by tightly coupling all the content. The following picture taken from the Dynamics 365 Microsoft marketing pack visualizes a specialized implementation versus a more general one:

A specialized implementation is not necessarily wrong, as some applications won't make sense if rendered generic, especially as some organizations work in siloed business units. That said, most organizations prefer a more flexible implementation.

This chapter will cover different schema-modeling techniques to deal with different business scenarios, along with their respective pros and cons. It will also cover out-of-the-box configurable business logic extensions that were introduced over the last few years, which drastically reduce the amount of code required to configure implementations.

To give context to our configuration, we will model our entities based on a college solution with a student/contact management system. The system will hold contacts that can either be generic individuals, students with graduation details, or contractors working for the college.

Modeling denormalized entities

Typically, account and contact entities are the most commonly used entities in a Dynamics CRM implementation. In large implementations, those entities are usually also reused for multiple purposes. To illustrate the modeling pattern, this recipe will leverage the college solution described in the introduction. We shall concentrate on creating contacts that can either be individuals or students. Each type of contact requires a different set of attributes.

The easiest way of modeling a multi-purpose entity is to add all the required attributes for the different types to the same entity.

Getting ready

In order to configure the schema, you will need to have access to a Dynamics 365 instance along with a **System Customizer** or higher security role . As a best practice, it is always recommended that you implement your configuration within a solution. For the purpose of this book, it is expected that you already have a solution created called `Packt` with a publisher prefix of `packt_`.

How to do it

1. Navigate to **Settings** | **Solutions** | **Packt**.
2. Click on **Add Existing** | **Entity** and select **Contact**, as shown in the following screenshot:

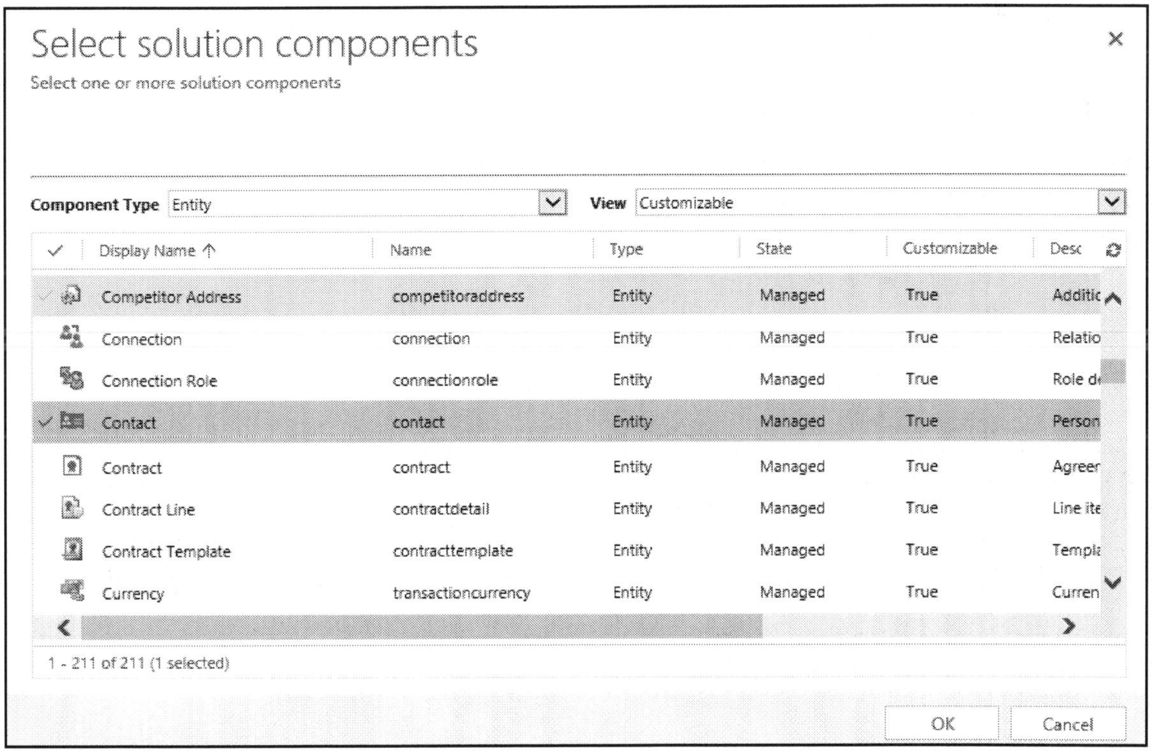

3. Select the necessary assets that support your configuration and add them to your solution, or, for simplicity, select **Add All Assets** and click on **Finish**:

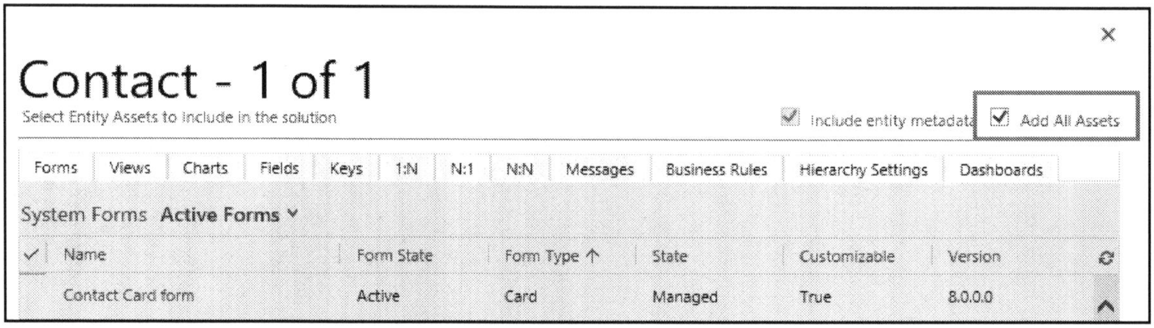

4. Click on **No, do not include required components**.
5. Navigate to **Entities** | **Contacts** | **Fields**.
6. Click on **New**, and create an attribute called `Student Id` of type **Single Line of Text**, and click on **Save and New**.
7. Create an **Option Set** attribute called `Contact` Type that contains two values; `Student` and `Other`. Then click on **Save and Close**.
8. Back in the solution, navigate to **Entities** | **Contact** | **Forms** and click on **New** | **Main Form** as per this screenshot:

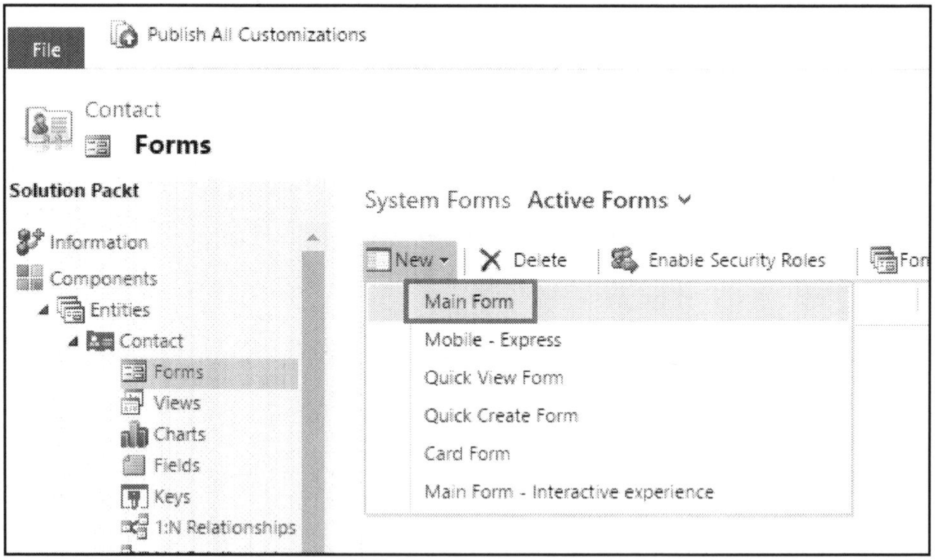

9. In the newly created form, add the two newly created fields to your form by dragging and dropping the entities from the right-hand window onto the form.
10. Click on the **Publish All Customizations** button for your solution.

How it works...

Just like database modeling, entities can be normalized or denormalized. Normalizing a structure is the action of separating it into several related tables to reduce redundant data or empty fields. Denormalizing a structure is the opposite: we merge two or more tables together to simplify the structure and improve query performance, whilst adding redundant or empty fields. In this recipe, the entity was denormalized to allow different types of contacts to be surfaced through the same contact entity.

In step 1 to step 4, we added the existing contact entity to the `Packt` solution. Notice that in step 3, we had the option to either add the necessary assets or add all assets. For this recipe's simplicity, we added all assets. With the recent granular solution enhancements, we can simply add what is required.

TIP

It is a best practice to minimize the number of unnecessary attributes and relationships in a solution to avoid conflicts and dependencies.

In step 5 to step 7, we created the attributes, and in step 8 and step 9, we added the attributes to a new contact form. In step 10, we published the configuration we implemented.

To avoid multi-solution dependencies and scenarios where a form is overwritten with an updated version from another solution, best practice dictates that you create a new form for your solution and mark it as default. Unnecessary forms can always be hidden by using Apps as described in `Chapter 9`, *Dynamics 365 extensions*.

Looking at the design of the updated entity, we have now configured the contact entity to fulfill more than one purpose: it is a generic contact as well as a student one.

A simplifiedEntity Relationship (ER) diagram is depicted in the following screenshot:

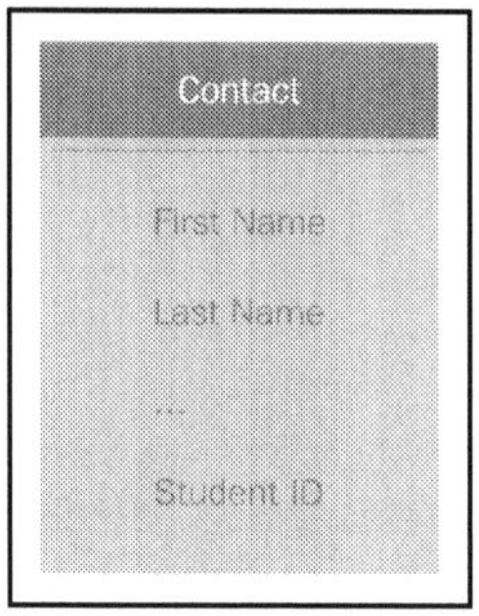

The advantages of a denormalized model are:

- Views will appear in the same combined list
- A quick and advanced find will include both types and display the results in the same list
- Positive form user experience, driven by the form configuration

The disadvantages of a denormalized model are:

- Security roles cannot easily be made specific to types
- Configuration/customization is required to show/hide irrelevant attributes or to mark them as mandatory or optional
- Records will contain blank fields when not applicable

See also

- *Modeling normalized entities with a common parent*
- *Modeling independent normalized entities*
- *Using Business Rule to show and hide attributes*
- The *Dynamics 365 applications* recipe of `Chapter 9`, *Dynamics 365 Extensions*

Modeling normalized entities with a common parent

Similar to database modeling, the alternative to a denormalized model, is, you guessed it, a normalized model. Normalizing a structure is the action of separating a table into two or more structures. Normalization reduces the number of redundant or unnecessary fields in a form. In the Dynamics 365 context, normalizing will help avoid overcrowding one entity by spreading the attributes across different entities whilst keeping a common parent.

In this recipe, we will carry on using the contact entity and extending its relationships to include additional attributes: student graduation details.

Getting ready

Similar to the previous recipe, **System Customizer** or higher security role is required to perform the configuration as well as a solution to contain the changes.

How to do it

1. Navigate to **Settings** | **Solutions** | **Packt**.
2. Click on **New** | **Entity**.
3. Enter `Graduation Details` in the **Display Name** field, and `Graduations Details` under the **Plural Name** field.

4. Before saving the new entity, untick all the check boxes on the form:

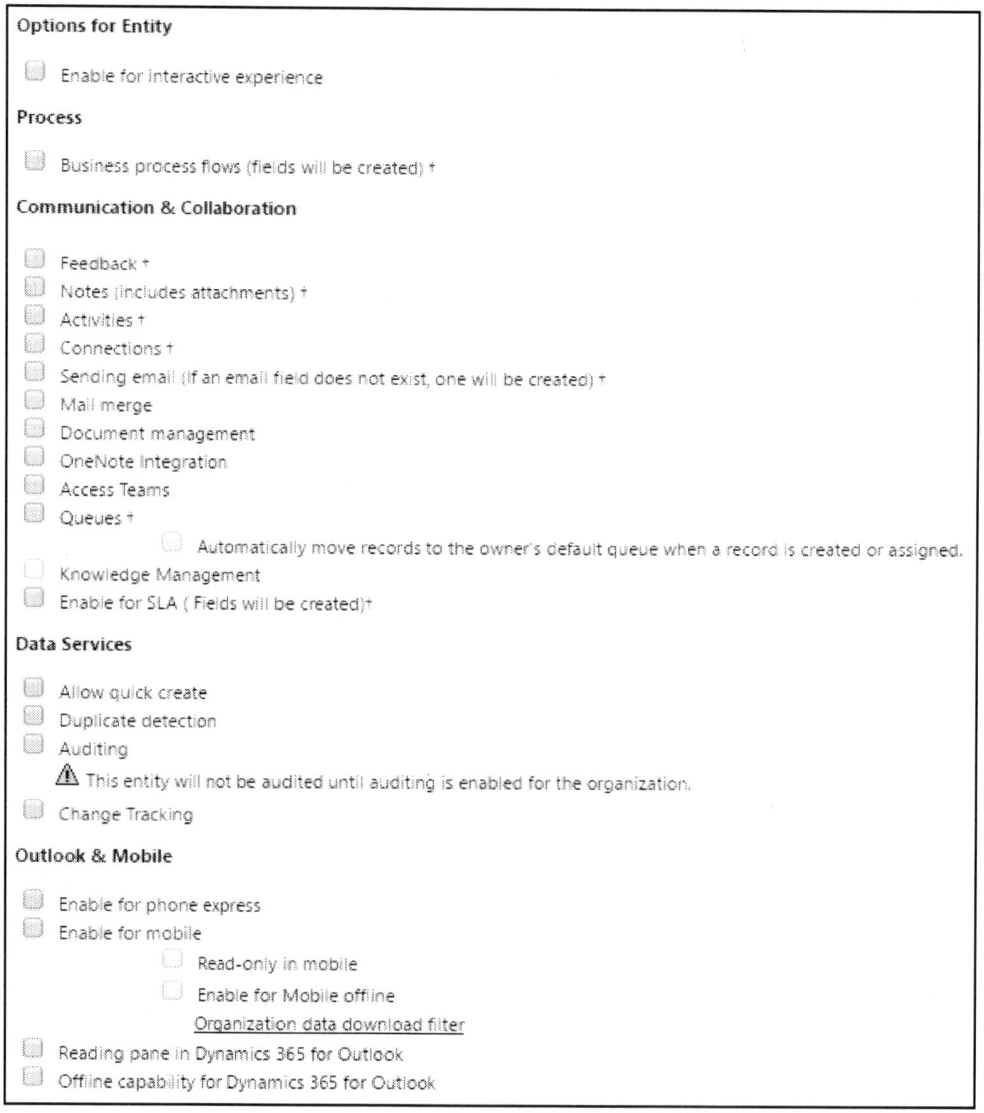

5. Click on the **Save** button.
6. Navigate to **Fields** on the left-hand side and click on **New**.
7. Create an attribute called `Supervisor` of type **Lookup** with a **Target Record Type** set to `user` and click on **Save and Close**.
8. Create another attribute called **Post Graduate Start Date** of type **Date and Time** and click on **Save and Close**.
9. Navigate to **Forms** and double-click the **Quick View Form** option.
10. Add the two attributes on your form by dragging and dropping them from the right-hand **Field Explorer**, then click on **Save and Close**.
11. Click on **Save and Close** on the entity as well to go back to your solution.
12. Navigate to **Entities** | **Contacts** | **N:1 relationships** | **New Many-to-1 Relationship**.
13. Enter **Graduation Details** in the primary contact field, **Display Name**: **Graduation Details** and click on **Save and Close**.
14. Navigate to the contact's **Forms** and double-click the **Main Information** form.
15. Add the newly created field to your form by dragging and dropping the **Graduation** attribute from the right-hand window on to the form.
16. Click on the **Insert** tab at the top followed by **Quick View Form**:

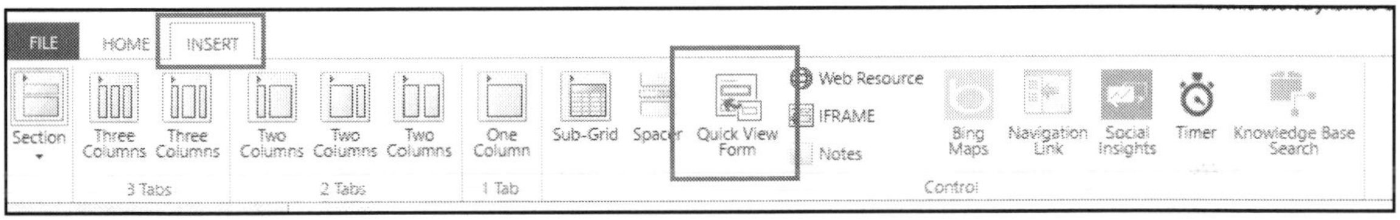

17. Enter the following details in the **Quick View Control Properties** window:
    - **Name**: `Graduation_Details`
    - **Label**: `Graduation Details`
    - **Lookup Field**: `Graduation Details`
    - **Quick View Form**: `Information`

18. Click on **OK**:

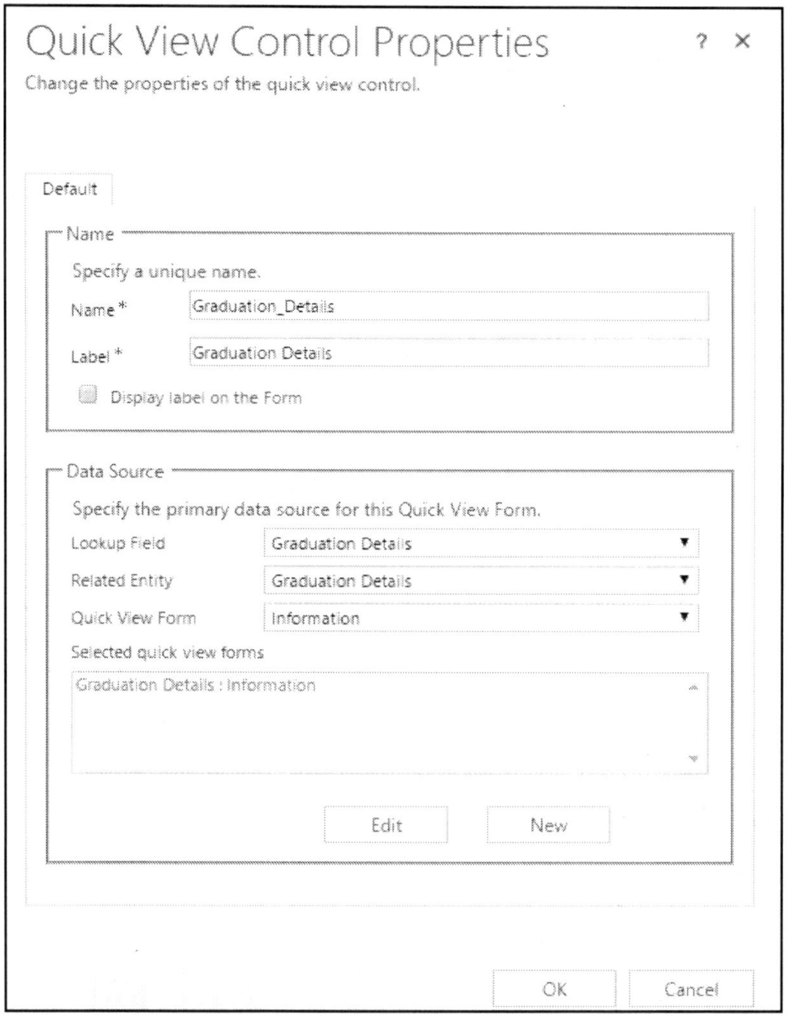

19. Click on **Save and Close**.
20. Click on the **Publish All Customizations** button for your solution.

How it works...

Although this recipe is simplified, typical normalized models will contain more than one attribute, as well as more than one entity.

In step 2 to step 11, we created a normalized entity that contains the employee details along with its Quick View. In step 4, we avoided keeping the checkboxes ticked. All the checkboxes with a † symbol depict options that cannot be reverted. We can always enable them later if required. As a best practice, if they are not required, don't enable them, otherwise your choice will be irreversible. In step 12 and step 13, we created a relationship between contacts and the newly created entity to provide a navigation path between the parent contact entity and the additional attributes for the specific types (Supervisor and Post Graduate Start Date). In the last steps, step 14 to step 18, we added the lookup as well as the Quick View on the contact form. A Quick View is a simplified sub-view of another record that can be placed on the parent record's form to display the child's subset of attributes in read-only. The red box in the following screenshot highlights the Quick View related to the **Graduation Details** lookup record:

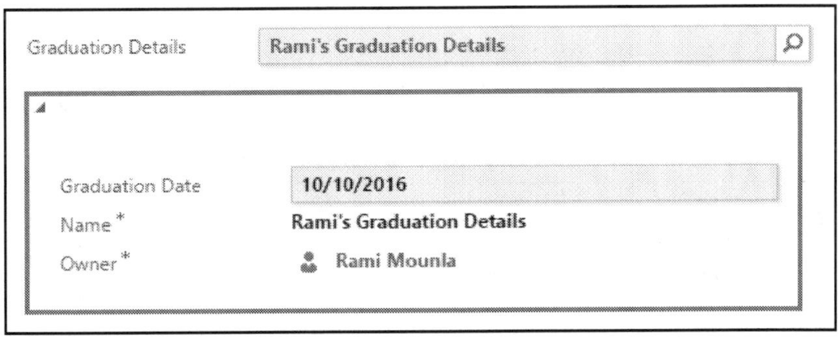

With this design we can now see the graduate details on the contact form without creating the attributes on the entity itself.

Our ER diagram now looks like this:

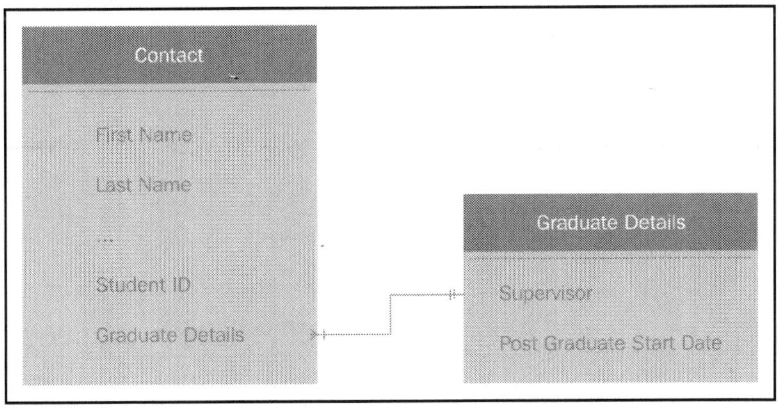

The advantages of normalizing your data with a common parent are:

- Lighter multipurpose parent entity
- Security roles can control the normalized entities with the additional attributes

> TIP
> However, the primary field value will still appear on the parent form, even if the user does not have read rights to the child entity. Moreover, field level security can be used to obfuscate the lookup's text.

- Quick Views help display the normalized data on the parent form (read-only)
- Advanced search can still retrieve and filter information from the related entities
- Views can contain data from the related entities (non-sortable)

> TIP
> With quick Views, a user can retrieve data that is two levels deep. Attributes from the related record as well as its 1:N or N:N related lists.

This model also has some cons, which are as follows:

- Degraded user experience as the Quick Views are read-only
- May require some customization to show and hide irrelevant details
- Quick search cannot search attributes across the different normalized entities

See also

- *Modeling denormalized entities*
- *Modeling independent normalized entities*
- *Using a Business Rule to show and hide attributes*
- The *Building cumulative security roles* recipe of `Chapter 7`, *Security*

Modeling independent normalized entities

The third modeling technique is similar to the second, except that the entities are completely independent. This scenario is typically used when there is a logical separation between the entities and there are few commonalities between them, to the point where reusability is not justified.

In this recipe, we will create a new entity called contractor that mirrors the contact entity with some additional attributes.

Getting ready

Similar to the previous recipes, a **System Customizer** or higher security role is required to perform the configuration, as well as a solution to contain the changes.

How to do it

1. Navigate to **Settings** | **Solutions** | **Packt**.
2. Click on **New** | **Entity**.
3. Enter `Contractor` in the **Display Name** field, and `Contractors` under the **Plural Name** field, and click on **Save**:

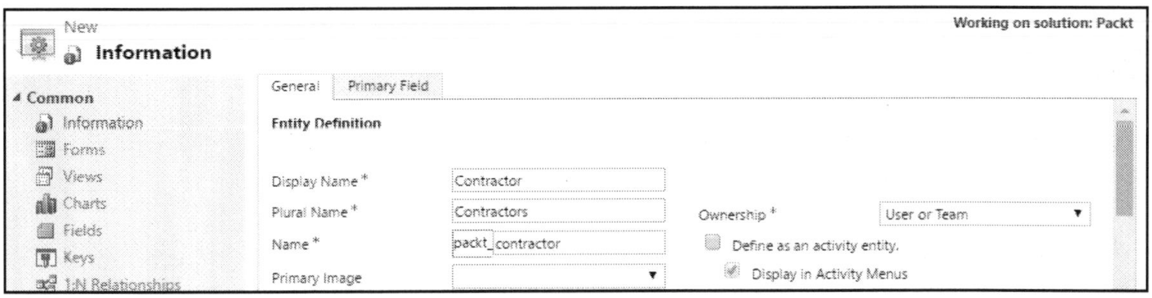

4. Navigate to **Fields** on the left-hand side and click on **New**.
5. Create an attribute called `Hourly Rate` of type **Currency** and click on **Save and Close**:

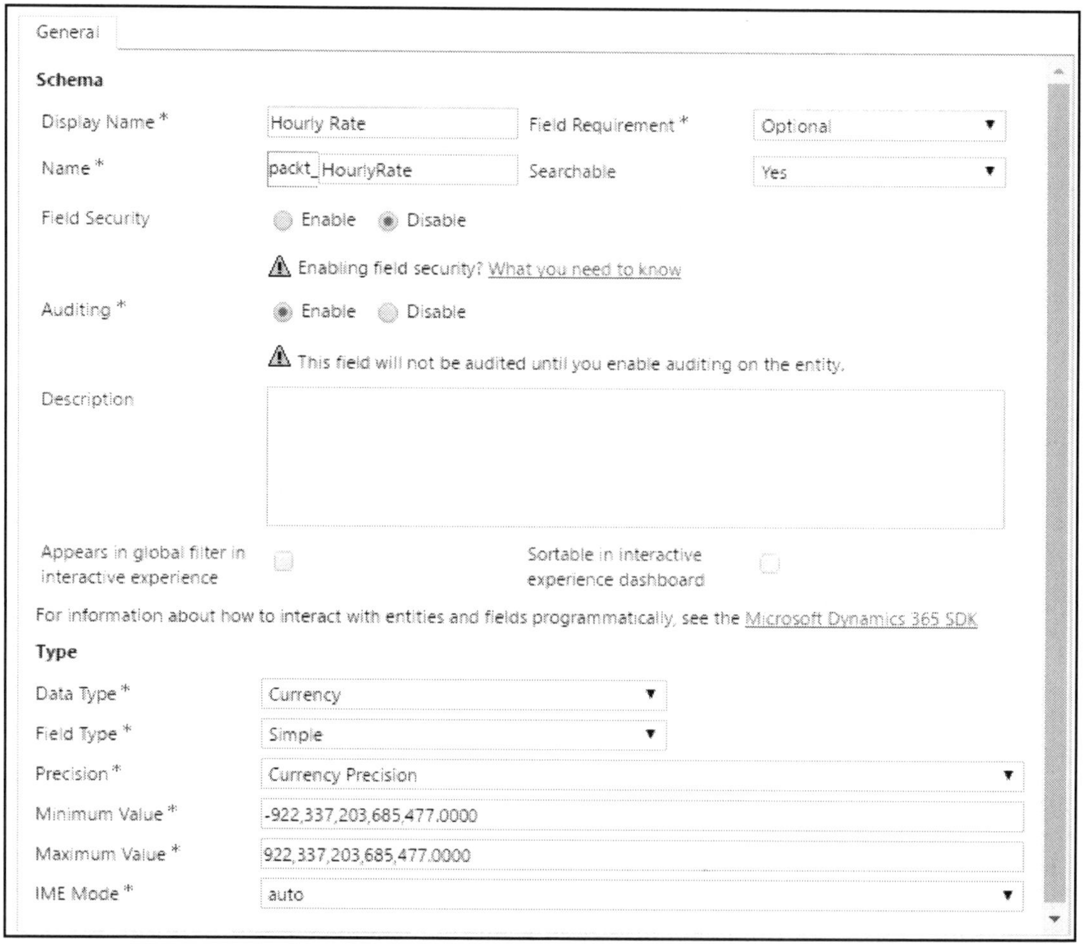

6. Navigate to **Contractor** | **Forms** and open the **Main Information** form.
7. Add the newly created field to your form by dragging and dropping the attributes from the right-hand window on to the form.
8. Click on the **Publish All Customizations** button for your solution.

How it works...

The alternative to the previous two modeling patterns is to keep your entities completely separate. This could prove to be an efficient design as it maximizes your instance's diversity. You can create a multitude of entities without overcrowding and without overlapping functionality. Nonetheless, as a best practice, promote reusability where possible. Keep in mind that a Dynamics 365 online instance has a limit on the number of custom entities that can be created. The limit also includes custom entities introduced by deploying third-party solutions. At the time of writing, the limit is 300 custom entities per Dynamics 365 instance. You can check your limit by navigating to **Settings** | **Administration** | **Resources In Use**:

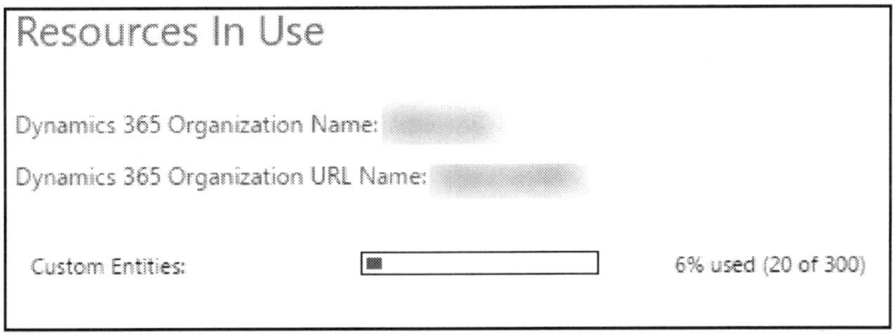

Your new ER diagram is highlighted in the following screenshot:

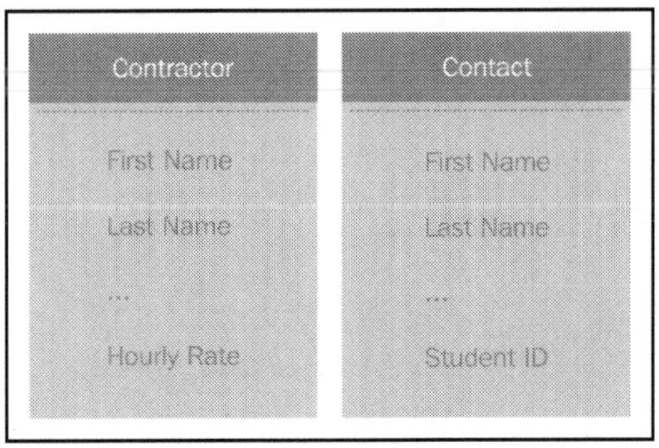

The advantages of a completely normalized model are:

- No coupling between entities, resulting in cleaner and easier to manage solutions
- Full independent control using security roles for each of the entities

- Positive user experience with clean independent forms
- No need for complex configuration or customization to show and hide irrelevant sections

This model also has some cons, some of which are:

- Search results will appear in different lists
- Cannot combine views with both entities
- Some out-of-the-box entities (contact, account, and activities, among others) have well-defined core structures that could be difficult to recreate (for example, the regarding field on activities).

See also

- *Modeling denormalized entities*
- *Modeling normalized entities with a common parent*
- *Using a Business Rule to show and hide attributes*
- The *Building cumulative security roles* recipe of `Chapter 7`, *Security*

Using a Business Rule to show and hide attributes

Business Rules are a Power User's dream come true. They minimize the amount of custom JavaScript required on forms and they can replace some simple calculation plugins when the rule is scoped at the entity level.

In this example, we will create a simple Business Rule to show and hide the `Student Id` attribute based on the contact types defined in the first recipe of this chapter.

Getting ready

Similar to the previous recipes, a **System Customizer** or higher security role is required to perform the configuration as well as a solution to contain the changes.

How to do it

1. Navigate to **Settings** | **Solutions** | **Packt**.
2. Navigate to **Entities** | **Contact** | **Forms** and open the previously created **Contact** form.
3. Double-click on **Contact Type** and uncheck the **Visible by default** checkbox.
4. Click on **OK**, then click on **Save and Close**.
5. Navigate to **Entities** | **Contact** | **Business Rules** and click on **New**.
6. Under **BUSINESS RULE: Contact**, enter the title, `Show/Hide Student Id`.
7. Click on the first available **CONDITION** and enter the following details in the right pane:
    - **Display Name**: `Check Contact Type Student`
    - **Source**: `Entity`
    - **Field**: `Contact Type`
    - **Operator**: `Equals`
    - **Type**: `Value`
    - **Value**: `Student`
8. Click on the **Apply** button.
9. Back in the main editor, click on **Add** | **Add Set Visibly** and select the + sign adjacent to the tick sign:

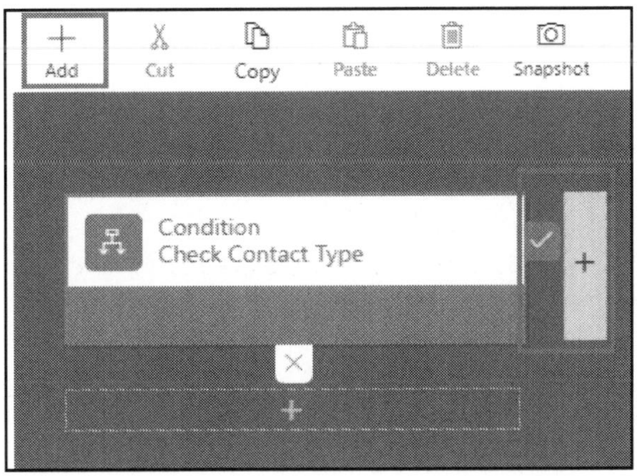

Enter the following details, followed by a click on **Apply**:

- **Display Name**: `Show Student Id`
- **Field**: `Student Id`
- **Status**: `Show field`

10. Back in the main editor again, click on **Add** | **Add Condition** and select the **+** sign adjacent to the **X** sign:

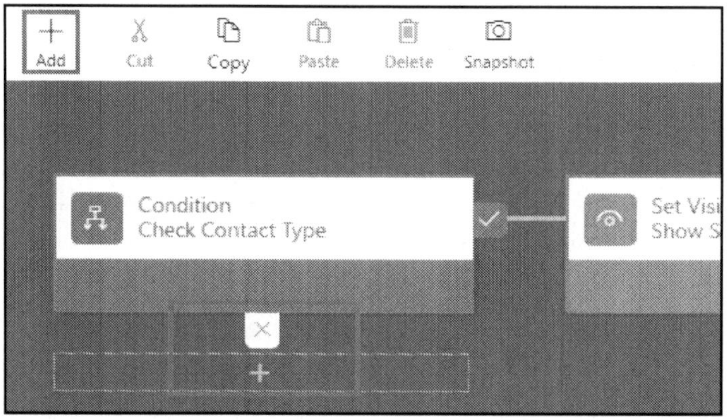

Enter the following details:

- **Display Name**: `Check Contact Type Other`
- **Source**: `Entity`
- **Field**: `Contact Type`
- **Operator**: `Equals`
- **Type**: `Value`
- **Value**: `Other`

11. Click on **Apply**.

12. Click on **Add action** | **Add Set Visibility** and select the **+** sign adjacent to the tick sign for the new condition:

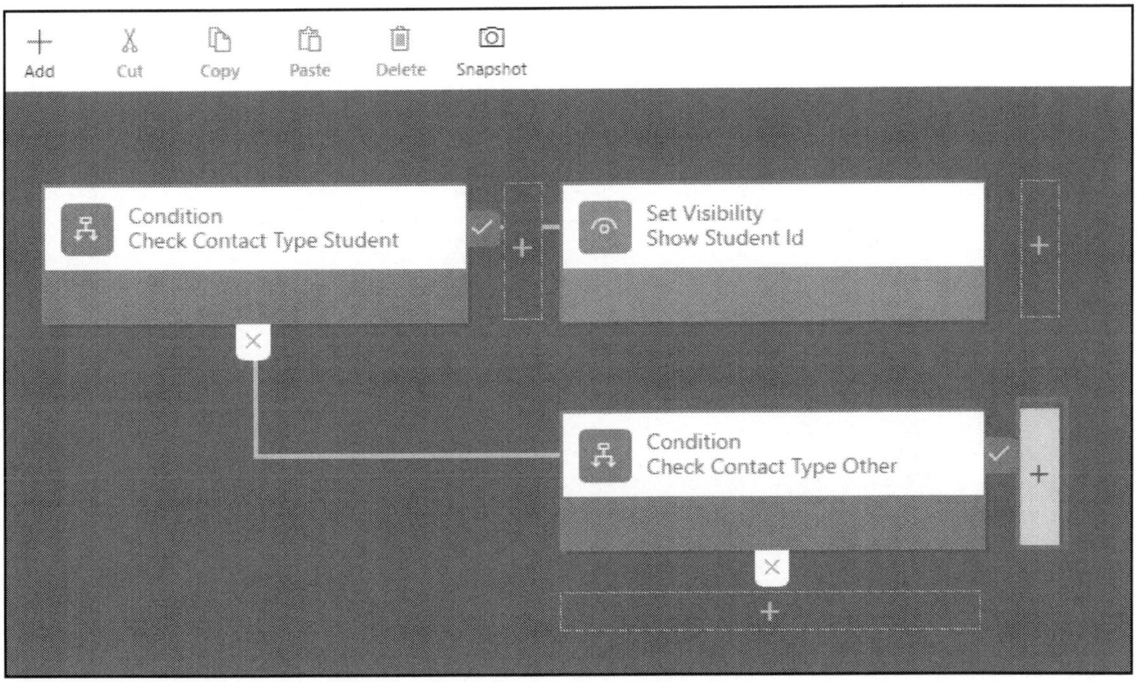

Enter the following in the right-hand pane:

- **Display Name**: `Hide Student Id`
- **Field**: `Student Id`
- **Status**: `Hide field`

13. Click on **Apply** in the right navigation pane, followed by **Save** in the main editor in the top left:

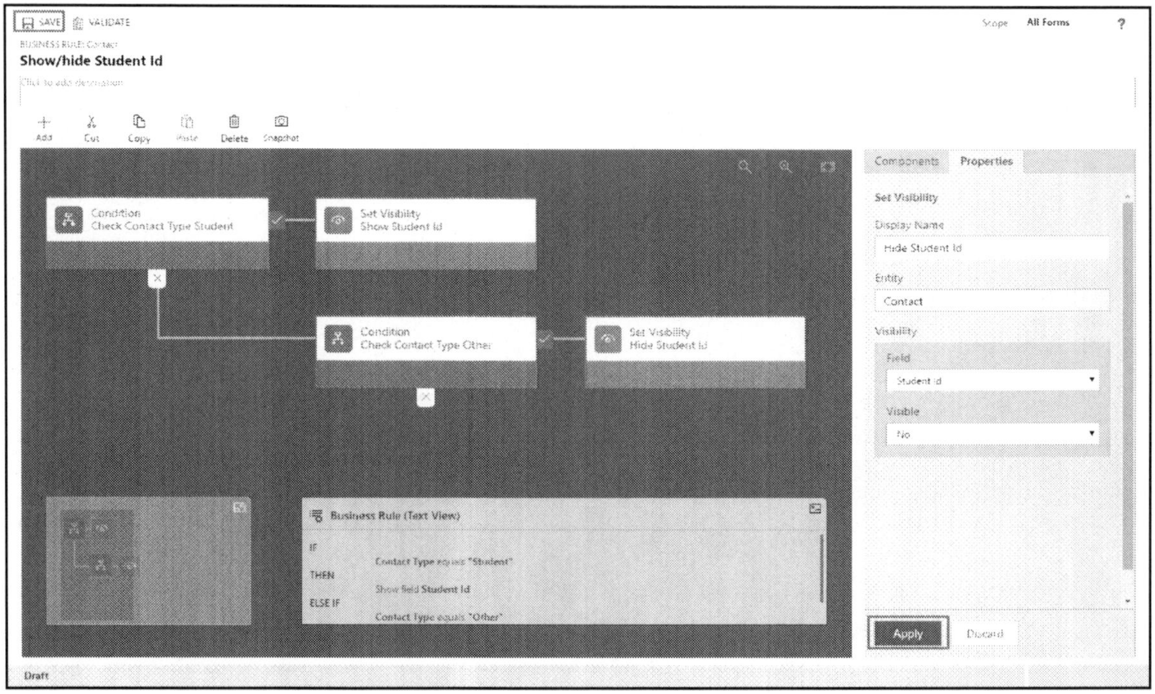

14. Once saved, click on **Activate** on the main editor followed by **Activate** in the **Process Activate Confirmation** prompt:

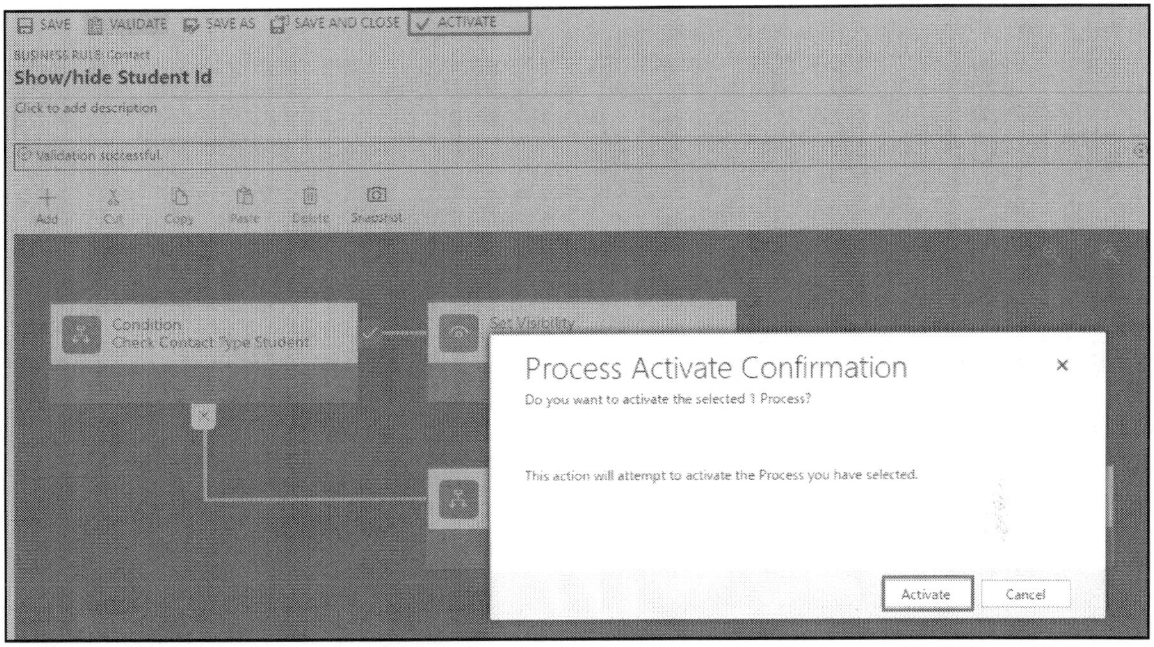

15. You can optionally click on the **VALIDATE** button to ensure that your business rules do not have any issues.

How it works

We started by marking the field as hidden by default in step 3. As a best practice, it always makes for a better user experience when hidden fields are revealed, as opposed to hiding visible fields on loading a record. In step 7 and step 8, we created the condition and rule to show the field; in step 9 and step 10, we created the converse condition and rule to hide the field. Always think about the reverse scenario when implementing business rules, otherwise, you will be faced with an irreversible action.

Given that the scope of the business rule was set to the default **All Forms** (top-right corner when editing the business rule), all forms will now respect that rule. If the scope was set to **Entity**, the rule would also trigger on the server side, which could be useful if implementing calculation rules that need to be respected when manipulating the data outside of a form (for example editable grids, bulk import, or through the Web API or SDK):

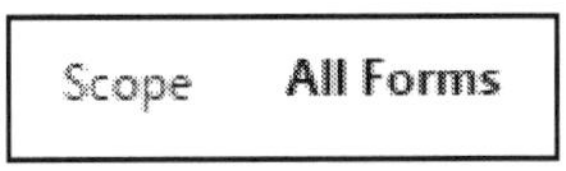

Behind the scenes, JavaScript functionality is created to address the rules' requirements. This is also respected in all form factors following the *configure once, deploy everywhere* design pattern.

Business Rules also have limitations, as follows:

- There is a limit of 10 `If Else` conditions per business rule
- Business Rules cannot control sections and tabs
- If not set to a scope of Entity, a Business Rule will only run on load and on changes to the field, not on save.
- Conditions cannot be a mixture of AND and OR; it's a set of one or the other

For additional limitations, visit `https://technet.microsoft.com/en-us/library/dn531086`.

There's more...

Business Rules provide a wide range of actions that can be performed. Among them are the following:

- Show error message
- Set field value (using another field's value, a static value, a formula, or simply clear it; it's good for simple plugin replacements)
- Set visibility
- Set default value
- Lock or unlock a field

The TechNet article (`https://www.microsoft.com/en-us/Dynamics/crm-customer-center/create-business-rules-and-recommendations-to-apply-logic-in-a-form.aspx`) covers more details about Business Rule.

Building a configurable e-mail notification workflow

Workflows are one of the most powerful no-code extensions you can configure in Dynamics 365; without any code, you can automate repetitive business processes.

Workflows are versatile and can fulfill a wide range of functionalities, ranging from creating entities and sending e-mails to calling actions. In this recipe, we will create a workflow that sends an e-mail to any new students after 24 hours of their record being created.

Getting ready

Similar to the previous recipe, a **System Customizer** or higher security role is required to perform the configuration as well as a solution to contain the changes.

How to do it

1. Navigate to **Settings** | **Solutions** | **Packt**.
2. Under **Processes**, click on **New**.
3. Fill in the following details:
   - **Process name**: `Send Student Welcome Email`
   - **Category**: `Workflow`
   - **Entity**: `Contact`
   - Tick **Run this workflow in the background**
   - **Type**: `New blank process`
4. In the **Process** editor tick **Record is created** and **As an on-demand**. Keep the rest as is with their default values.
5. Click on **Add Step** | **Wait Condition**.
6. Click on **<condition> (click to configure)** and select the following:
   - Process in the first column
   - Execution time in the second column
   - Equals in the third column
   - In the last column, use the form assistance on the right-hand side:
     1. Select **1** under **Day**
     2. Select **After**
     3. Look for **Process**
     4. Double click **Execution Time** in the last list

7. Click on **Save and Close**.
8. Back in your process, click on **Select this row and click Add Step**, then click on **Add Step** | **Check** condition.
9. Click on <condition> (click to configure) and enter the following details:

    - **Contact**, **Email**, and **Contains Data**
    - **Contact**, **Contact Type**, **Equals**, and **Student** (created in the previous recipe)
    - **Contact**, **Status**, **Equals**, and **Active**
    - Click on **Save and Close**:

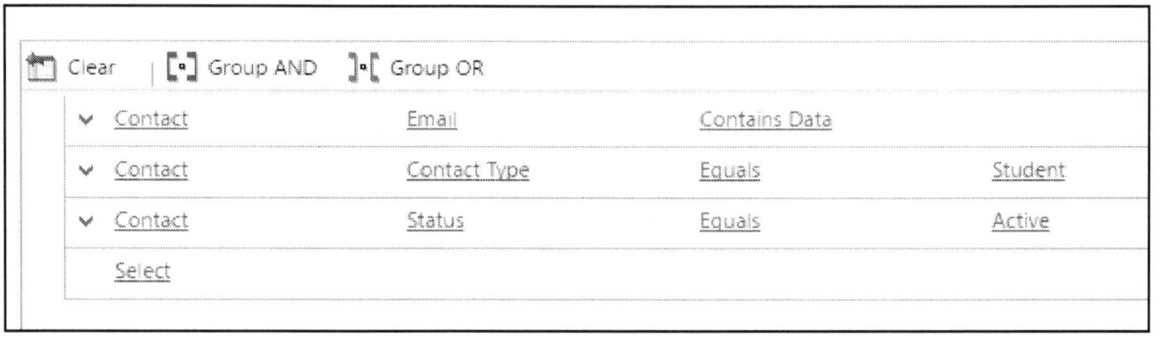

10. Click on **Select** this row and click **Add Step,** followed by **Add Step** | **Send Email**.
11. Select **Create New Message** from the drop-down and click on **Set Properties**.
12. Enter the details of the e-mail as follows:

    - **From**: `<your name>`
    - **To**: using **Form Assistance** on the right, select **Contact** under **Look for** followed by **Contact** from the next dropdown, then click on the **Add** button followed by the **OK** button at the bottom:

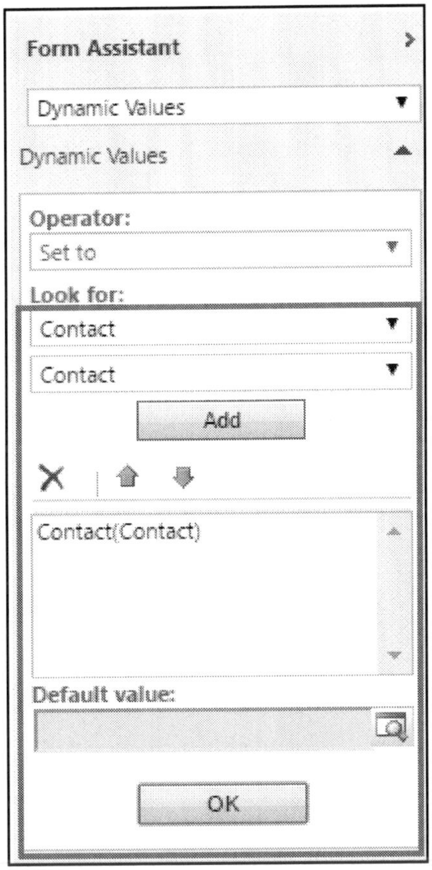

- Enter `Welcome to Packt University` in the **Subject Line** option
- Enter `Hi`
- Using the right **Form Assistance**, select **Contact**, **Last Name**, and click on **Add**, then **OK**
- Follow the salutation with a carriage return (*Enter*) and `Welcome to Packt University`

13. **Save and Close** the dialog.

14. Click on **Activate** at the top of the workflow:

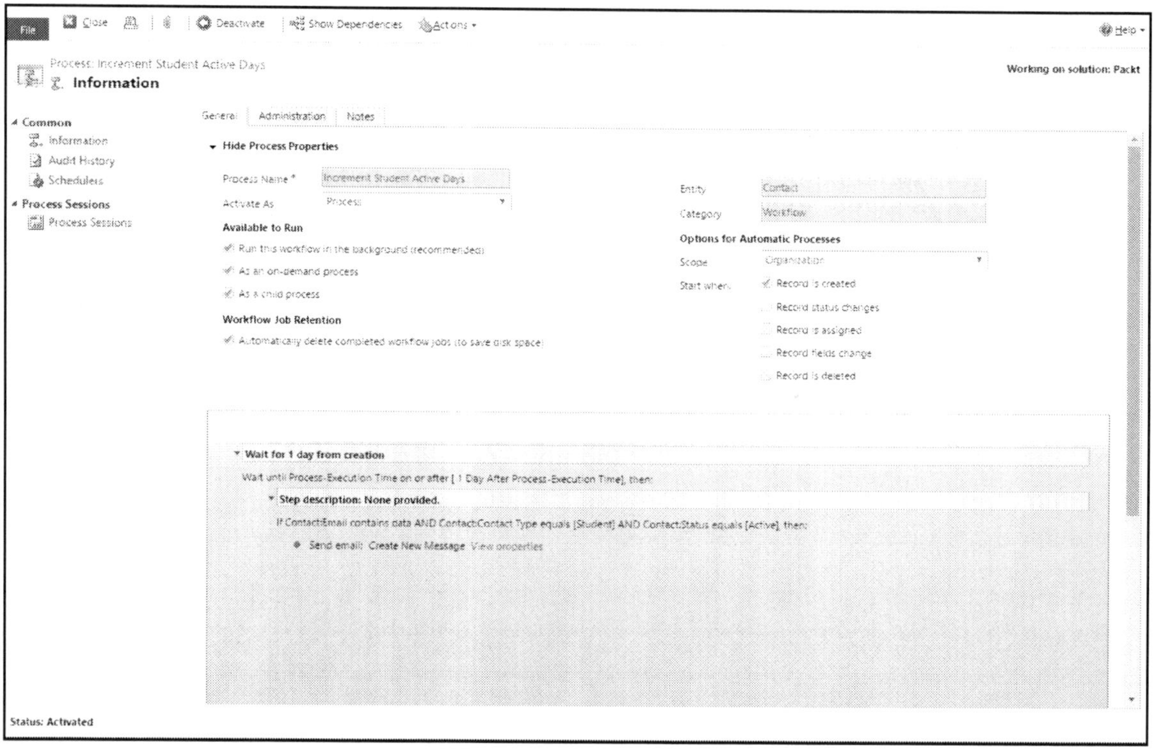

How it works...

In step 2 to step 4, we created a workflow that triggers on creation (when the contact record is first created, the workflow will start waiting). The workflow can also be called on demand in case we want to trigger it again. In this example, the contact might already be created but not as a Student. Once the contact is set as a Student, the workflow can be triggered manually to send the welcome e-mail.

In step 5 and step 6, we set up the wait condition to wait for a day.

In step 7 and step 8, we checked if the contact is an active student with an e-mail address.

In step 9 to step 12, we created a personalized e-mail for the contact and welcomed them.

In step 13, we activated the workflow.

As a good practice, always add descriptions to your workflow, and to each step, to understand at a high level what the workflow is doing.

When asynchronous workflows are triggered, they enter into a pool to be processed when the asynchronous service is free. Asynchronous workflows are typically executed within seconds or minutes. If the execution is taking hours, then you might want to raise a support ticket with Microsoft to investigate. Executing workflows asynchronously is a great way to lighten the load on your Dynamics instances.

When workflows instances are waiting for a condition to be satisfied, they do not consume resources or affect your instance's performance. However, it is generally agreed by the community that it is a bad practice to have too many workflow instances in a waiting status.

There's more

In more recent releases, synchronous workflows that turn your workflow into a configurable plugin became available. Microsoft does not recommend synchronous workflows for long processes due to the load that is associated with them. Furthermore, online instances have a limit of 2 minutes per synchronous workflow or plugin. Nevertheless, synchronous workflows are there to be used. Use them wisely.

See also

- The *Creating your first custom workflow activity* recipe of `Chapter 4`, *Server-Side Extensions*

Building your first action

Have you ever wanted to call a workflow from your JavaScript? If you have, then you will be pleased to learn about Actions. Actions, introduced with Dynamics CRM 2013, are yet another great addition to the configurable extensions. It was created to allow a business logic to be called from within workflows, as well as from JavaScript and Plugin customization.

Actions can be built using a point and click interface, as well as using .NET code. In this recipe, we will create a configured action that takes a few string values, creates a student record, and returns that record as an output parameter.

Getting ready

Similar to the previous recipes, a **System Customizer** or higher security role is required to perform the configuration as well as a solution to contain the changes.

How to do it

1. Navigate to **Settings** | **Solutions** | **Packt**.
2. Under **Processes**, click on **New**.
3. Fill in the following details:
    - **Process name**: `Create Student`
    - **Category**: `Action`
    - **Entity**: `None (global)`
4. Click on **OK**.
5. Click on the + button below **Hide Process Arguments** and add the following four arguments:
    - **Name**: `FirstName`, **Type**: `String`, and **Direction**: `Input`
    - **Name**: `LastName`, **Type**: `String`, and **Direction**: `Input`
    - **Name**: `EmailAddress`, **Type**: `String`, and **Direction**: `Input`
    - **Name**: `CreatedStudent`, **Type**: `EntityReference`, **Entity**: `Contact`, and **Direction**: `Output`
6. Click on **Add Step** | **Create Record**.
7. In the drop-down next to **create**, select **Contact** and click on **Set Properties**.

8. Enter the following details:
    - **First Name**: From the right form assistance, select **Arguments** in the **Look For** dropdown, followed by **FirstName** in the drop down, click on **Add**, and then **OK**
    - **Last Name**: From the right form assistance, select **Arguments** in the **Look For** dropdown, followed by **LastName** in the drop down, click on **Add**, and then **OK**
    - **Email Address**: From the right form assistance, select **Arguments** in the **Look For** dropdown, followed by **EmailAddress** in the dropdown, click on **Add**, and then **OK**
    - **Contact Type**: `Student`
9. Click on **Save** and **Close**.
10. Click on **Add Step | Assign Value**.
11. Select **Set Properties** next to **Assign Value**.
12. Enter the following details:
    - **Statement Label**: `Assign a created student`
    - **Name**: `Created student`
    - Go to **Value** from the right-hand **Form Assistance** and select **Create (Contact)** from the **Look For** dropdown and **Contact** from the next drop down
    - Click on **Add** and **OK**, and then **Save and Close**

13. Click on **Activate** and then **Save and Close**:

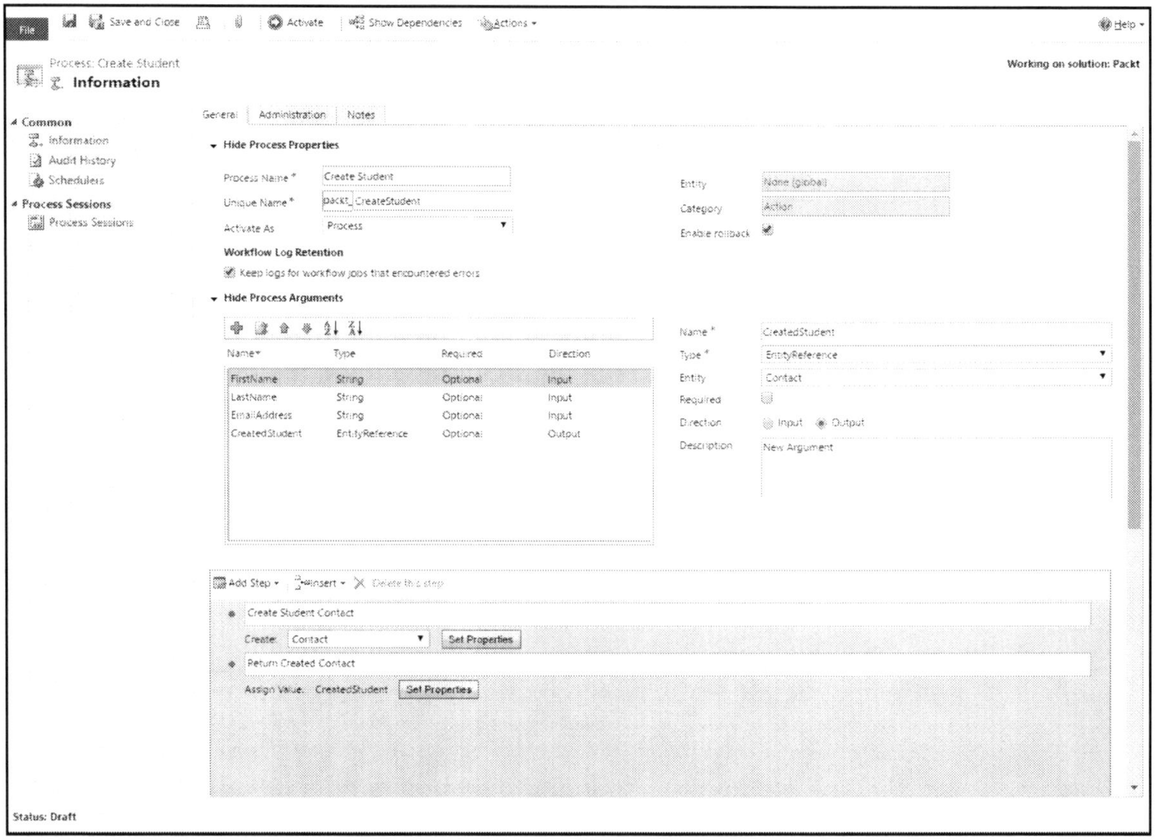

How it works...

In step 2 and step 3, we created the blank action. We ensured that the action's entity is set to **None (global)**, meaning that the process is not bound to any entities (the way workflows are).

In step 4, we created three input parameters and one output parameter.

In step 5 to step 7, we created the student contact record using the input parameters.

In step 8 to step 10, we assigned the created record to the output parameter.

In step 11, we activated the process.

As mentioned previously, actions can be called from workflows, JavaScript, Plugins, or using the Dynamics 365 web services. Every time an action is created, Dynamics 365 creates a message that can be called externally. In the *Creating your first custom action* recipe in `Chapter 4`, *Server-Side Extensions*, you will learn how to generate early-bound types for actions to call using managed .NET code.

Microsoft recommends naming your action using a verb describing what the action is about to ensure your application's vocabulary is something that makes sense from a business flow perspective.

For more information about actions, visit
`https://technet.microsoft.com/en-us/library/dn531060.aspx`.

See also

The *Creating your first custom action* recipe of `Chapter 4`, *Server-Side Extensions*

Setting up the rollup fields

Rollup fields are one of the most exciting new features that were introduced in recent years that significantly reduced the amount of custom code required. Rollup fields can aggregate values from other attributes. You can calculate sums, averages, minimums, maximums, and counts.

In this recipe, we will create a rollup field that counts how many active activities are associated with a contact.

Getting ready

Similar to the previous recipes, a **System Customizer** or higher security role is required to perform the configuration as well as a solution to contain the changes.

How to do it

1. Navigate to **Settings** | **Solutions** | **Packt**.
2. Create a new field by clicking on **Entity** | **Contact** | **Fields** | **New** and enter the following details:
    - **Display Name**: `Number of Activities`
    - **Data Type**: `Whole Number`
    - **Field Type**: `Rollup`
3. Click on **Edit** next to the **Field Type** dropdown.
4. In the **Rollup Field** dialog, under **Related Entity**, select **Activities (Regarding)** and click the tick box.
5. In the **Filters** section, select the following:
    - `Activity Status` under **Field**
    - `Equals` under **Operator**
    - `Value` under **Type**
    - Check `Open and Scheduled` under **Value**
6. Click on the tick box.
7. Under **Aggregation**, select the following:
    - `Aggregate Function` under **Count**
    - `Activity` under **Aggregated Related Entity** field
8. Click on the tick box. Your **ROLLUP FIELD** dialog will look as follows:

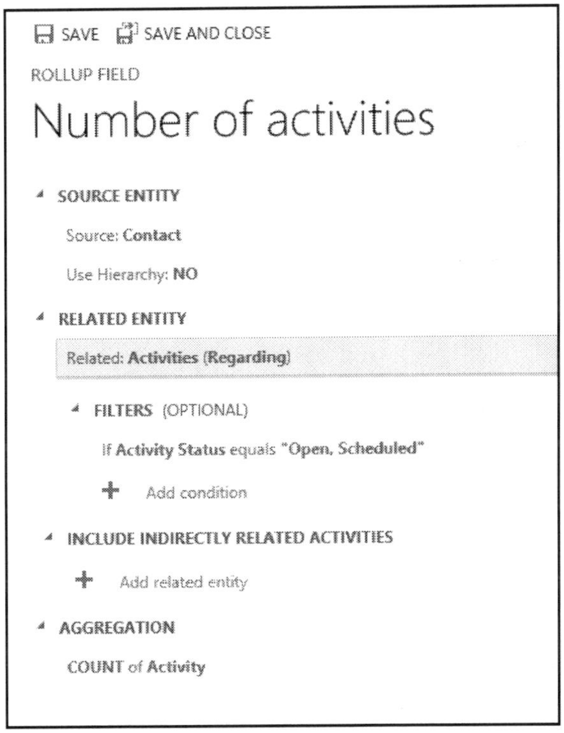

9. Click on **Save and Close** on the **ROLLUP FIELD** dialog and the attribute dialogue.
10. Click on the **Publish All Customizations** button for your solution.

How it works...

In step 2 to step 7, we created a new rollup field of type whole number that calculates the total count of active activities associated with a contact.

A couple of things to note about rollup fields: the fields are read-only and the calculation does not take into account a user's security roles.

Frequency

When a rollup field is created, behind the scenes, a system asynchronous job is scheduled to execute 12 hours after the field is created. Navigate to **Settings** | **System Jobs**; you will see a job of type **Mass Calculate Rollup** field with the name of your new field in **System Job Name**. You can force the job to run sooner by clicking on **Action** | **Postpone** and entering an earlier date/time. It is not recommended to do so when you have a large number of records in a production environment. The first time the job runs, it will have to update all fields, which might lead to a performance impact.

Subsequently, the **System Jobs** option will have a **Calculated Rollup** field per entity that has rollup fields configured. By default, subsequent rollup field calculations will take place every hour, (which is the fastest schedule). If an hourly update is not necessary, you can update the value by double-clicking on the **System Job** option, and selecting **Actions** | **Modify Recurrence**. This will present a dialog box that helps you redefine the recurrence of the execution:

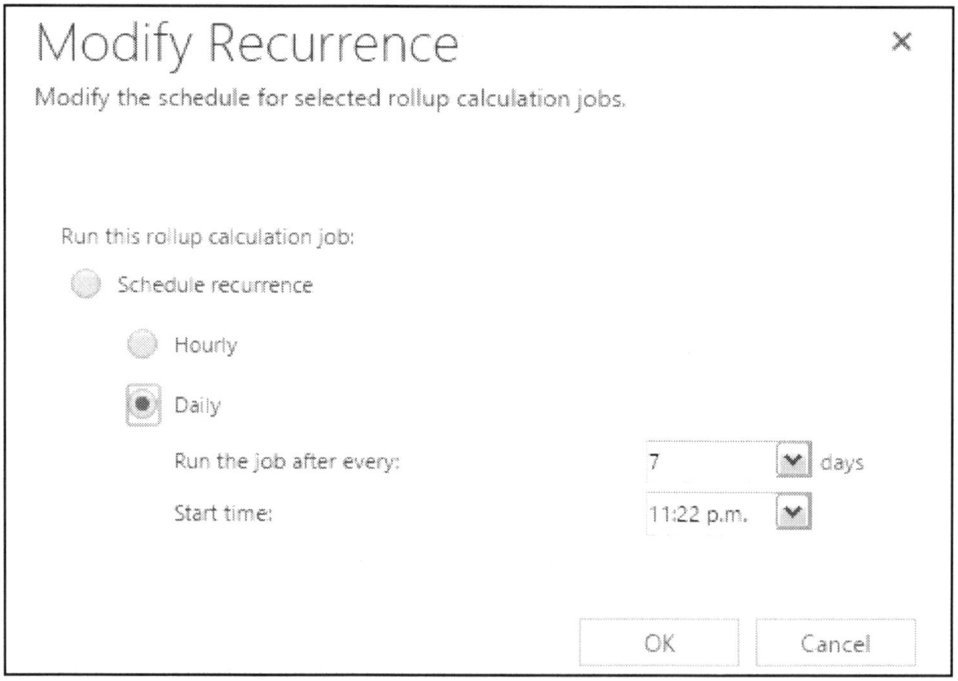

> Given that the rollup fields are executed as asynchronous jobs, if the calculation is not occurring, consider checking the status of the asynchronous service. For on-premise installation, log on to your backend server and check its status. For online implementations, log a support call with Microsoft to check the status of the service.

Programmatic Rollup Field execution

On top of the automated schedules, rollup fields can also be executed programmatically by executing `CalcualteRollupFieldRequest`. Furthermore, if you search online for "rollup field workflow", you will find custom workflow activities built by the community to force recalculations in your configurable workflows.

There's more...

Rollup fields are a powerful feature in Dynamics 365. On top of the counting capability described in this recipe, rollup fields offer other types of aggregations. Furthermore, in some cases (activities), the aggregation can span across multiple relationship levels.

Different types of aggregation

Counting the number of records is one of the many capabilities of a rollup field. You can also get the maximum, minimum, average, and sum of a field, assuming the field type allows it. As you select a different aggregate function, the entity fields will be filtered accordingly.

Indirectly related activities

Given that our rollup field is aggregating activities, the field can also include indirectly related activities by defining **Activity Parties** (activities) under indirectly related activities. This will expand the aggregation, not only when the contact is in the regarding field, but also in the parties field.

For more details about rollup fields, visit
`https://technet.microsoft.com/en-nz/library/dn832162.aspx`.

See also

- *Setting up calculated fields*

Setting up calculated fields

Similar to rollups fields, calculated fields are another recent addition to Dynamics 365's configuration capabilities that significantly reduces the need for custom code extensions.

As the name suggests, calculated fields allow you to set the value of an attribute based on another field, a function, or a formula. Furthermore, calculated fields may trigger based on a set of conditions.

In this example, we will configure a field to calculate the difference in months between two dates: (student start date, and student end date).

Getting ready

Similar to the previous recipes, a **System Customizer** or higher security role is required to perform the configuration as well as a solution to contain the changes.

How to do it

1. Navigate to **Settings** | **Solutions** | **Packt**.
2. Create two new fields by clicking on **Entity** | **Contact** | **Fields** | **New** as follows:
    - **Start Date** of type **Date Time**
    - **End Date** of type **Date Time**
3. Create a new **Calculated** field and enter the following details:
    - **Display Name**: `Months for graduation`
    - **Data Type**: `Whole Number`
    - **Field Type**: `Calculated`
4. Click on **Edit** next to the **Field Type** drop-down.
5. In the **Calculated** dialog under **Condition (Optional)**, click on **Add condition**.

6. In the **If** row, enter the following details and click on the tick box:
    - **Entity**: `Current Entity (Contact)`
    - **Field**: `Contact Type`
    - **Operator**: `Equals`
    - **Type**: `Value`
    - **Value**: `Student`
7. Under **Action**, click on **Add action,** enter `DIFFINMONTHS(packt_enddate, packt_startdate)`, and then click on the tick button:

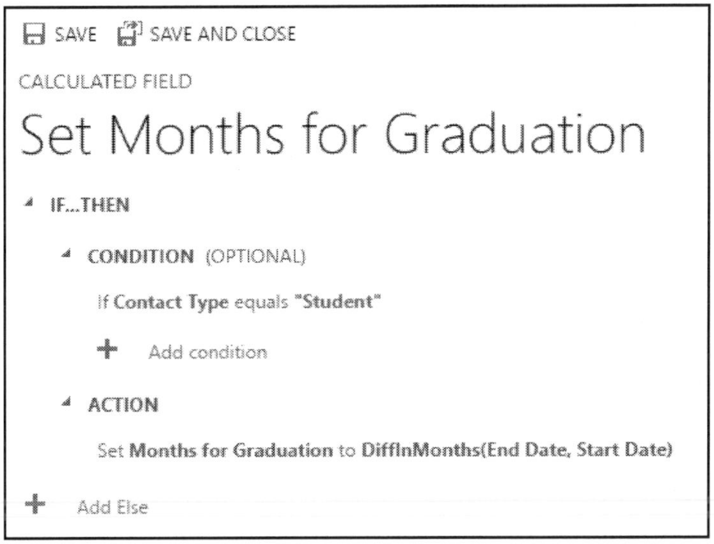

8. Click on **Save and Close** on the rollup field dialogue and the attribute dialogue.

How it works

In this recipe, we used a point and click configuration to set up a calculated field to calculate the number of months' difference between a graduate's start date and end date.

In step 5 and step 6, we defined the condition, and in step 7, we defined the calculation formula.

> **TIP**
> Calculated fields translate to synchronous server-side code executions. They are similar to plugins and are executed during stage 40 of the execution pipeline of a post update or create message.

Given that the execution takes place on the server side, the users will only see the changes right after a save event is triggered. Unlike business rules and JavaScript customization, the result is not instantaneous. They do not trigger after the condition is met on the form frontend.

Similar to rollup fields, calculated fields are read-only and do not take into account a user's security roles.

There's more...

Calculated fields are a powerful addition; they can be used in many scenarios, some of which are:

- Number calculations, (for accounting, weights, and so on)
- Retrieving values from related entities
- Constructing a string based on other attributes

The TechNet article (`https://technet.microsoft.com/library/dn832103.aspx`) covers calculated fields in a few examples. The article also covers some limitations of calculated fields. Among them are the following:

- Calculated fields cannot trigger a plugin or workflows
- Once a field is created as simple, you cannot convert it to a calculated field without deleting it; (something to consider when upgrading old versions)
- A calculated field cannot reference itself, but it can reference another calculated field or rollup field (limit of five chained fields)
- Values in the calculated formula can come from the current entity or a direct parent (no access to 1:N or N:N entities)
- Up to 10 unique calculated fields can be used in saved queries, charts, and visualizations
- You cannot define a maximum or minimum metadata property on a calculated field

At the time of writing, in addition to basic arithmetic operations, the Dynamics 365 supports the following built-in formulas with their respective return types:

Function syntax	**Return type**
`ADDDAYS (whole number, date and time)`	Date and Time
`ADDHOURS (whole number, date and time)`	Date and Time
`ADDMONTHS (whole number, date and time)`	Date and Time
`ADDWEEKS (whole number, date and time)`	Date and Time
`ADDYEARS (whole number, date and time)`	Date and Time
`SUBTRACTDAYS (whole number, date and time)`	Date and Time
`SUBTRACTHOURS (whole number, date and time)`	Date and Time
`SUBTRACTMONTHS (whole number, date and time)`	Date and Time
`SUBTRACTWEEKS (whole number, date and time)`	Date and Time
`SUBTRACTYEARS (whole number, date and time)`	Date and Time
`DIFFINDAYS (date and time, date and time)`	Whole Number
`DIFFINHOURS (date and time, date and time)`	Whole Number
`DIFFINMINUTES (date and time, date and time)`	Whole Number
`DIFFINMONTHS (date and time, date and time)`	Whole Number
`DIFFINWEEKS (date and time, date and time)`	Whole Number
`DIFFINYEARS (date and time, date and time)`	Whole Number
`CONCAT (single line of text, single line of text, ... single line of text)`	String
`TRIMLEFT (single line of text, whole number)`	String
`TRIMRIGHT (single line of text, whole number)`	String

See also

- *Setting up the rollup fields*

Duplicate detection using alternate keys

Duplicate detection has been around since the early versions of Dynamics CRM. In 2015, alternate keys were introduced to help identify a record based on a unique combination of attributes to perform an **upsert** request. An upsert is the action of inserting a record if it is new, or updating it if it already exists, based on the primary key identifier (`https://msdn.microsoft.com/en-us/library/dn932135.aspx`). Logically, this means whenever an alternate key is defined, any new records that are created with the same key combination will throw a duplicate exception.

This recipe will walk us though defining an alternate key for a contact, and testing the duplicate detection.

Getting ready

Similar to the previous recipes, a **System Customizer** or higher security role is required to perform the configuration as well as a solution to contain the changes.

How to do it

1. Navigate to **Settings** | **Solutions** | **Packt**.
2. Create a new field by clicking on **Entity** | **Contact** | **Keys** | **New**.
3. In the Key definition dialogue, type `Name and Email` in the **Display Name** field.
4. Double-click on the **First Name**, **Last Name**, and **Email Address** fields under **Available Attributes**:

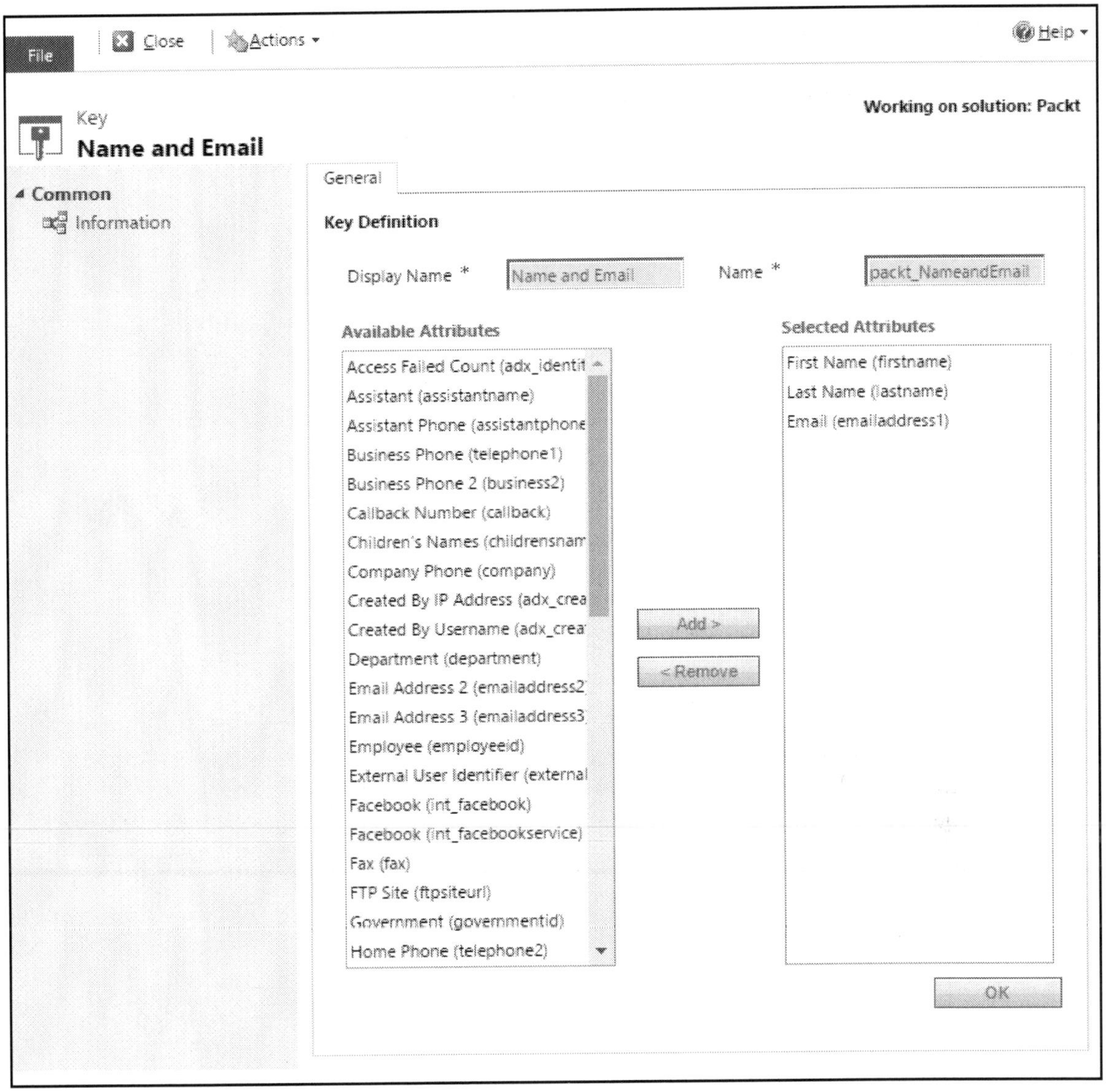

5. Click on **Save and Close**.

6. Navigate to contacts and try creating two contacts with the same first name, last name, and e-mail address. You will be prompted with the **Duplicate Record** error, as shown in the following screenshot:

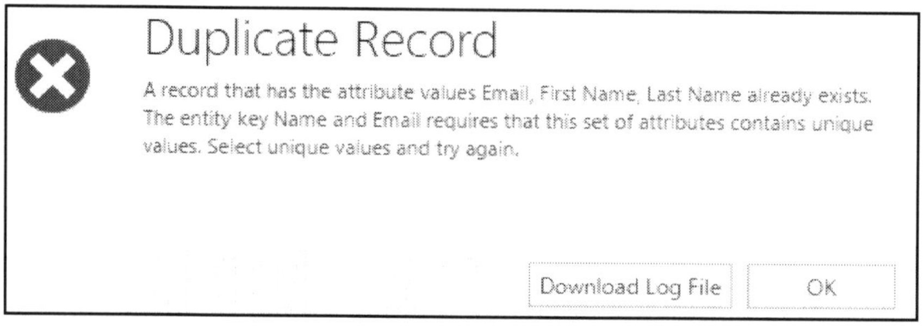

How it works

In step 2 to step 5, we created an alternate key using **First Name**, **Last Name**, and **Email** on an individual. In step 6, we tested the duplicate detection by creating two records with the same key combination.

Alternate keys have a similar behaviour to conventional duplicate detection, except the check happens at a lower level in the database (a unique nonclustered index). Additionally, if a duplicate is detected, primary keys will strictly stop a duplicate from being created, whereas, conventional duplicate detection functionality gives you the option to create it nonetheless. This is particularly important if you want to stop duplicates when using different channels than the frontend forms.

Behind the scenes, Dynamics CRM is creating a nonclustered unique index using the three fields defined in the key. If you have an on-premise deployment, you can run a SQL profiler to intercept commands that are executed on the database. A query similar to the following one will appear in your list:

```
CREATE UNIQUE INDEX [ndx_for_entitykey_packt_NameandEmail]
ON [ContactBase]
([EMailAddress1] ASC, [FirstName] ASC, [LastName] ASC)
INCLUDE ([ContactId])
WHERE [EMailAddress1] is not null
AND [FirstName] is not null
AND [LastName] is not null
WITH (FILLFACTOR = 80, MAXDOP = 4, SORT_IN_TEMPDB = ON)
```

The preceding query creates a unique nonclustered index on the `ContactBase` (the contact table) on the three columns: `FirstName`, `LastName`, and `EmailAddress1`. For more information on nonclustered indexes, read the following article at `https://docs.microsoft.com/en-us/sql/relational-databases/indexes/create-nonclustered-indexes`

During the duplicate detection process, if a field has an empty value (translated to NULL in the database) in one of the fields, the record will not be identified as a duplicate.

Note that alternate key creation can fail sometimes. Always check, after creating your key, whether the creation has been successful. If a duplicate already exists in your dataset, the key creation will fail. To check the status of a newly created key, in your solution, navigate to **Entities** | <your entity> | **Keys** and ensure the **Status** column states **Active**. If the creation fails, it will state **Failed**:

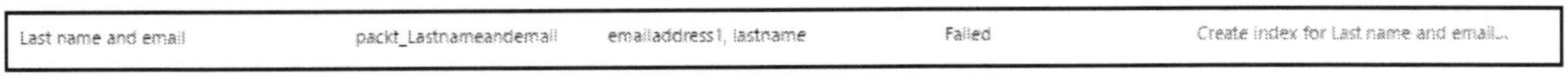

2
Client-Side Extensions

In this chapter, we will cover the following recipes:

- Creating your first JavaScript function
- Wiring your event programmatically
- Writing reusable JavaScript functions
- Querying 365 data using the Web API endpoint
- Querying the 365 metadata services
- Building a custom UI using AngularJS
- Debugging your JavaScript with Edge
- Debugging your JavaScript with Chrome
- Unit testing your JavaScript
- Customizing the Ribbon

Introduction

One of the greatest advantages of the Dynamics 365 suite is its web-based frontend. Users do not need a fat client installed on their machines to access the platform; a web browser is enough to access it. Most end users consider frontend user experience paramount to their day-to-day job. Dynamics 365 Sales offers a wide range of configurable extensions to enhance frontend user experience. In the previous chapter, we covered some no-code extensions; however, sometimes, customer requirements go beyond what Dynamics 365 offers out of the box. This is where JavaScript comes into the picture. JavaScript is currently the most popular web frontend scripting language. It is widely used in the industry and, thus, makes it easy for developers to pick up and start using.

Most online resources and training materials you find typically cover the bare minimum to achieve your extensions. Very few actually give you guidance on how to use modern industry standards to build enterprise-scale client-side extensions. Over the years, I have inherited a great deal of Dynamics CRM implementations with poorly written client-side extensions, making them difficult to maintain and enhance.

Not only does this chapter cover some simple recipes to leverage the power of JavaScript extensions, but it also focuses on code structuring techniques and debugging capabilities to assist you in implementing scalable JavaScript whilst also helping you improve your frontend development efficiency.

Creating your first JavaScript function

In this first recipe, we will set up our environment and write a simple JavaScript method that automates generation of a date field with today's date when another field is populated, using the custom Graduation Details entity created in the previous chapter. Ensure the entity has a form with the `Supervisor` and the `Post Graduate Start Date` attributes to apply our customization on it. Even though we are using the entity from the first chapter, the customization can be applied to any lookup and date field of your choice.

Getting ready

In addition to the usual access to Dynamics 365, the correct security role (**System Customizer** or higher), and a solution to contain your customization, it is highly recommended that developers use a mature **integrated development environments** (**IDE**) to develop JavaScript. You can opt to use the out-of-the-box limited Dynamics 365 web resource editor; however, using an IDE such as Visual Studio (2015. or even the free equivalent Visual Studio Code) greatly increases your productivity when writing your code. This includes debugging, unit testing, and integrating your code with source control.

Visual Studio and Developer Tool Kit

Visual Studio is one of the most mature IDEs available in the market. It greatly simplifies the task of writing your JavaScript code. Furthermore, the Dynamics 365 team implemented the Developer Tool Kit add-on for Visual Studio to help developers integrate Dynamics 365 with Visual Studio. The add-on helps you retrieve and deploy customizations from, and to, Dynamics 365. The only limitation with this combination is the lack of publishing capabilities from within Visual Studio.

Developers will still need to go to Dynamics 365 to publish their changes manually. Refer to *Creating a solution using the Dynamics CRM Developer Toolkit template* recipe in `Chapter 4`, *Server-Side Extensions* for detail about the Developer Toolkit.

XrmToolBox's Web Resources Manager

Another popular choice is the `XrmToolBox`. The `XrmToolBox` is a project originally started by Microsoft MVP Tanguy Touzard. It's an extensible plugin-based Windows application used to manage, configure, and customize Dynamics 365. The Web Resource Manager plugin helps write, deploy, and publish web resources with a few shortcuts to speed up your work. Developers quickly get into the habit of pressing *Ctrl* + *S* and *Ctrl* + *U* to save, push, and publish their customizations. Additionally, the Web Resource Manager allows the persistence of web resources to disk, giving the developers the choice of using a separate editor, such as Sublime or Visual Studio, to do the meaty development.

How to do it...

1. Navigate to **Settings** | **Solutions** | **Packt**.
2. Click on **Web Resources** and click on **New**, enter `packt_common.js` as the name, select **JScript** from **Type**, and then click on **Text Editor**.
3. Copy the following code:

```
var packtNs = packtNs || {};
packtNs.common = packtNs.common || {};

/**
* A method that populates the post graduate start date
* when the supervisor lookup is populated.
* @returns {Void}
*/
packtNs.common.populateWithTodaysDate =  function()
 {
    if (Xrm.Page.getAttribute("packt_supervisor").getValue() !==
null &&
Xrm.Page.getAttribute("packt_postgraduatestartdate").getValue() ===
null)
    {
      Xrm.Page.getAttribute("packt_postgraduatestartdate").
      setValue(new Date());
    }
}
```

4. Back in your **Packt** solution in Dynamics 365, navigate to **Entities** | **GraduationDetails** | **Forms** and double-click on the **Main** form.
5. Click on **Form Properties**, and under **Form Libraries**, click on the add symbol (+).
6. Select your JavaScript library created in step 2 from the list (you can use the search functionality to filter the values). Click on **Add** and then click on **OK**.
7. Double-click on the **Supervisor** field and, in the **Field Properties** dialog, select the **Events** tab.
8. Under **Form Libraries**, click on the add symbol (+), select your JavaScript library from the list (you can again use the search functionality to filter the values), and click on **Add**.
9. Under **Event Handlers**, click on the add symbol (+) and enter `populateWithTodaysDate`. Keep the rest as is and click on **OK**.
10. In your form edit, click on **Publish**, followed by **Save and Close**:

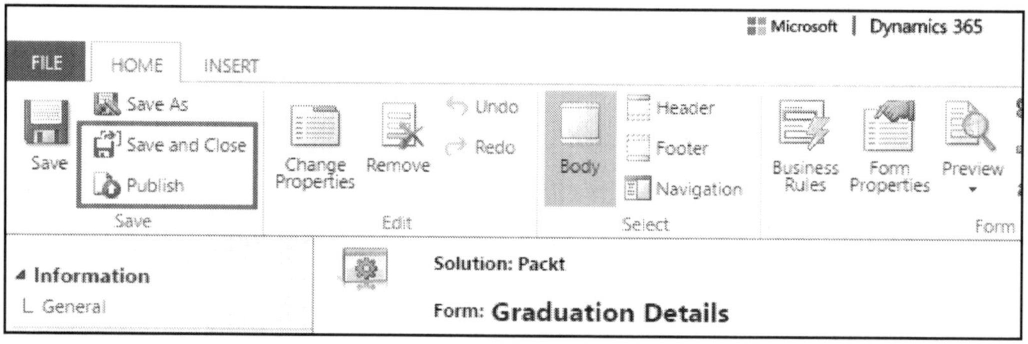

How it works...

In the first three steps, we created our JavaScript function. Notice how we introduced a namespace at the beginning of the file. JavaScript namespaces are a good practice when creating enterprise applications. Namespaces will ensure that different libraries with the same function names can coexist, and that your code calls the correct method. Furthermore, the way we declared the namespace, which is shown in the following line of code, ensures that if the namespace is already declared in a different file, the content does not get overridden:

```
var packtNs = packtNs || {}
```

This practice is particularly important when you refactor your large JavaScript library into a collection of files.

Notice the conventional JsDoc comments: `/** */`. JsDoc is the standard documentation style for JavaScript. Visual Studio autogenerates the skeleton of your comments when you start typing `/**`. In the remaining recipes of this book, we will omit the comments to make our code more concise.

In step 5 and step 6, we added the JavaScript library to the form to ensure it is loaded when the form is loaded.

In step 7 to step 9, we manually wired the function to trigger during the `OnChange` event of the **Post Graduate Start Date** field.

In step 10, we saved and published the changes. The publishing step is important to reflect your changes on the instance. Until the **Publish** button is pressed, your changes will not be available for use.

The function itself looks at the content of the hardcoded fields, **Supervisor** and **Post Graduate Start Date**, and sets the value of **Post Graduate Start Date** to today's date if the **Supervisor** field is not null and the **Post Graduate Start Date** field is null.

Behind the scenes, Dynamics 365 saves your web resources in its database and loads the necessary resources when the form is loaded, as if they are a part of the web application content. It then calls the `populateWithTodaysDate` function when the value of the **Supervisor** field is changed.

As a first simple JavaScript function, it is straightforward; however, when building enterprise applications, try to avoid hardcoded values and consider maximizing the reuse of your functions by making them generic.

There's more...

The Dynamics 365 client-side API is broad and diverse. The following diagram from MSDN (`https://msdn.microsoft.com/en-us/library/gg328474.aspx`) highlights the high-level namespaces:

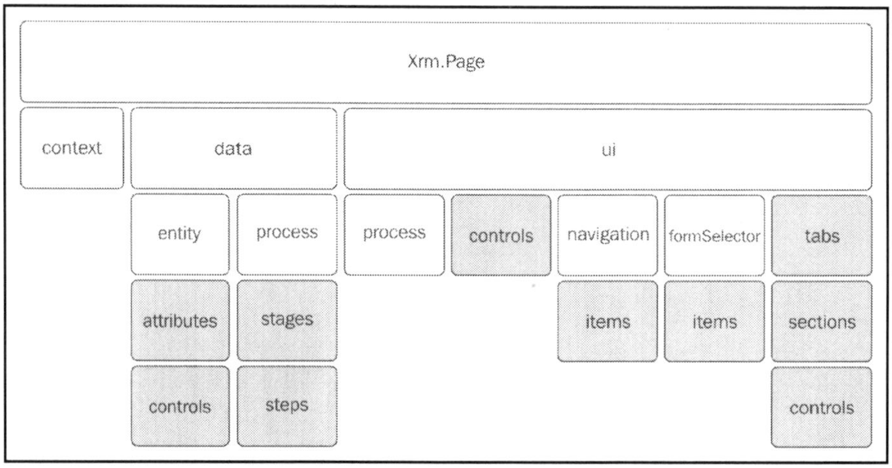

For a frontend scripting reference guide and a list of client-side capabilities, visit `https://msdn.microsoft.com/en-us/library/jj602964.aspx`.

See also

- *Wiring your event programmatically*
- *Writing reusable JavaScript functions*

Wiring your event programmatically

In the previous recipe, we wrote our first JavaScript function and wired it manually. If you are going down the custom development path, always keep in mind future maintenance tasks. Rather than wiring your events manually through the user interface, consider doing it programmatically. Not only will that reduce the manual steps to configure your extensions, but it will also give you one location to view/maintain all the event wiring.

Getting ready

In order to wire your event programmatically, you'll need a candidate function to wire (we will use the function from the previous recipe), an IDE to write your code, and, of course, access to a Dynamics 365 instance with the **System Customizer** or higher security role.

How to do it...

1. Navigate to **Settings** | **Solutions** | **Packt**.
2. Click on **Web Resources** and double-click on `packt_common.js`.
3. Click on **Text Edit** and add the following lines of code to your library:

```
packtNs.graduateForm = packtNs.graduateForm || {};
packtNs.graduateForm.loadEvent = function(){
  Xrm.Page.getAttribute("packt_supervisor").addOnChange(
     populateWithTodaysDate);
}
```

4. Click on **OK**, followed by **PUBLISH**, and then close the dialog.
5. In your solution, navigate back to **Entities** | **Graduation Details** | **Forms** and double-click on the **Main** form.
6. Double-click on the **Supervisor** field and, in the **Field Properties** dialog, select the **Events** tab.
7. Select the row with the `populateWithTodaysDate` function and click on **Remove**.
8. Click on **OK**, and then click on the **Form Properties** button at the top of your form designer.
9. Under **Event Handlers**, click on the add symbol (+).
10. Verify that `packt_common.js` is selected in the **Library** dropdown and then enter `packtNs.graduateForm.loadEvent` in the function field.
11. Click on **OK** twice, and then click on **Publish** and **Save and Close** in your form designer.

How it works...

In step 3, we extended our JavaScript to include the `loadEvent` function as the only method to manually wire up on the load event of the form. The function programmatically wires up the `populateWithTodaysDate` function to fire during the `OnChange` event of the **Supervisor** field.

We then proceeded to remove the existing manual function call in step 6 to step 8 (if we had already wired it previously), and then we introduced the `loadEvent` function as the only function called during the form's `OnLoad` event in step 9 and step 10.

As mentioned in the introduction, this pattern ensures that all the necessary setup is done in one location, giving you one place to see all the wired events in case you need to enhance/maintain your extensions. Furthermore, this will simplify your wiring when you have a large number of events to set up.

There's more...

The `OnChange` event is not the only one that can be wired; you can also programmatically wire an `OnKeyPress` event using the `addOnKeyPress` event to add behavior as the user types into a field. Form-level events can also be wired using `addOnLoad` and `addOnSave`.

See also

- *Writing reusable JavaScript functions*

Writing reusable JavaScript functions

Fool me once, shame *on you; fool me twice, shame on me!*

Whenever you see yourself copying and pasting code more than once, consider refactoring your code into reusable functions. In the first two recipes of this chapter, we built single-purpose functions with hardcoded values. We can refactor our code into a collection of reusable functions.

In this recipe, we will refactor our two functions into generic ones by parameterizing them.

Getting ready

As per the previous recipe, you will need an IDE and access to a Dynamics 365 instance with the **System Customizer** or higher security role.

How to do it...

1. Navigate to **Settings** | **Solutions** | **Packt**.
2. Click on **Web Resources** and double-click on `packt_common.js`.
3. Click on **Text Edit** and change the `populateWithTodaysDate` code to the following:

```
packtNs.common.populateWithTodaysDate =
function(attributeToMonitor, dateAttributeToChange)
{
  if (Xrm.Page.getAttribute(attributeToMonitor).getValue() !== null
&&
     Xrm.Page.getAttribute(dateAttributeToChange).getValue() ===
null)
  {
    Xrm.Page.getAttribute(dateAttributeToChange).setValue(
       new Date());
  }
}
```

4. Add the following function:

```
packtNs.common.wireOnChangeEvents =
   function(eventAttributeTuples){
for (var i in eventAttributeTuples) {
  Xrm.Page.getAttribute(eventAttributeTuples[i].attribute)
     .addOnChange(eventAttributeTuples[i].function);
  }
}
```

5. Replace the `loadEvent` function with the following code:

```
packtNs.graduateForm.loadEvent = function(){
  packtNs.common.wireOnChangeEvents([
    {attribute: "packt_supervisor",
      function:
        packtNs.common.populateWithTodaysDate("packt_supervisor",
        "packt_postgraduatestartdate")
    }
  ]);
}
```

6. Click on **OK**, followed by **PUBLISH**, and then close the dialog.

How it works...

In this recipe, we refactored our existing functions into something more generic and reusable.

In step 3, we removed the hardcoded attribute names of our `populateWithTodaysDate` function and replaced them with the function's parameters.

In step 4, we created a new function to write a parameterized attribute to an `onChange` event and execute a parameterized function. Notice how the function is expecting an array of elements and loops through them. The function also leverages the dot notation for each object in the array to retrieve the attribute name and the function to execute `OnChange`.

In step 5, we replaced the `loadEvent` event with a call to our newly created function from step 4, and we passed it a **JSON** (**JavaScript Object Notation**) object that actually constitutes the function and the attributes of each element to be wired.

In step 6, we saved and published our changes.

The result is a generic set of functions that enriches your common library. They can be reused across multiple solutions simply by plugging in the name of the attributes that need to be monitored and changed.

See also

- *Creating your first JavaScript function*
- *Wiring your event programmatically*

Querying 365 data using the Web API endpoint

As the Dynamics platforms evolved over the years, new features were introduced to keep the platforms modern and up to date. In older versions, the only way to communicate with Dynamics CRM programmatically was through SOAP web services. In later years, the Microsoft Dynamics product team introduced OData endpoints that greatly simplified and modernized the communication mechanism.

In this recipe, we will retrieve the list of activities associated with a contact, and then display a warning message if any of the activities are open and assigned to the current logged-in user.

Getting ready

To perform the customization, you will require access to a Dynamics 365 module along with a **System Customizer** or higher role. An IDE or a JavaScript editor of your choice is also recommended. To test your OData queries, consider using the **CRM REST Builder** solution written by Microsoft MVP, Jason Lattimer. Also, consider a REST query tool to rapidly test your queries. Chrome's REST Console add-on is a good one.

Additionally, users will require the appropriate access to the relevant entities being queried.

How to do it...

1. Navigate to **Settings** | **Solutions** | **Packt**.
2. Click on **Web Resources** and click on **New**, enter `contact.js` next to the name, select **Script (JScript)** from **Type**, and click on **Text Editor**.

3. Copy and insert the following code and click on **OK**:

```
var packtNs = packtNs || {};
packtNs.contact = packtNs.contact || {};
packtNs.contact.checkActiveTasksAssignedToMe = function()
 {
  var uniqueNotificationId = "OutstandingTasks";
  Xrm.Page.ui.clearFormNotification(uniqueNotificationId);
   var contactId =
     Xrm.Page.data.entity.getId().replace(/[{}]/g,"");
  var currentUserId =
     Xrm.Page.context.getUserId().replace(/[{}]/g,"");
  var req = new XMLHttpRequest();
  var requestUrl = Xrm.Page.context.getClientUrl() +
     "/api/data/v8.2/tasks?$filter=_regardingobjectid_value
     eq " + contactId + " and _ownerid_value eq " +
     currentUserId + " and  statecode eq 0";
  req.open("GET", requestUrl, true);
  req.setRequestHeader("OData-MaxVersion", "4.0");
   req.setRequestHeader("OData-Version", "4.0");
   req.setRequestHeader("Accept", "application/json");
  req.setRequestHeader("Prefer", "odata.include-
     annotations=\"OData.Community.Display.V1.FormattedValue\"");
  req.onreadystatechange = function () {
     if (this.readyState === 4) {
       req.onreadystatechange = null;
       if (this.status === 200) {
         var results = JSON.parse(this.response);
         if(results.value.length > 0){
           Xrm.Page.ui.setFormNotification("You have
           outstanding tasks assigned to you.", "WARNING",
           uniqueNotificationId)
         }
      }
      else {
        //.. handle error
      }
    }
  };
  req.send();
}
```

4. Click on **Save**, and then close your window.
5. Back in your **Packt** solution, navigate to **Entities** | **Contact** | **Forms** and double-click on the Main form.
6. Click on **Form Properties** and, under **Form Libraries**, click on the add symbol (**+**).
7. Select your JavaScript library, `packt_contact.js`, from the list (you can use the search functionality to filter the values). Click on **Add** and then click on **OK**.
8. Under **Event Handlers**, verify that **Control** is set to **Form** and **Event** is set to **OnLoad**, then click on +.
9. Ensure that `packt_contact.js` is selected in the **Library** dropdown, and then enter `packtNs.contact.checkActiveTasksAssignedToMe` in the **Function** field.
10. Click on **Save and Close**, followed by **Publish All Customizations** in your solution window.

How it works...

In order to call the Web API from our function, we first prepared the query URL, used `XMLHttpRequest` to build and execute our request, and then displayed a warning if the result met a specific criterion. The last few steps described the manual wiring as per the first recipe of this chapter.

Setting up the GET URL

In step 3 of our custom JavaScript extension, we constructed the `requestUrl` parameter as follows:

```
Xrm.Page.context.getClientUrl() +
 "/api/data/v8.2/tasks?$filter=_regardingobjectid_value eq " +
contactId + " and _ownerid_value eq " + currentUserId + " and
statecode eq 0"
```

The `getClientUrl()` function returns the base URL of your Dynamics 365 instance. We then appended `/api/data/v8.2`, which is the address of the Web API endpoint, as defined under **Settings** | **Customizations** | **Developer Resources** | **Instance Web API**:

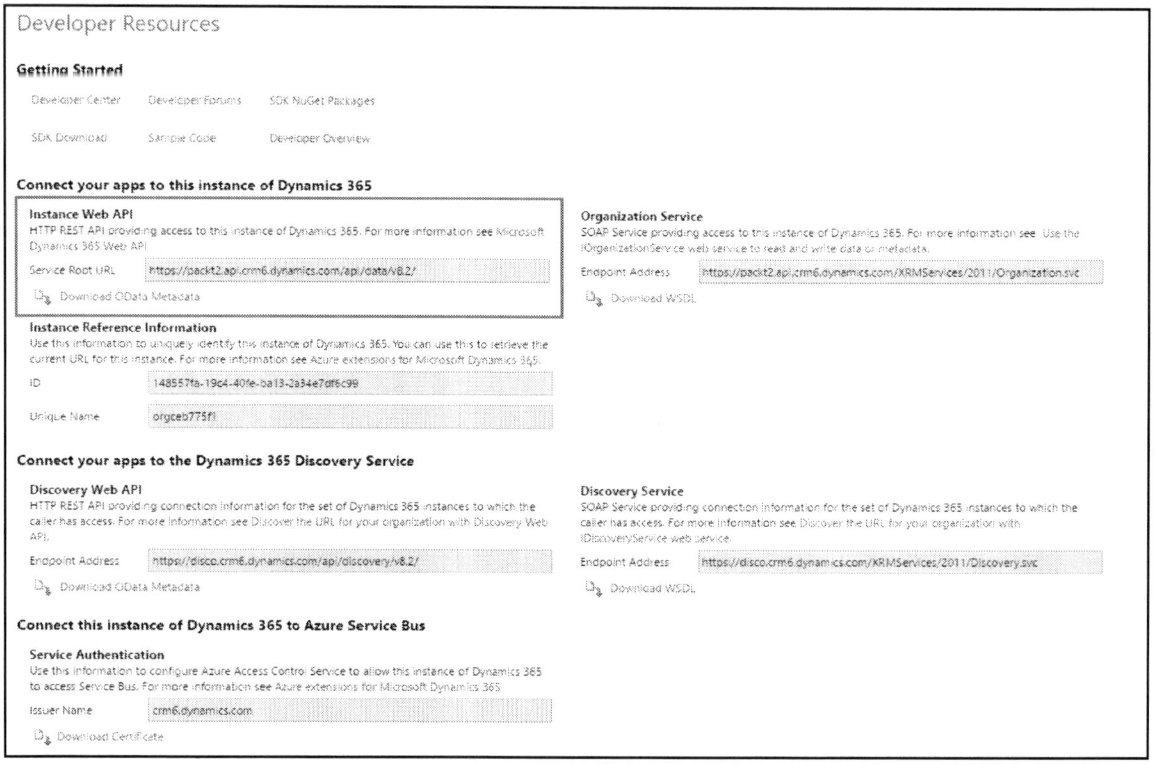

> **TIP:** The URL construction will be different when running your query using an on-premise Dynamics 365 instance. It is highly recommended to refactor the URL construct in its own method.

Notice how `currentUserId` and `contactId` are extracted as variables to better understand the flow and for debugging purposes.

The URL looks for the task activity and uses the `$filter` keyword to only retrieve records related to the current record, owned by the current user with a `statecode` of 0 (Open).

REST request

Additionally, in step 3 of our custom JavaScript extension, we used the cross-browser `XMLHttpRequest` (an API that helps communicate between client and server) to call the Dynamics 365 Web API endpoint. We opened the connection using the following line:

```
req.open("GET", requestUrl, true);
```

The first parameter is a "verb" that defines we are performing a GET request to retrieve data using the constructed URL. The Boolean value at the end ensures that the request is performed asynchronously.

> TIP: Asynchronous calls are the recommended way to call the Web API endpoint on the client side to ensure your pages are responsive.

The callback function is defined in the `onreadystatechange` element later in the code.

In setting up the request, we ensure that we are requesting the OData v4.0, and that we accept JSON.

The following lines of code ensure that we get the formatted value as it would appear on your screen:

```
req.setRequestHeader("Prefer", "odata.include-
 annotations=\"OData.Community.Display.V1.FormattedValue\"");
```

Finally, we send the request by executing the `send()` function.

Notifications

At the beginning of the function, we cleared all notifications associated with a predefined unique. Towards the end, we checked whether the JSON result contains more than one value. If it does, we set a warning notification using the unique key and a text message.

Wiring

In step 5 to step 9, we wired our extension to the `OnLoad` event of the contact entity.

There's more...

The OData Web API is used for much more than retrieving data. In fact, the Microsoft product team's aim is to have it on par with the SOAP web services. The differences are minor and every release narrows the gap even further. The new OData v4.0 endpoint is the main candidate to build custom-rich applications with a Dynamics 365 backend.

> The SOAP endpoint (also referred to as the CRM 2011 endpoint) has been deprecated as of February 2017 (`https://msdn.microsoft.com/en-us/library/dn281891.aspx`).

If you are planning on using the Web API outside Dynamics 365, within a separate web application, the *Using Cross-Origin Resource Sharing with CRM Online* recipe from `Chapter 6`, *Enhancing Your Code*, explains how to set up **Cross-origin resource sharing** (**CORS**).

The aim of this recipe is to demonstrate the different steps to connect to the OData endpoint. Given that most of the code can be reused, it is a good candidate to be refactored into a library. In fact, there are some libraries already out there that can help you encapsulate some of that logic, such as the `SDK.REST.js` library included in the SDK samples.

See also

- *Using Cross-Origin Resource Sharing with CRM Online*, in `Chapter 6`, *Enhancing Your Code*.

Querying the 365 metadata services

In the previous recipe, we used the Web API to query data available in our Dynamics 365 instance. As we previously mentioned, the Web API is almost on par with the SOAP endpoint. This includes for querying Dynamics 365 metadata; retrieving the metadata is key to building custom frontends driven by Dynamics 365 configuration.

In this recipe, we will walk through how to query metadata associated with the contact entity to view the entity details as well as attribute details.

Getting ready

On top of your Dynamics 365 access, you will require "read" access on the **Entity** and **Field** privileges located under the **Customization** tab in security roles.

How to do it...

1. Using Chrome, navigate to this URL:

```
[your organization
URL]/api/data/v8.2/EntityDefinitions?$filter=SchemaName eq
'Contact'
```

2. In a different tab, navigate to the following URL:

```
[your organization
URL]/api/data/v8.2/EntityDefinitions(608861bc-50a4-4c5f-
a02c-21fe1943e2cf)?$select=LogicalName&$expand=Attributes($select=L
ogicalName;$filter=AttributeType eq
Microsoft.Dynamics.CRM.AttributeTypeCode'Picklist')
```

How it works...

The Web API provides a RESTful service that can be queried using the GET HTTP verb and a URL to select and filter the content. In step 1, we queried the entity definitions and filter red on contact. The JSON result contained all the metadata associated with the contact entity. We can expand the URL to include further OData statements, such as the `$select` keyword, to filter the number of fields returned.

The first query returned a list of elements including the `MetadataId` of the entity. We then fed the ID into the second query to retrieve the attributes related to the contact entity. We limited the number of elements returned to `LogicalName`, as depicted by the `$select` statement. The `$expand=Attributes` statement is similar to a SQL join statement. It includes all the related attributes. We then further refined the content to only include the `LogicalName` of each attribute and filtered the expand statement to only include `Picklist`.

There's more...

The metadata services introduce a new dimension of customization that goes beyond basic data manipulation. It opens new doors for user-interface customizations as well as generic processing where the schema of the entities you are dealing with is unknown until runtime.

On top of the two queries we described in this recipe, you can query specific-attribute details, relationships, global option sets, and much more.

For further details, visit the following MSDN article at `https://msdn.microsoft.com/en-us/library/mt607522.aspx`.

See also

- *Querying 365 data using the Web API endpoint*

Building a custom UI using AngularJS

Web resources were introduced in Dynamics CRM 2011. One of the reasons for introducing HTML and JavaScript web resources was to get rid of ASPX ISV pages that needed to be deployed on the Dynamics CRM server. An action was not possible in a cloud environment. ISV pages were replaced with custom HTML **user interfaces** (**UI**) that can be embedded in iFrames on a form.

As a developer, you have the choice to build your own UI libraries to retrieve content and display it on custom user interfaces, or you can leverage industry standard frameworks that help produce clean, maintainable user interface extensions using proven design patterns. In this recipe, we have selected AngularJS as a popular framework to build a custom web resource to embed in an iFrame. We will focus on Angular version 1, since version 2 is still to gain popularity.

This recipe's custom user interface will leverage the metadata queries discussed in the previous recipe to build a page that displays the logical names of picklists associated with the contact entity.

Getting ready

To develop the custom UI, you will need the usual access to a Dynamics 365 instance with the **System Customizer** or higher security role. An IDE, or a modern text editor of your choice, is highly recommended to facilitate the development of your Angular page.

You also need to download the latest Angular 1 libraries available from `https://angularjs.org/`.

In this recipe, we will be using Angular 1.5.0.

How to do it...

1. Navigate to **Settings** | **Solutions** | **Packt**.
2. Click on **Web Resources** and click on **New**.
3. Create a JScript called `packt_/js/angular.min.js` and upload the `angular.min.js` file that you have downloaded from `https://angularjs.org/`.
4. Create a JScript called `packt_/js/packt.app.js` with the following content:

```
var app = angular.module("packtApp", []);
```

5. Create a JScript called `packt_/js/packt.controller.js` with the following content:

```
app.controller('packtController', function
 ($scope,  packtCrmService) {
  $scope.dataLoading = true;
  packtCrmService.loadAttributesFromCurrentEntity().then(
      function (result) {
       if (result.status == 200) {
         $scope.attributes = result.data;
       }
       else{
         alert("Error while loading attributes. " +
             result.status);
       }
     }).finally(function () {
       $scope.dataLoading = false;
     });
});
```

6. Create a JScript called `packt_/js/packt.services.js` with the following content:

```
app.service('packtCrmService', function ($http, $location)
 {
  this.loadAttributesFromCurrentEntity = function () {
    var entityGuid =
window.location.href.substring(window.location.href.indexOf("=")+1)
;
      var attributesUrl = window.location.origin +
       '/api/data/v8.2/EntityDefinitions(' + entityGuid +
       ')?$select=LogicalName&$expand=Attributes(
       $select=LogicalName;$filter=AttributeType eq
       Microsoft.Dynamics.CRM.AttributeTypeCode\'Picklist\')';
      var attributesRequest = {
        method: 'GET',
        url: attributesUrl,
        headers: {
        'Prefer': 'odata.include-
         annotations="OData.Community.Display.V1.FormattedValue"'
      }
    }
    var attributesPromise = $http(attributesRequest).then(
      function (response) {
        return {
          "status": response.status,
          "data": response.data.Attributes
                };
            },
            function (response) {
               return {
                    "status": response.status,
                    "data": response.statusText
                };
            }
        );
        return attributesPromise;
    }
});
```

7. Create an HTML resource with the name `packt_/attributes.htm` and the following content:

```
<html>
<head>
    <script type="text/javascript"
src="js/angular.min.js"></script>
```

```
    <script type="text/javascript" src="js/packt.app.js"></script>
    <script type="text/javascript"
src="js/packt.controller.js"></script>
    <script type="text/javascript"
src="js/packt.service.js"></script>
    <meta charset="utf-8">
        <title>Attributes V1.14</title>
    </meta>
</head>
<body>
    <div ng-app="packtApp" ng-controller="packtController">
        <div ng-if="dataLoading">Loading analysis...</div>
        <ul ng-repeat="attribute in attributes" ng-
 if="dataLoading === false">
            <li>{{ attribute.LogicalName }}</li>
        </ul>
    </div>
</body>
</html>
```

8. Under **Entities** | **Contact** | **Forms**, double-click on the **Main** form.
9. Click on **INSERT** | **Web Resource** and enter the following details:
    - **Web**: `resource packt_attributes.htm`
    - **Name**: `WebResources_attributehtm`
    - **Label**: `Attributes`
    - **Custom Parameter (data)**: `<Contact entity MetadataId in this example: 608861bc-50a4-4c5f-a02c-21fe1943e2cf>`
10. Click on **OK**, and then on the **HOME** tab, click on **Save and Close**.
11. Back in your solution, click on **Publish All Customizations**.

How it works...

The AngularJS application is divided into five layers: an HTML user interface with embedded ng directives, an application JavaScript file that initializes the Angular application, a service layer that retrieves the data, a controller that coordinates the communication between your data access layer and your user interface, and, finally, the AngularJS library.

In step 3, we started by adding the AngularJS libraries to ensure that the browser's JavaScript engine understands the ng directives.

In step 4, we defined the app--a simple AngularJS app with the name `packtApp`.

In step 5, we built the controller with one built-in function. We injected the `$scope` variable into our controller, which will help us access variables from the global scope. We also injected `packtCrmService`, the service layer that we will define in the next step. The result from the service layer is then passed to the `$scope.attributes` variable accessible from the HTML View. The controller also set the `$scope.loading` variable to true and false. This will be used later in the HTML binding to show and hide sections, as the request is executing asynchronously.

In step 6, we defined the service layer that calls the metadata query from the previous recipe and returns the attribute's `LogicalName` values. Given that the result is in JSON format, the JavaScript engine is flexible enough to treat it as an array with attributes for each record. Notice how we are retrieving a value from `windows.location.href`. This attribute is defined in step 9, where we pass the entity GUID as a parameter. We can potentially use the Dynamics 365 metadata services to query the GUID of the entity and make the library completely generically, with minimal setup required. However, to reduce chattiness between client and server and improve performance, we are passing it as a static parameter value. As for the method to retrieve the query string value, we are simply using `indexOf` and the substring function. AngularJS provides better alternatives by enabling HTML5 mode. That said, to compact the code, and for simplicity, this has been omitted.

In step 7, we built our `HTML` file. Notice the relative path used to reference the JavaScript libraries, as we introduced a hierarchy using the forward slashes (/) in the name of the web resources.

> **TIP:** Using a hierarchical web resource structure helps when debugging your code using web browsers' development tools, or when using other editing tools such as the XrmToolBox's Web Resources Manager.

In the `HTML` file, we use the `dataLoading` value to show and hide the relevant sections as the asynchronous calls are retrieving the data. Once the results are returned, the list <ul> appears. The `ng-repeat` directive loops through all the attributes and creates one list item, <li>, to display the `LogicalName` value of each attribute.

Finally, in step 9, we inserted the HTML web resource into the contact's form and we included the entity `Metadata ID` (retrieved in the previous recipe for the contact entity) as a parameter to avoid calling the metadata services twice. In case you are using the application on a different entity, you will have to retrieve the correct GUID for your entity using the technique from the previous recipe. There is always a compromise between how much you query, and how much you provide. It's a balance between performance and setup overhead.

There's more...

AngularJS is one of the many frameworks you can use within Dynamics 365. There are numerous other frameworks that are also good candidates to integrate with your extensions. Common ones are Knockout, React, TypeScript, and jQuery.

> Microsoft recently announced the custom controls feature to be included in future Dynamics 365 versions. This feature will allow developers to build their own controls using a Microsoft-defined frameworks. In fact, custom controls have been available in Dynamics CRM for a while. They were introduced as (non-customizable) rich mobile controls in Dynamics CRM 2016.

See also

- *Query CRM data using the Web API endpoint*

Debugging your JavaScript with Edge

Debugging is one of the essential skills a developer needs to master when building JavaScript extensions. This recipe covers the steps required to debug your extensions using Microsoft Edge.

Getting ready

To get ready, you'll need a form that calls a custom JavaScript function. You can use the **Graduation Details** client-side customization from the first recipe in this chapter as an example. Ensure the **Graduation Details** entity is accessible from the **Sales** module.

You can do so by ticking the **Sales** checkbox in the entity configuration general tab. You will also need the Edge browser (available by default on Windows 10 and above). If you prefer Internet Explorer, the two browsers have very similar debugging interfaces.

How to do it...

1. Navigate to an entity that has a form that uses your JavaScript using Edge (in our example, **Sales** | **Graduation Details**).
2. Open an existing record by double-clicking one from the list, or create a new one by click on the **+ New** option.
3. Press *F12* on your keyboard, or go to your Edge menu by clicking on the ellipsis **...**, on the top right-hand side of the browser's window and click on **F12 Developer Tools**.
4. Select the **Debugger** tab, and then look for your JavaScript file in the left navigation.

   Alternatively, you can simply start typing the first part of your JavaScript file name, and it will filter the content based on your input. Once you locate your file, select it.

5. Click the line number on the left-hand side of your script content corresponding to the line where you want the debugger to break.
6. Perform the action that will trigger the JavaScript function call:

```
var packtNs = packtNs || {};
packtNs.common = packtNs.common || {};

packtNs.common.populateWithTodaysDate  = function()
{
    if (Xrm.Page.getAttribute("packt_supervisor").getValue() !== null && Xrm.Page.ge
    {
        Xrm.Page.getAttribute("packt_postgraduatestartdate").setValue(new Date());
    }
}
```

7. Once the debugger breaks on your breakpoint line, you can highlight the expressions you want to inspect and hover over them to view their values:

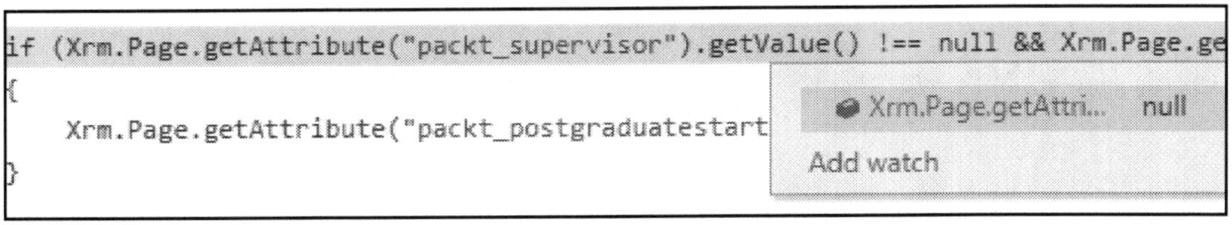

8. Press *F10* to step to the next line.
9. Press *F5* to resume your script execution.

How it works...

In step 4, we searched for the JavaScript we would like to debug. If you are looking for your custom script manually, they usually sit under a folder with your organization URL followed by a subfolder with a number between curly brackets, as shown in the following screenshot:

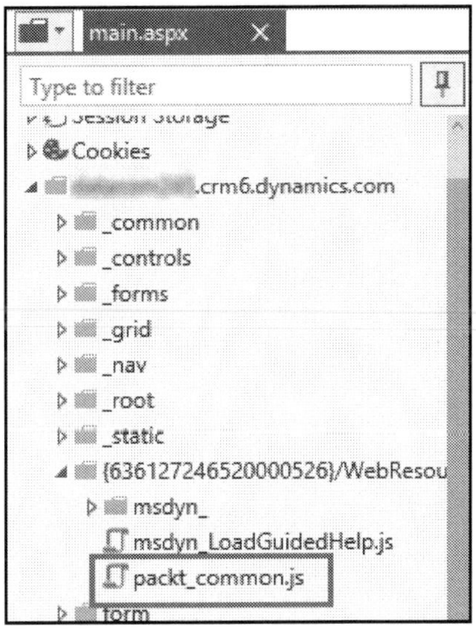

In step 5, we set the breakpoint at the line where we would like the debugger to break.

In step 7, we inspected the values of an expression. We can also add it to the **Watch** list by clicking on the **Add watch** link under the value. Any changes to that expression will then be highlighted in the watch list.

> The console is a developer's best friend. It can maximize your development velocity by testing your code live rather than going through a cycle of update/save/push/publish/refresh every time you change your script. You can also edit your JavaScript on the fly to address issues, and retest your code, granted you do not refresh the page. This feature is experimental in edge and might not work as expected.
> In scenarios where your script is executed during `the OnLoad` event, consider using Telerik's Fiddler to intercept calls from Dynamics 365 to replace the JavaScript with an updated version until you are satisfied with the outcome, before going back to the usual channels.

Finally, in step 8 and step 9, we used the keyboard shortcuts to step over the breakpoint line or continued running the script. We can also use *F11* to step into a function and *Shift* + *F11* to step out of a function.

There's more...

This recipe covers the basics of Edge's JavaScript debugging capabilities; the browser covers far greater capabilities than simple debugging. For example, the **Network** tab displays useful details on how long each file took to load. The following screenshot shows the different cached GET requests:

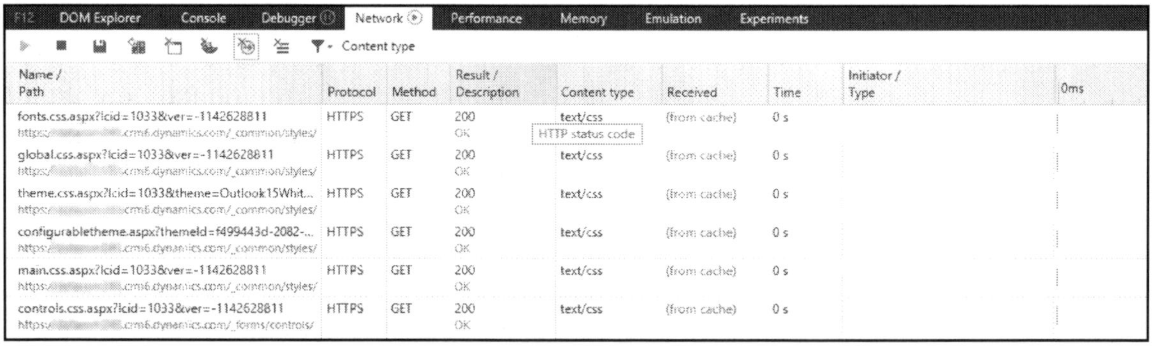

This is particularly important when troubleshooting performance issues to identify the root cause of your problem (network, large files, anything else).

The **Performance** tab is another good feature that allows you to record a portion of your session and display metrics on the browser's performance. The dashboard will not only display network values, but also script evaluation time, DOM rendering time, and much more:

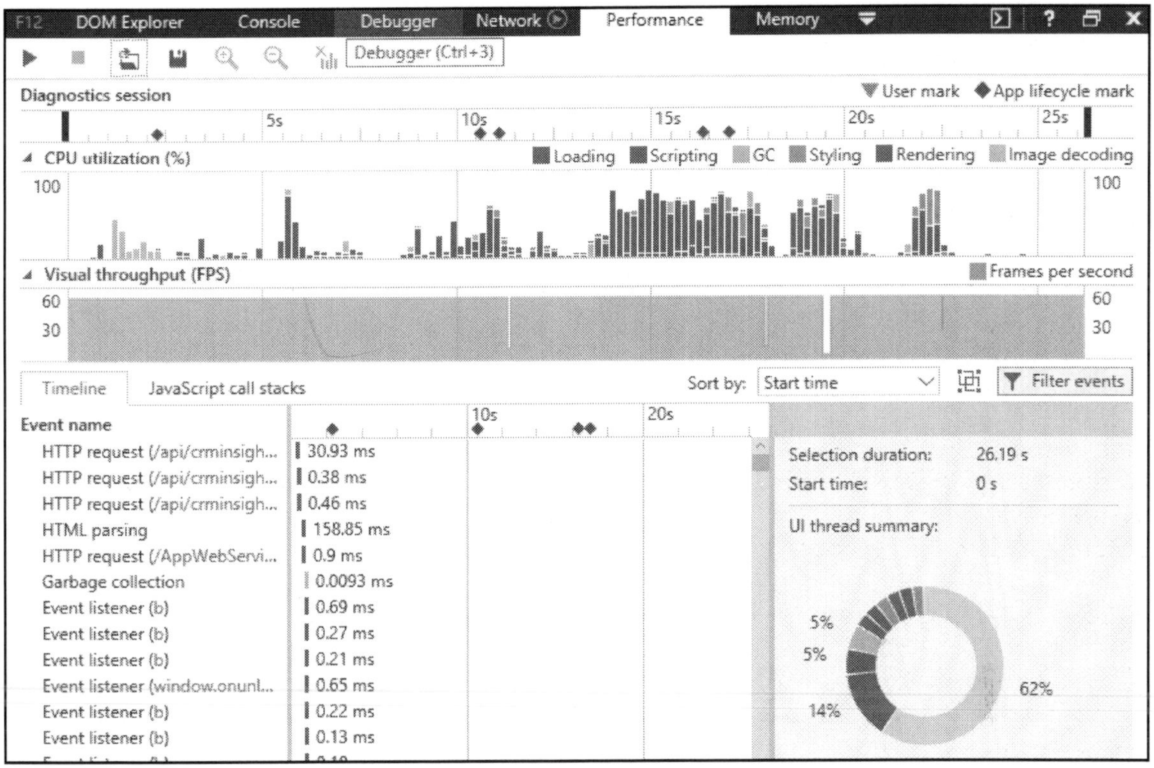

See also

- *Debugging your JavaScript with Chrome*

Debugging your JavaScript with Chrome

Given that Dynamics 365 is cross-browser compatible, developers can also debug their client-side code using Google Chrome. This recipe will cover a similar scenario to the previous one, except, the debugging will be done using Google Chrome.

Getting ready

Similar to the previous recipe, you'll need a form that calls a custom JavaScript function. You can use the first recipe in this chapter as an example. Of course, you'll also need a Google Chrome browser.

How to do it...

1. Navigate to an entity that has a form that uses your JavaScript using Google Chrome, in our example, **Sales** | **Graduation Details**.
2. Open an existing record by double-clicking a record in the list, or create a new one by clicking on the **+ New** option.
3. Press *F12* on your keyboard or *Ctrl* + *Shift* + *I*. Alternatively, go to your Chrome menu and navigate to **More tools** | **Developer tools**.
4. Select the **Sources** tab, and then look for your file in the left navigation **Sources** list or press *Ctrl* + *P* on your keyboard. Start typing a partial name of your file (`common`) to find your JavaScript file (in our example, `packt_common.js`).
5. Click on the line number on the left-hand side corresponding to the line where you want the debugger to break.
6. Perform the action that will trigger the JavaScript function call and the debugger will break at the breakpoint, as per the following screenshot:

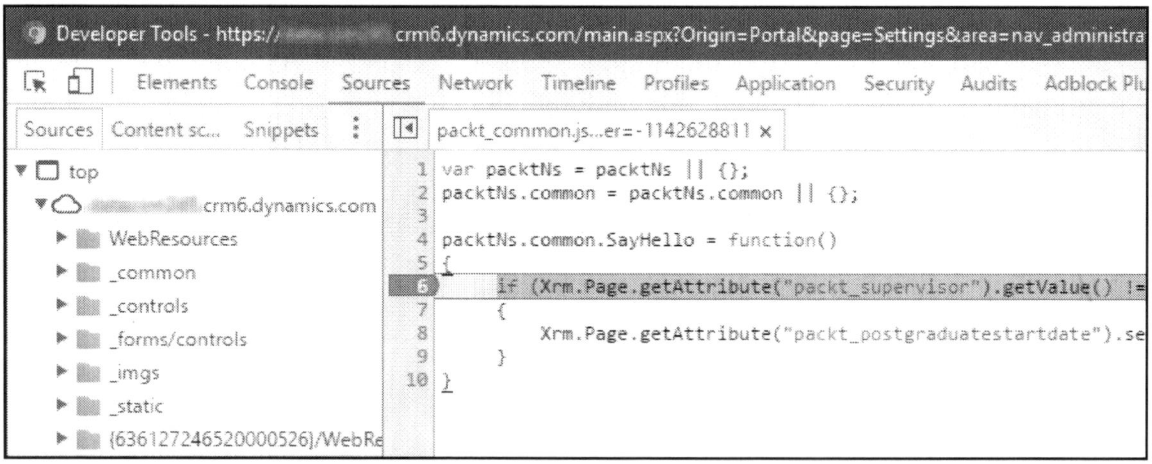

7. Once the debugger breaks on your breakpoint line, you can highlight expressions you want to inspect and hover over them to view their values.
8. Press *F10* to step to the next line.
9. Press *F8* to resume your script execution:

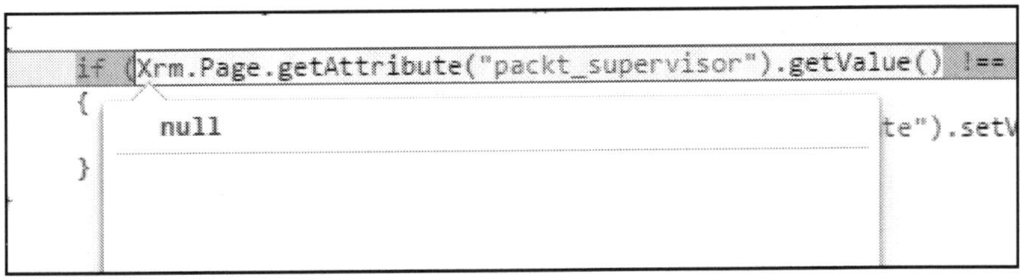

How it works...

In step 4, we searched for the JavaScript we would like to debug, and in step 5. we set the breakpoint at the line where we would like the debugger to break.

In step 7, we inspected the values of an expression. We can also add it to the **Watch** list by right-clicking on the expression and selecting **Add to watch**. Any changes to that expression will then be highlighted in the Watch list. We can furthermore add it to the console to run live queries on it.

Finally, in step 8 and step 9, we used the keyboard shortcuts to step over the breakpoint line or continue running the script. We can also use *F11* to step into a function.

There's more...

This recipe covers the basics of Chrome's JavaScript debugging capabilities. The browser covers far greater capabilities than simple debugging. The **Network** tab, for instance, displays behind the scenes file-by-file download times that could be very useful to identify performance issues.

In the **Network** tab, you can also simulate a slow connection by selecting a profile under throttling (high latency, slow download/upload speed) as shown in the following screenshot:

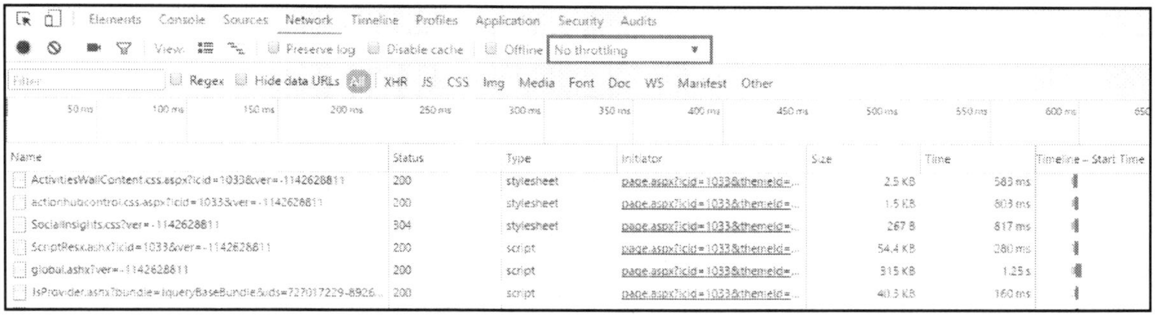

The **Timeline** tab displays further details about the time to evaluate the scripts and render the page. This is particularly useful if your page has a high number of elements and you'd like to understand which bits have the highest performance impact:

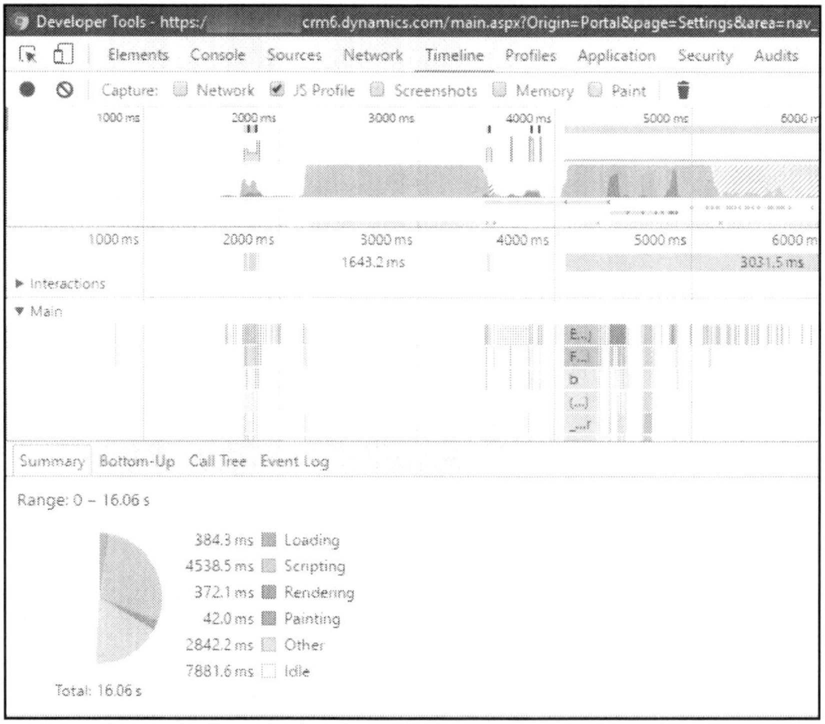

The other tabs in the developer tools cover further capabilities, such as DOM inspect, security, and much more.

See also

- *Debugging your JavaScript with Edge*

Unit testing your JavaScript

Nowadays, automated unit testing has become the norm on most projects. Unit testing is not only great at ensuring that your code is repeatedly and thoroughly tested, but it also provides a safety harness against future changes that might break your code. Furthermore, unit testing helps you improve code structure quality by building loosely coupled modules.

In this recipe, we will write a Visual Studio unit test for our Dynamics 365 JavaScript extension. More specifically, we will unit test the first JavaScript library we built in this chapter. We will check whether the conditions are correct and that the set value is called once on the `postgraduatestartdate` attribute. Given that the unit tests will run from Visual Studio with a fake `Xrm.Page` library, we won't need access to Dynamics 365.

Getting ready

Unlike managed .NET code unit tests, JavaScript unit testing requires a bit of preparation to get up and running. There are a few parts to your setup: you will need a tool to integrate your JavaScript unit test with Visual Studio, a JavaScript unit testing assertion framework, an `Xrm.Page` fake library, and optionally, a tool to run your JavaScript without a browser (headless). You will also need Visual Studio 2015.

Integration with Visual Studio

There are a few options available that can integrate your JavaScript unit tests into Visual Studio. **ReSharper** by *JetBrains* and **Chutzpah** are among the most popular ones. Given the richness of the ReSharper tool, and its seamless integration with Visual Studio, we will be using it in this recipe. ReSharper is not a free tool, but JetBrains does offers a 30-day trial for its products. The regular version of ReSharper should suffice for this exercise.

Assertion framework

There are a few JavaScript assertion frameworks in the market. **QUnit** and **Jasmine** are among the popular ones that integrate well with ReSharper and Chutzpah. In this recipe, we will be focusing on QUnit.

Faking Xrm.Page

There are a few available mocking/stubbing frameworks, **sinon.js** (`http://sinonjs.org/`) being one of them.

There are even Xrm-specific ones, such as **Fake Xrm Page** (`https://fakexrmpage.codeplex.com/`).

To better understand how we are interacting with what is happening behind the scenes in our unit test, we will build our own fake `Xrm.Page` library.

Headless browser

The headless browser is optional but highly recommended, especially, if you are going down the Continuous Integration/Continuous Deployment route. Headless browsers allow you to run JavaScript without a browser. One of the most popular headless JavaScript execution tools is **PhantomJS** (`http://phantomjs.org/`). PhantomJS is based on the WebKit engine used in Safari and Chrome.

ReSharper, by default, executes the JavaScript unit test in your default browser. In order to change this behaviour, navigate to **ReSharper** | **Options** | **JavaScript Tests** | **Run Tests With** and add the location of the downloaded `phantomjs.exe` file in the **Path to PhantomJS executable** option:

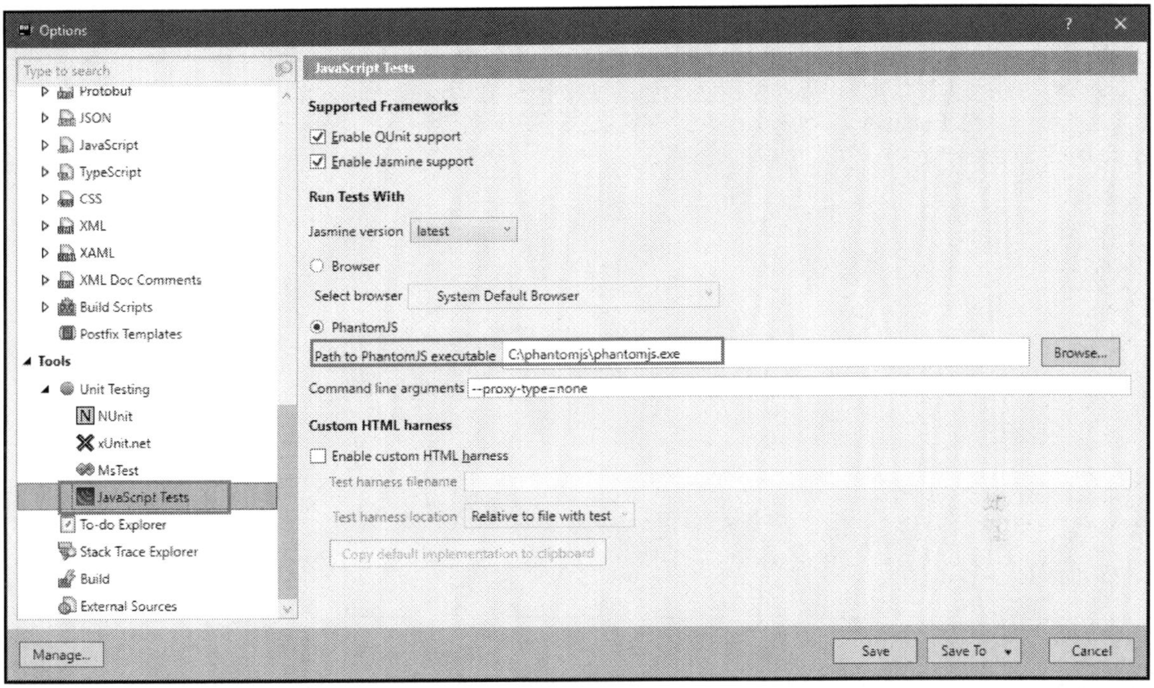

How to do it...

1. Create a new empty **ASP.NET Web Application** in Visual Studio, as shown here:

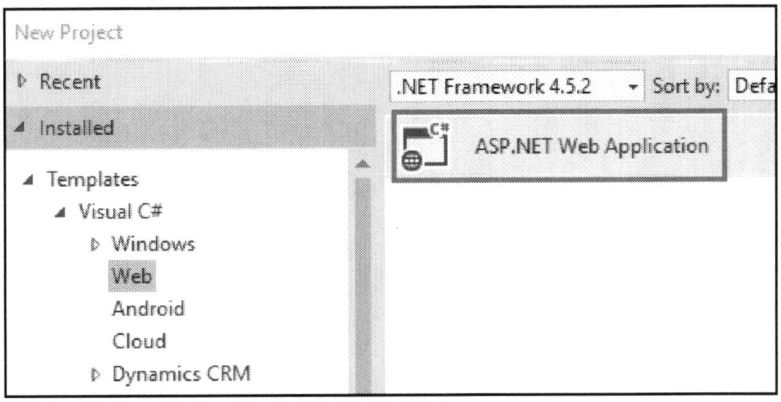

2. Download and add `Qunit.js` from `https://qunitjs.com/`.

3. Under the `scripts` folder, add the `common.js` library created in the first recipe of this chapter:

```
var packtNs = packtNs || {};
packtNs.common = packtNs.common || {};

packtNs.common.populateWithTodaysDate =  function()
{
  if (Xrm.Page.getAttribute("packt_supervisor").getValue()
      !== null &&
Xrm.Page.getAttribute("packt_postgraduatestartdate").
      getValue() === null)
  {
    Xrm.Page.getAttribute("packt_postgraduatestartdate").
     setValue(new Date());
  }
}
```

4. Add the following code in the `Xrm.Fake.js` file:

```
var Xrm = {};
Xrm.Page = {}
var Attribute = function (attributeName) {
  this.attributeName = attributeName,
   this.setValueCounter = 0;
  this.getValue = function () {
    if (this.attributeName === ("packt_supervisor")) {
      return "Sample Value";
    }
    return null;
  },
  this.setValue = function (value) {
    this.setValueCounter += 1;
  },
  this.getCountFunctionCalls = function () {
    return this.setValueCounter;
  }
}
var pageAttributes = {}
Xrm.Page.getAttribute = function (attributeName) {
  if (pageAttributes[attributeName]) {
    return pageAttributes[attributeName];
  }
  pageAttributes[attributeName] = new
     Attribute(attributeName);
  return pageAttributes[attributeName];
}
```

5. Add the following code in the `common.test.js` file:

```
/// <reference path="common.js"/>
/// <reference path="qunit-2.0.1.js" />
/// <reference path="FakeXrmPage.js"/>
test("Xrm test populateWithTodaysDate", function () {
  // Act
  packtNs.common.populateWithTodaysDate();

  //Assert
equal(Xrm.Page.getAttribute("packt_postgraduatestartdate")
   . getCountSetValueCalls(), 1, "PostGraduate attribute
   setValue called exactly once");
});
```

6. Run the test by clicking on the ReSharper icon next to your test method and select **Run**:

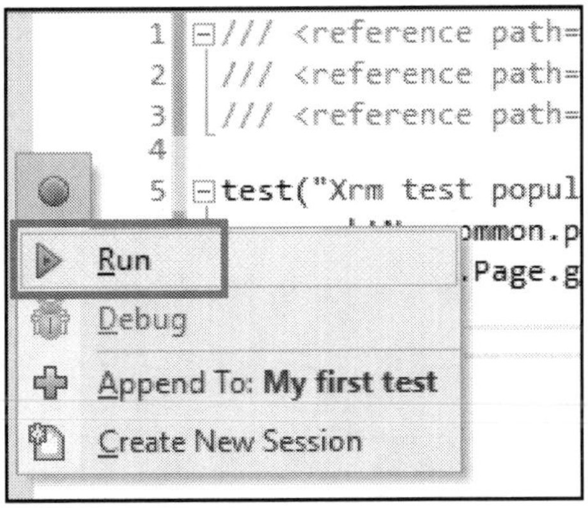

How it works...

In step 1 to step 3, we set up our blank ASP.NET solution. We added the JavaScript unit testing assertion framework (QUnit.js) and the JavaScript Web Resource we are unit testing. Note that if you already have a Visual Studio solution with your web resources, you can reuse it; no need to recreate a new solution specifically for unit testing.

In step 4, we created the fake library. We first created the `Xrm` and `Xrm.Page` namespaces, then defined the stub for each of `getAttribute`, `setValue`, and `getValue`.

The `getAttribute` function creates a custom object that has `setValue`; `getValue`, a new method, `getCountSetValueCalls`; and some attributes. Notice how `getAttribute` stores the newly created objects in an array to ensure that we do not recreate it every time we call the `getAttribute` function with the same attribute name.

The `getValue` function fakes the result based on the attribute name to simulate what Dynamics 365 would actually do in a specific scenario.

The `setValue` function is actually used as a mock, not a stub. All it does is increment the number of times the method has been called.

Finally, the `getCountSetValueCalls` function is a helper function that returns the number of times `setValue` was called.

In step 5, we started by referencing all the JavaScript required for the unit tests using the `/// <reference path="..."/>` notation. This ensures that the correct fake library is called, and arranges our unit test correctly in case we create more than one for different scenarios.

Each test starts with the function test that helps ReSharper identify your unit tests. We give our unit test a name, `Xrm test populateWithTodaysDate`, and pass it a callback function to act on and execute our function under the `populateWithTodaysDate` test. We then assert that the `setValue` function is called exactly once and displays a text describing the expected result, **PostGraduate attribute setValue called exactly once**.

Once executed in step 6, the final result will look like this:

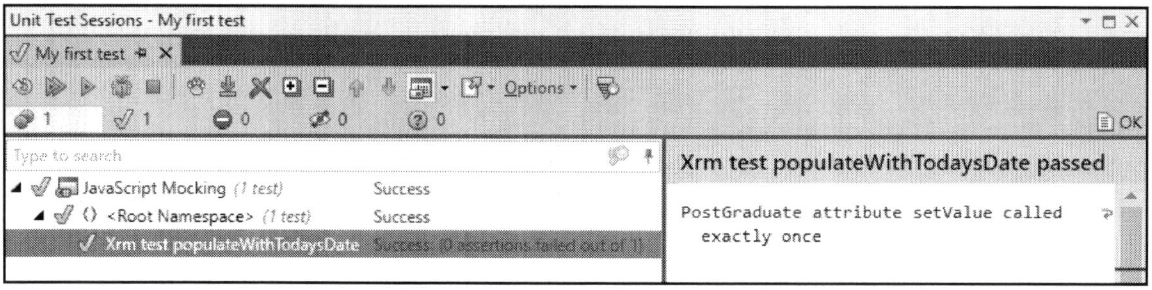

There's more...

This recipe just scratches the surface of JavaScript unit testing. It highlights the different components available to get it working and demonstrates a working combination using some popular choices. There are quite a few possible combinations of frameworks/libraries/tools that can harness the power of unit testing, especially, when using modern JavaScript frameworks such as AngularJS, React, or Knockout. Choose the one you are most comfortable with and give it a go. Also, consider using a mocking/stubbing framework to make your setup easier.

See also

- The *Unit testing your plugin business logic* recipe of `Chapter 6`, *Enhancing Your Code*
- The *Unit testing your plugin with an in-memory context* recipe of `Chapter 6`, *Enhancing Your Code*
- *Building a custom UI using Angular*

Customizing the Ribbon

Reducing the number of clicks to perform an action is always at the top of any customer's priority list. One way to achieve this is to add buttons to the Dynamics 365 ribbon. In this recipe, we will keep the extension simple and add a button labeled `Packt` to open a new browser window that navigates to the Packt website.

Getting ready

In order to customize the Dynamics 365 ribbon, you can either edit the XML manually or you can use a ribbon editing tool. Microsoft MVP Scott Durow has done such a good job implementing his Ribbon Workbench that I seldom use anything else to edit Dynamics 365 ribbons. In order to get the Ribbon Workbench, you can either get it as part of the Microsoft MVP Tanguy Touzard's XrmToolBox, or you can download the managed solution from `https://www.develop1.net/public/rwb/ribbonworkbench.aspx`. A **System Customizer** or higher role is required to edit the ribbon XML.

How to do it

1. Import the **Ribbon Workbench** solution into your Dynamics 365 instance.
2. Navigate to **Settings** | **Solutions** and click on **Ribbon Workbench**.
3. Select **Packt** as your solution and click on **OK**.
4. Ensure that the **Contact** entity is selected under **Entities**.
5. Right-click on **Commands** and select **Add New**.
6. Select the newly created command from under the **Command** parent.
7. Click on the lookup next to **Actions**, then click on **Add** and select **Open Url Action**, followed by **OK**.
8. Under **Address**, enter `https://www.packtpub.com`, and then click on **OK**.
9. From the left-hand **Toolbox**, drag and drop the **Button** item into your desired location on the lower ribbon-labeled form:

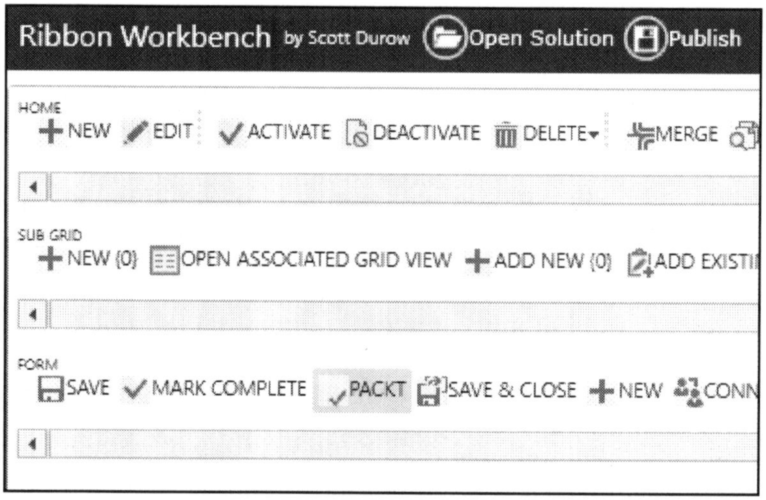

10. Select the newly added button and on the right-hand side under **Command** and select the command you just created with the default name `packt.contact.Command0.Command`.
11. Enter `Packt` under **LabelTextText**:

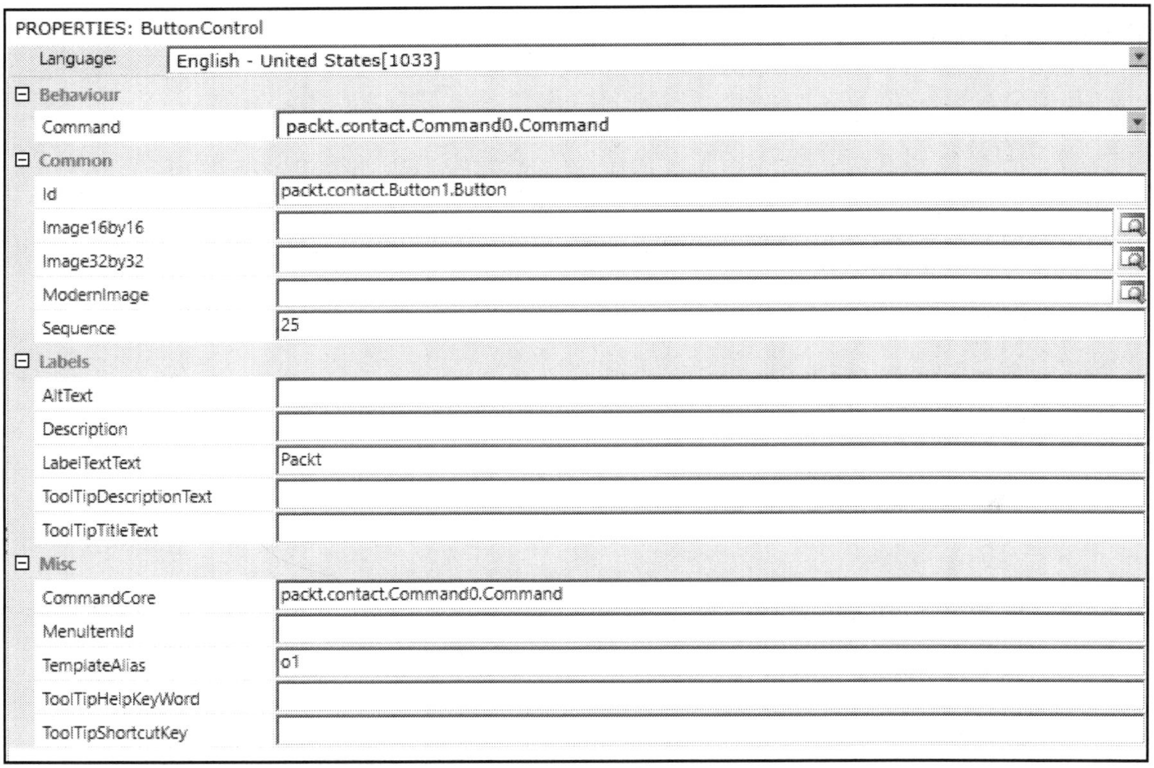

12. Click on **Publish**.

How it works...

The Ribbon Workbench is a tool that downloads and modifies the XML fragment responsible for rendering the Dynamics 365 entities' ribbon.

We started by creating the command in step 5 to step 8 to navigate to the Packt website in a new window. Notice that we can also call a `JavaScript Function` action, which can harnesses the power of client-side scripting.

In step 9 to step 11, we created the button that will execute the command and gave it a specific label. We added the button on the form ribbon. Alternatively, you can also add it to entity ribbons or subgrid ribbons.

When we clicked on **Publish** in step 12, the ribbon workbench uploaded the changes back to the solution and published them.

There's more...

Typically, ribbon buttons are used to quick-launch workflows, execute calculations/transformations, perform complex on-demand validations, and much more. Custom ribbon buttons are also used to redirect users to external locations when integrating Dynamics 365 with other systems.

Although the ribbon editor is a great tool, sometimes unexpected behavior can occur, which would require you to take a look at the underlying XML for debugging purposes and manual edits. In case you want to learn how to edit the ribbon manually, refer to the MSDN article at `https://msdn.microsoft.com/en-us/library/gg309639.aspx`.

3

SDK Enterprise Capabilities

In this chapter, we will cover the following recipes:

- Server-side concurrency control
- Client-side concurrency control
- Executing a request within a transaction
- Batch requests
- Staging data imports
- Creating early bound entity classes
- Extending CrmSvcUtil with filtering
- Extending CrmSvcUtil to generate option-sets enum
- Migrating configuration across instances using the CRM configuration migration tool

Introduction

Looking back at the history of Dynamics CRM, the product has evolved over the years to adapt to the latest trends. The first few releases of Dynamics CRM were meant for on-premises deployments and internal use. Later releases introduced internet-facing deployments and the Microsoft Cloud SaaS offering.

As ongoing releases introduced new enterprise features to cater for large implementations, additional capabilities and tooling were also introduced to enhance the Dynamics enterprise strength.

This chapter will cover a few of the SDK gems that can be useful when implementing enterprise-scale solutions. We will cover server-side and custom client-side optimistic concurrency control, transactional and batch requests, large data import using the new data loader services, configuration data transfer between instances, and finally `CrmSvcUtil` extensions.

Server-side concurrency control

Optimistic concurrency control is one of the top asks for enterprise-scale users of Dynamics 365. The moment multiple users have the potential to update records concurrently, concurrency control becomes important. After all, concurrent usage is one of the main reasons why organizations moved away from tracking their work in spreadsheets.

Optimistic concurrency control is the mechanism of detecting concurrent changes when a user tries to update a record that has already been updated since the last time it was loaded. This is opposed to pessimistic concurrency control, where records are locked when read to stop other users from accessing them. Locking can sometimes lead to deadlocks.

At the time of writing, Dynamics 365 only offers server-side optimistic concurrency control. In this recipe, we will demonstrate how to enable optimistic concurrency control when updating a record.

Getting ready

In order to test this code, you will need read/write access to the account entity of Dynamics 365, a Visual Studio IDE with .NET 4.5.2, and the Dynamics 365 NuGet packages to access the SDK libraries. The entity being tested must have its optimistic concurrency control enabled. In order to check whether your entity (account in this example) has optimistic concurrency control enabled, inspect its metadata by navigating to the following URL:

```
<OrganizationUrl>/api/data/v8.2/EntityDefinitions?$filter=SchemaName eq
'Account'&$select=IsOptimisticConcurrencyEnabled
```

Don't forget to replace <OrganizationUrl> with your instance's URL.

How to do it...

1. Create a new console application in Visual Studio called Packt.Xrm.ConcurrencyControl.
2. Right-click on **References,** click on **Manage NuGet Packages,** and search and install Microsoft.CrmSdk.XrmTooling.CoreAssembly:

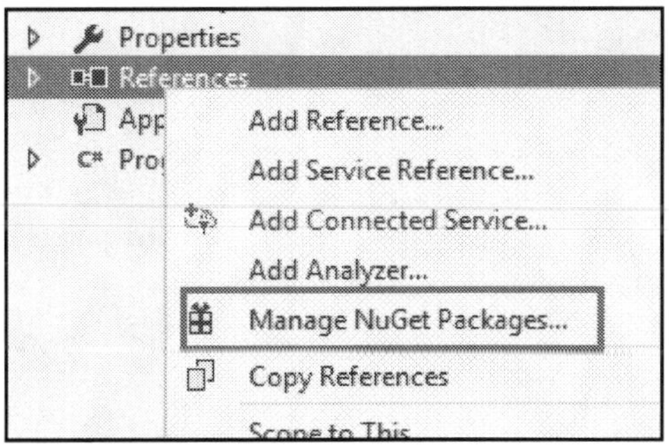

Your final set of **References** will look similar to this screenshot:

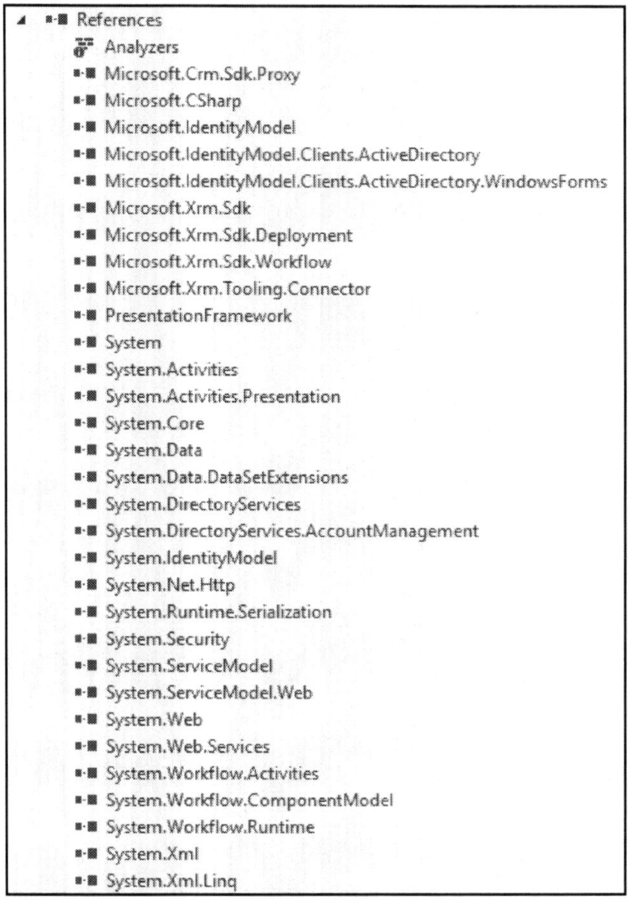

3. Include the following `using` statements to your `.cs` file:

```
using Microsoft.Xrm.Sdk;
using Microsoft.Xrm.Sdk.Messages;
using Microsoft.Xrm.Sdk.Query;
using Microsoft.Xrm.Tooling.Connector;
```

4. Copy and insert the following code into your main function (don't forget to update the connection string):

```
var connectionString ="AuthType=Office365;Username=
@.onmicrosoft.com; Password=;Url=https://.crm6.dynamics.com";
var crmSvc = new CrmServiceClient(connectionString);
using (var serviceProxy = crmSvc.OrganizationServiceProxy)
{
    var accountToCreate = new Entity("account");
    accountToCreate["name"] = "Packt V1.0";

    //Create an account
    var accountGuid = serviceProxy.Create(accountToCreate);

     // Retrieve the account
    var account = serviceProxy.Retrieve("account", accountGuid, new
ColumnSet("name"));

    account["name"] = "Packt v2.0";

    // Built the request
    UpdateRequest accountUpdate = new UpdateRequest()
    {
        Target = account,
        ConcurrencyBehavior =
ConcurrencyBehavior.IfRowVersionMatches
    };

    // Update the account
    UpdateResponse accountUpdateResponse1 =
(UpdateResponse)serviceProxy.Execute(accountUpdate);

    account["name"] = "Packt v3.0";

    // Update the account again
    UpdateResponse accountUpdateResponse2 =
(UpdateResponse)serviceProxy.Execute(accountUpdate);

    serviceProxy.Delete("account", accountGuid);
}
```

How it works...

In step 1 and step 2, we started by adding the necessary NuGet package to ensure that the correct libraries are referenced.

We then referenced the namespaces, notably `Microsoft.Xrm.SDK`, which provides the organization service class, allowing us to perform the necessary create, read, update, and delete CRUD operations.

> The `CrmServiceClient` class from the `Microsoft.Xrm.Tooling.Connector` namespace provides the preferred way to connect to Dynamics 365. This connection method is best practice, as it is future proof. Connecting straight to the web services using the endpoint URL is not considered good practice as the endpoint might change over time. The `Xrm.Tooling` connection takes care of the piping behind the scenes.

In the code, we start by building our connection string using Office 365 credentials. Make sure you change the values in the connection string to reflect your credentials and organization. For more details about connection strings, visit `https://msdn.microsoft.com/en-nz/library/mt608573.aspx`.

Once we have our organization service created, we start by creating an account that returns the account GUID. We then retrieve the account and try to save it twice, using an update request with the `ConcurrencyBehavior` set to `ConcurrencyBehavior.IfRowVersionMatches`. This ensures that if the version number does not match, an exception is thrown. Given that we don't reload the record in between the updates, the version number remains the same and the second save throws the exception.

Behind the scenes, the SDK is leveraging the `VersionNumber` column in the underlying SQL tables to check whether the version matches the one submitted. If you have an on-premise Dynamics 365 instance, a SQL profiler session will show the following SQL query before the exception is thrown:

```
exec sp_executesql N'select
convert(bigint, "account0".VersionNumber) as "versionnumber"
from AccountBase as "account0" (UPDLOCK)
where ("account0".AccountId = @AccountId0) ',
N'@AccountId0   uniqueidentifier',
@AccountId0='DCEAF3CF-C1B3-E611-9428-0050569228E8'
```

There's more...

In order to avoid this exception, you will have to reload your record before running your third update. Insert the following code after the first update to retrieve the record again with the latest version, before submitting the third update:

```
account = serviceProxy.Retrieve("account", accountGuid, new
ColumnSet("name"));
accountUpdate.Target = account;
```

TIP: If you are using `OrganizationServiceContext`, you can set `ConcurrencyBehavior` at the context level, which affects all update and delete requests.

See also

- *Batch requests*

Client-side concurrency control

As described in the previous recipe, sever-side concurrency control can be enabled when making a server-side `UpdateRequest` or `DeleteRequest`, however, client-side concurrency is not currently available while using the frontend UI.

In this recipe, we will create a custom JavaScript library that checks for concurrency when saving the record, essentially enabling a client-side optimistic concurrency control mechanism. We will then enable it for the contact entity being used.

Getting ready

In order to build this customization, you will require the **System Customizer** or higher security role. End users, however, will only require read/create/update access to the entities.

How to do it...

1. Navigate to **Settings** | **Solutions** | **Packt**.
2. Click on **Web Resources** and click on **New**, enter `packt_/js/concurrency.js` as the name, select **JScript** from **Type**, and then click on **Text Editor**.
3. Copy and insert the following piece of code:

```
var packtNs = packtNs || {};
packtNs.concurrency = packtNs.concurrency || {};
var _recordLoadedVersion;
var _schemaName = "";
var _saving = false;

 packtNs.concurrency.init = function (schemaName)
 {
     _schemaName = schemaName;
    var modifiedResult =
 packtNs.concurrency.checkLastModified("0");
    _recordLoadedVersion = modifiedResult.modifiedVersion;
    Xrm.Page.ui.clearFormNotification("concurrency");
Xrm.Page.data.entity.removeOnSave(packtNs.concurrency.checkConcurre
ncy);
Xrm.Page.data.entity.addOnSave(packtNs.concurrency.checkConcurrency
);
}

packtNs.concurrency.checkConcurrency = function (executionObj)
{
     if(_saving){
         return;
    }
     var saveMode = executionObj.getEventArgs().getSaveMode();
    executionObj.getEventArgs().preventDefault();

     var modifiedObject =
packtNs.concurrency.checkLastModified(_recordLoadedVersion);

     if (!modifiedObject.hasChanged) {
         packtNs.concurrency.callSecondSave(executionObj,
saveMode);
        return;
    }

    if (saveMode === 70) {
        Xrm.Page.ui.setFormNotification("Seems like this record has
been updated by " + modifiedObject.modifiedBy + ". AutoSave has
```

```
been aborted.", "WARNING", "concurrency");
      }
      else if (saveMode === 59 || saveMode === 2 || saveMode === 1)
{
         Xrm.Utility.confirmDialog("Seems like this record has been
updated by " + modifiedObject.modifiedBy + ".\nAre you sure you
still want to save it?",
         function () {
packtNs.concurrency.callSecondSave(executionObj,saveMode);
          },
         null);
     }
}

packtNs.concurrency.callSecondSave = function (executionObj,
saveType){
   //Omitted code. Call the correct save method.
 }

packtNs.concurrency.checkLastModified = function
(recordLoadedVersion)
 {
    //Omitted code. Compare the result from JSON @odata.etag with
recordedLoadedVersion
}
```

4. Back in your `Packt` solution in Dynamics 365, navigate to **Entities** | **Contact** | **Forms** and double-click on the **Main** form.
5. Click on **Form Properties** and under **Form Libraries**, click on **+ Add**
6. Select your JavaScript library created in step 2 from the list (you can use the search functionality to filter the values) and click on **Add**, then click on **OK**.
7. Under **Event Handlers**, verify that **Control** is set to `Form` and **Event** is set to `OnLoad`, then click on **+Add**.
8. Ensure that `packt_/js/concurrency.js` is selected in the **Library** dropdown and then enter `packtNs.concurrency.init` in the **Function** field.
9. Enter `contacts` in the parameter field.
10. Click on **Save and Close**, followed by **Publish All Customizations** in your solution window.

How it works...

In step 3 of this recipe, we created the function that checks whether the record has been updated in the background since it was opened. The `init` JavaScript function was wired to the `OnLoad` event of form, which in turn wires the `OnSave` event to call the `checkConcurrency` function (step 7 and step 8).

The `checkConcurrency` function has two behaviors. If a save is in progress, it exists. If it isn't, it checks whether the record has changed since it was first loaded by calling the `checkLastModified` function, which in turn calls the **Web API** to retrieve the record's server version and compares it with the current version.

> The constant version checking retrieval triggered on every save will have a performance impact on your Dynamics 365 instance.

If no changes are detected, the default save is cancelled and replaced with one that has a callback method to retrieve the latest version after the save is done.

> Given that the save event is replaced by an alternative one, you will have to pay extra attention to any additional wired `OnSave` function. Make sure the order is registered correctly and that when the save is called twice, the methods are not called twice.

If a concurrent update is detected, depending on the event, the following notification or a confirmation message is displayed to the user to check whether they truly want to save:

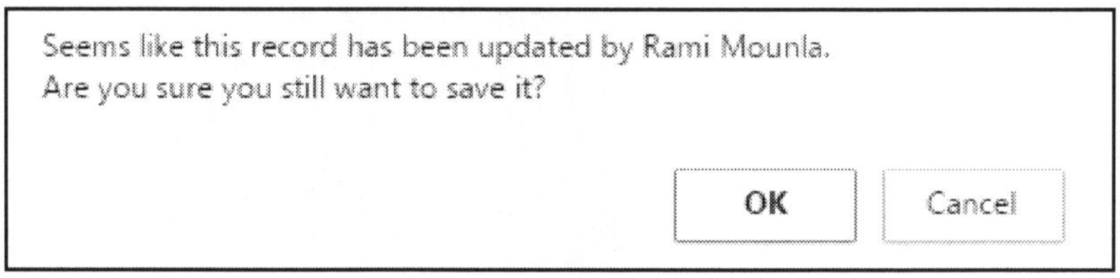

An unobtrusive notification is also displayed at the top of the record when an auto-save is triggered:

Note that this will only enable concurrency control when using the specific form that has the JavaScript enabled on it. Other means, such as updating records from an editable grid or bulk edit, will not trigger the control routine.

Known limitations

This customization works best with Internet Explorer (Chrome has an issue with the save and close event). The script is also adapted for online instances. In case you want to change it to on-premise Dynamics 365 instances, you'll have to ensure that the Web API URL construction under `checkLastModified` updates accordingly and includes your organization's name.

The script is also concise and only works with **Save**, **Save and Close**, and **Auto Save** calls. In order to adapt it to other save methods, you'll have to add the extra save modes.

Another limitation of this customization is that it only works on updated entities--most entities in new Dynamics 365 instances (`https://msdn.microsoft.com/en-us/library/gg328261.aspx#BKMK_UpdatedEntties`)--as it uses the `Xrm.Page.data.save()` function for its callback capabilities.

Given the list of limitations and performance impact, the code in this recipe is focused more on understanding the potential Dynamics 365 client-side API capabilities as opposed to production use.

See also

- *Server-side concurrency control*

Executing a request within a transaction

When Dynamics 365 is used to its full enterprise capacity, often a composite operation will span multiple CRUD operations and will need to be executed atomically. Such requirements typically dictate that if any of the operations were to fail, the entire process must roll back to ensure data integrity.

As of Dynamics CRM 2015, `ExecuteTransactionRequest` was introduced in the SDK libraries, allowing custom code to execute within a single database-level transaction.

In this recipe, we will create an account and a contact within the scope of a single transaction.

Getting ready

In order to test this code, you will need write access to the account and contact entities, a Visual Studio IDE, and the Dynamics 365 NuGet packages to access the SDK libraries (please refer to the first recipe in this chapter for details on how to set up your Visual Studio solution).

How to do it...

1. Create a new console application in Visual Studio called `Packt.Xrm.Transaction`.
2. Right-click on **References** and click on **Manage NuGet Packages**, and search and install `Microsoft.CrmSdk.XrmTooling.CoreAssembly`.
3. Include the following `using` statements in your .cs file:

```
using Microsoft.Xrm.Sdk;
using Microsoft.Xrm.Sdk.Messages;
using Microsoft.Xrm.Tooling.Connector;
```

4. Copy and insert the following code in your main function (don't forget to update the connection string):

```
var connectionString =
"AuthType=Office365;Username=@.onmicrosoft.com;Password=;
Url=https://.crm6.dynamics.com";

var crmSvc = new CrmServiceClient(connectionString);

using (var serviceProxy = crmSvc.OrganizationServiceProxy)
{
    //Create request collection
    var request = new OrganizationRequestCollection()
    {
            new CreateRequest
            {
                Target = new Entity("account")
                {
                    ["name"] = "Packt Account"
                }
```

```
                },
                new CreateRequest
                {
                    Target = new Entity("contact")
                    {
                        ["firstname"] = "Packt",
                        ["lastname"] = "Contact"
                    }
                }
        };

        //Create Transaction and pass previously created request
collection
        var requestToCreateRecords = new ExecuteTransactionRequest()
        {
            // Create an empty organization request collection.
            Requests = request,
            ReturnResponses = true
        };

        //Execute requests within the transaction
        var responseForCreateRecords =
(ExecuteTransactionResponse)serviceProxy.Execute(requestToCreateRec
ords);

        // Display the results of each response.
        foreach (var responseItem in
responseForCreateRecords.Responses)
        {
            Console.WriteLine("Created record with GUID {0}",
responseItem.Results["id"].ToString());
        }
    }
```

How it works...

Similar to the first recipe, we started by creating a new solution and referenced the correct NuGet packages. We then added the correct library references in step 3.

In step 4, we started by connecting to Dynamics 365 by injecting a simple connection string into the `CrmServiceClient` class from the `Microsoft.Xrm.Tooling` namespace.

We then created a collection of requests: a create request for an account and a create request for a contact record. We then passed the request collection to the `ExecuteTransactionRequest` class. `ExecuteTransactionRequest` provides the transaction in which to execute the list of requests.

If any of the requests fail, all the other requests roll back. In our example, if the contact-create request fails, the account creation request rolls back.

Given that we have indicated in `ExecuteTransactionRequest` to return the responses by setting `ReturnResponses` to `True`, we can now loop through each of the responses and display the GUID of each of the records created. We can then correlate each of the responses to the requests, as they are returned in the same order as the requests.

There's more...

To learn more about the `ExecuteTransactionRequest` class, visit `https://msdn.microsoft.com/en-us/library/microsoft.xrm.sdk.messages.executetransactionrequest.aspx`.

See also

- *Server-side concurrency*
- *Batch requests*

Batch requests

Often in enterprise applications, large amounts of data needs to be manipulated in batches to increase performance. Batch data processing patterns were observed in Microsoft SQL's evolution (and many other database engines), where batch-SQL executions were introduced to improve efficiency.

In this recipe, we will use the same request collection from the previous recipe to create an account and a contact; however, the execution will be done in a batch request as opposed to a transaction request.

Getting ready

In order to test this code, you will need write access to the account and contact entities, a Visual Studio IDE, and the Dynamics 365 NuGet packages to access the SDK libraries (please refer to the first recipe in this chapter for details on how to set up your Visual Studio solution).

How to do it...

1. Create a new console application in Visual Studio called `Packt.Xrm.Batch`.
2. Right-click on **References** and click on **Manage NuGet Packages,** and search and install `Microsoft.CrmSdk.XrmTooling.CoreAssembly`.
3. Include the following `using` statements in your `.cs` file:

```
using Microsoft.Xrm.Sdk;
using Microsoft.Xrm.Sdk.Messages;
using Microsoft.Xrm.Tooling.Connector;
```

4. Copy and insert the following code in your main function (don't forget to update the connection string):

```
var connectionString =
"AuthType=Office365;Username=@.onmicrosoft.com;Password=;Url=https:
//.crm6.dynamics.com";

var crmSvc = new CrmServiceClient(connectionString);

using (var serviceProxy = crmSvc.OrganizationServiceProxy)
{
    //Create request collection
    var request = new OrganizationRequestCollection()
    {
            new CreateRequest
            {
                Target = new Entity("account")
                {
                    ["name"] = "Packt Account"
                }
            },
            new CreateRequest
            {
                Target = new Entity("contact")
                {
```

```
                    ["firstname"] = "Packt",
                    ["lastname"] = "Contact"
                }
            }
        };

      //Create Transaction and pass previously created request
collection
        var requestToCreateRecords = new ExecuteMultipleRequest()
        {
            // Create an empty organization request collection.
            Requests = request,
            Settings = new ExecuteMultipleSettings()
            {
                ContinueOnError = true,
                ReturnResponses = true
            }
        };

        //Execute requests within the transaction
        var responseForCreateRecords =
(ExecuteMultipleResponse)serviceProxy.Execute(requestToCreateRecord
s);

        // Display the results of each response.
        foreach (var responseItem in
responseForCreateRecords.Responses)
        {
            Console.WriteLine("Created record with GUID {0}",
responseItem.Response.Results["id"].ToString());
        }
}
```

How it works...

Similar to the first recipe and the transaction recipe, we started by creating a new solution and referenced the correct NuGet packages. We then added the correct library references to our class file in step 3.

In step 4, we started by connecting to Dynamics 365 by injecting a simple connection string into the `CrmServiceClient` class from the `Microsoft.Xrm.Tooling` namespace.

We then created a collection of requests: a create account request and a create contact request. We passed the request collection to the `ExecuteMultipleRequest` class. We also set the `ExecuteMultipleSettings` property to the request to continue the execution if an error is encountered and to return all responses.

We executed the request and finally displayed the ID of each response, as we set up the create requests to return the GUID of the created records.

Behind the scenes, the SDK is leveraging the low-level SQL transaction capabilities. If you have an on-premise instance of Dynamics 365, a SQL-profiler session reveals a batch start and batch complete event with the following execution:

```
SET TRANSACTION ISOLATION LEVEL READ COMMITTED
```

There's more...

The number of requests executed within a batch request is capped at 1000.

> If you try to execute a batch that is larger than your maximum allowed, an exception will be thrown. However, you can catch the exception, read the maximum allowed number from the exception, and resize your batch accordingly. This MSDN article highlights the code to retrieve the maximum batch size: `https://msdn.microsoft.com/en-us/library/jj863631.aspx#fault`.

Just like with SQL Server's batching, you'll have to find the sweet spot while tuning your batch parameters. There is a point where increasing the number of requests executed in a batch and the number of parallel executions actually degrades your performance.

As for the request settings implications, the following article highlights the different response scenarios based on the request settings:

`https://msdn.microsoft.com/en-us/library/jj863631.aspx#options`

See also

- *Executing a request within a transaction*
- *Server-side concurrency control*

Staging data imports

Most of the enterprise Dynamics implementations I have worked on require some kind of data migration from legacy systems. Dynamics 365 offers an out-of-the-box files import through its web interfaces. This conventional data import mechanism is typically criticized as laborious to set up and slow, especially if you have errors.

Recently, a point-and-click data loader web tool was introduced to enhance the old capabilities by allowing staging, error reconciliation, and batch processing. At the time of writing, the data loader tool is still in preview mode and is not recommended for production usage. It is also only available in North American Dynamics 365 instances.

In this recipe, we will create a simple data load using a contact `CSV` file.

Getting ready

To get the data loader working, you will need an Office 365 user as well as a Dynamics 365 user (not necessarily the same as the Office 365 one) with the correct privileges to read/write to the entities you are loading to.

How to do it...

1. Navigate to `https://integrator.lcs.dynamics.com/DataLoader/Index`.
2. Click on **Sign in** and log in using your Office 365 credentials.
3. Log in using your Office 365 credentials.
4. Click on **CRM Connections** as shown in following diagram:

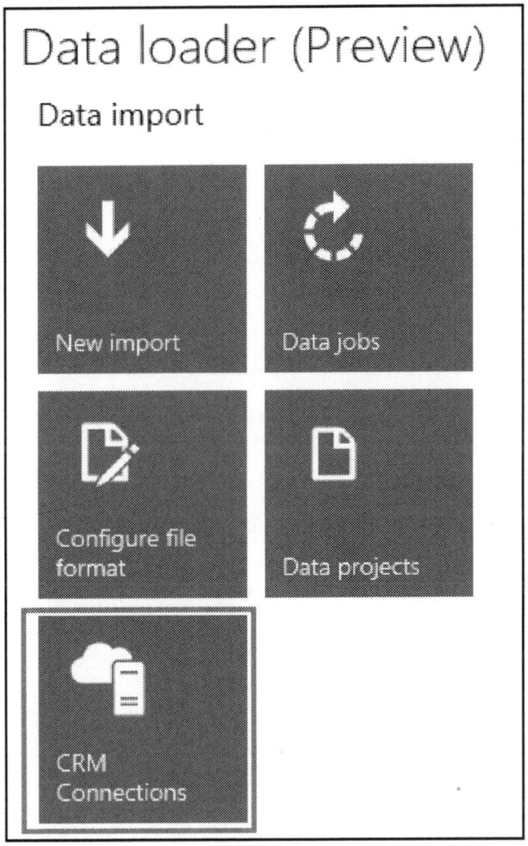

5. In the **CRM Connections** page, click on the **+** sign and enter the following details:
    - **CRM Username**: `<your Dynamics 365 username>`
    - **CRM Password**: `<your Dynamics 365 password>`
    - Then, click on **Fetch CRM instances**.

6. Once the instances are loaded, select the correct instance you want to connect to and click on **Create**:

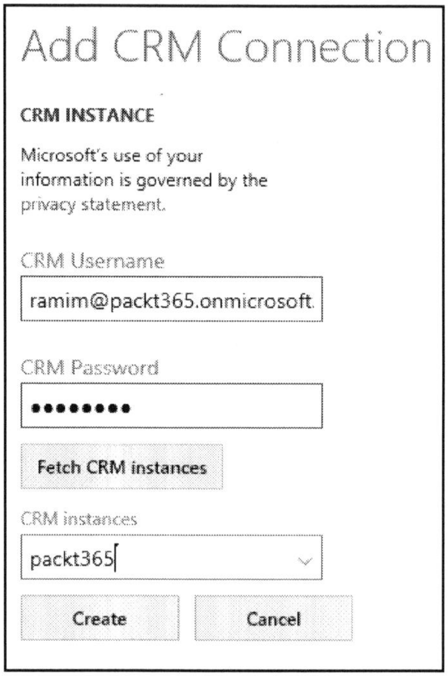

7. Wait until the connection status in the CRM Connections page turns to **Running**:

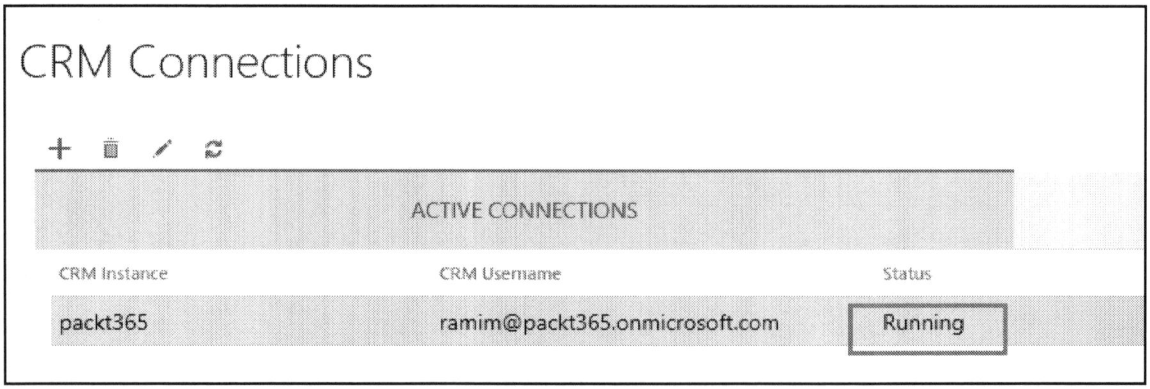

8. Back on the main screen, click on **New import** and follow these steps:

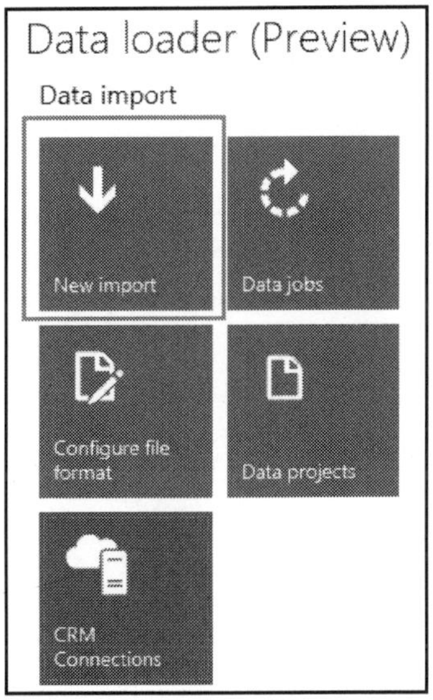

8.1. Create a new project by giving it a name and selecting the instance, then clicking on **Next**:

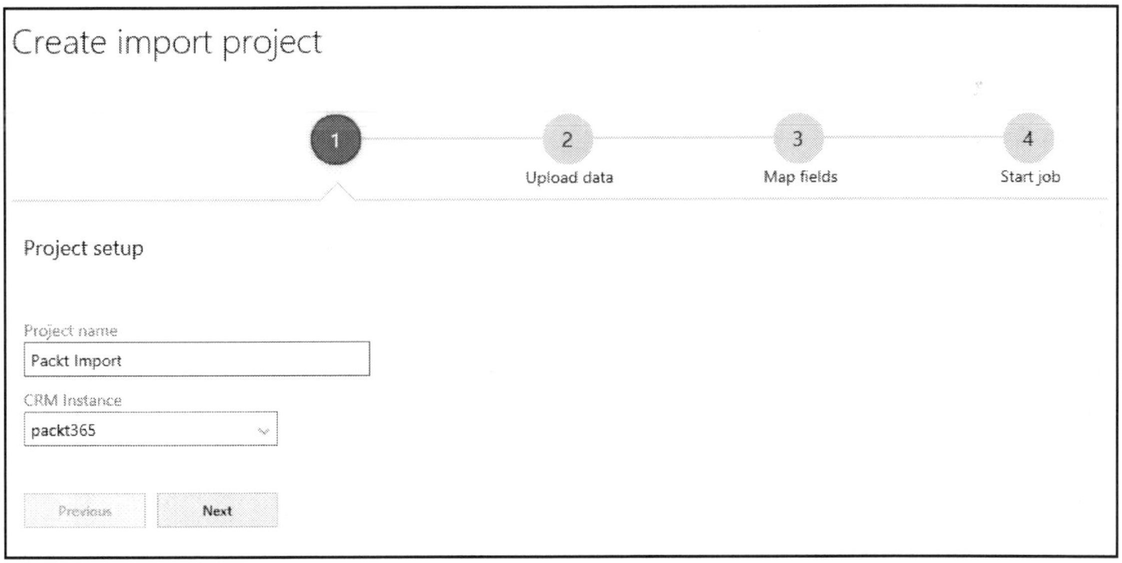

8.2. In step 2, select the file format of your choice and the entity type, and then click on **upload** to upload the file based on your preferred format. Wait until the file status is completed before clicking on **Next**.

8.3. In step 3, define the mapping that was not automatically matched, and then click on **Next** when you are satisfied with the mapping.

8.4. In step 4, give your job a name and click on **Start job**.

9. On the main screen, click on **Data jobs** and then select the job you just created.
10. In your job window, on the **STAGING** tab, click on **Validate**:

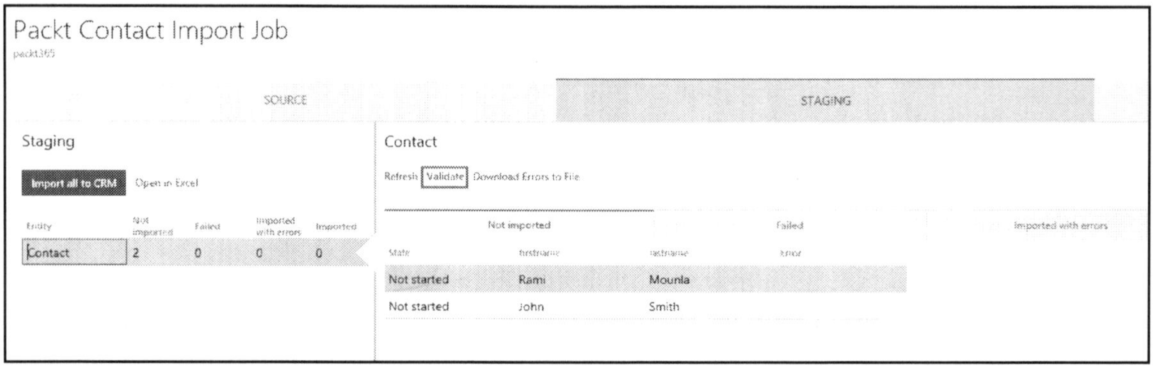

11. Once the records are marked as **Valid**, click on **Import all to CRM**.

How it works...

We started in step 5 to step 7 by creating our CRM connection simply by specifying our credentials. The connection manager automatically identifies the instances we have access to. Don't forget to replace <your Dynamics 365 username> and <your Dynamics 365 password> with your actual Dynamics 365 username and password.

In step 8, we created our file import. More specifically, in step 8.2, we uploaded a file to be mapped to a specific entity. Note that the data load can include more than one file. In step 8.3, the data loader will try to match the column names automatically to the correct destination attributes.

If we try to load data without using the primary key combinations, we will be prompted with a warning message stating that all the records will be created and not **upserted** (update or inset if the record is not found):

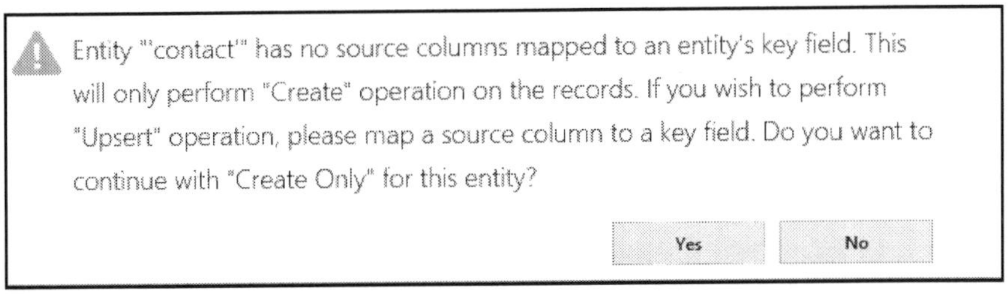

For more details about the **upsert** functionality, read the *Duplicate detection using primary keys* recipe of `Chapter 1`, *No Code Extensions*.

By the end of step 8, our data is not loaded into Dynamics 365 yet; it is staged for validation.

In step 10, we performed a data validation to ensure that all attributes are compatible with the schema and all lookups can be resolved.

We finally loaded the data into Dynamics 365 in step 11.

The advantage of using the data loader over the conventional CSV import is its simple configuration and its staging validation capabilities that allow you to revisit incorrect records and fix them and, most importantly, the speed with which the data is loaded using batch requests in the background.

There's more...

The data loader services also provide an error fixing feature as well as a schema refresh capability, in case your instance's schema gets updated.

Fixing errors

When you encounter loading errors, you can download an Excel spreadsheet containing the offending records, modify them, and then publish them back from within Excel. After you log in using your Office 365 account in Excel, the data connector add-on will allow you to publish the changes back to Dynamics 365 using the **Publish** button, as per the following screenshot:

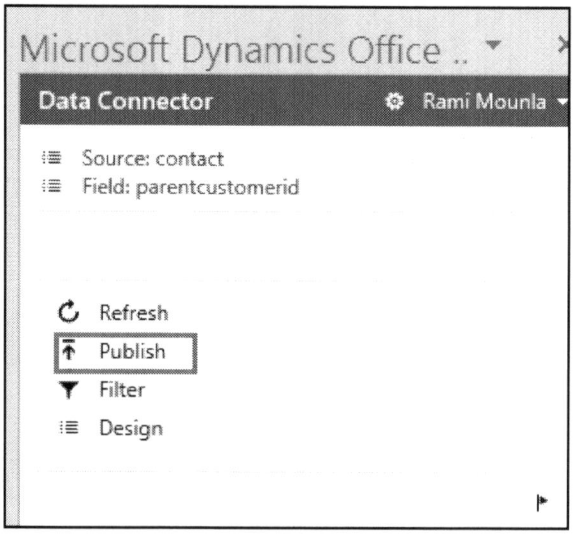

Refreshing your instance's schema

When we created the CRM connection in step 5, the instance's metadata was loaded. When you change your Dynamics 365 schema, you will have to refresh your connection.

To do so, go to you CRM connections from the data loader landing page and click on the **refresh** button.

See also

- The *Duplicate detection using primary keys* recipe of `Chapter 1`, *No Code Extensions*
- *Batch requests*

Creating early bound entity classes

Manipulating entity records in your server-side customization can be done using early bound or late bound classes. Early bound classes allow you to use Visual Studio intellisense and dot notations to access and validate entity names and attribute names at compile-time. On the other hand, with a late bound entity, a developer will have to type the entity and attribute's names manually which will be validated at runtime. Nonetheless, late bound entities have an advantage; they give you the flexibility to write **generic** code unbound to specific entities and attributes.

Getting ready

In order to generate early bound entity classes, you will need to download a version of the Dynamics 365 SDK that matches your Dynamics 365 instance. You will also need an active Dynamics 365 user with **System Customizer** or higher privileges.

How to do it...

1. Navigate to the `<SDK folder location>\bin` folder in a command prompt.
2. Run the following command:

```
CrmSvcUtil.exe /connectionstring:"AuthType=Office365;
Username=@.onmicrosoft.com;
Password=;Url=https://.crm.dynamics.com"
/namespace:Packt.Xrm.Entities /out:Entities.cs /language:CS
/serviceContextName:OrganisationServiceContext
```

How it works...

`CrmSrvUtil` checks all the schema that are applied to your Dynamics 365 instance and generates early bound classes for each one of them.

In this recipe, we fed a collection of arguments to `CrmSrvUtil`:

The `/connectionstring` parameter holds your instance connection string. It includes the URL, the authentication mechanism, and the credentials to connect. The `/out` parameter defines the name of your output class. Make sure there are no spaces between the parameters and their values.

The namespace to use for your classes is defined in the `/namespace` parameter (in our instance, we followed the same convention as the previous recipe). The language in which the code will be generated is defined in the `/language` parameter (we selected CS for C#, which is the default; the alternative is VB). Finally, the service context name that will be used later to run LINQ queries is defined in the `/serviceContextName` parameter.

There's more...

`CrmSvcUtil` has a few other parameters that can be used. To view all the possible parameters and further details, including the short forms, type `CrmSvcUtil /help` in the command prompt.

Interactive login

Among those parameters is the **interactive login** parameter (shortened to **il**). When set to `true`, you will be prompted with the familiar login mechanism that we've seen in many other recipes:

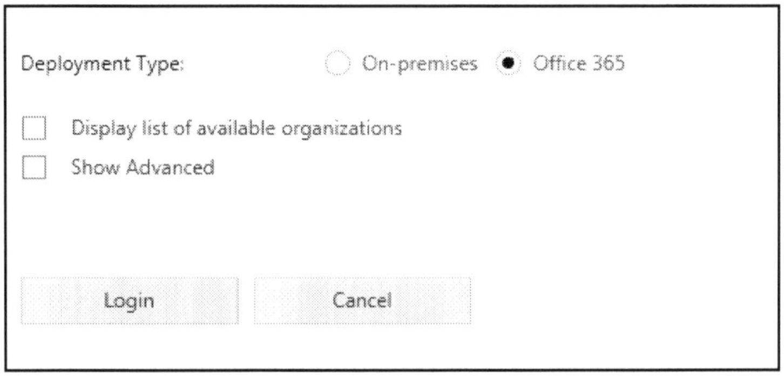

Your new command line should look like this:

```
CrmSvcUtil.exe /namespace:Packt.Xrm.Entities /out:Entities.cs
/language:CS /serviceContextName:OrganisationServiceContext /il:true
```

This is good practice if you do not want to have your password displayed in plain text; however, as a compromise, you'll have to deal with the login prompt and enter the details somehow.

Generate action messages

The `/generateActions` parameter instructs the tool to generate custom action request and response messages as per the *Creating your custom action* recipe of `Chapter 4`, *Server-Side Extensions*.

Developer Toolkit entity generation

You can define early bound entities on a class-by-class basis using the Developer Toolkit Visual Studio add-on, as defined in the *Creating a solution using the Dynamics CRM Developer Toolkit template* recipe of `Chapter 4`, *Server-Side Extensions.*

Extending CrmSvcUtil

`CrmSvcUtil` can be extended by creating .NET extensions assemblies. Extensions can be used to filter the entities that can be created in your generated class, adding option-set enumerations, manipulating the generated code, and so on.

> TIP: It is best practice to filter the number of entities created, otherwise, your class will be too large.

The *Extending CrmSvcUtil with filtering* and *Extending CrmSvcUtil to generate option-sets enum* recipes, later in this chapter, cover a couple of scenarios.

See also

- *Extending CrmSvcUtil with filtering*
- *Extending CrmSvcUtil to generate option-sets enum*
- The *Creating a solution using the Dynamics CRM Developer Toolkit template* recipe of `Chapter 4`, *Server-Side Extensions*

Extending CrmSvcUtil with filtering

As described in *Creating early bound entity classes*, `CrmSvcUtil` is a great utility to generate early bound entities that improve your development productivity.

`CrmSvcUtil`, as it is, generates all entities associated with a Dynamics 365 instance. The generated file is usually quite large and onerous to inspect. In this recipe, we will write a small extension to only generate early bound classes for custom entities that have a prefix of our choice, in this example, the `packt_` prefix (our Dynamics 365 publisher prefix).

Getting ready

In order to create the extension, you will need an IDE such as Visual Studio with .NET 4.5.2, a reference to the `Microsoft.CrmSdk.CoreAssemblies` NuGet package, and a reference to the `CrmSvcUtil.exe` executable.

How to do it...

1. Create a new Visual Studio solution called `Packt.Xrm.CrmSvcUtilExensions` with a project of type class library.
2. Using the NuGet package manager, install the latest version of `Microsoft.CrmSdk.CoreAssemblies` that is relevant to your instance.
3. Using the reference manager, add a reference to `CrmSvcUtil.exe`.
4. Create a new `C#` class called `PacktFiltering` and insert the following code:

```
using System;
using System.Collections.Generic;
using System.Linq;
using Microsoft.Crm.Services.Utility;
using Microsoft.Xrm.Sdk.Metadata;

namespace Packt.Xrm.CrmSvcUtilExensions
{
    public sealed class PacktFiltering : ICodeWriterFilterService
    {
        private ICodeWriterFilterService DefaultService { get; }
        public PacktFiltering(ICodeWriterFilterService
defaultService)
        {
            DefaultService = defaultService;
```

```
        }

    //Omitted code for default behavior interfaces

   //Custom filtering value defined in GetFilter()
// Ensure to only include elements with a schema name that start
with the value defined in GetFilter
        bool ICodeWriterFilterService.GenerateEntity(EntityMetadata
entityMetadata, IServiceProvider services)
        {
            return
entityMetadata.SchemaName.StartsWith(GetFilter()) &&
DefaultService.GenerateEntity(entityMetadata, services);
        }

//Get the filter value from the command argument
        private static string GetFilter()
        {
            var filterArgument =
Environment.GetCommandLineArgs().FirstOrDefault(p =>
p.ToLower().StartsWith("/filter"));
            return
filterArgument?.Substring(filterArgument.IndexOf(":") +
1).Trim('"').Trim() ?? string.Empty;

        }
    }
}
```

5. Compile your solution.
6. Run the `CrmSvcUtil` command from the `bin\Debug` folder with the following parameter:

```
CrmSvcUtil.exe
/codewriterfilter:"Packt.Xrm.CrmSvcUtilExensions.PacktFiltering,
Packt.Xrm.CrmSvcUtilExensions" /connectionstring:"
AuthType=Office365;Username=@.onmicrosoft.com;
Password=;Url=https://.crm.dynamics.com"
/namespace:Packt.Xrm.Entities /out:Entities.cs /filter:packt_
```

How it works...

In step 1 to step 3, we set up our solution to generate an assembly that we can reference in the `CrmSvcUtil` command line. In step 3, we added a reference to the `CrmSvcUtil.exe` executable that includes the `Microsoft.Crm.Services.Utility` library required in the development of our extension. The executable can be found under the `Bin` folder of the Dynamics 365 SDK.

In step 4, we created the extension class that implements `ICodeWriterFilterService`. This requires all six interfaces to be implemented, with most of them referencing the default service behavior (omitted code). The only method we changed is `GenerateEntity`, which that now returns `false` if the entity's schema name does not start with the value that was entered for the `/filter` command-line argument: `packt_`.

Finally, in step 6, we ran `CrmSvcUtil.exe` with the `/codewriterfilter` argument that intercepts the execution pipeline and checks for each entity executed whether it is prefixed with `packt_` before calling the default behavior. The filter value is passed through a custom argument called `/filter`.

Don't forget to replace the connection string with the correct value. Check the following article to understand how to construct your connection string:

`https://msdn.microsoft.com/en-nz/library/mt608573.aspx`

There's more...

In this abridged recipe, we entered a simple filter to only include entities that start with a specific prefix. This can be further enhanced to include a XML whitelist/blacklist, or even to only include entities that belong to a specific solution.

`CrmSvcUtil` is quite a powerful utility; the next recipe will cover how to build an extension to the tool to generate typed option-set enums.

Consider wrapping the `CrmSvcUtil` command in a batch file, a Visual Studio extension (or external tool), or some other integrated mechanism.

See also

- *Extending CrmSvcUtil to generate option-set enums*
- *Creating early bound entity classes*

Extending CrmSvcUtil to generate option-sets enum

In this recipe, we will build a `CrmSvcUtil` extension that generates a clean class file with a filtered set of option-set enumerations.

Getting ready

Just like the previous recipe, to create the extension you will need an IDE such as Visual Studio with .NET 4.5.2, a reference to the `Microsoft.CrmSdk.CoreAssemblies` NuGet package, and a reference to the `CrmSvcUtil.exe` executable. You can leverage the existing solution created in the previous recipe.

How to do it...

1. Using the same solution used for the previous recipe, create a new class called `PacktOptionSetFiltering` with the following code:

```
using System;
using System.Collections.Generic;
using System.Linq;
using Microsoft.Crm.Services.Utility;
using Microsoft.Xrm.Sdk.Metadata;

namespace Packt.Xrm.CrmSvcUtilExensions
{
    public sealed class PacktOptionSetFiltering :
ICodeWriterFilterService
    {
        private ICodeWriterFilterService DefaultService { get; }
        private Dictionary<string, bool> GeneratedOptionSets { get;
}
        public PacktOptionSetFiltering(ICodeWriterFilterService
```

```
defaultService)
        {
            DefaultService = defaultService;
            GeneratedOptionSets = new Dictionary<string, bool>();
        }
 //Only include piclists, state, and status attributes
        bool
ICodeWriterFilterService.GenerateAttribute(AttributeMetadata
attributeMetadata, IServiceProvider services)
        {
return (attributeMetadata.AttributeType ==
AttributeTypeCode.Picklist
    || attributeMetadata.AttributeType == AttributeTypeCode.State
    || attributeMetadata.AttributeType ==
AttributeTypeCode.Status);
        }

        bool
ICodeWriterFilterService.GenerateOptionSet(OptionSetMetadataBase
optionSetMetadata,
            IServiceProvider services)
        {
            if (!optionSetMetadata.Name.StartsWith(GetFilter()) ||
GeneratedOptionSets.ContainsKey(optionSetMetadata.Name))
                return false;
            if (optionSetMetadata.IsGlobal.HasValue &&
optionSetMetadata.IsGlobal.Value)
                GeneratedOptionSets[optionSetMetadata.Name] = true;
            return true;

        }

// Omitted code GenerateServiceContext returns false
// GenerateRelationship returns flase
  // GenerateEntity same as previous recipe
     // GetFilter same as previous recipe
  // GenerateOption default behavior

    }
}
```

2. Create a new class called `CodeCustomizationService.cs` with the following piece of code:

```
using System;
using System.CodeDom;
using Microsoft.Crm.Services.Utility;

namespace Packt.Xrm.CrmSvcUtilExensions
{
    public sealed class CodeCustomizationService :
ICustomizeCodeDomService
    {
        public void CustomizeCodeDom(CodeCompileUnit codeUnit,
IServiceProvider services)
        {
            for (var i = 0; i < codeUnit.Namespaces.Count; ++i)
            {
                var types = codeUnit.Namespaces[i].Types;
                for (var j = 0; j < types.Count;)
                {
                    if (!types[j].IsEnum || types[j].Members.Count
== 0)

                    {
                        types.RemoveAt(j);
                    }
                    else
                    {
                        j += 1;
                    }
                }
            }
        }
    }
}
```

3. Compile your code.
4. Run the `CrmSvcUtil` command in the `bin\Debug` folder with the following parameters:

```
CrmSvcUtil.exe
/codewriterfilter:"Packt.Xrm.CrmSvcUtilExensions.PacktOptionSetFilt
ering, Packt.Xrm.CrmSvcUtilExensions"
/codecustomization:"Packt.Xrm.CrmSvcUtilExensions.CodeCustomization
Service, Packt.Xrm.CrmSvcUtilExensions"
/connectionstring:"AuthType=Office365;Username=@.onmicrosoft.com;
Password=;Url=https://.crm.dynamics.com"
/namespace:Packt.Xrm.Entities /out:OptionSets.cs /filter:packt_
```

How it works...

In this recipe, we enhanced the previous entity filtering extension to only include option-sets, state, and status attributes by altering the behavior of `GenerateAttribute`. We also changed the `GenerateOptionSet` behavior to return `true` to all optionsets that start with a prefix of our choice (the prefix value is passed as parameter to the command line using `/filter` as per the previous recipe) while ensuring that no duplicates are created.

In step 2, we created `CodeCustomizationService`, which implemented `ICustomizeCodeDomService` and changed `CustomizeCodeDom` to remove anything from the generated code that is not an enum or has no members. This ensures that only enums are included. This fragment is based on the code provided by the SDK.

Finally, when calling `CrmSvcUtil` from the command line, we passed `PacktOptionSetFiltering` and `CodeCustomizationService` to the `codewriterfilter` and `codecustomization` arguments, respectively. Similar to the previous recipe, we also included a custom filter argument.

The result is a class that only contains enums with schema names that start with `packt_` and no duplicates.

There's more...

Again, this recipe is abridged and can be extended even further. As an example, the SDK contains further extensions, such as customizing the generated attributes' names by implementing an `INamingService` extension. The sample code is available in the SDK under `SDK\SampleCode\CS\CrmSvcUtilExtensions`.

See also

- *Extending CrmSvcUtil with filtering*

Migrating configuration across instances using the CRM configuration migration tool

Quite often, as you are working on enterprise applications with different **software development life cycle** (**SDLC**) environments (development, test, user acceptance testing, pre-production, production, and so on), your configuration data needs to be consistent between environments. Luckily, the Dynamics 365 SDK contains a configuration migration tool specifically designed to migrate small amounts of configuration data from one environment to the other.

The configuration migration tool is not designed to migrate large amounts of data between environments. For large data migrations, consider alternatives, such as the out-of-the-box CSV import, the data loader web tool, or even third-party tools, such as the **Scribe** and **KingswaySoft** SSIS packages.

In this recipe, we will export simple account and contact data from one instance and import it to another.

Getting ready

The configuration migration tool is included in the Dynamics 365 SDK under **SDK** | **Tools** | **ConfigurationMigration**. You also need read access to the entities you are trying to export and write in the destination.

How to do it...

1. Start the `DataMigrationUtility.exe` application that is included in the Dynamics 365 SDK under **SDK** | **Tools** | **ConfigurationMigration**.
2. Click on **Create schema**, then **Continue**:

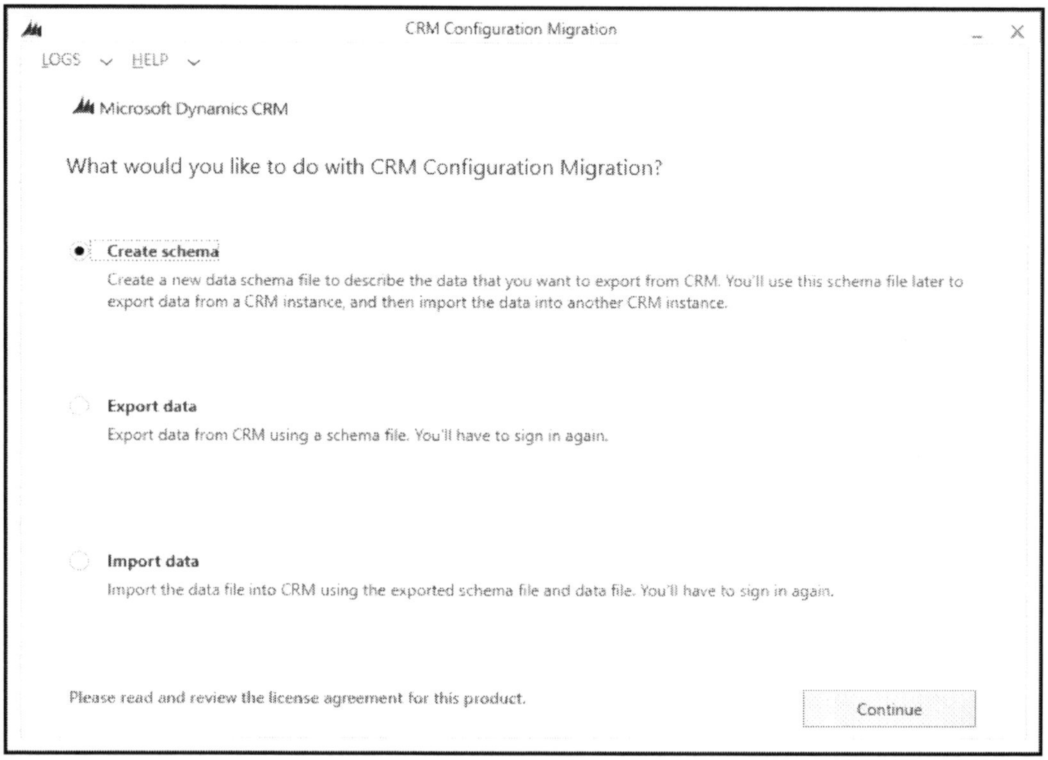

3. On the login screen, click on **Login** and enter your credentials.
4. On the create configuration schema, select the solution, entities, and attributes you would like to create a schema for, and then click on **Save and Export**. You can include more than one entity:

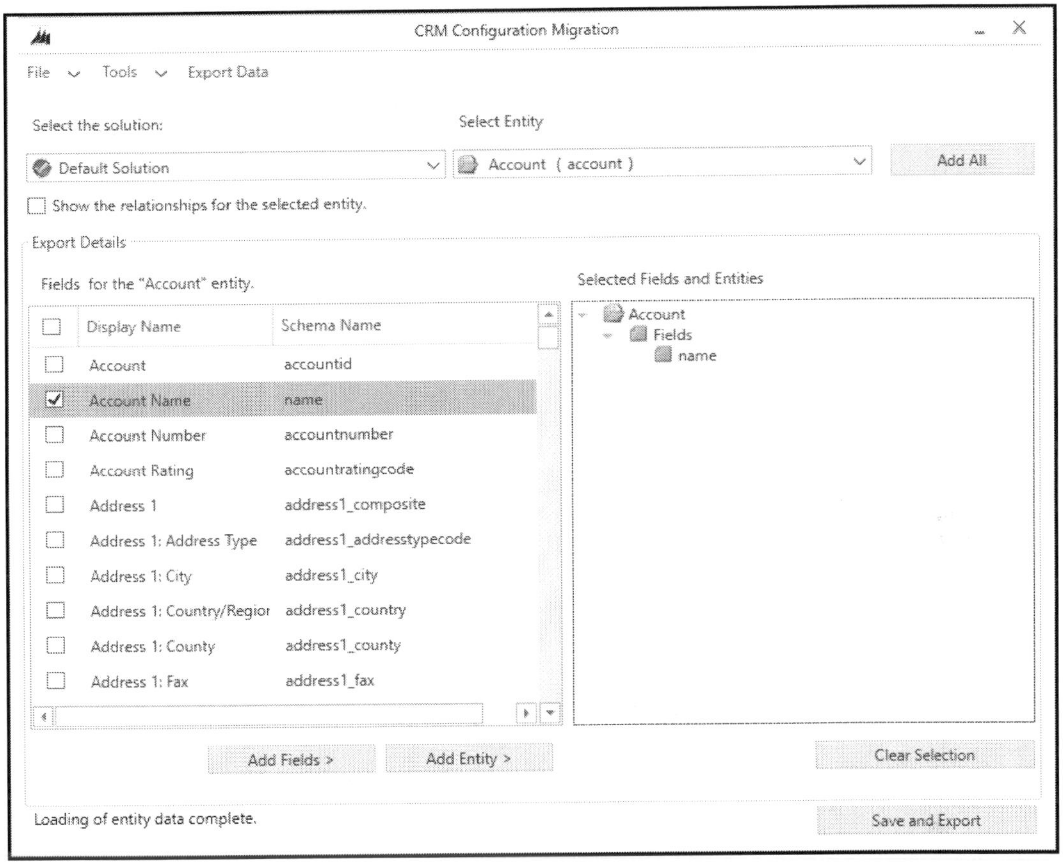

5. On the export dialog, give your XML file a name and navigate it in your preferred location, and then click on **Save**.
6. When prompted with a dialog asking you to export the data, click on **Yes**.
7. Click on **...** next to the **Save to data file** field and enter a name for the data zip file, and then click on **Save**.
8. In the export data screen, click on **Export Data**.
9. Click on **Exit** after the export is complete.
10. On the main page of the Configuration Migration utility, click on **Import data**, followed by **Continue**.
11. Log in as per step 3 to your destination instance.
12. Once logged in, click on **...** next to the **Zip file** text field and select the data zip file created in step 8 and then click on **Import Data**.

How it works...

We started the recipe by creating the schema for the data we are exporting. In step 3, we logged in.

> Notice how the logging mechanism only asked for our credentials and identified the Dynamics 365 instance we have access to? This is the preferred way to connecting to Dynamics 365 as it automatically detects the best way to access your organization. This is a best practice compared to explicitly defining the web service endpoint, which might change over time.

In step 4 and step 5, we selected the attributes we are after and exported the schema. This prompted us in step 6 to export the data as well, which we did in step 7 and step 8.

In step 10 to step 12, we imported the configuration data into a different organization.

There's more...

The configuration tool can migrate data that is otherwise difficult to import using other conventional methods. This includes business units, users, themes, and much more.

See also

- *Staging data imports*
- The *Running a no code scheduled synchronization using Scribe* recipe of `Chapter 5`, *External Integration*
- The *Integration with SSIS using Kingswaysoft* recipe of `Chapter 5`, *External Integration*

4
Server-Side Extensions

In this chapter, we will cover the following recipes:

- Creating a Visual Studio solution for Dynamics 365 customization
- Creating a solution using the Dynamics CRM Developer Toolkit template
- Creating a LINQ data access layer
- Creating your first plugin
- Impersonating another user when running your plugin
- Creating your first custom workflow activity
- Creating your first custom action
- Deploying your customization using the plugin registration tool
- Debugging your plugin in Dynamics 365 on-premise
- Debugging your plugin in Dynamics 365 online

Introduction

One of the strengths of the Microsoft Dynamics 365 platform is its server-side extensibility. The out-of-the-box functionality of Dynamics CRM is great, but most enterprise implementations require further logic to validate, automate, or integrate.

At the time of writing this book, Dynamics 365 provides three different kinds of server-side extensibility: plugins, custom workflow activities, and custom actions. Each of them fits a specific set of scenarios.

Plugins

Plugins are typically used for custom logic that executes on the server before or after specific events, such as create, update, delete, assign, and more. Post-event plugins can also trigger synchronously or asynchronously.

Custom workflow activities

Custom workflow activities are reusable activities that can be added to a configured workflow business process. If a custom logic is to be reused multiple times and needs to be configured by power users, then custom workflow activities is the way to go.

> Power users are Dynamics 365 users with elevated privileges which can configure the system using point and click features.

Custom workflow activities have input and output parameters, making them ideal for data processing and returning computed values.The following diagram, taken from the *Event execution pipeline* MSDN article (`https://msdn.microsoft.com/en-us/library/gg327941.aspx`), shows the different types of plugins and custom workflows:

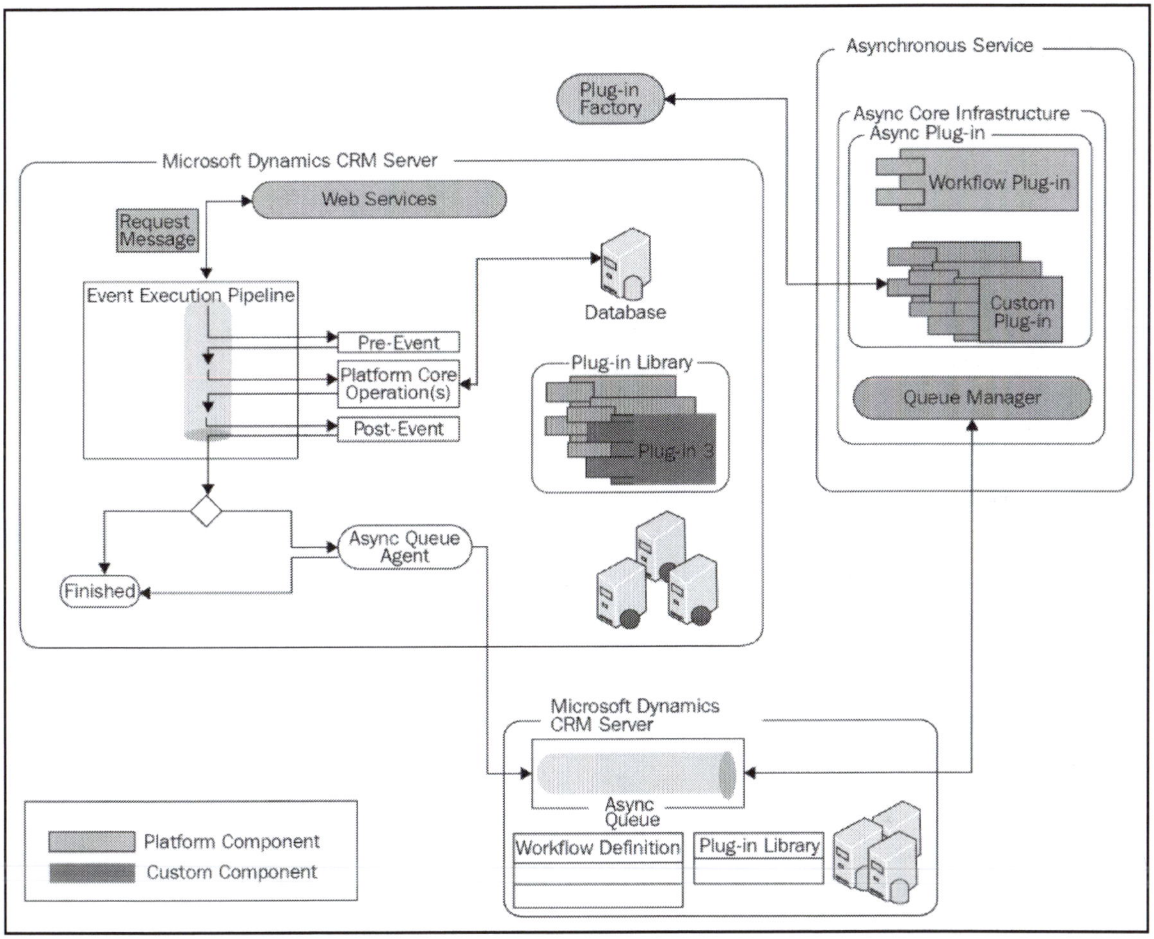

Custom actions

Custom actions are similar to custom workflow activities as they can be used in configured workflows. That said, custom activities can also be used in client-side JavaScript customization. If a custom logic is easier to implement using .NET code, but needs to be called from client-side extensions, then custom actions are your best bet.

The recipes in this chapter will guide you through implementing the different types of server-side customization, deploying them, testing them, and refining them.

Creating a Visual Studio solution for Dynamics 365 customization

Visual Studio is the preferred IDE to build Microsoft Dynamics 365 server-side customization. Visual Studio is a very powerful IDE that improves productivity and facilitates customization development. A Visual Studio Solution will contain Visual Studio Projects that will ultimately generate **Dynamic Linked Libraries** (**DLL**) that will be deployed on your Dynamics 365 instance.

In this recipe, we will demonstrate the setup of a Visual Studio solution with the required .NET Dynamics 365 library references as a basis for other recipes.

Getting ready

As a prerequisite for this recipe, you need to have a version of Visual Studio installed on your development machine (preferably 2015, the version used in this recipe; you can also use Visual Studio code and the express edition, although not the preferable option) and an internet connection to get the SDK DLLs packages using NuGet.

TIP

Alternatively, you can manually add the DLLs from the SDK, which requires a pre-downloaded version of the Dynamics 365 SDK that is compatible with your instance.

How to do it...

1. Start Visual Studio.
2. Create a new solution by selecting **New** | **Project** from the **File** menu.
3. In the **New Project** dialog, select **Blank Solution** from the **Visual Studio Solutions** templates.
4. Ensure that the selected .NET framework version matches the recommended version of your Dynamics 365 instance. In our example, Dynamics 365 uses .NET 4.5.2.
5. Give your solution a name, following your project's convention. Type `Packt.Xrm.Extensions` in the **Name** field.

6. It is highly recommended that you keep the **Add to source control** checkbox ticked to store your source code in source control:

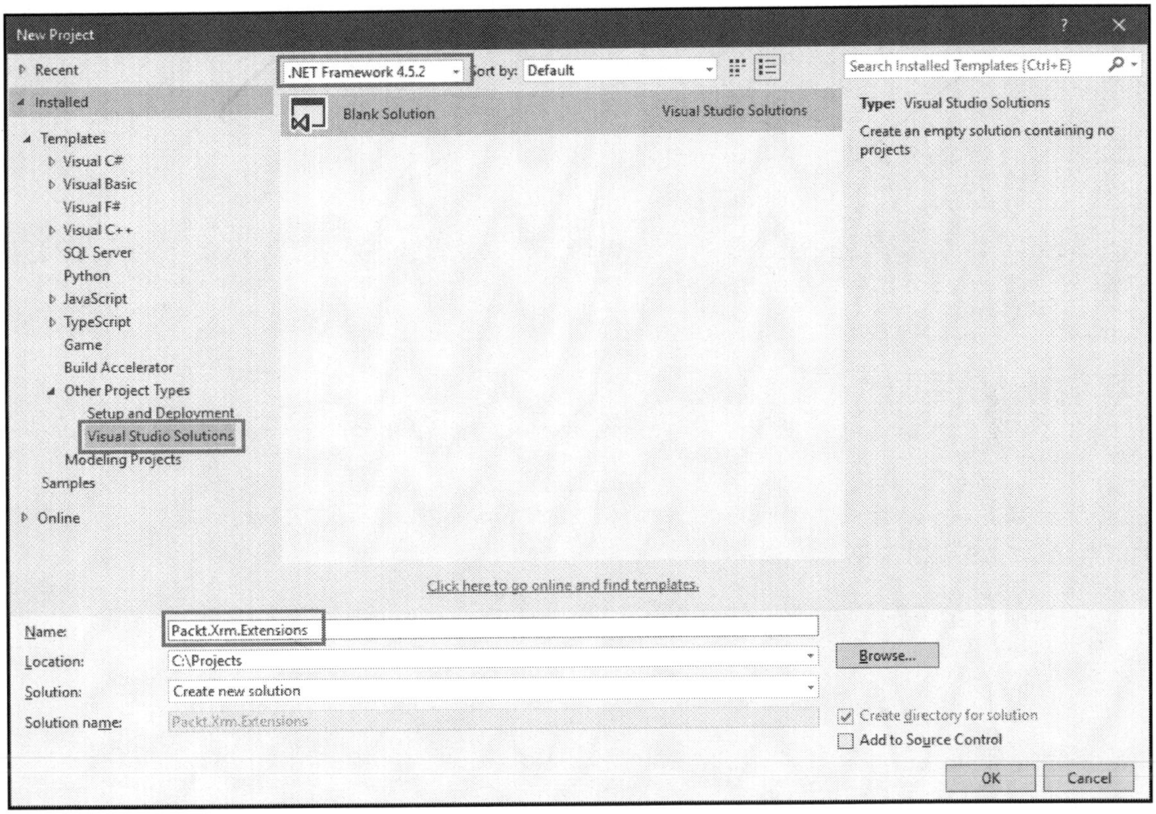

7. Click on **OK**.
8. Right-click on your solution in the Visual Studio Solution explorer window and select **Add** | **New Project**.
9. Select **Class Library** and give your project the name `Packt.Xrm.Extensions.CoreCrm`.
10. Click on **OK**.
11. Right-click on your new project's references and select **Manage NuGet Packages...**.

12. Search for `CRM XrmTooling core assemblies` using the top-right search field in the **Manage Nuget Packages** dialog:

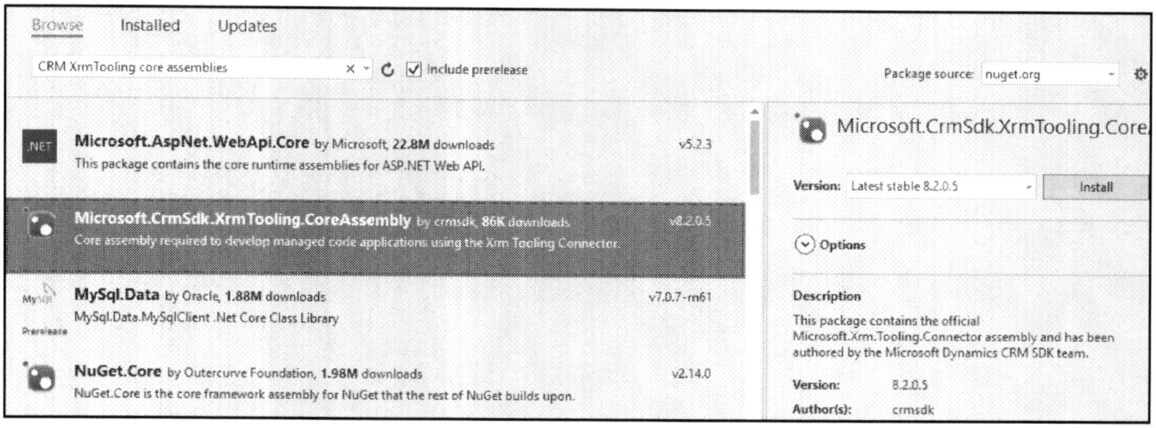

13. Locate the **Microsoft.CrmSdk.XrmTooling.CoreAssemblies** package that matches your Dynamics CRM instance version and install it by clicking on the **Install** button.
14. Click on the **I Accept** button after having read and agreed to the license details in the **License Acceptance** dialog.
15. Right-click on your project and select **properties**.
16. Click on the **Sign the assembly** tick box in the **Signing** tab and select an existing signing key, or create a new one. You can optionally create a password for your signing key.

How it works...

In this recipe, we started by creating a solution and a project that will contain our customizations in step 1 through step 10. Visual Studio will create containers that will hold the code and the required references, along with code analysis and all the required build steps. The naming conversion used in this recipe follows the Microsoft MSDN namespace guidelines (`https://msdn.microsoft.com/en-us/library/ms229026(v=vs.110).aspx`):

```
<Company>.(<Product>|<Technology>)[.<Feature>][.<Subnamespace>]
```

It is important to get the .NET version correct in step 4, otherwise, you will face incompatibility issues when adding your SDK core assembly NuGet package.

Step 11 through to step 13 helped us locate the Dynamics CRM SDK NuGet package from the public NuGet repository and install it in our Visual Studio project. The NuGet package contains the core DLLs required to build our solution and any dependencies to any other NuGet packages. Visual Studio automatically resolves missing dependencies and installs them in your project. As a result, the solution will have several packages installed, including the Microsoft Dynamics CRM 365 SDK core assemblies.

The final step was to sign the assembly, a required step as any code deployed on your Dynamics 365 instance needs to be strongly typed. Protecting your signing key with a password is considered good practice to protect your identity.

There's more...

The Dynamics 365 product team also released the Dynamics 365 Developer Toolkit, which can be downloaded from `https://marketplace.visualstudio.com/items?itemName=DynamicsCRMPG.MicrosoftDynamicsCRMDeveloperToolkit`. The next recipe focuses on the usage and capabilities of the Developer Toolkit Visual Studio add-on.

The toolkit facilitates the integration from and to Dynamics 365. Using the **Navigation** menu, you can select web resources to add to your solution, generate early bound entity classes, create new plugins for an entity, and more.

From the Visual Studio Solution, you can also register plugins and push customization to your Dynamics 365 instance.

At present, the Developer Toolkit is not compatible with Visual Studio 2017.

See also

- *Creating a solution using the Dynamics CRM Developer Toolkit template*

Creating a solution using the Dynamics CRM Developer Toolkit template

The developer toolkit for Dynamics 365 is a Visual Studio add-on that simplifies building customization extensions for Dynamics 365, as well as helps deploying them to different Dynamics 365 instances.

In this recipe, we will walk you through installing the developer toolkit and starting a new solution using the template.

Getting ready

You will need to download the developer toolkit from `https://marketplace.visualstudio.com/items?itemName=DynamicsCRMPG.MicrosoftDynamicsCRMDeveloperToolkit` and install it on a development machine that has Visual Studio and the Dynamics 365 SDK already installed. You will also require the .NET framework 4.5.2 installed.

At the time of writing, the developer toolkit is not compatible with Visual Studio 2017. It is recommended that you use the 2015 version. Older versions, 2012 and 2013, are also supported.

Once installed, you will need to set up the path to the SDK by navigating to **Tools** | **Options** | **Tools Path** and configuring the required values. As shown in the following screenshot, the **Plug-in Registration Tool** path is set to `<SDK folder>\Tools\PluginRegistration` and the **Bin** path is set to `<SDK folder>\Bin`:

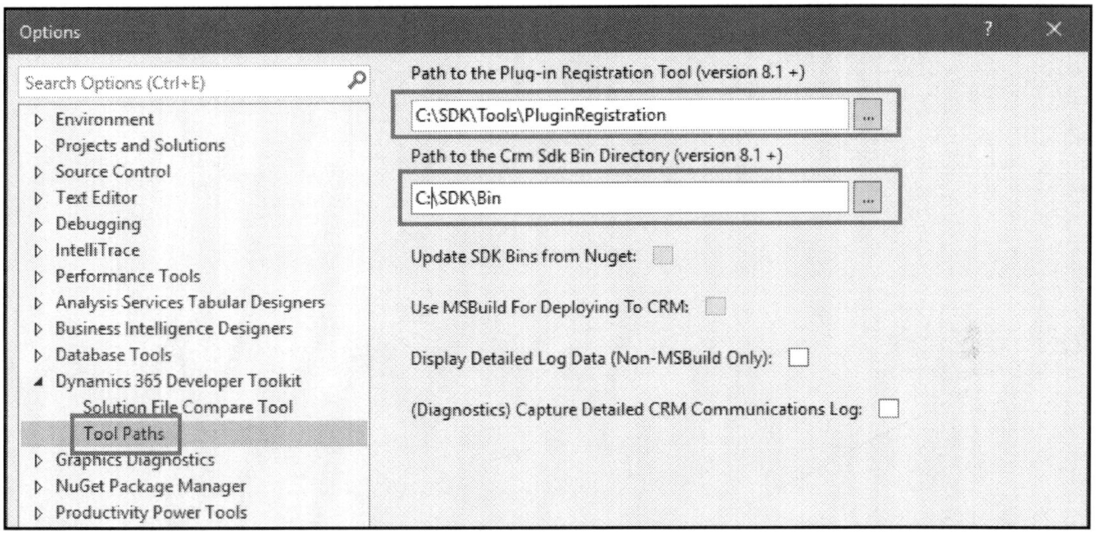

You will also require the usual instance of Dynamics 365 with a solution containing your customization, and at least the **System Customizer** security role applied to the user connecting to the instance.

How to do it...

1. Start Visual Studio.
2. Create a new solution by selecting **New** | **Project** from the **File** menu.

3. In the **New Project** dialog, select **Installed** | **Templates** | **Visual C#** | **Dynamics 365** | **New Visual Studio Solution Template for Dynamics 365** from the list of templates and give it the name `Packt.Xrm.Extensions`. Ensure that .NET Framework 4.5.2 is selected at the top, as shown here:

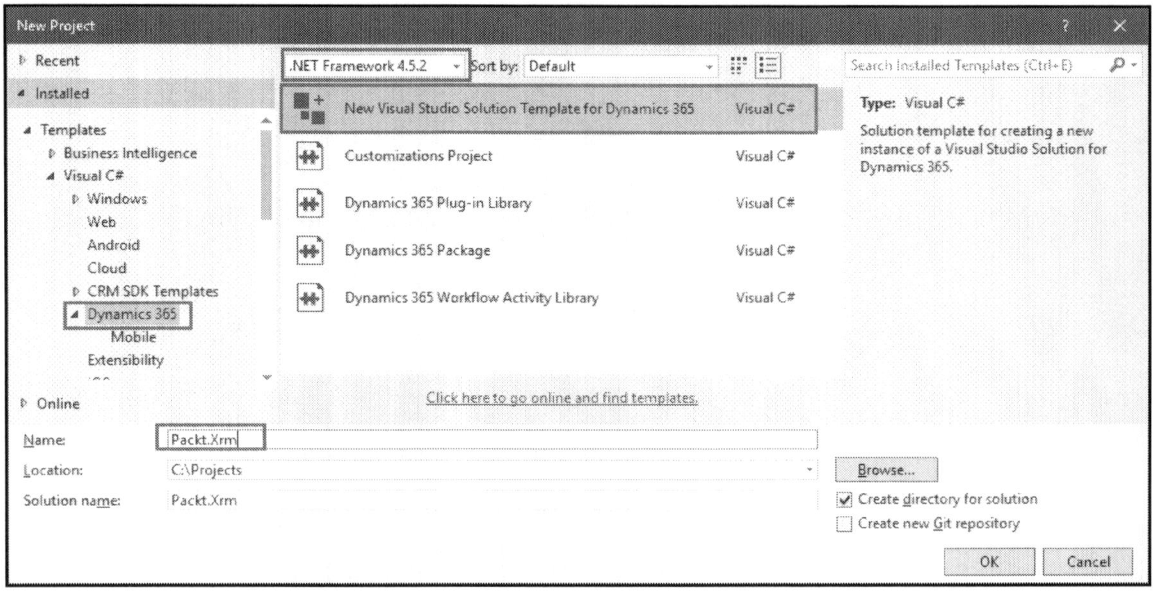

4. You will be prompted to connect to Dynamics 365. If you have already logged in, you can leverage the existing connection; otherwise, you can follow the familiar prompt to connect.
5. In the **Configure Microsoft Dynamics 365 Solution** dialog select **Start from CRM**:

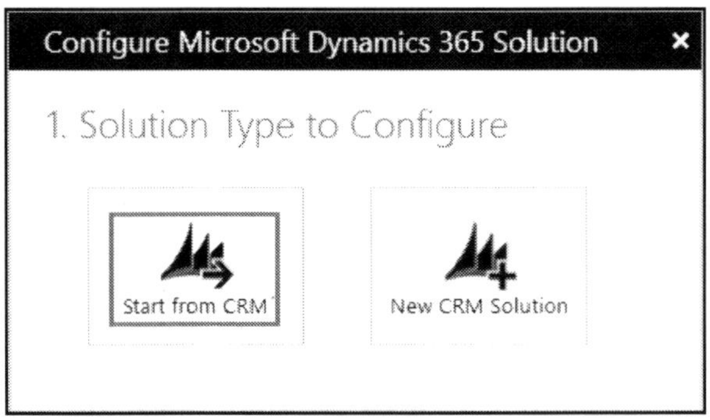

6. You will then be prompted with the connection details that you can change or accept by pressing **Next**. Then select your preferred solution as per this screenshot and click on **Done**:

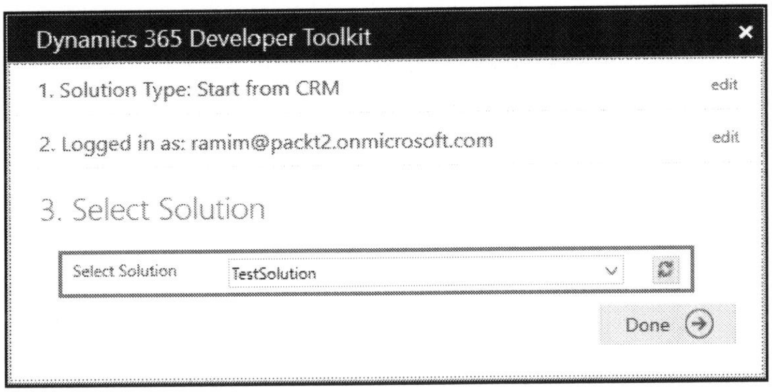

7. In the Visual Studio Template Selection dialog, select **Add New Templates**.
8. In the next step of the dialog, select **Add Plugin Project** then click on **Next**, as highlighted here:

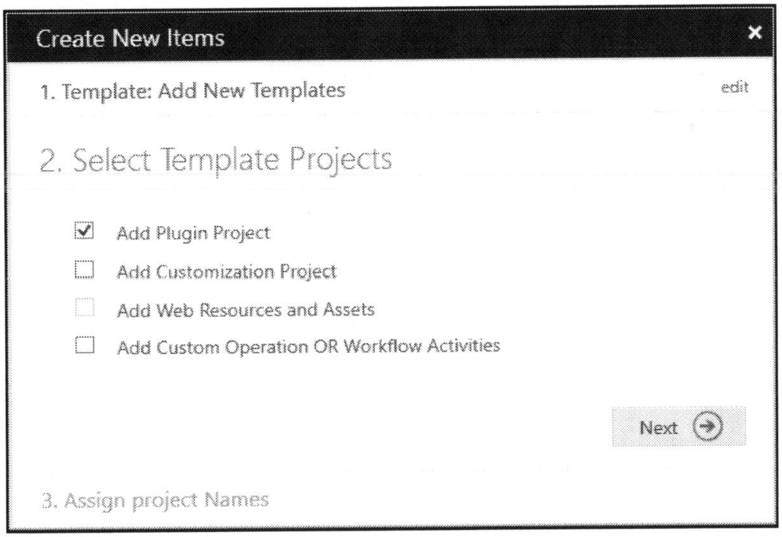

9. In the final step, give your project a name, such as `Packt.Xrm.Extensions.Plugins`. Your final solution will look something like this:

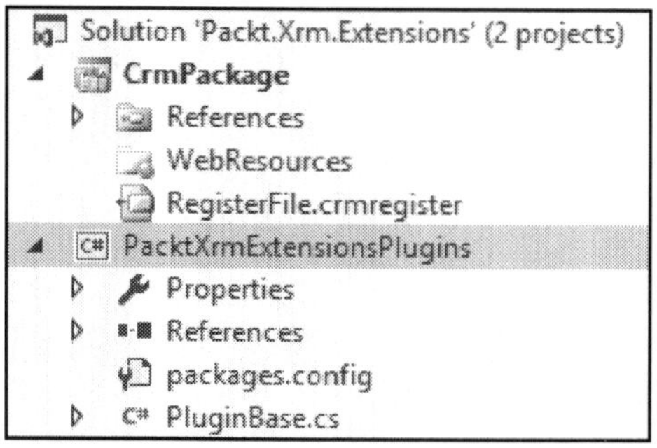

How it works...

In the first three steps, we created a Visual Studio solution using the template included in the developer toolkit, and we gave it the name `Packt.Xrm.Extensions`, as per the first recipe in this chapter.

In step 4 to step 6, we opted to start from a Dynamics 365 solution. This will help us deploy our customization to an existing solution in Dynamics 365. Alternatively, we could have created a new solution.

In step 7 to step 9, we created a new project under the solution to hold our plugins. We could also create custom operations workflow activities or customization projects, each with a different set of libraries referenced. A sample code file is included in the plugin and custom workflow projects.

The Developer toolkit is currently in Beta release. It still has a few minor debugs that will hopefully be addressed in the final version. For instance, you will notice that the plugin project created is missing the dots in the namespace. This can easily be fixed by renaming the project and changing its properties.

In step 9, we ended up with a Visual Studio solution that contains two projects: a class library project for our plugins, and a **CrmPackage** project that contains our Dynamics 365 artefacts and an XML `RegisterFile.crmregister` that will help deploy our customization.

If you missed adding a project of a specific type during the initial setup, you can always add it later the normal way you add a project to your Visual Studio solution. The Dynamics 365 project templates will be available as demonstrated in step 3.

There's more

The developer toolkit is a powerful tool that can help you increase your Dynamics 365 customization productivity. From within the tool, you can create early bound classes, create and manipulate plugins and plugin steps, create and edit custom actions, create workflow activities as well as deploy your changes to your Dynamics 365 solution, and much more.

Create early bound classes

In order to create early bound classes, navigate to `<Your Instance Name>` | **Entities** and right-click on the entity of your choice. Then select **Create Class for Entity**, as highlighted in this screenshot:

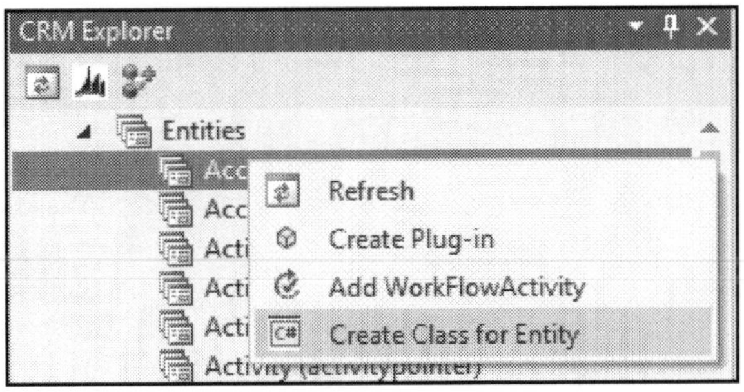

If you cannot find the **CRM Explorer** dialog, you can bring it back by navigating it to **CRM Explorer** under the **View** Visual Studio menu.

You will be prompted with the **Create Strong Type** dialog. Enter the following details (make sure that you update the namespace correctly).

- **Project to Add to**: `PacktXrmEntensionsPlugins` (this is project the that will include the newly generated class in case you have multiple customization projects within your Visual Studio solution)
- **Service Context Name**: `PacktContext` (this is the context class name used for LINQ queries, for example)
- **Filename to Create**: `Account.cs`
- **Namespace to use**: `Packt.Xrm.Entensions.Plugins` as shown here:

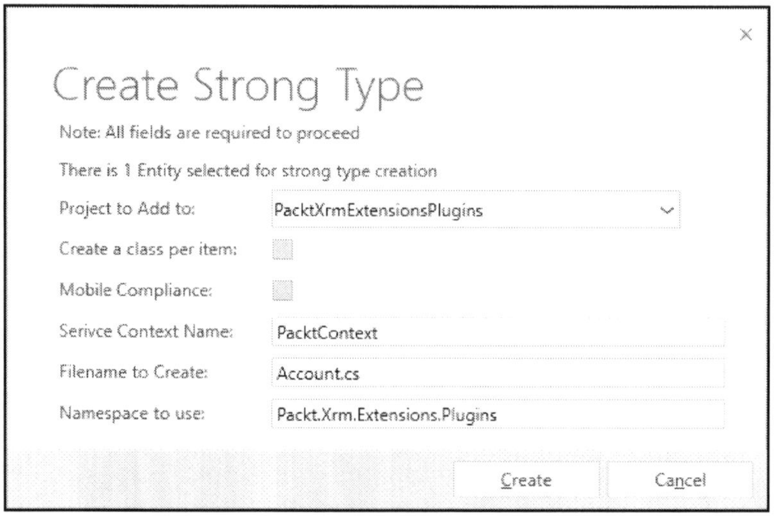

Finally, click on the **Create** button.

Deploy changes to Dynamics 365

To deploy your artefacts to your Dynamics 365 instance, right-click on **CrmPackage** and select `Deploy` from the context menu. In the **Select What to Deploy** dialog, ensure that the **Target Organization** and the **Solution Name** values are correct. Then, either select **Deploy All** or select which components you want to deploy, as shown here:

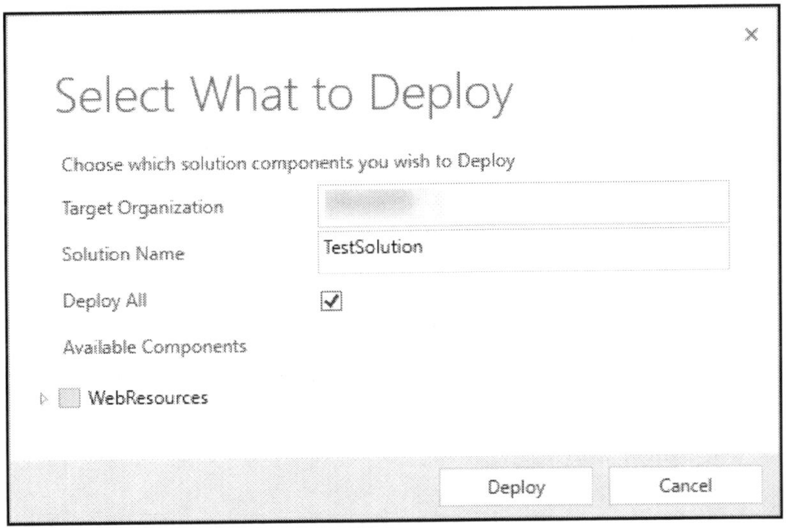

At the time of writing, the developer toolkit does not allow you to publish your changes from Visual Studio.

If you are having problems deploying, ensure that all your projects are compiling. If you are still facing issues, review the content of `RegisterFile.crmregister` and ensure that the XML references are correct.

See also

- *Creating a Visual Studio Solution for Dynamics 365 customization*

Creating a LINQ data access layer

In preparation for writing our first plugin in the next recipe, we will start in this recipe by creating a simple data access layer. A sample functional requirement states that; any e-mails associated with a specific account with no subject are to be closed, and the rest are to have an updated due date ten days from today's date when an account name is changed. In this recipe, we will only focus on retrieving the e-mails associated with a specific record, closing e-mails as canceled, and updating the rest.

This recipe will also leverage the unit of work pattern provided with the organization service context generated with the early bound entity generation. The patterns is explained in the *How it works...* section.

Getting ready

To write your data access layer, you will need the early bound entities generated as per the *Creating early bound entity classes* recipe from `Chapter 3`, *SDK Enterprise Capabilities*; optionally, you can generate the enums for the status codes.

> The status code enums are generated by default if you generate the class using the Developer Toolkit add-on for Visual Studio.

Additionally, you will require the solution created in *Creating a Visual Studio Solution for Dynamics 365 customization.*

To execute the code, you will require the appropriate privileges on the entities you are manipulating.

How to do it...

1. Leverage the solution created earlier in this chapter and add a class called `UpdateActivity`.
2. Import the following namespaces:

```
using System;
using System.Collections.Generic;
using System.Linq;
using Microsoft.Xrm.Sdk;
```

```
using Microsoft.Xrm.Tooling.Connector;
using Packt.Xrm.Entities;
using Microsoft.Crm.Sdk.Messages;
```

3. Initialize a service context and `IOrganizationService` at the class scope level:

```
OrganisationServiceContext _organizationContext;
IOrganizationService _organizationService;
```

4. Add a `GetEmails` method that takes a `Guid` as a parameter:

```
public IEnumerable<Email> GetEmails(Guid parentEntityId)
{
var query = from email in _organizationContext.EmailSet
         where email.RegardingObjectId.Id == parentEntityId
                &&
                email.StateCode == EmailState.Open
                select new Email
                {
                  Id = email.Id,
                  Subject = email.Subject
       };

return query.ToList();
}
```

5. Add a `closeEmailAsCancelled` method that takes an e-mail as a parameter:

```
public void CloseEmailAsCancelled(Email email)
{
    email.StateCode = EmailState.Canceled;

    var setStateRequest = new SetStateRequest()
    {
        Status = new
OptionSetValue((int)email_statuscode.Canceled),
        State = new OptionSetValue((int)EmailState.Canceled),
        EntityMoniker = new
EntityReference(Email.EntityLogicalName, email.Id)
    };
    _organizationContext.Execute(setStateRequest);
}
```

6. Add an `UpdateEntity` method that takes an entity as a parameter:

```
public void UpdateEntity(Entity entity)
{
_organizationContext.UpdateObject(entity);
```

```
}
```

7. Add a `Commit()` method that calls the `SaveChanges` on the context:

```
public void Commit()
{
_organizationContext.SaveChanges();
}
```

How it works...

In this recipe, we only focused on the data access layer to retrieve and update records in Dynamics 365.

The `GetEmails` method uses a LINQ query to retrieve the e-mails associated with the records' GUID.

> To test your LINQ queries outside your code, consider using LINQPad (`https://www.linqpad.net/`).

Notice how we opted to select a few attributes instead of returning all of them. Attribute filtering is considered best practice to keep performance under control; however, you might turn your methods into single-usage methods. You'll have to find the right balance between how many attributes you can return and how often you can reuse your method.

The query and the `ToList` are separated intentionally to demonstrate that the query is not executed until `ToList()` is called. At the time of writing, if you run fiddler in the background, you will notice that behind the scenes the query is converted into a `RetrieveMultipleRequest` namespace. `QueryExpression` requests point to `https://<organizationame>.api.crm.dynamics.com/XRMServices/2011/Organization.svc`.

The `CloseEmailAsCancelled` method uses a `SetStateRequest` request to change the state of the e-mail, which is then passed to be executed by the organization service context. This request is executed straight away when the `execute` method is called.

In contrast, the `UpdateEntity` method does not update the record straight away. The method encapsulates the organization service context, the `UpdateObject` method, and uses polymorphism to accept any entity that requires its changes to be updated.

The changes are only committed when the `SaveChanges` method is called on the organization service context, which is implemented in the `Commit` method. This is known as the repository in the unit of work design pattern. This pattern is typically used in Microsoft's Entity framework.

> `SaveChanges` does not execute the changes in a transaction. It just bundles them to be executed in one call.

Even though as it currently stands the code is not usable, some simple modifications to pass the organization service into the constructor changes that. However, given that this will be part of a plugin later, we won't venture into refactoring it yet.

There's more...

You can opt not to use the organization service context and replace it with the organization service proxy instead, which will simplify the implementation. Nevertheless, this recipe highlights the repository pattern and how to use it.

The advantage of having a separate class for your data access layer is that you can alter its internals without affecting the consumer, as we will observe in *Replacing your LINQ data access layer with QueryExpress* recipe of `Chapter 6`, *Enhancing Your Code*; a perfect example of object-oriented encapsulation at its best.

See also

- The *Creating early bound entity classes* recipe of `Chapter 3`, *SDK Enterprise Capabilities*
- *Creating your first plugin*
- The *Refactoring your plugin using a three-layer pattern* recipe of `Chapter 6`, *Enhancing Your Code*
- The *Executing a request within a transaction* recipe of `Chapter 3`, *SDK Enterprise Capabilities*

Creating your first plugin

Plugins are some of the most powerful extensions Dynamics 365 offers. They allow you to execute a process before or after an entity's event, such as create, update, assign, and so forth.

In the previous recipe, we created a data access layer class that retrieves e-mails and updates entities. In this recipe, we will leverage this layer and convert the class into a plugin that retrieves e-mails associated with a specific account, closes the ones with no subject, and updates the start date of the rest to ten days from today's date.

Getting ready

For this recipe, you will need the Visual Studio solution created in this chapter's *Creating a Visual Studio Solution for Dynamics 365 customization*, the early bound entities with the optionset enum values created in the *Creating early bound entity classes* and *Extending CrmSvcUtil to generate optionsets enum* recipes of `Chapter 3`, *SDK Enterprise Capabilities*, and the data access layer defined in *Creating a LINQ data access layer* from this chapter as well. None of those components are mandatory, but they form a good basis to build your plugin on.

To run the plugin, you need the appropriate access to the account and e-mail entities.

How to do it

1. Add the following import statement to your previously created `UpdateActivities`:

```
using System.ServiceModel;
```

2. Implement the `IPlugin` interface, as follows:

```
public class UpdateActivities : IPlugin
```

3. Implement the `Execute` method, as follows:

```
public void Execute(IServiceProvider serviceProvider)
        {
            var tracingService =
(ITracingService)serviceProvider.GetService(typeof(ITracingService)
);
```

```
            var context =
(IPluginExecutionContext)serviceProvider.GetService(typeof(IPluginE
xecutionContext));

            if (!context.InputParameters.Contains("Target") ||
!(context.InputParameters["Target"] is Entity))
                return;

            Entity entity =
(Entity)context.InputParameters["Target"];

            if (entity.LogicalName != "account")
                return;

            try
            {
                IOrganizationServiceFactory serviceFactory =
(IOrganizationServiceFactory)serviceProvider.GetService(typeof(IOrg
anizationServiceFactory));
                _organizationService =
serviceFactory.CreateOrganizationService(context.UserId);

                _organizationContext = new
OrganisationServiceContext(_organizationService);

                var emails = GetEmails(entity.Id);
                foreach (var email in emails)
                {
                    if (string.IsNullOrEmpty(email.Subject))
                    {
                        CloseEmailAsCancelled(email);
                    }
                    else
                    {
                        email.ScheduledStart =
DateTime.Today.AddDays(10);
                        UpdateEntity(email);
                    }
                }

                Commit();
            }
            catch (FaultException<OrganizationServiceFault> ex)
            {
                throw new InvalidPluginExecutionException("An error
occurred in the FollowupPlugin plug-in.", ex);
            }
            catch (Exception ex)
```

```
                {
                    tracingService.Trace("FollowupPlugin: {0}",
        ex.ToString());
                    throw;
                }
            }
```

How it works...

We first started by importing an additional namespace that contains `FaultException` that we caught in our code.

In step 2, we implemented the `IPlugin` interface. This interface indicated to Dynamics 365 that this class can execute a plugin and follows the expected plugin signature.

In step 3, we implemented the `Execute` method required by the `IPlugin` interface. Within this method, we did some standard checks to ensure that we have the target entity as an input parameter, then we validated that the entity is an account (this is not necessary if we want the plugin to execute on any entity), then we retrieved the organization service that we assigned to a local variable and also instantiated the organization service context class.

The rest of the method contains some business logic and leverages the methods created in the previous recipe to close the e-mails with no subject, and to update the ones with a subject with a new date. Once all e-mails were updated, we committed our changes.

Towards the end of the method, we introduced some error handling to trace and throw exceptions. To display a user-friendly error message, we threw an exception using `InvalidPluginExecutionException`.

> Throwing a sanitized exception message is a good practice to ensure that a user-friendly error message is displayed to the user.

There's more...

There are many things you can do with plugins. Common plugin examples include: validation, automation, integration, auto-numbering, and auditing.

See also

- *Impersonate another user when running your plugin*
- The *Creating early bound entity classes* recipe of `Chapter 3`, *SDK Enterprise Capabilities*
- The *Refactoring your plugin using a three-layer pattern* recipe of `Chapter 6`, *Enhancing Your Code*
- The *Executing a request within a transaction* recipe of `Chapter 3`, *SDK Enterprise Capabilities*

Impersonate another user when running your plugin

Often, when running a plugin, you would want to execute a server-side transaction that might require additional privileges that the current logged in user does not have. For example, when a plugin passes or fails, you want to record the outcome of your process in a custom entity. Normal users would typically have limited-to-no access to such entities to avoid tampering. In such a scenario, even though the plugin is running in the context of a user, you would want that user to temporarily run as a different user with the correct privileges.

There are two ways to impersonate within plugins: you can either do it in your plugin code or when registering your plugin. In this recipe, we will cover the in-code example.

Getting ready

You will need a plugin already created, such as the one in the previous recipe. When running the code, the users must have the **Act On Behalf Of Another User** privilege (under **Business Management** | **Miscellaneous Privileges** in security roles) or be a member of the `PrivUserGroup` group in Active Directory:

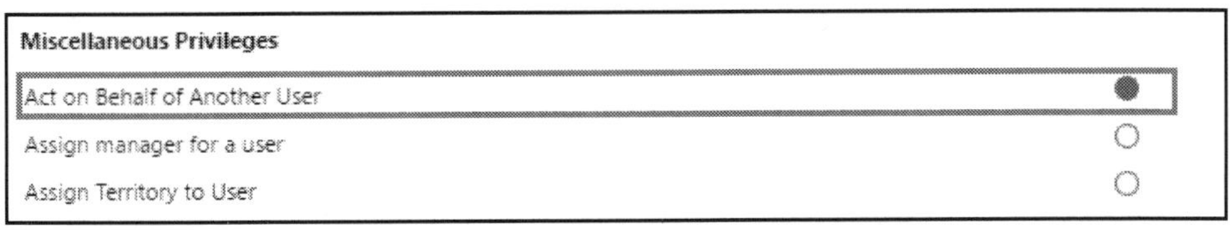

How to do it...

In your plugin, replace the `CreateOrganizationService` command with the following line where `<UserGuid>` is the actual GUID of the user you want to impersonate:

```
_organizationService =
serviceFactory.CreateOrganizationService(<UserGuid>);
```

How it works...

By passing another user's GUID to the `CreateOrganizationService` method, we impersonated that user while executing our plugin. Alternatively, we can pass null to impersonate a System User. In this abridged example, we used a hardcoded GUID; however, typically, you will have a separate method call to resolve the GUID given a set of attributes. For example, we might resolve the GUID based on a key, the name of the user, or the role of the user.

> It is important to note that hardcoding the GUID is bad practice and an SDLC maintenance nightmare.

There's more...

The alternative to in-code impersonation is to define it at the plugin registration level.

This can be done at the registration level step using the **Run in User's Context** attribute, as per this screenshot:

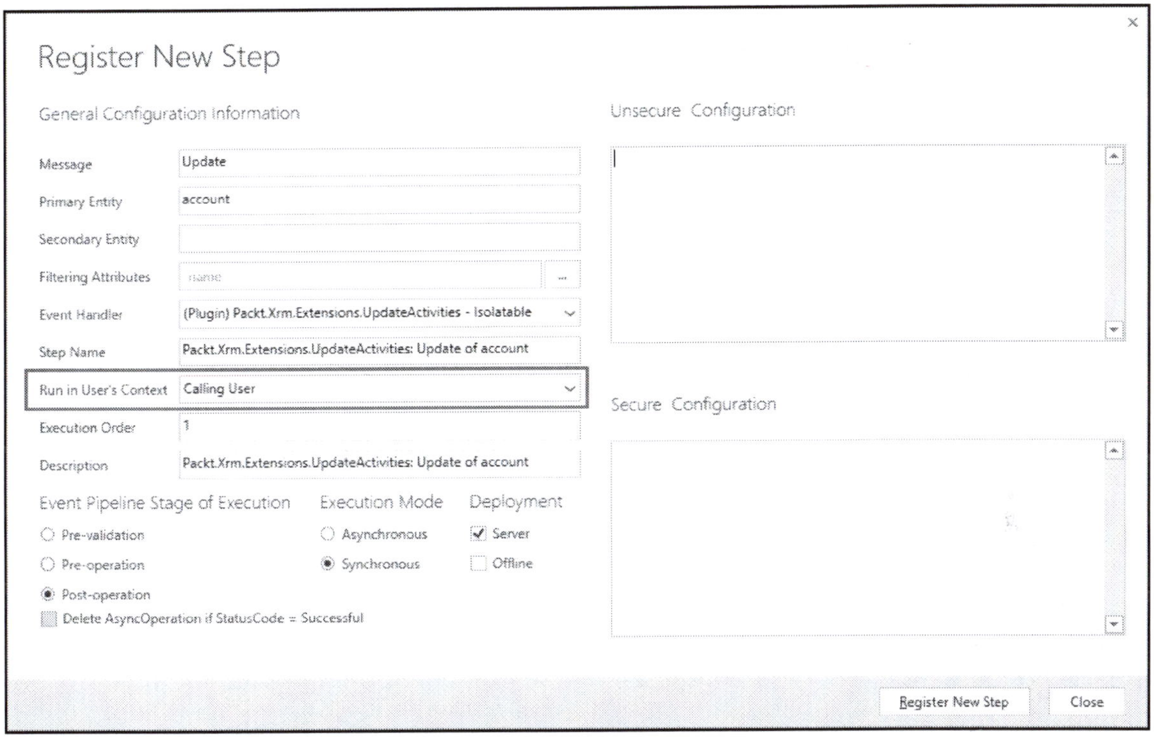

Unlike the in-code scenario, this value will be static as opposed to having the option to resolve the GUID at runtime.

See also

- *Deploying your customization using the plugin registration tool*
- *Creating your first plugin*

Creating your first custom workflow activity

A custom workflow activity allows you to add complex processing steps to your configurable workflows. Workflows are ideal for long-running processes as they do not face the two-minute timeout limitation that plugins have. Workflows can be run on demand as well as after triggering an event. Workflows can be configured by power users using a point and click user interface. Once custom activities are defined they can also be used as a point and click configuration without requiring additional .NET coding.

Creating a customer workflow activity is very similar to plugins. In this recipe, we will create a custom workflow activity that executes the exact same functionality as the plugin described in the previous section. In fact, rather than writing the workflow from scratch, we will turn the plugin into a workflow.

One of the great features of a custom workflow activity is that it can take input parameters and generate output parameters; a great feature if you want to process some data and pass the output to another workflow step.

Getting ready

Similar to plugins, to start writing a custom workflow activity you'll need to have a Visual Studio solution as per the first recipe in this chapter. Optionally, you can generate early bound entity classes to improve your coding productivity, as described in the previous chapter.

How to do it...

1. Add the following `using` statements to your `UpdateActivities.cs` file:

```
using Microsoft.Xrm.Sdk.Workflow;
using System.Activities;
```

2. Inherit from `CodeActivity` instead of implementing `IPlugin`, as follows:

```
public class UpdateActivities : CodeActivity
```

3. Add the following workflow input parameter:

```
[Input("Account Guid")]
[Default("00000000-0000-0000-0000-000000000000")]
public InArgument<string> AccountGuid { get; set; }
```

4. Change the signature of the `Execute` method to the following line of code:

```
protected override void Execute(CodeActivityContext
executionContext)
```

5. Replace the initialization of the tracing service, the organization service, and the organization service context with the following piece of code:

```
var tracingService =
  executionContext.GetExtension<ITracingService>();

var context = executionContext.GetExtension<IWorkflowContext>();
var serviceFactory =
  executionContext.GetExtension<IOrganizationServiceFactory>();
_organizationService =
  serviceFactory.CreateOrganizationService(context.UserId);
```

6. Replace the account and account ID instantiation with the following, and add the trace statement:

```
var input = AccountGuid.Get<string>(executionContext);
var accountId = input == Guid.Empty.ToString().Trim('{').Trim('}')
?
 context.PrimaryEntityId : Guid.Parse(input);
tracingService.Trace("Input value {0}", input);

var emails = GetEmails(accountId);
```

7. Remove the **catch fault exception** block.
8. The rest remains the same.

How it works...

As you can see, the structure behind a workflow is very similar to a plugin. The syntax and the objects to retrieve the organization proxy service and the context are different, and the way to access the input parameters is also different. However, once inputs are established, the business logic and the data access layer remain untouched.

In step 1, we started by importing namespaces specific to workflows that give us the parent `CodeActivity` class, and the input parameter class and attributes.

In step 2, we changed the class definition to inherit from `CodeActivity`, which helps Dynamics 365 identify that this is a custom workflow activity.

In step 3, we defined a workflow input parameter to feed the workflow activity the account GUID. This step is not necessary for the workflow, but it will be used in the next recipe.

In step 4, we changed the signature of the `Execute` method to override the `CodeActivity` parent class `Execute` method.

In step 5, we refactored the code to allow us to extract the organization proxy service from the workflow context.

In step 6, we retrieved the account GUID from the context primary entity ID if the input parameter is an empty GUID (not set). We then traced the value that was passed to the input parameter (again, this last step is optional). We passed the GUID to the `GetEmails` method. The rest remained the same.

There's more...

Custom workflow activities are a powerful extension to Dynamics 365 as they convert complex processing into a simple reusable point and click configurable component.

Coupled with the input and output parameters, the workflow can also be used for complex calculations or transformations.

Furthermore, given the asynchronous nature of workflows, you can also use them for non-time critical long-running processes, such as document generation and integration tasks.

In CRM 2013, synchronous real-time workflows were introduced, allowing them to run straight after an event, turning workflows into synchronous plugin analogues.

> Synchronous workflows are transactional, meaning that, if a step in the workflow fails, the workflow rolls everything back to their original states.

See also

- *Creating your first plugin*
- The *Creating early bound entity classes* recipe of `Chapter 3`, *SDK Enterprise Capabilities*
- *Creating your first custom action*

Creating your first custom action

Custom actions are the most recent addition to server-side extensions. They belong to the family of processes and are similar to custom workflow activities. One advantage of using a custom action, as opposed to a custom workflow activity, is that not only can they be called from a workflow, but they can also be easily called from JavaScript and even be early bound and called as an SDK message call.

In this recipe, we will convert the previously created custom workflow into a custom activity.

Getting ready

You will first need a custom workflow activity to convert into a custom action. The workflow activity created and deployed in the previous two recipes is a good candidate. Similar to previous extensions done from within Dynamics 365, a **System Customizer** role is required, along with a Dynamics 365 solution to contain your extension. We will reuse the existing Packt solution created in the previous chapters.

How to do it...

1. In Dynamics 365, navigate to **Settings** | **Solutions** | **Packt** | **Processes** and click on **New**.
2. In the **Create Process** dialog, enter the following details:
    - **Process name**: `Update Activities`
    - **Category**: `Action`
    - **Entity**: `Account`
    - Click on **OK**

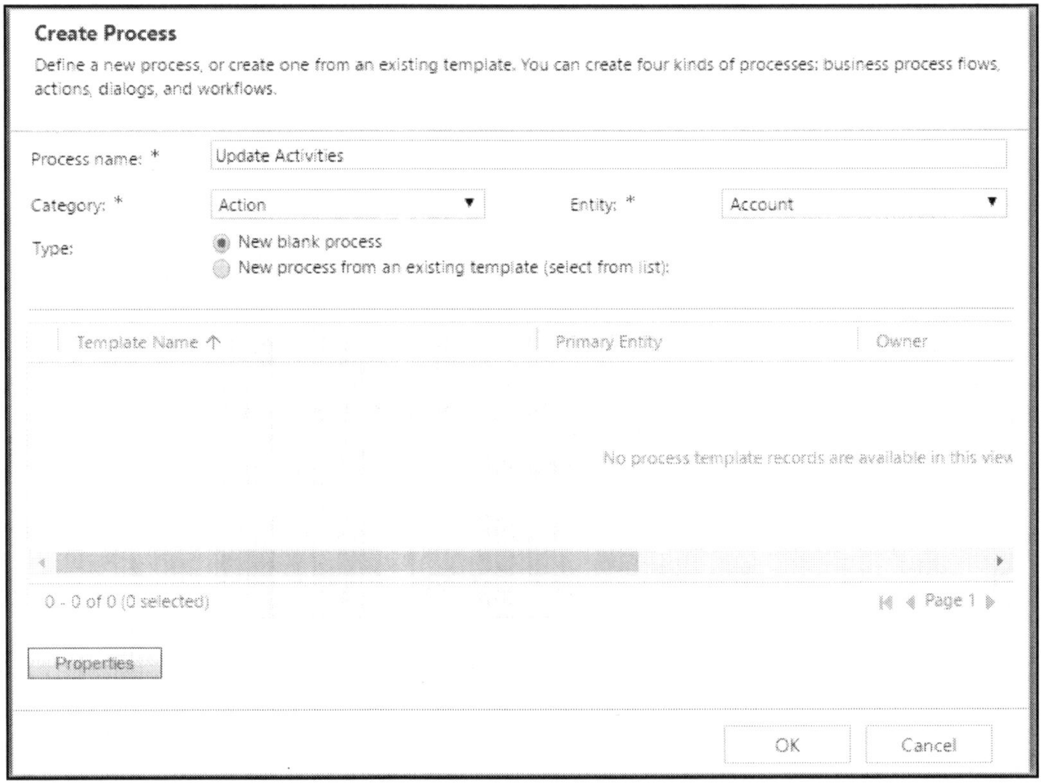

3. In your workflow dialog, under **Hide Process Arguments**, click on the **+** and create an input argument with the following details:
    - **Name:** `AccountGuid`
    - **Type:** `String`
    - **Required:** `True`
    - **Direction:** `Input`
    - **Description:** `Parent Account GUID related to the activities to be updated.`
4. In your workflow steps, click on **Add Step** and select the following custom workflow activity created in the previous recipe:

```
Packt.Xrm.Entensions |
  Packt.Xrm.EntensionsUpdateActivitiesWorkflow
```

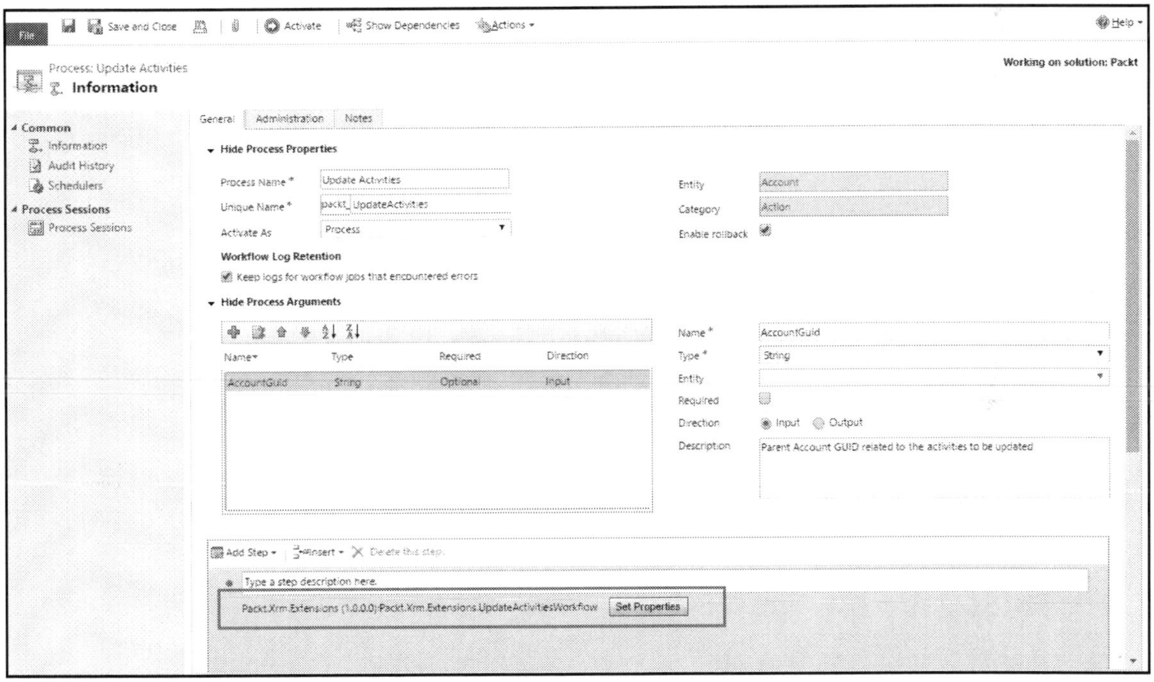

5. Click on **Set Properties**, and, in the **Update Activities** dialog, set the `AccountGUID` value using the right **Form Assistance** by selecting **Arguments** under **Look for**, followed by **AccountGuid** from the next dropdown, then click on the **Add** button followed by the **OK** button at the bottom. The value will show `{AccountGuid(Arguments)}`, as shown here:

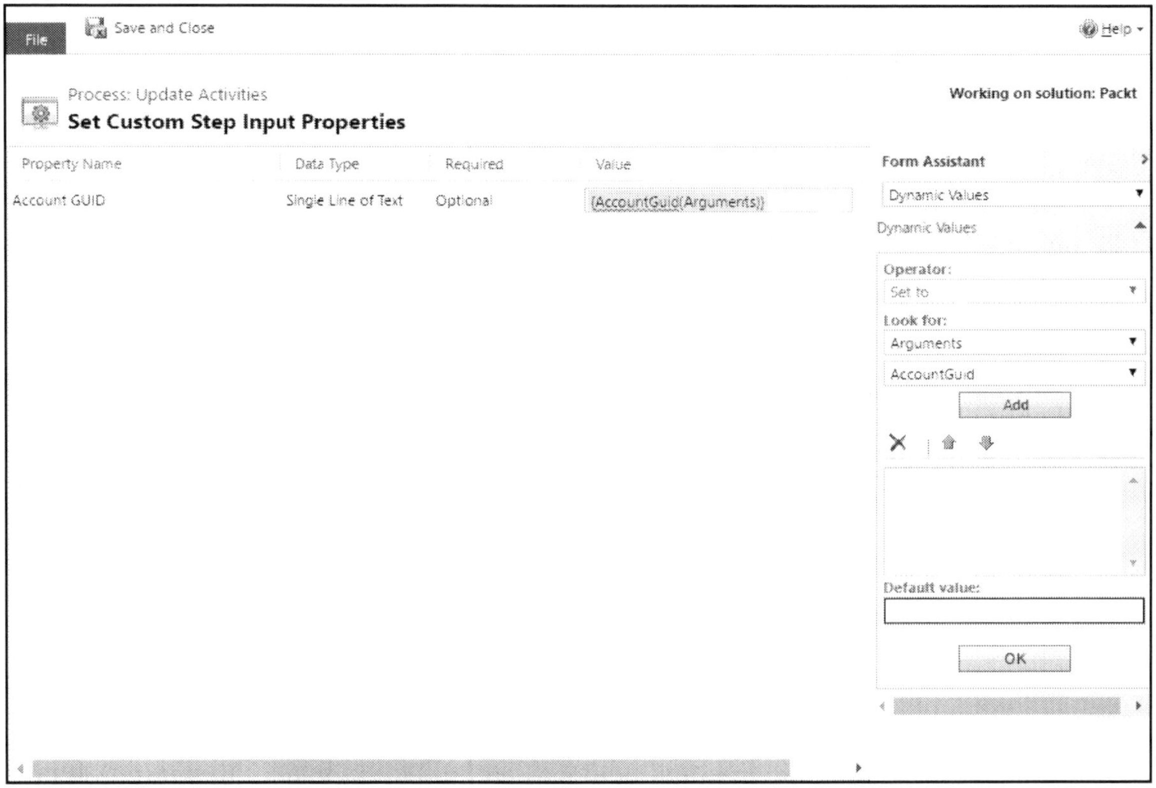

6. Click on **Save** and **Close**.
7. Click on the **Activate** button.

How it works...

In step 1 and step 2, we created our custom action process.

Next in step 3, we defined an input parameter to our action (we can also have output parameters). The parameter is of type string, which matches what our custom workflow activity expects.

In step 4, we added the custom workflow activity created in the previous recipe to our action steps.

Finally, in step 5, we relayed our input value to the newly added custom workflow activity.

There's more...

The alternatives discussed in this section can improve your productivity when implementing custom actions.

Wiring an IPlugin as a custom action

A plugin can also be wired as a custom action. Follow these steps to register your plugin as a custom action:

1. Create a plugin that implements the `IPlugin` interface.
2. Create an empty action in Dynamics 365 and give it a meaningful name, for example, `UpdateActivities`.

3. Using the plugin registration tool, add a step to your plugin using the name of your action as the message, as highlighted in the following screenshot:

In your code, using the `IPluginExecutionContext` class (which holds the plugin context), you can retrieve and set the input and output parameters using `context.InputParameter` and `context.OutputParameters`.

The **Primary Entity** value must match the value defined in your Dynamics 365 action. Nonetheless, you can create a global action not related to any entity.

Calling a custom action from your JavaScript

Once your activity is created, you can call it from your JavaScript extensions by sending a POST HTTPS request to the following Web API URL, with the body of your request containing the expected arguments in `JSON` format:

```
<OrganizationURL>/api/data/v8.2/<actionName>
```

Generate early bound custom action messages

Using `CrmSvcUtil`, you can also generate early bound request and response messages to facilitate the usage of the custom activity in your code. You can add custom action messages to your early bound generated classes using the `/generateActions` parameter, as shown in the following code snippet:

```
CrmSvcUtil.exe /namespace:Packt.Xrm.Extensions
/out:EntitiesWithActions.cs /language:CS
/serviceContextName:OrganisationServiceContext /il:true
/generateActions
```

See also

- *Creating your first custom workflow activity*
- The *Building your first action* recipe of `Chapter 1`, *No Code Extensions*

Deploying your customization using the plugin registration tool

Once you have a server-side extension implemented, you'll want to deploy it into your Dynamics 365 instance. The **Plugin Registration Tool** has been around since the early days of Dynamics CRM and is a great tool to master. It helps you deploy your .NET customization to your Dynamics 365 instances, and also helps register Azure Service Bus endpoint, enable profiling, and much more.

In this recipe, we will deploy the plugin implemented earlier in this chapter to a Dynamics 365 online instance using the plugin registration tool.

Getting ready

In order to deploy your server-side customization, you'll first need an existing assembly to deploy. We will leverage the one created in *Creating your first plugin* earlier in this chapter. This recipe will use the Plugin Registration Tool to register the plugin. The Plugin Registration Tool can be found in the Dynamics 365 SDK under `Tools\PluginRegistration`.

When deploying sandbox plugins on-premises, you must be part of the deployment administrators in the **Dynamics 365 Deployment Manager**.

How to do it...

1. Launch the `PluginRegistration.exe` application located in the SDK under `Tools\PluginRegistration`.
2. Click on **+ CREATE NEW CONNECTION**, as shown in the following screenshot, and you will be prompted with a familiar dialog:

3. Enter the details to connect to your Dynamics 365 instance.

4. Once connected, click on **Register** | **Register New Assembly**, as highlighted here:

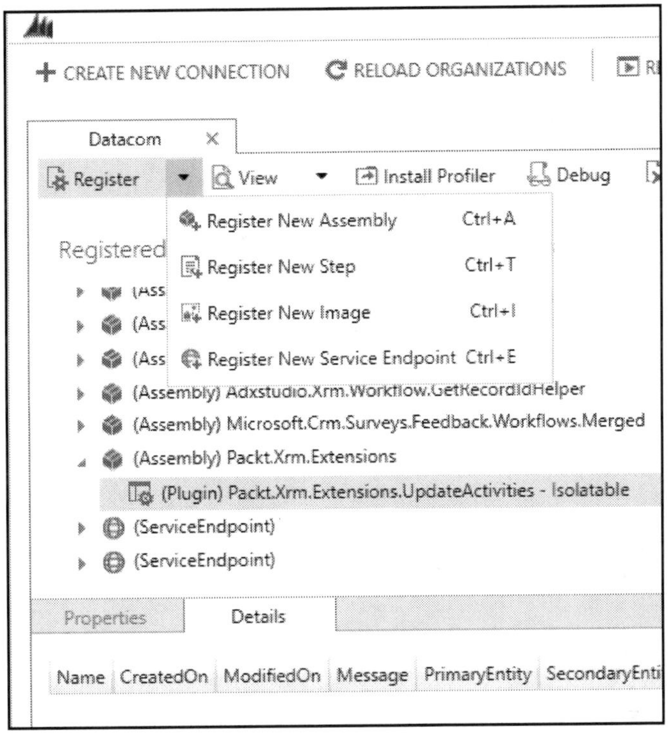

5. In the registration dialog, enter the location of your assembly in step 1. The following screenshot highlights a sample assembly location:

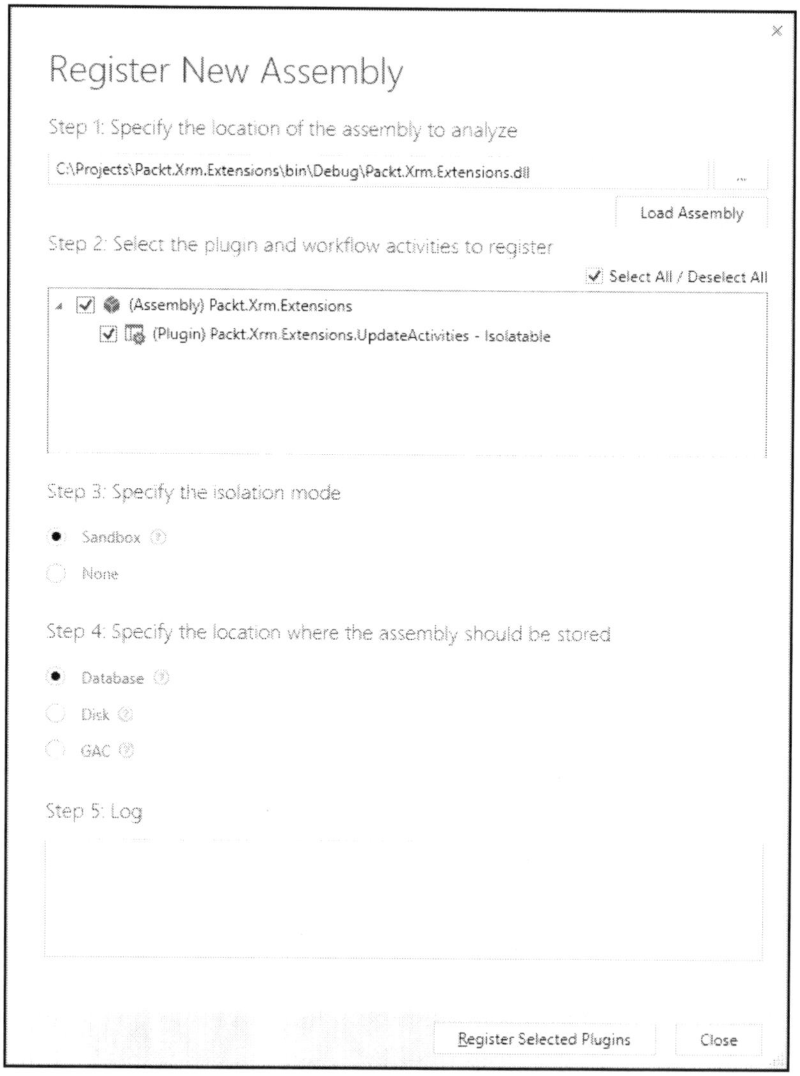

6. Once the assembly is loaded, enter the following details:
    - Ensure that your plugin class is selected in step 2
    - In step 3 set the isolation mode to sandbox
    - In step 4 set the storage location to database
    - Click on **Register Selected Plugins**

7. Once your assembly is registered, expand it from your list of registered plugins, select the plugin and, from the menu, select **Register** | **Register New Step**.
8. Enter the following details in your new step:
    - **Message**: `Update`
    - **Primary Entity**: `Account`
    - **Filtering Attributes**: `name`
    - **Event Pipeline Stage of Execution**: `Post-operation`
    - **Execution Mode**: `Synchronous`
    - Click on **Register New Step**

Your step should look like the following screenshot:

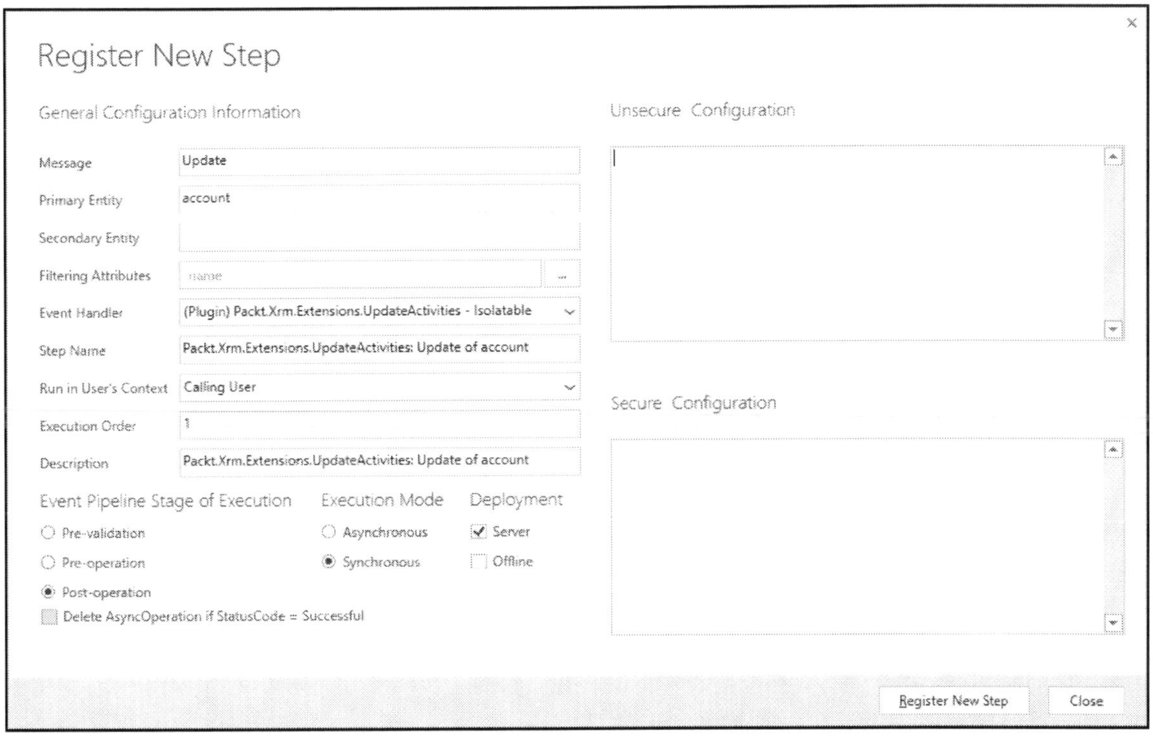

9. Now, click on the step registered in step 8 and select **Register** | **Register New Image**.
10. In the **Register New Image** dialog, enter the following details:
    - **Name**: `PreAccountUpdateImage`
    - **Entity Alias**: `Pre Account Update Image`
    - **Parameters**: `name`
    - Click on **Register Image**.

How it works...

Firstly in step 1 to step 3, we launched the Plugin Registration tool and connected to our Dynamics 365 instance.

In step 4 to step 6, we registered the assembly that holds our plugin. For online instances, we are bound to use the sandbox isolation mode and database registered assemblies. Step 6 uploads our assembly to a Dynamics 365 instance's database.

Next, in step 7 and step 8, we registered a plugin step. This specific step allows the plugin to execute after an account is updated, and specifically when the account name is changed. There are a few events that the plugin can register to including: create, delete, assign, and more, as well as custom action messages. The message field has an autocomplete function to assist you when typing the message name. A plugin can be built in a generic fashion and registered to more than one entity by registering multiple steps for different entities or simply not specifying any entities in the **primary entity** field (not recommended due to the overhead of executing the logic for all entities).

Finally, in step 9 and step 10, we registered an image that will include the attributes we are interested in inspecting in our plugin. These steps are not required but were added just to illustrate how to register images. The images can be in the form of a pre-image (state of the record before any changes are applied) or post-image (state the record is in after the changes have been applied).

There's more...

The Plugin Registration Tool offers a wide range of features when registering your server-side extensions.

Plugin registration

When registering a plugin, you can select whether it needs to execute within a sandbox isolation mode. This mode is mandatory for online instances, as users will not have access to the server resources.

> It is recommended that you register your plugins in sandbox mode on-premises as well, unless you have specific resources you are trying to access, which is usually considered bad practice.

The location of your plugin can also vary from database, disk, or GAC. Online instances only allow database deployments. With on-premise installations, the **Global Assembly Cache** (**GAC**) is a viable option if your assemblies are used across several applications. Disk deployments are also an option when debugging and constantly changing the assemblies. Nevertheless, database deployment is the preferred method of deploying your solution, as everything is contained within the database and can easily be recovered and promoted across instances using solutions.

Plugin step registration

When registering a plugin step, users have the flexibility to select from a few configuration options. The plugin can trigger at different stages of the execution pipeline, which are as follows:

- **Pre-validation**: It is used for validation purposes
- **Pre-operation**: It is used to alter the record before saving it
- **Post-operation**: It is used to update other entities once the execution is done

> Unless limited by some constraints, avoid re-updating the record that initiated the plugin in the post-operation stage. This will cause the record to save twice and it can potentially enter a loop if not configured properly (using image attribute filtering).

The introduction to this chapter contains a diagram highlighting the different events in the execution pipeline. The following table lists the different stages, their number, a short description, and whether they are executed within a transaction:

Stage Name	Stage Number	Description	Within Transaction
Pre-validation	10	The validation event that takes place before the operation.	Not guaranteed
Pre-operation	20	The event that takes place right before the operation.	Yes
MainOperation	30	An event that cannot be overridden. It represents the main operation when the changes are persisted in the database.	Yes
Post-operation	40	The stage that triggers after the operation. This event can be synchronous or asynchronous.	Yes, if synchronous

Both, synchronous and asynchronous, plugins have a two-minute execution limit when registered in sandbox mode.

To learn more about the Microsoft Dynamics 365 event execution pipeline, check out the following MSDN article at `https://msdn.microsoft.com/en-us/library/gg327941.aspx`

The plugin registration tool also allows you to enter the order in which plugins are executed, in case you have a collection of plugins executing on the same record with the same configuration.

The plugin can also be registered synchronously or asynchronously. Synchronous plugins can enhance the user experience as the results appear straight away. Asynchronous plugins are great for long--running processes.

Plugins can be registered to execute offline as well, by ticking the **Offline** checkbox in the **Deployment** option. Offline plugins are great to execute logic on disconnected mobile devices; however, caution must be applied when using the offline option, especially if the user does not have access to all records offline.

Finally, plugin steps can have a (secure or non-secure) configuration string associated with them (typically XML). This is useful when you want to pass static data to your plugin (usually configuration data).

Register actions

As per the *Creating your first custom action* recipe in this chapter, you can also use the plugin registration tool to wire a plugin as an action. Please refer to the previous recipe for details.

See also

- *Create your first plugin*

Debugging your plugin in Dynamics 365 on-premise

In this recipe we will demonstrate how to debug your server-side extensions with an on-premises Dynamics 365 instance. For simplicity, this recipe assumes that you have Visual Studio and your Dynamics 365 instance is running on the same server. It is also assumed that the plugin is running synchronously and not in sandbox mode. For other scenarios, read the *There's more...* section of this recipe.

Getting ready

In order to debug your server-side extension, you will need an instance of Visual Studio 2015 or 2017 (express edition is not recommended), your code, and the compiled **Dynamic-link library** (**DLLs**) and **program database** (**PDBs**) of your code deployed on the server.

Your plugin must be registered either on disk or the database. Either way, the corresponding `PDB` files must go under `<Dynamics 365 Server Folder>\bin\assembly`.

> **TIP:** When deployed to disk, the worker process can sometimes lock the files. If this happens, restart your application pool (or IIS) to release the locks.

How to do it...

1. Create a breakpoint in your plugin by clicking on the margin on the left of the line where you want the debugger to break. Your editor will highlight the breakpoint line, as depicted here:

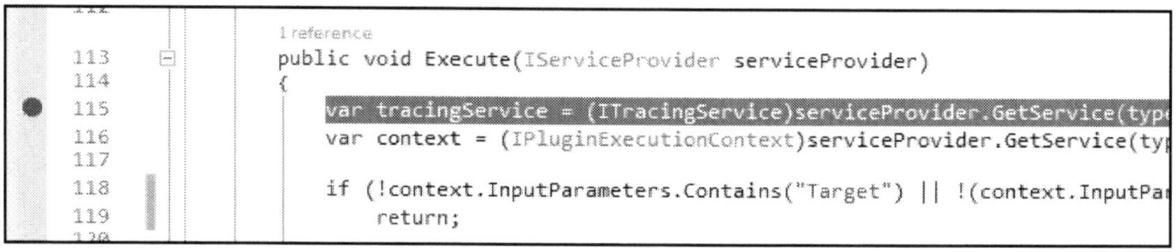

2. In Visual Studio, click on **Debug** | **Attach to Process** from the menu.
3. Find the worker process (`w3wp.exe`) that matches your Dynamics 365 web application. If unsure, attach to all worker processes. If you cannot find the process, tick the **Show processes from all users** checkbox.
4. Run your plugin.
5. The debugger will then break when the execution reaches the breakpoint line.

How it works...

Similar to other types of .NET web development, Dynamics 365 uses the same technology stack under the hood. It is no surprise that debugging your custom code is similar to debugging a web application or service you have written.

After we enabled the breakpoint in the first step, we attached the Visual Studio debugger to the correct process that will be running your code.

Once your plugin is executed, the Visual Studio debugger will catch the event and break at the line that you have highlighted in step 1. You can then debug the code as you would debug any .NET application by stepping into the relevant sections, monitoring your variables, and following the call stack.

For further details, check out the following MSDN article: `https://msdn.microsoft.com/en-us/library/gg328574.aspx`.

There's more...

In this recipe, we demonstrated how to debug a synchronous plugin in non-sandbox mode. Asynchronous plugins, custom workflow activities, offline plugins, and sandboxed customizations can also be debugged. The difference lies in the process we are trying to attach our debugger to. The following table highlights the different processes associated with each scenario:

Customization Type	**Service Process**
Synchronous online	`w3wp.exe`
Synchronous offline	`Microsoft.Crm.Application.Hoster.exe`
Asynchronous and custom workflow Activities	`CrmAsyncService.exe`
Sandboxed	`Microsoft.Crm.Sandbox.WorkerProcess.exe`

Debugging on a remote server

If your Visual Studio instance and your Dynamics 365 instance do not reside on the same server, you will need to ensure that the Visual Studio remote debugging tool is installed in the Dynamics 365 server and that you have the correct privileges to access it.

To install the debugging tool, follow the instructions at `https://msdn.microsoft.com/en-us/library/y7f5zaaa.aspx`.

In the properties of your Visual Studio project, under **Debug**, enter the name of the remote server under **Use remote machine,** as highlighted here:

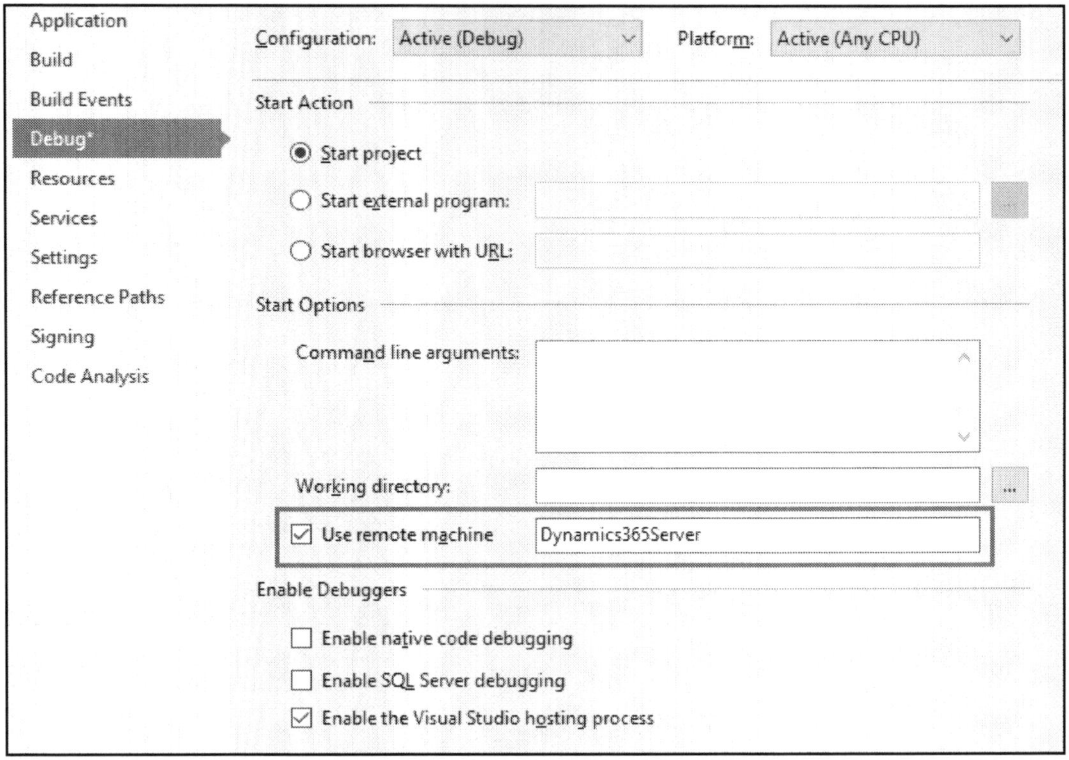

For more details about remote debugging, check out the following MSDN article:

`https://msdn.microsoft.com/en-us/library/y7f5zaaa.aspx`

Debugging a sandbox plugin

As defined previously, sandboxed plugins are executed by the Dynamics 365 Sandbox Processing Service (`Microsoft.Crm.Sandbox.WorkerProcess.exe`) on the sandbox server. In order to debug a sandbox plugin, follow the same steps as this recipe and attach your debugger to the correct process.

You will also need to disable the auto-shutdown feature that shuts down the process if it is unresponsive for more than 30 seconds, which is usually the case when you are debugging. To do so, set the `HKEY_LOCAL_MACHINE\SOFTWARE\Microsoft\MSCRM\SandboxDebugPlugins` registry key to the value of 1.

For further details, visit `https://msdn.microsoft.com/en-us/library/gg328574.aspx`.

See also

- *Debugging your plugin in Dynamics 365 online*
- *Creating your first plugin*

Debugging your plugin in Dynamics 365 online

Given that the server processes are not accessible when using Dynamics 365 online, debugging your server-side customization can be a bit trickier. In the past, we used to rely on custom log tracing to debug a plugin. We also had the option of using the plugin profiler to replay a defect in a development environment. However, with Dynamics CRM 2016, a new debugging technique was introduced.

In this recipe, we will explain how you can debug a Dynamics 365 online plugin using the online plugin and custom workflow activity trace log.

Getting ready

In order to trace your custom plugin or workflow activity, you will need to ensure that the correct tracing level is enabled in the system settings.

In order to change the level, navigate to the **Settings** | **Administration** | **System Settings** | **Customization** tab and level to **Exception** or **All**, as per the following screenshot:

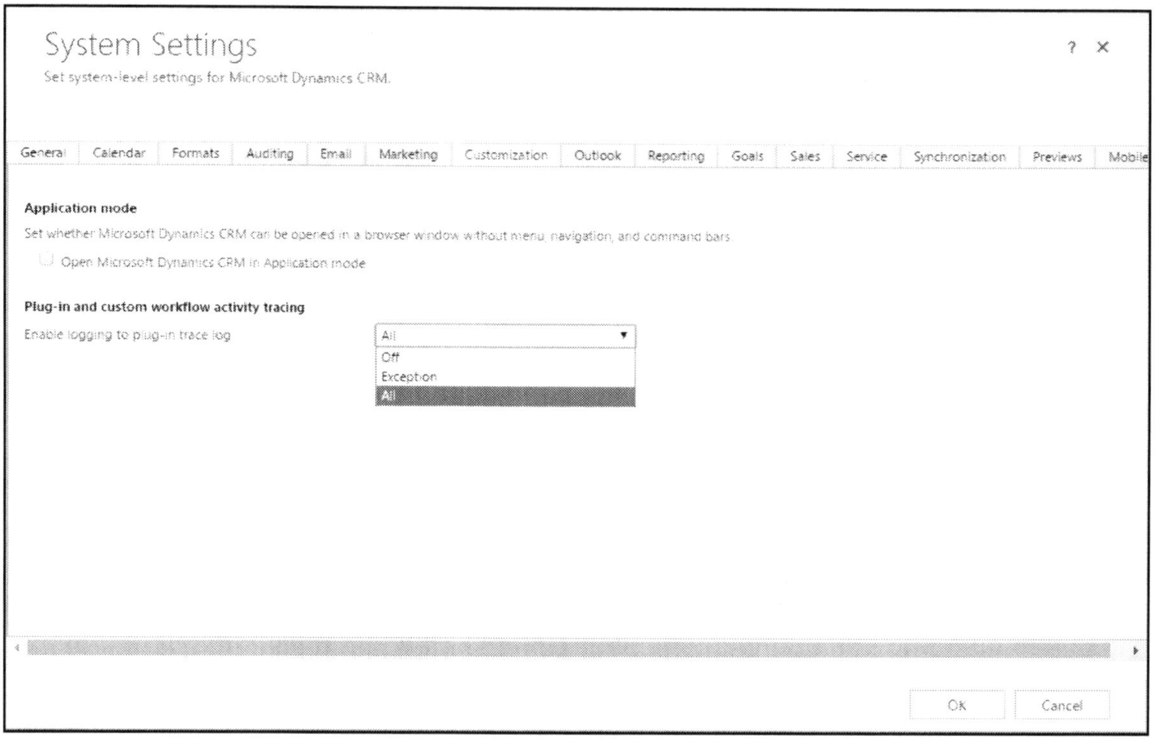

You will also need a plugin or custom workflow activity to run.

How to do it...

1. Trigger an event that executes a plugin in its pipe.
2. Using advanced find, look for **Plug-In Trace Log**, demonstrated as follows:

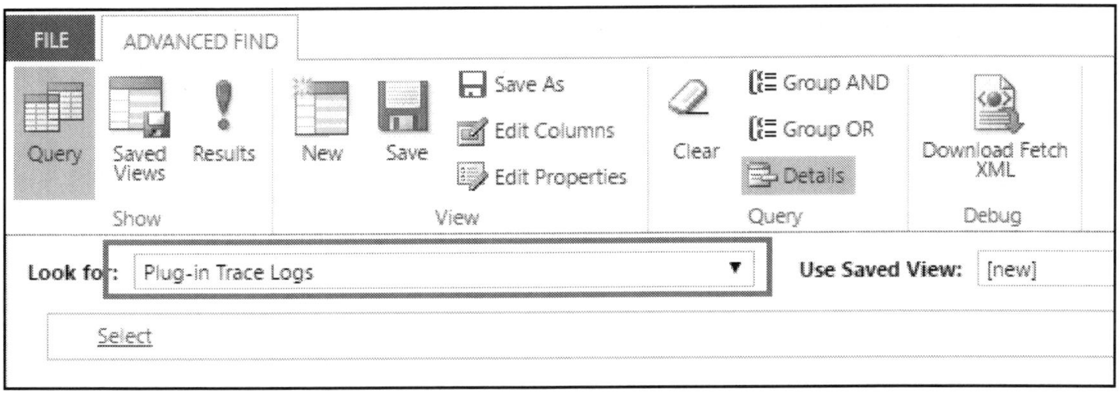

3. Open the record that has a time stamp that matches your plugin execution time.
4. Inspect **Message Block** and **ExceptionDetails**. The following screenshot demonstrates a sample record:

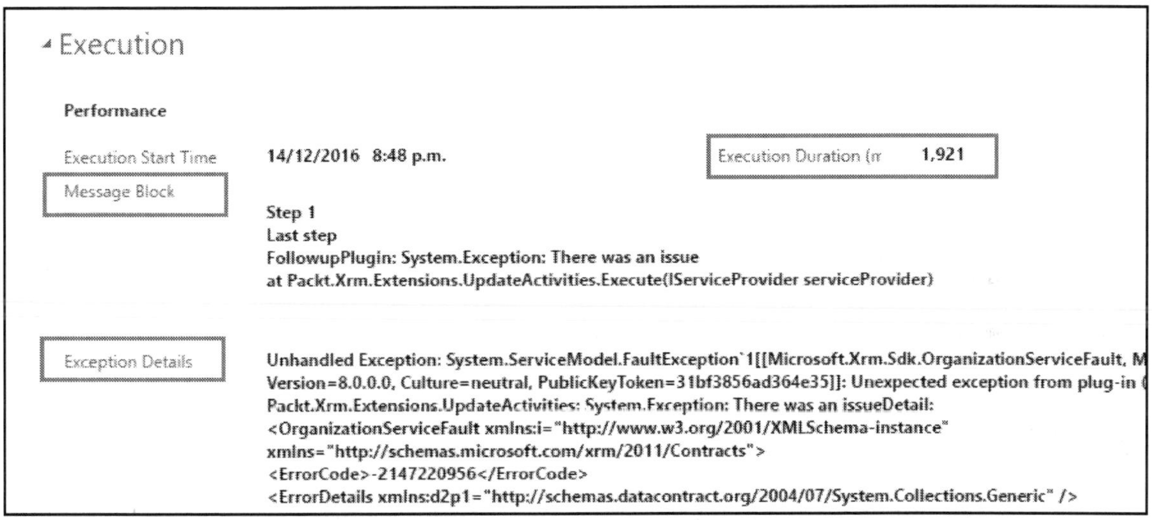

How it works...

Depending on your setting (Exception, All), the logs are either created when an exception is thrown or anytime a plugin is executed. If you are only recording the exceptions, both the trace and exception details are recorded.

In this recipe, we caught a plugin execution that threw an exception. The **Message Block** field under the **Execution** section displayed all your trace details, whereas the **Exception Details** field included the exception message as well as the stack trace.

You will also see some useful details about the plugin, such as some of the information you entered during the registration but, most importantly, you will see the execution duration in milliseconds, which might help when investigating performance issues.

Always remember to set tracing back to **Off**, or at least to **Exception**, when you are done with your debugging, as it has a performance impact on top of consuming space, although out of the box, there will be a **Bulk Record Deletion** job to delete all logs older than 1 day, which runs daily. To check the status of this job, navigate to **Settings** | **Data Management** | **Bulk Record Deletion** | **View: Recurring Bulk Deletion System Jobs** | **Delete Plug-in Trace Log Records**.

See also

- *Debugging your plugin in Dynamics 365 on-premise*
- *Creating your first plugin*

5
External Integration

In this chapter, we will cover the following recipes:

- Connecting to Dynamics 365 from other systems using .NET
- Connecting to Dynamics 365 from other systems using OData (Java)
- Retrieving data from external sources using external libraries
- Connecting to Dynamics 365 using web applications
- Running Azure Scheduled tasks
- Setting up an Azure Service Bus endpoint
- Building near real-time integration with Azure Service Bus
- Consuming messages from an Azure Service Bus
- Running no code scheduled synchronization using Scribe
- Integrating with SSIS using KingswaySoft

Introduction

One of the main strengths of the Dynamics 365 platform is its capability to easily integrate with other systems. Integration is an appealing feature that makes the platform a true enterprise contender. Most Dynamics CRM and Dynamics 365 implementations I have worked on in the public sector require a degree of integration with another system. Portals, batch processing, and data synchronization are some of the typical integration examples.

With integration comes challenges. Some systems are only available on-premise, whereas others are exposed to the public but have strict security restrictions.

In this chapter we will look at a few design patterns that address different scenarios. We will target Dynamics 365 online however, most patterns are also applicable to Dynamics 365 on-premise or IFD instances.

We will start with the client/server pattern where a fat client application (.NET or Java) connects to Dynamics 365 as its backend, as depicted in the following diagram. The arrows represent application dependencies:

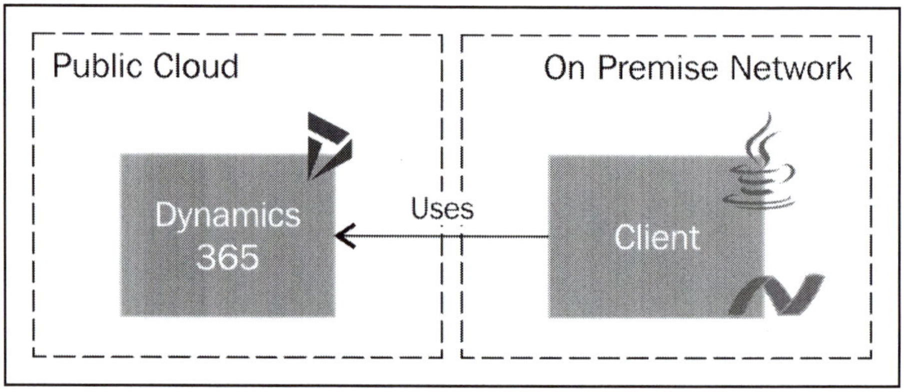

We will also look at a message queuing pattern using the Azure Service Bus queues. The following figure shows how data is written to the Azure Service Bus and how on-premise listeners consume messages from the Azure Service Bus and broadcast them to other local systems. This pattern can also work with on-premise Dynamics 365 deployments:

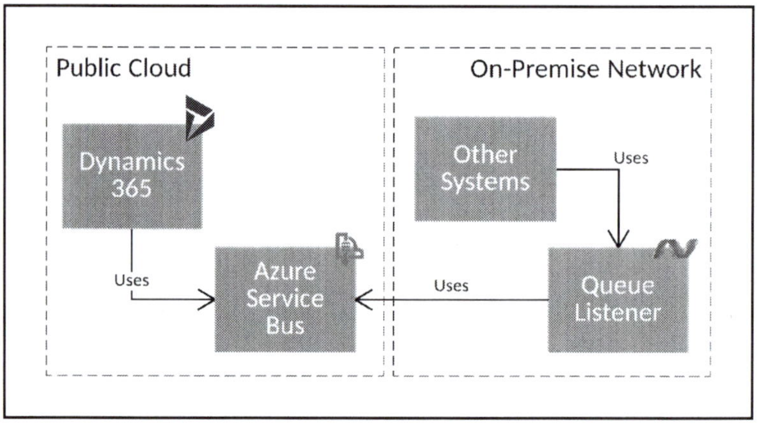

Next, we will look at running a scheduled task that calls a custom built façade to our Dynamic 365 endpoints. The MVC application in the following diagram represents a façade to Dynamics 365, which is consumed by the Azure Scheduler:

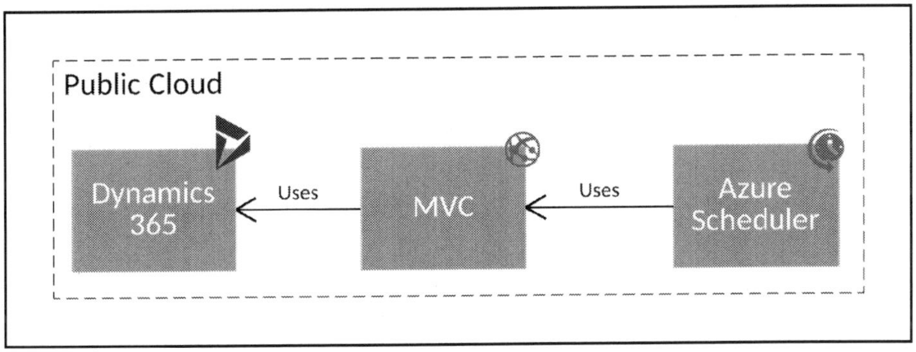

We will also cover some third-party tools:

- Scribe (`https://www.scribesoft.com`), which uses a controller/agent pattern. The following diagram shows a Scribe Agent connecting to Dynamics 365 online to retrieve data and push it into an on-premise application. The Scribe tool is described further in *Running no code scheduled synchronization using Scribe*:

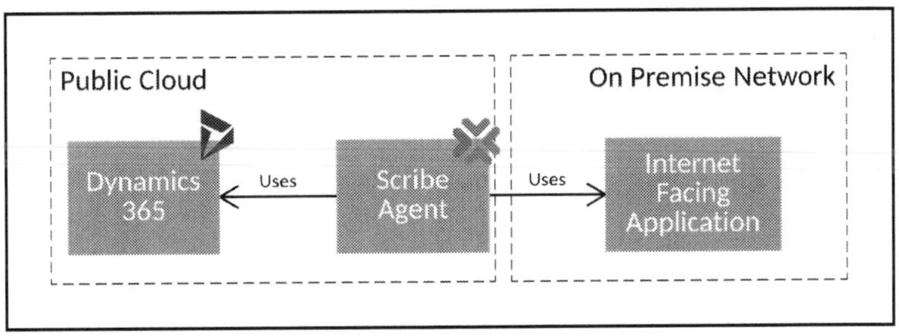

- KingswaySoft SSIS Dynamics CRM extensions (`http://www.kingswaysoft.com/products/ssis-integration-toolkit-for-microsoft-dynamics-365`) leverage the power of **Sql Server Integration Services** (**SSIS**). The following is a diagram that highlights how an SSIS package using KingswaySoft hosted on-premise extracts data from an on-premise application and pushes it to Dynamics 365 online:

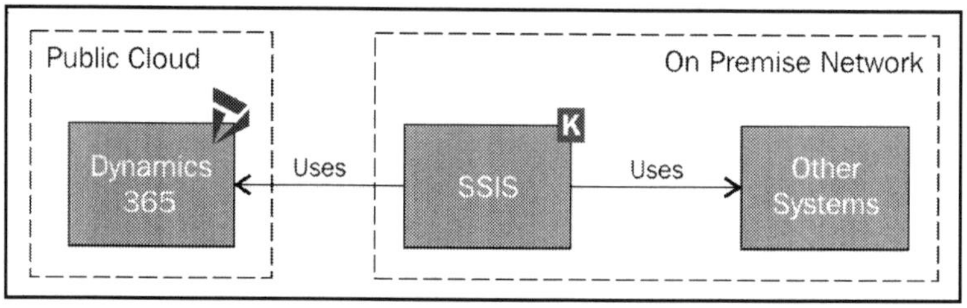

Finally, we will look at how Dynamics 365 can be the consumer and reach external resources. This image shows Dynamics 365 accessing a public resource:

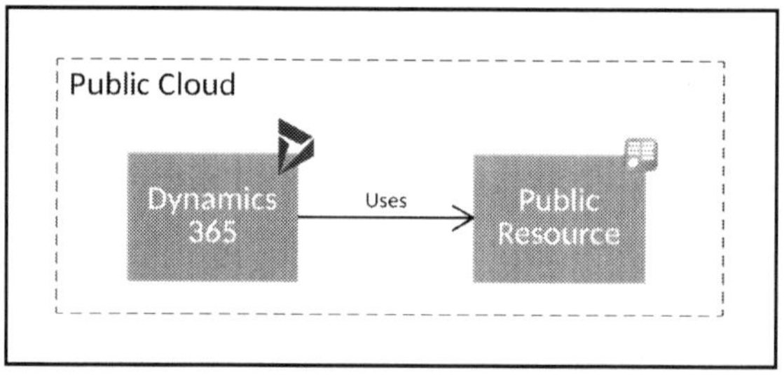

Connecting to Dynamics 365 from other systems using .NET

In this recipe, we will cover a simple data access layer that allows you to connect to Dynamics 365 from an external .NET application using the Dynamics 365 SDK.

Getting ready

To get going with this recipe, you will require a Visual Studio IDE and the Dynamics CRM NuGet packages to access the SDK libraries. Alternatively, you can download the SDK and reference the assembly manually.

If you want to use the unit of work pattern using the organization service context, you will also need to generate the early bound classes with an organization service context. Refer to the *Creating early bound entity classes* recipe of `Chapter 3`, *SDK Enterprise Capabilities*, for further details.

How to do it...

1. Create or reuse a new C# library solution in Visual Studio called `Packt.Xrm.Extensions`.
2. Create a new public class called `Dynamics365DataAccessLayer`.
3. Right-click on the **References** and click on **Manage NuGet Packages**. Search and install `Microsoft.CrmSdk.XrmTooling.CoreAssembly`.
4. Include the following `using` statements at the top of your .cs class and private variable in your DAL class.:

```
using Microsoft.Xrm.Sdk;
using Microsoft.Xrm.Sdk.Messages;
using Microsoft.Xrm.Tooling.Connector;
using Packt.Xrm.Entities;

private CrmServiceClient _crmSvc;
```

5. Copy and insert the following code in the class's constructor (don't forget to update the connection string, as shown here):

```
public Dynamics365DataAccessLayer(string conn) {
  var connectionString = string.IsNullOrEmpty(conn)
  ? "AuthType=Office365;Username=@.onmicrosoft.com;
  Password=;Url=https://.crm6.dynamics.com": conn;
  _crmSvc = new CrmServiceClient(connectionString);
}
```

6. Create a new method called `Connect` that returns void:

```
using (var serviceProxy = _crmSvc.OrganizationServiceProxy)
{
  serviceProxy.EnableProxyTypes();
  using (var organisationContext = new
  OrganisationServiceContext(serviceProxy))
  {
    //Your code goes here
  }
}
```

How it works...

We first started by creating a simple solution following the convention discussed in *Creating a Visual Studio Solution for Dynamics 365 customization* recipe of `Chapter 4`, *Server-Side Extensions*.

In step 3, we added the necessary assemblies that encapsulate all the connection management details.

In step 4, we included all the namespaces required to connect. Note `Packt.Xrm.Entities`, a namespace generated using `CrmSvcUtil`.

In step 5, we defined the constructor that generates `CrmServiceClient` which takes the connection string that will then allow us to generate the organization service proxy.

Finally, in step 6, we instantiated the organization service proxy as well as the organization service context. The service proxy enables us to execute methods such as `Retrieve`, `RetrieveMutiple`, `Create`, `Update`, `Delete`, `Associate`, `Execute`, and many others. The service context allows us to leverage the unit of work design pattern where your changes are not sent to Dynamics 365 until the `SaveChanges` method is called.

By calling `EnableProxyTypes`, we enabled support for early bound entities.

There's more...

Given that we are using the .NET managed code libraries from the SDK, any disaster recovery scenarios for Dynamics 365 online are handled by the SDK. If the primary site fails and the failover site become primary, the libraries take care of the switch without any additional coding . This is not the case when using other connection means and other languages (Java). This MSDN article describes the different scenarios: `https://msdn.microsoft.com/en-nz/library/hh771583.aspx`.

See also

- The *Creating early bound entity classes* recipe of `Chapter 3`, *SDK Enterprise Capabilities*
- *Connecting to Dynamics 365 from other systems using OData (Java)*

Connecting to Dynamics 365 from other systems using OData (Java)

As we have already seen in previous recipes, accessing OData is relatively straightforward. The power of RESTful services is in their simplicity. We issue a request with a specifically formatted URL, along with some headers, to get a `JSON` response. In *Querying Dynamics 365 Data using the Web API endpoint*, recipe of `Chapter 2`, *Client-Side Extensions*, we used JavaScript to generate our `GET` request. However, even though Java applications follow the same mechanism, we will need to deal with authentication as we don't have an existing session to leverage.

In this recipe we will write a Java console application to connect to Dynamics 365 online and retrieve the top three accounts ordered by name. The focus of this recipe will be on how to prepare your Azure tenancy to accept calls from a Java application and how to authenticate to receive your token that will be used to issue the correct HTTP `GET` request to Dynamics 365.

Getting ready

There are a few steps required to get up and running.

Java

In order to connect a Java application to Dynamics 365, you will need to have `Java JDK` installed to compile your application, `Azure ADAL` and its dependencies to connect to Azure, and a JSON parsing library such as `org.json.jar` to parse the JSON responses. Optionally, you can use **Maven** to resolve your dependencies by creating a `pom.xml` file or even use an IDE, such as Eclipse, to improve your productivity.

Azure tenancy

Through your Azure tenancy, you will require to retrieve some necessary details as well as set up some permissions.

Tenant GUID

The first item you will need is **Active Directory Domain's GUID** of your Azure tenancy associated with Office and Dynamics 365. To get this ID, you will need to log in to your Azure tenancy as an administrator. If you are using the old portal, you will have a list of the directories under **ACTIVE DIRECTORY**. Click on the name of the correct directory and the GUID will be in the URL.

If you are using the new Azure portal, click on the help menu at the top right, **?** | **Show diagnostics** (as per the following screenshot), and you will be prompted with a JSON dialog. Locate the tenant object with the correct domain name. The GUID will be the ID of that JSON object in the array:

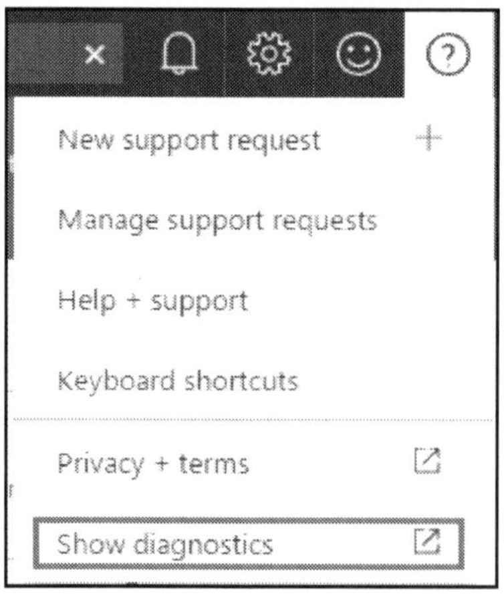

The JSON object will contain an array of tenants that look like the following:

```
"tenants": [
    {
      "id": "00000000-0000-0000-0000-000000000000",
      "domainName": "packt.onmicrosoft.com",
      "displayName": "Packt",
      "isSignedInTenant": true
    }
  ]
```

TIP: You can access your Azure tenancy from Office 365 by navigating to **Admin Centers** | **Azure AD**.

Alternatively, you can also retrieve your tenant GUID using the following PowerShell script:

```
Login-AzureRmAccount
```

Check this article for details at `https://support.office.com/en-us/article/Find-your-Office-365-tenant-ID-6891b561-a52d-4ade-9f39-b492285e2c9b`

Application GUID

In order to get an application GUID, we will need to create it in Azure AD. Using the new portal, navigate to **Azure Active Directory** | **App registration** | **+ Add**.

In the **Create** dialog, enter the following details:

- **Name**: `Pack Java 365`
- **Application Type**: `Native`
- **Sign-on URL**: `http://localhost/Signon`

The name can be anything you like; the application type is native as opposed to web app/API as we are building a console application and not a web application/web API. Since we are not going to use a sign-on URL in this recipe, we just need is populate the filed with a correctly formatted URL.

Once created, we have our GUID in the **APPLICATION ID** column in the **App registration** list. The following screenshot highlights the navigation path to get to the **APPLICATION ID**:

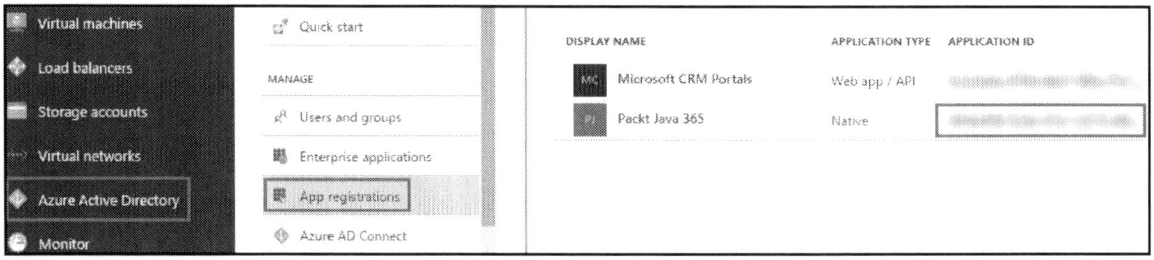

Application permissions

After creating your application, you need to set the correct permissions. Navigate to <the newly created application> | **Required permissions** | **+ Add**. In the **Select an API** list, select **Dynamics CRM Online (Microsoft.CRM)**, followed by **Select**. In the second step, click on **Access CRM Online as organization users** followed by **Select**. Finally, click on **Done**.

Once the permission is created, select it from the list and click on **Grant Permissions** to grant permissions to all users.

Failure to grant permission to all users will result in an `AADSTS65001` error in our console application (the user or administrator has not consented to use the application with the ID).

If you are building an end user application (mobile, desktop, and so on), it is recommended that you do not click on the **Grant Permissions** button. This will not grant all users permissions by default and will prompt them for approval the next time they log in.

Dynamics 365

From a Dynamics 365 perspective, you will need to grant the user with the correct privileges on the entities you are manipulating. In our example, we will need read access to the account entity.

How to do it...

1. Create a new `JavaDynamics365.java` Java class. Use the following package name:

```
package com.packt.dynamics365;
```

2. Add the following import statements:

```
import java.io.BufferedReader;
import java.io.IOException;
import java.io.InputStream;
import java.io.InputStreamReader;
import java.io.Reader;
import java.net.URL;
import java.nio.charset.Charset;
import java.net.HttpURLConnection;
import java.net.URLConnection;
import org.json.JSONException;
import org.json.JSONObject;
import org.json.JSONArray;
import com.microsoft.aad.adal4j.AuthenticationContext;
import com.microsoft.aad.adal4j.AuthenticationResult;
import java.util.concurrent.ExecutorService;
import java.util.concurrent.Executors;
import java.util.concurrent.Future;
import javax.naming.ServiceUnavailableException;
```

3. In your `JavaDynamics365` public class, add the following parameters:

```
private final static String CLIENT_ID =
"00000000-0000-0000-0000-000000000000";
private final static String DYNAMICS365_URL =
"https://organizationName.crm.dynamics.com";
private final static String USERNAME = "username@domain.com";
private final static String PASSWORD = "password";
private final static String AUTHORITY =
"https://login.microsoftonline.com/00000000-0000-0000-0000-00000000
0000";
```

4. Add the `getAccessTokenFromUserCredentials` method:

```
private static AuthenticationResult
getAccessTokenFromUserCredentials() throws Exception {
  AuthenticationContext context = null;
  AuthenticationResult result = null;
  ExecutorService service = null;
  try {
    service = Executors.newFixedThreadPool(1);
    context = new AuthenticationContext(AUTHORITY, false,
      service);

    Future<AuthenticationResult> future =
      context.acquireToken(DYNAMICS365_URL,
      CLIENT_ID,
      USERNAME,
      PASSWORD, null);
    result = future.get();
  } finally {
    service.shutdown();
  }
  if (result == null) {
    throw new ServiceUnavailableException("authentication result
      was null");
  }
  return result;
}
```

5. Add the `getAccounts` method:

```
public static void getAccounts(String token, String surl) throws
IOException, JSONException{
  URLConnection connection = new URL(surl).openConnection();
  connection.setRequestProperty("User-Agent", "Mozilla/5.0 (Windows
NT 6.1; WOW64) AppleWebKit/537.11 (KHTML, like Gecko)
Chrome/23.0.1271.95 Safari/537.11");
  connection.setRequestProperty("OData-MaxVersion", "4.0");
  connection.setRequestProperty("OData-Version", "4.0");
  connection.addRequestProperty("Authorization", "Bearer " +
token);
  connection.setRequestProperty("Content-Type", "application/x-www-
form-urlencoded");
  connection.connect();

  BufferedReader r  = new BufferedReader(new
InputStreamReader(connection.getInputStream(),
Charset.forName("UTF-8")));
  StringBuilder sb = new StringBuilder();
```

```
      String line;
      while ((line = r.readLine()) != null) {
        sb.append(line);
      }

      JSONObject json = new JSONObject(sb.toString());
      JSONArray arr = new JSONArray(json.getString("value"));

      for (int i=0; i <  arr.length()  ; i++) {
        JSONObject object = arr.getJSONObject(i);
        System.out.println(object.getString("name"));
      }
    }
```

6. Populate your main method as follows:

```
public static void main(String[] args) throws IOException,
JSONException, Exception {
  AuthenticationResult authenticationResult =
getAccessTokenFromUserCredentials();
  getAccounts(authenticationResult.getAccessToken(),
DYNAMICS365_URL +
"/api/data/v8.2/accounts?$top=2&$select=name&$orderby=name");
}
```

7. Compile your code by referencing all the `.jar` prerequisites in your classpath:

```
javac -cp .\target\dependency\*
com\packt\dynamics365\JavaDynamics365.java
```

8. Run your application by referencing all the `.jar` prerequisites in your classpath:

```
java -cp .;.\target\dependency\*
com.packt.dynamics365.JavaDynamics365
```

How it works...

This abridged Java code is a simple example of how you can use non-.NET code to connect to your Dynamics 365 instance. For the sake of simplicity, let's say the code is far from following Java code best practices. For instance, you would expect connection values to be configurable rather than hardcoded. You would also expect the application to be divided into layers.

In step 1, we started by creating a Java class called `JavaDynamics365` with the package name `com.packt.dynamics365` (make sure you store your Java file in the correct folder `com\packt\dynamics365` to abide by the convention). The package name follows the Oracle-recommended reversed Internet domain convention:
`https://docs.oracle.com/javase/tutorial/java/package/namingpkgs.html`.

In step 2, we referenced the libraries that we will be using in our code. We've got `java.net` libraries to manipulate our HTTP request, `org.json` libraries to deal with JSON parsing, `com.microsoft.aad.adal4j` for the Azure AD authentication, and finally, some `java.util` libraries to help with the authentication method.

In step 3, we defined some static strings, such as our connection details, the client ID, and the login URL with the tenant GUID, as defined in the *Getting ready* section. As explained previously, it's best practice to extract these into a secure configurable container.

In step 4, we got the authentication token from Azure AD by calling the `acquireToken` method. This method from the ADAL library encapsulates the mechanism required to log in to Azure AD and get the required token. The `getAccessTokenFromUserCredentials` method is reused from the Microsoft Azure Samples GitHub repository:
`https://github.com/Azure-Samples/active-directory-java-native-headless`.

In step 5, we issued an HTTP `GET` request with an `Authorization` header to contain the retrieved token. We then parsed the result into JSON arrays and looped through each returned object to display the name of the retrieved organizations. This method is similar to the Web API request discussed in *Querying Dynamics 365 Data using the Web API endpoint* recipe of `Chapter 2`, *Client-Side Extensions.*

In step 6, we created a main method to call the token retrieval method and call the `getAccounts` method with the retrieved token.

Finally, in step 7 and step 8, we compiled and ran the console application. Note how we referred to a wild card `*` for referenced dependencies. The list of dependencies is as follows:

- `activation-1.1.jar`
- `adal4j-1.1.1.jar`
- `bcprov-jdk15on-1.51.jar`
- `commons-codec-1.10.jar`
- `commons-lang3-3.3.1.jar`
- `gson-2.2.4.jar`
- `jcip-annotations-1.0.jar`
- `json-smart-1.1.1.jar`

- `lang-tag-1.4.jar`
- `mail-1.4.7.jar`
- `nimbus-jose-jwt-3.1.2.jar`
- `oauth2-oidc-sdk-4.5.jar`
- `org.json.jar`
- `slf4j-api-1.7.5.jar`

However, the main three libraries are `adal4j`, `oauth2-oidc-sdk`, and `json`.

If you have Maven installed, you can retrieve all the necessary libraries and their dependencies using the `copy dependencies` command, as follows:

```
mvn dependency:copy-dependencies
```

To do so, you will need a `pom.xml` file with the following dependencies:

```
<dependencies>
   <dependency>
    <groupId>com.microsoft.azure</groupId>
    <artifactId>adal4j</artifactId>
    <version>1.1.1</version>
  </dependency>
   <dependency>
    <groupId>com.nimbusds</groupId>
    <artifactId>oauth2-oidc-sdk</artifactId>
    <version>4.5</version>
    <type>jar</type>
  </dependency>
  <dependency>
    <groupId>org.json</groupId>
    <artifactId>json</artifactId>
    <version>20090211</version>
  </dependency>
</dependencies>
```

There's more...

Jason Lattimer Business Solutions Microsoft MVP wrote a list of posts that explain how to connect to Dynamics 365 from different languages (C#, Java, Python, and more). For more detail, visit his blog at `http://jlattimer.blogspot.co.nz/`.

In fact, you can use any language that can issue a properly formatted HTTP request and deal with the Active Directory authentication. Microsoft provides an Active Directory library for most of them (OS X, iOS, Node.js, JavaScript, Java, .NET, Android, among others): `https://docs.microsoft.com/en-us/azure/active-directory/active-directory-authentication-libraries`.

See also

- The *Querying Dynamics 365 data using the Web API endpoint* recipe of `Chapter 2`, *Client-Side Extensions*
- *Connecting to Dynamics 365 using web applications*
- The *Using Cross-Origin Resource Sharing with CRM online* recipe of `Chapter 6`, *Enhancing Your Code*

Retrieving data from external resources using external libraries

In this recipe, we will extend Dynamics 365 online to access external resources; more specifically, we will be reading data from a RESTful feed. The results will be retrieved in a JSON format and require an external .NET library to easily manipulate the JSON stream. We will implement the external connection within the account update plugin created in the *Creating your first plugin* recipe in `Chapter 4`, *Server-Side Extensions*.

Getting ready

For this recipe, you will need access to a publicly available RESTful service of your choice. We will be using the freely available service at `https://jsonplaceholder.typicode.com`.

In order to easily manipulate the JSON results, we will use an external library called Json.NET by Newtonsoft. The library provides serialization, deserialization, and parsing capabilities between JSON and .NET objects. This lightweight library will save us a significant amount of unnecessary development. For more details about Json.NET visit `http://www.newtonsoft.com/json`.

Given that Dynamics 365 online only allows database plugin deployments and that we are using an external .NET library, we will need to merge the external library with our plugin assembly. `ILMerge` (`https://www.microsoft.com/download/details.aspx?id=17630`) is a well-known utility that can merge several .NET assemblies into one.

Since our code will log the results using the Dynamics 365 tracing capabilities, you need to ensure that your plugin verbose tracing is enabled. Check out the *Debugging your plugin in Dynamics 365 Online* recipe of `Chapter 4`, *Server-Side Extensions* for details.

Finally, given that we will be deploying an updated plugin, you will need the **System Customizer** or higher role within Dynamics 365. To run the code, we also need the correct privileges to access and update an account. The plugin will trigger when the account name is updated.

How to do it...

1. In the existing plugin project, use the NuGet package manager to get the latest stable version of `Newtonsoft.Json`.
2. In the plugin code, add the following `using` statements:

```
using System.Net;
using Newtonsoft.Json.Linq;
```

3. In the plugin's try statement, add the following code snippet:

```
using (var webClient = new WebClient())
{
    var jsonResult =
webClient.DownloadString("https://jsonplaceholder.typicode.com/user
s");
    var parsedResult = JArray.Parse(jsonResult);
    tracingService.Trace("Number of users retrieved: {0}",
parsedResult.Count);
}
```

4. Compile your code.
5. Ensure that you have `ILMerge`, and your signing key is in the correct `Debug` or `Release bin` folder. Run the following from the command line:

```
ilmerge /out:Packt.Xrm.Extensions_Merged.dll
Packt.Xrm.Extensions.dll Newtonsoft.Json.dll
/targetplatform:"v4,c:\windows\Microsoft.NET\Framework\v4.0.303
19" /keyfile:Packt.snk
```

6. Deploy your newly created assembly (note how we changed the assembly name).
7. Run an update on the account entity and check the plugin logs.

How it works...

This recipe has two purposes; the first is to demonstrate how you can access external resources, and the second is to demonstrate how you can use extra assembly dependencies by merging them into your own assembly using `ILMerge`.

In step 1 to step 3, we prepared our plugin to call the external resource using a simple `WebClient DownloadString` method that effectively sends a GET request to the defined URL. The URL is hardcoded for simplicity; however, in your code, avoid hardcoding external dependency values. Instead, use the plugin configuration as described in *Building near real-time integration with Azure Service Bus* in this chapter (or some other flexible means). Once we receive the JSON response, we parse it into a JSON array using **JArray** from the `Newtonsoft.Json.Linq` namespace and then use the Dynamics 365 tracing service to display the count.

In step 5, we merged our assembly with the `Newtonsoft.Json.dll` assembly into a new one called `Packt.Xrm.Extensions_Merged.dll`. Note the name difference. If you have already deployed `Packt.Xrm.Extensions.dll` in your Dynamics 365 instance, make sure you tidy up your plugin to avoid duplicate plugin executions. Also, note how we sign the new assembly using the `/keyfile` argument.

Any assembly going to Dynamics 365 online needs to be signed, including merged ones.

In the last two steps, we ran the plugin and observed the tracing output. For more details on how to retrieve tracing logs in Dynamics 365 online, read the *Debugging your plugin in Dynamics 365 Online* recipe of `Chapter 4`, *Server-Side Extensions*. For on-premise instances, read the following TechNet article:
`https://technet.microsoft.com/en-us/library/hh699694.aspx`.

There's more...

Generally speaking, it is bad practice to introduce such coupling between systems; however, some business requirements might require such external access. When required, make sure you run your plugins in an asynchronous mode in order to avoid the online plugin limitations and also to enhance user experience. If you need to write to an external source, best practice dictates that you use the Azure Service Bus, as described in *Setting up an Azure Service Bus Endpoint* later in this chapter. The Service Bus has many advantages, including scalability, queuing, better error handling mechanisms, and loose coupling.

As for merging different assemblies with your assembly, ensure the external libraries can run in the sandbox mode (check out this article to test your assembly `https://msdn.microsoft.com/en-us/library/bb763046(v=vs.110).aspx`).

While writing this recipe, I tried to access Azure's `DocumentDB` using the `WindowsAzure.Storage` NuGet package from within the plugin. An exception was thrown when trying to instantiate the object (even before connecting) due to the constructor trying to access the server's resources (more specifically, the default tracing services). Even using the `System.Data.SqlClient` library will throw a security restriction exception. This is due to the sandbox mode limitations that do not permit some classes' instantiations. To address this issue, you'll have to create a supported façade to your SQL database or other storage platform. The pattern is similar to what we discussed in *Connecting to Dynamics 365 using web applications* in this chapter, but for your repository as opposed to Dynamics 365.

See also

- The *Creating your first plugin* recipe of `Chapter 4`, *Server-Side Extensions*
- *Setting up an Azure Service Bus endpoint*
- *Building near real-time integration with Azure Service Bus*
- The *Debugging your plugin in Dynamics 365 Online* recipe of `Chapter 4`, *Server-Side Extensions*

Connecting to Dynamics 365 using web applications

This recipe reuses some of the previously built bits in preparation for the next scheduled task recipe.

In this recipe, we will build a one-page MVC application that creates an account when it is called, effectively creating a façade with some business logic to your Dynamics 365 endpoints. We will reuse the **Data Access Layer (DAL)** built in *Connecting to Dynamics 365 from other systems using .NET* earlier in this chapter, in our MVC application. We will add an additional method called `CreateAccount` and call it when the `CreateNewAccount` action is called from the account controller.

Getting ready

Since we are building an MVC application, it is strongly recommended that you use the latest stable Visual Studio version; we will be using Visual Studio 2015. We also need an existing DAL class; we will reuse the one from the *Connecting to Dynamics 365 from other systems using .NET* recipe. You just need to update the constructor to accept the connection string as a parameter as opposed to hard coding it. We can also reuse the same solution from that recipe.

On the Dynamics 365 side, we will need a publicly accessible Dynamics 365 instance (online or IFD) and a service account that will have the appropriate privileges. In this recipe, the service account requires write access to the account's entity.

TIP

You can use a non-interactive user in Dynamics 365 as a service account; therefore, you do not need an additional license for service accounts. Microsoft MVP **George Doubinski** published a PowerShell script to create such users. Refer to `http://crmtipoftheday.com/2015/12/22/create-non-interactive-user-like-a-boss/`.

Finally, from an Azure hosting perspective, you will need an **App Service** application to deploy the web application on. You will also need a deployment username and password. Alternatively, you can always create an App Service as you create your project. Along with the Azure components, you will also need an Azure account with enough credits to create an App Service. Nonetheless, you can spin an Azure trial to test the capabilities.

Optionally, you will need a basic understanding of the **ASP.NET MVC** solution and pattern to help you follow this recipe.

How to do it...

1. Create a new **Empty** web application project in your existing solution of type MVC called `Packt.Xrm.WebApplication`. The following screenshot shows the application creation dialog in Visual Studio with the correct solution template:

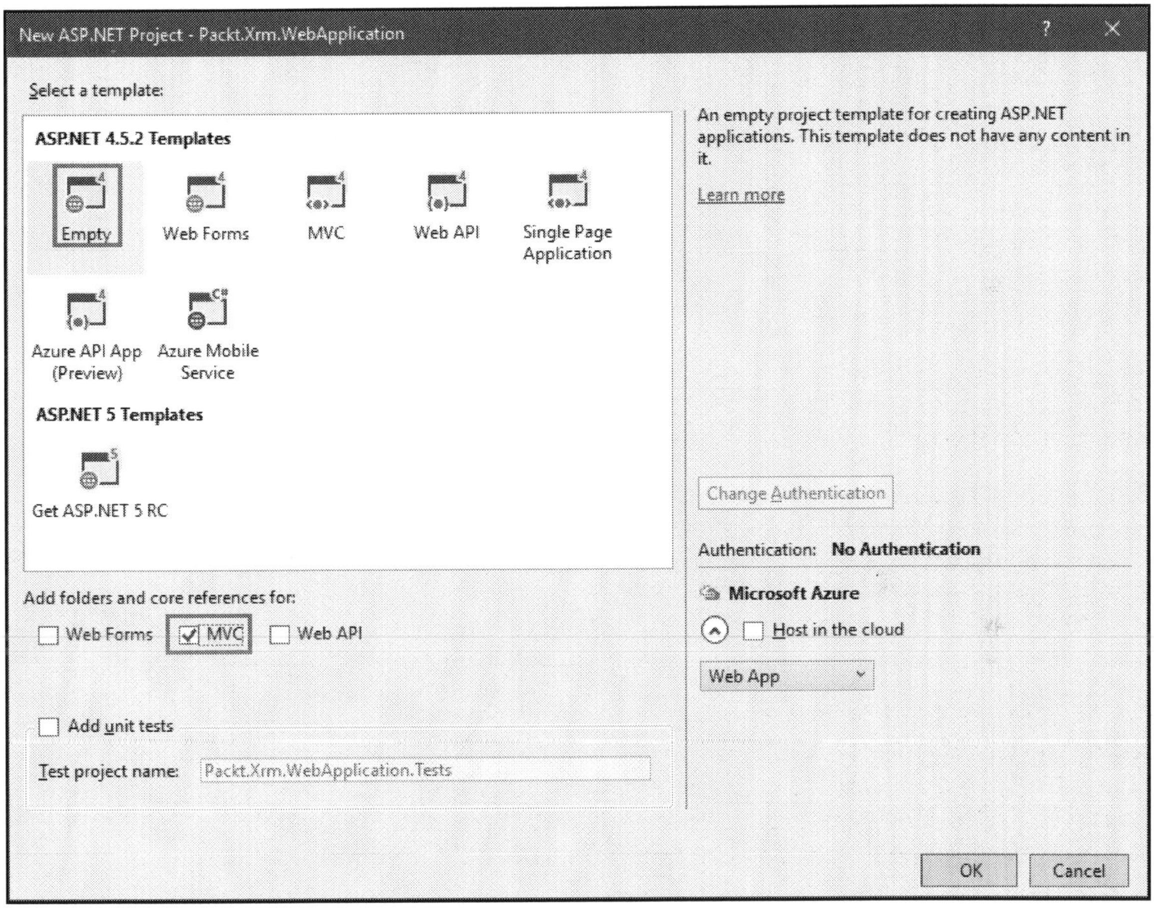

2. Using the NuGet package manager, add the `Microsoft.IdentityModel v6.1.7600.16394` package if it cannot be resolved from the DAL assembly.

3. Add a reference to the previously built assembly where your `Dynamics365DataAccessLayer` class is, or, if you are starting fresh, create a new data access layer similar to the `Dynamics365DataAccessLayer` created in *Connecting to Dynamics 365 from other systems using .NET* earlier in this chapter (don't forget the reference to the `Microsoft.CrmSdk.XrmToolingCoreAssembly` package).
4. Add the following method to your DAL:

```
public void CreateAccount()
{
  using (var serviceProxy = _crmSvc.OrganizationServiceProxy)
  {
    serviceProxy.Create(new Account
    {
        Name = string.Format("MVC account {0}",
DateTime.UtcNow)
    });
  }
}
```

5. Create a new empty controller called `AccountConroller` by right-clicking on the **Controllers** folder in your Visual Studio solution explorer and navigating to **Add** | **Controller**, as shown here:

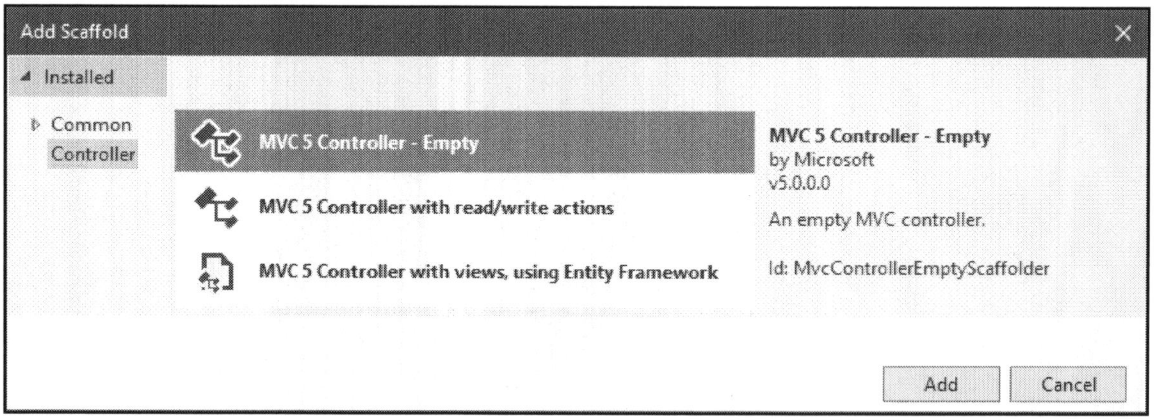

6. Add the following `using` statements at the top of your controller class:

```
using Packt.Xrm.Extensions;
using System.Configuration;
```

7. Create a new method in your controller:

```
public ActionResult CreateAccount()
{
    var connectionString =
      ConfigurationManager.AppSettings["D365ConnectionString"];
    var updateActivity = new
      Dynamics365DataAccessLayer(connectionString);
    updateActivity.CreateAccount();
    return Content("Success!");
}
```

8. Add your Dynamics 365 connection string in your `web.config` app settings:

```
<configuration>
  <appSettings>
<add key="D365ConnectionString" value="<Your Connection String>" />
  </appSettings>
```

9. Build and publish your solution to **Azure AppService** by right-clicking on the project and selecting **Publish**. The following screenshot highlights where the **Publish** button is on the context menu:

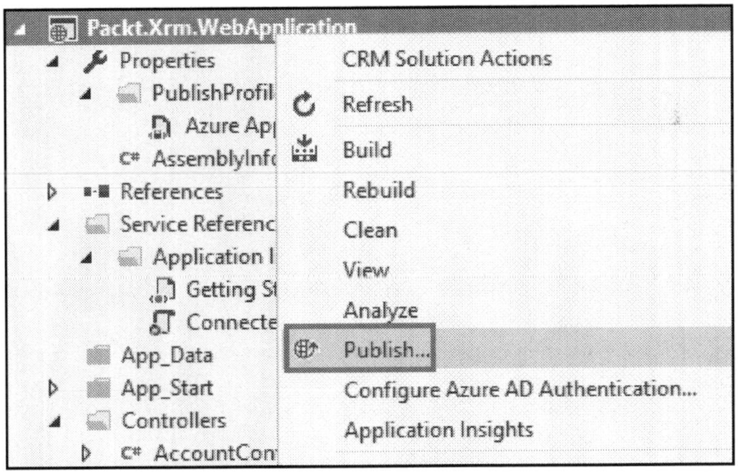

Enter the following details in the publish dialog:

- **Name**: `Azure App Service`
- **Publish method**: `Web Deploy`
- **Server**: `<AppName>.scm.azurewebsites.net:443`
- **Site name**: `<AppName>`
- **User name**: Deployment user name
- **Password**: Deployment user password
- **Destination**: `<AppName>.azurewebsites.net`

Your publish profile should look similar to this screenshot:

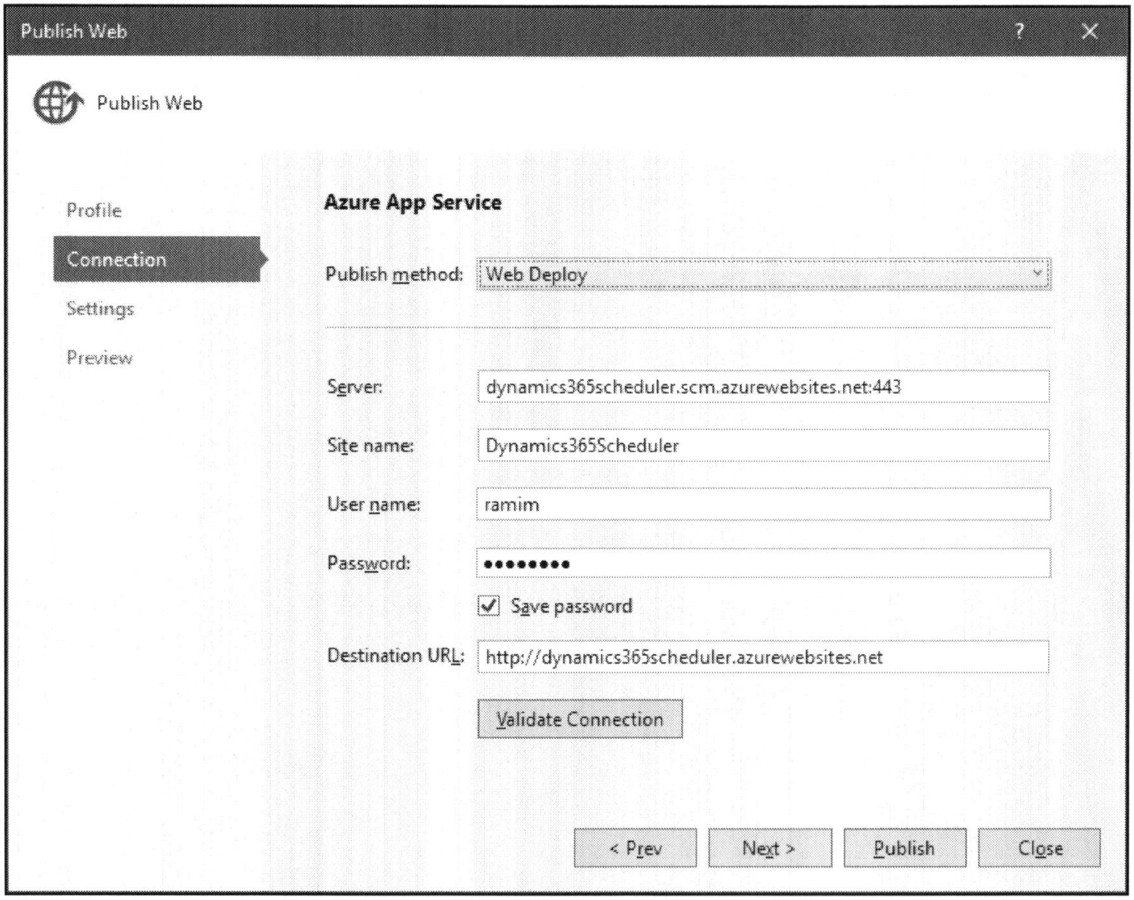

How it works...

This recipe is not about building an MVC web application following best practices, but rather about getting an MVC application up and running as quickly as possible. For instance, it is not considered best practice to have username and password details in your `config` file. We also did not leverage the dependency injection pattern. If you are interested in best practices, `Chapter 6`, *Enhancing Your Code*, deals with techniques and guidance on how to structure your code.

We started by creating an empty MVC application and added the correct library references in step 1 to step 3. In step 4, we enhanced our existing DAL. We added a simple `CreateAccount` method that creates a new account with a name populated with the current date and time. As a best practice, it would be a good idea to reuse the organization service proxy as opposed to recreating it every time and implementing `IDisposable` to dispose of the connections when done with the class.

We then created a controller in step 5 to step 8 with an action that instantiates the DAL, calls the `CreateAccount` method, and returns a success string message. Again, it's probably not best practice to instantiate a DAL every time we call a method, instead, it would be best to use a dependency injection pattern and a factory pattern to return a reusable object. In step 8 specifically, we added the connection string in our configuration file. If you include the username and password, make sure the file is encrypted. Best practice dictates that you don't use plain text credential details in `web.config`, rather use a secure container instead. For more details about connections strings, visit `https://msdn.microsoft.com/en-nz/library/mt608573.aspx`.

We then compiled and deployed to our App Service resource in Azure in step 9. Our application is now hosted and publicly available using the chosen URL: `http://dynamics365scheduler.azurewebsites.net`. Our action is now accessible at `http://dynamics365scheduler.azurewebsites.net/Account/CreateAccount`.

Your publishing profile will certainly look different given the way you have configured it. You will need to replace **<AppName>** with your Azure App Service name when you first configure it in Azure.

There's more...

This recipe covered a scenario where we created an account with a UTC timestamped name every time a URL is called. Although not very useful, the code can easily be enhanced to run a more complex job. Nonetheless, the recipe deals with how to connect to Dynamics 365 from an MVC application and how to deploy this application to an Azure App Service. We will reuse the application as a façade in the next recipe.

See also

- *Connecting to Dynamics 365 from other systems using .NET*
- The *Refactoring your Plugin using a three-layer pattern* recipe of `Chapter 6`, *Enhancing your code*
- *Running Azure Scheduled tasks*

Running Azure scheduled tasks

In the previous recipe, we created an Azure-hosted web application that was accessible publicly. The façade encapsulated some Dynamics 365 business logic to create a timestamped account with a specific name format. In this recipe, we will leverage this application to create an Azure Scheduler task that will send an HTTP request on an interval to execute the code behind our MVC application.

Getting ready

For this recipe, you will need an existing public application that executes some business logic which does not require any dynamic input. We will leverage the Azure-hosted MVC application created in the previous recipe.

From an Azure perspective, you will require a valid Azure subscription to create a **Scheduler**.

> The basic job collection is free of charge (limited to a minimum of hourly intervals between executions).

You will also need a preexisting job collection to use in your Scheduler; alternatively, you can create one when creating your first Scheduler.

How to do it...

1. In Azure's new portal, create a new Scheduler resource by clicking on the top-left corner followed by navigating to **Monitoring + management** | **Scheduler**.
2. Enter a name of your choice that easily identifies the purpose of your scheduled job and select appropriate **Job collection**.
3. Click on **Action settings** and enter the following details:
    - **Action**: HTTP
    - **Method**: Get
    - **Url**: http://<applicationname>.azurewebsites.net/Account/CreateAccount
    - Click on **OK**

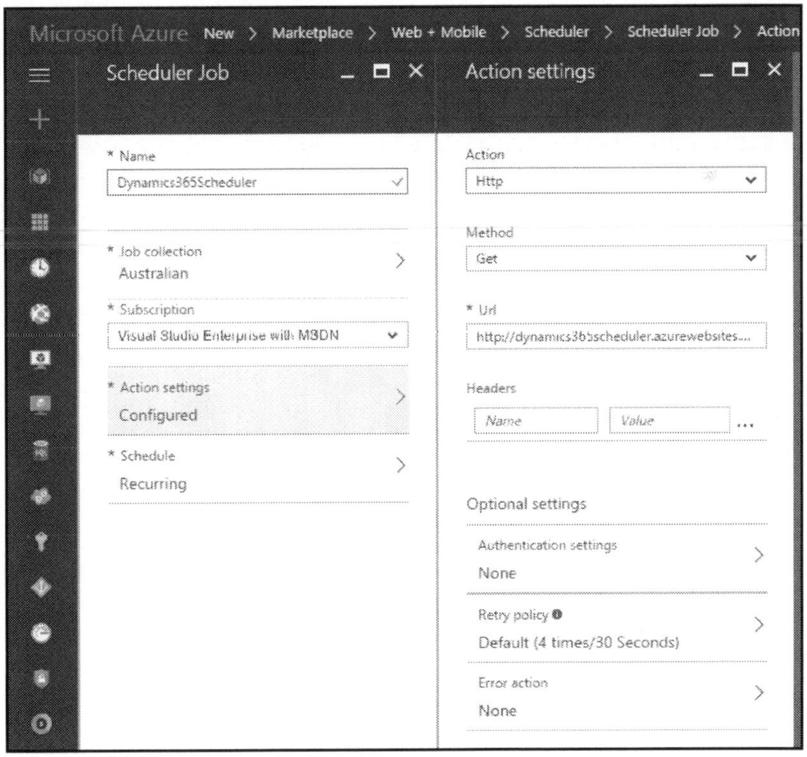

4. Click on **Schedule** and enter the following details:
    - **Recurrence**: `Recurring`
    - **Recur every**: `1 hours`
    - **End**: `Never`
    - Click on **OK**

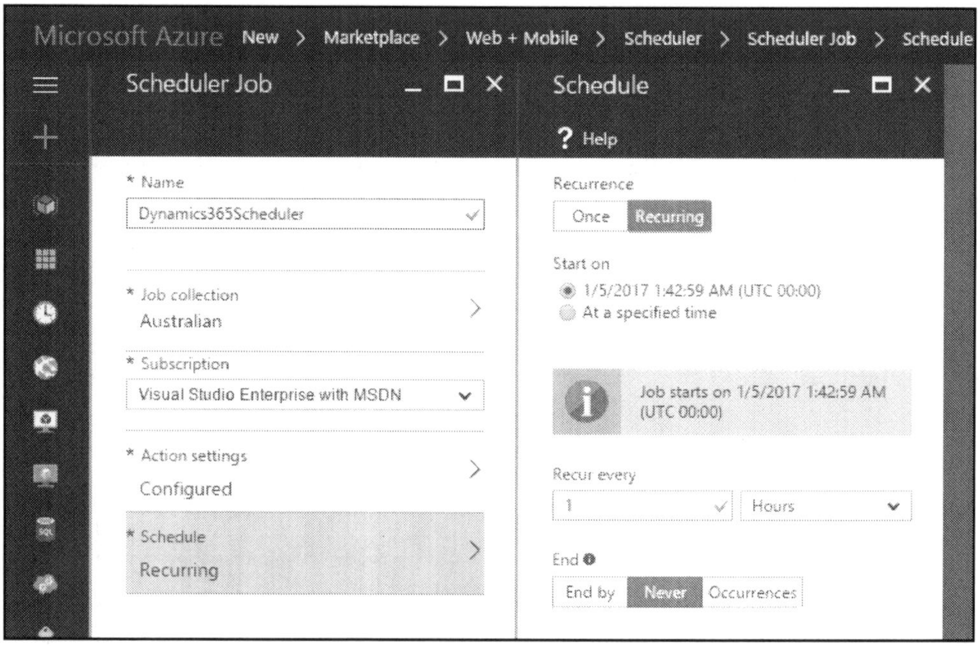

5. Click on **Create**.

How it works...

In this recipe, we created an Azure Scheduler task that calls the URL published in the previous recipe. We configured the Scheduler to run every hour.

In step 2, we reused an existing **Job Collection**. Alternatively, you can create your own **Job Collection**.

In step 3, we defined the action of the task to call the HTTP `GET` request on the MVC application that we created in the previous recipe.

There's more...

In step 3, we defined an HTTP `GET` method. You can also look at other alternatives, for example, you can use a POST request with a static body content or a request to an Azure Service Bus queue as designed in the *Setting up an Azure Service Bus endpoint* recipe in this chapter. Each alternative has its advantages and is built on slightly different design patterns.

You can make your Scheduler more secure by implementing an authentication mechanism. For simplicity, we did not implement an authentication mechanism, which is bad practice for public environments.

Finally, in step 4, you can create a more elaborate schedule. Options include one-off, once a day, and different combinations per week and per month.

See also

- *Connecting to Dynamics 365 using web applications*
- *Setting up an Azure Service Bus endpoint*

Setting up an Azure Service Bus endpoint

In this recipe, we will walk you through the setup and registration of an **Azure Service Bus**. This is in preparation for the next recipe where we write a **remote service context** to the Service Bus. This example is specific for Dynamics 365 online; on-premise instances may require some certificate configuration, as well as Internet access to the asynchronous service.

Getting ready

On the Azure side, you will need a user with enough privileges to create a new service bus. On the Dynamics 365 side, you will need a user with a **System Customizer** or **Administrator** privileges to register the endpoint in your instance. You will also need the plugin registration tool available from the Dynamics 365 SDK.

How to do it...

1. Log in to the new Azure portal (`https://portal.azure.com`) with an account that has the correct privileges.
2. From the left-hand side navigation, go to **+** | **Enterprise Integration** | **Service Bus**, as shown here:

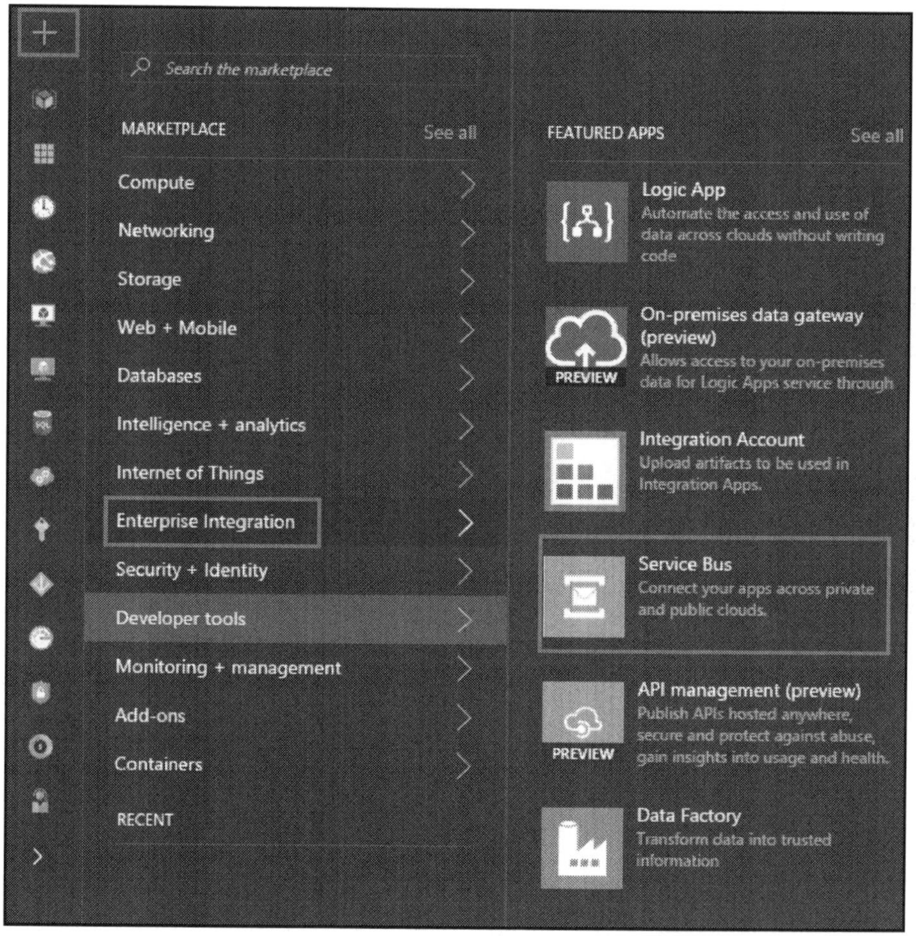

3. Enter the following details:
    - The namespace name of your choice (for example, `PacktDynamics365ServiceBus`)
    - Select a price tier
    - The appropriate subscription
    - The appropriate resource group
    - A location that is closest to your Dynamics 365 data center and your service bus consumers
    - Click on **Create**
4. Once the service bus is created, go to **All resources** and click on the newly created **Service Bus**.
5. Click on **+ Queue** at the top of the overview form and enter `Dynamics365Queue` in the **Name** field. Click on **Create**.
6. Once the queue is created, click on the queue name in the **Service Bus** overview followed by **Shared access policies**, then click on **+ Add** on top of **Shared access policies**.
7. Enter `Dynamics365SharingPolicy` and select **Send** and **Listen.** Then, click on the **Create** button.
8. Once the policy is created, click on it and copy **CONNECTION STRING-PRIMARY KEY**, shown as follows:

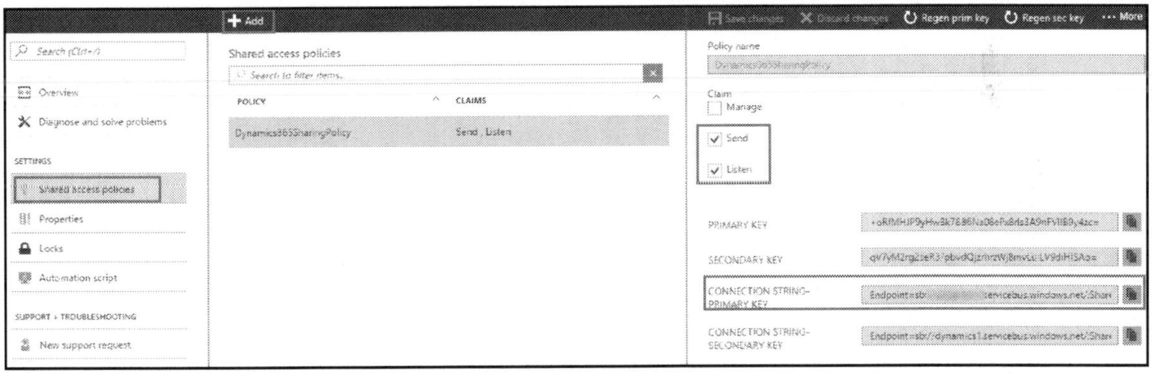

Now that we have created our queue and configured it, we are ready to register it on our Dynamics 365 instance.

9. Launch the plugin registration tool located in the Dynamics 365 SDK under `SDK\Tools\PluginRegistration` and connect to your instance.
10. Navigate to **Register** | **Register New Service Endpoint**:

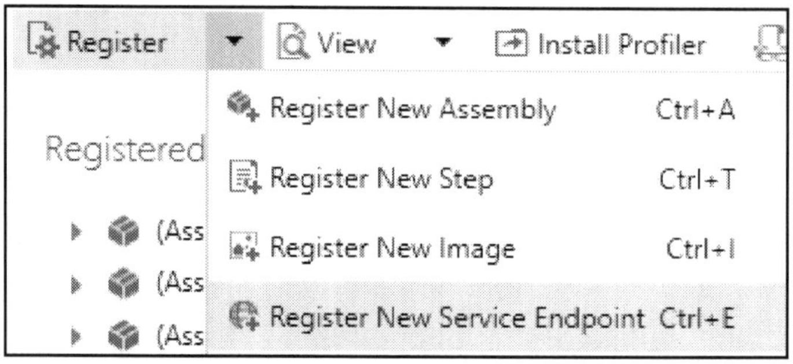

11. Paste the connection string we copied in step 8 and click on **Next**, followed by **Save**.
12. Right-click on the newly registered endpoint in your list and select **Register New Step**.
13. Enter the following details in the **Register New Step** dialog:
    - **Message**: `Update`
    - **Primary Entity**: `account`
    - **Filtering Attributes**: `Account Name`
    - **Execution Mode**: `Asynchronous`
14. Click on **Register New Step**

How it works...

From step 1 to step 6, we created an Azure service bus, a queue, and a shared access policy. Throughout the process, ensure that the names are generic but that they make sense in your context. In step 3, ensure that the pricing tier capabilities meets your non-functional requirements.

In step 7, the **Send** claim is necessary for one-way communication.

Both, the **Send** and **Listen** claims are necessary if you want to implement a two-way communication.

In step 9 to step 13, we registered the endpoint in our Dynamics 365 instance and registered a step to pass the context when an account name is updated. In step 11, the default message format is .NET binary, which works well if your consumer is a .NET application capable of reading a .NET binary object. For consumers written in other languages (JAVA, Python, or any other language that can connect to an Azure Service Bus), change the value to the more universal JSON or XML options.

In step 13, we registered the step as Asynchronous, which is the only possible option. If you try to register your step as synchronous, you will receive the following error:

Behind the scenes, Dynamics 365 has an internal plug-in named `ServiceBusPlugin` that sends the plugin context as `RemotePluginContext` when the **Account Name** attribute is updated. The context will sit in the Azure Service Bus queue and wait until it is consumed. We'll cover a consumer example code in *Consuming messages from an Azure Service Bus* later in this chapter.

There's more...

There are two ways to authenticate with your Azure Service Bus: **Shared Access Signature** (**SAS**) and **Access Control Service** (**ACS**). The latter has been deprecated in favor of SAS due to SAS's simple, flexible, and easy-to-configure advantages. For further details, check out the MSDN article at `https://docs.microsoft.com/en-us/azure/service-bus-messaging/service-bus-authentication-and-authorization`.

If you are using ACS with an on-premise or Internet-facing deployment of Dynamics 365, you will need to further configure your instance to communicate with the Azure Service Bus, as described in `https://msdn.microsoft.com/en-us/library/gg328249.aspx`. Dynamics 365 online is preconfigured. As for SAS authorization, no special configuration is required.

This book is not about Microsoft Azure Services, and as you can see, Azure services change often. Nonetheless, this recipe is important to understand the end-to-end process of Azure integration.

See also

- The *Deploying your customization using the plugin registration tool* recipe of `Chapter 4`, *Server-Side Extensions*
- *Consuming messages from an Azure Service Bus*

Building near real-time integration with Azure Service Bus

In the previous recipe, we mainly used configuration to connect Dynamics 365 to an Azure Service Bus. If you want to implement a custom plugin code before communicating with the Service Bus, or if you want to send something other than the plugin context, you can create your own **Azure aware plugin**.

In this recipe, we will augment an existing custom plugin's capabilities to also connect to an Azure Service Bus. We will reuse the plugin built in *Creating your first plugin* recipe of `Chapter 4`, *Server-Side Extensions,* as the basis of our work.

Getting ready

Using NuGet in Visual Studio, you will need to retrieve the usual Dynamics 365 assemblies. Alternatively, you can try to source the DLL manually from the SDK. Refer to the *Creating your first plugin* recipe in `Chapter 4`, *Server-Side Extensions* for details.

Your plugin requires a register service endpoint in your Dynamics 365 instance. We can reuse the endpoint created in the previous recipe. You will need the GUID of that endpoint. The easiest way to get the GUID is to run the following query in a Chrome browser:

```
<YourDynamics365OrganizationURI>/api/data/v8.2/serviceendpoints?$select
=name,serviceendpointid
```

Finally, you will need the usual Dynamics 365 security role of **System Customizer** or higher in order to register the plugin.

How to do it...

1. Open a previously created plugin solution in Visual Studio.
2. Add the following private variable:

```
private Guid serviceEndpointId;
```

3. Ensure that the public constructor of your class accepts a string parameter called `config` and add the following code to you constructor:

```
if (string.IsNullOrEmpty(config) || !Guid.TryParse(config, out
serviceEndpointId))
{
    throw new InvalidPluginExecutionException("Service endpoint ID
should be passed as config.");
}
```

4. In your Execute method add the following code:

```
var cloudService =
(IServiceEndpointNotificationService)serviceProvider.GetService(typ
eof(IServiceEndpointNotificationService));
if (cloudService == null)
    throw new InvalidPluginExecutionException("Failed to retrieve
the service bus service.");
string response = cloudService.Execute(new
EntityReference("serviceendpoint", serviceEndpointId), context);
```

5. Compile your code and register the assembly in your Dynamics 365 instance.
6. Using the Plug-in Registration Tool add a post-update step to your plugin with the following details:
    - **Message**: `Update`
    - **Primary Entity**: `account`
    - **Filtering Attributes**: `Account Name`
    - **Execution Mode**: `Synchronous`
    - **Unsecure Configuration**: `<Your endpoint GUID>`
    - Click on **Update Step**

How it works...

In step 2 to step 4, we added the code to write to the Azure Service Bus using `IServiceEndpointNotificationService` from the plugin service provider. The method requires an entity reference to our Dynamics 365 service endpoint record, which we resolved using the GUID passed by the plugin configuration.

> TIP: Alternatively, you can write a method to query and resolve the service endpoint record and return the required GUID instead of passing it throught the configuration.

Finally, the plugin context is passed to the `IServiceEndpointNotificationService Execute` method.

In step 5, don't forget to sign your assembly, as we have done in the *Creating your first plugin* recipe of `Chapter 4`, *Server-Side Extensions*.

In step 6, we also added a step that triggers synchronously. Generally speaking, registering a synchronous plugin dependent on external resources is not recommended as the external communication might take longer than expected, which might affect user experience and possibly exceed the 2 minutes timeout limitation. However, synchronous steps give you a near real-time integration between Dynamics 365 and consumers listening to incoming messages, whereas asynchronous steps will execute within a few seconds delay depending on the server load.

In step 6, we also added the service endpoint we retrieved in the *Getting ready* section of this recipe. The passed on configuration may contain other values as well, in which case you will have to write your own methods to extract the values you are after.

There's more...

When your plugin fails to post a message to the Azure Service Bus, if your plugin is asynchronous, the plugin will fail and retry by executing the entire plugin again. As for synchronous plugins, the plugin will simply fail, and you will have to handle the retry mechanism yourself. Read this MSDN article for more details at `https://msdn.microsoft.com/en-us/library/gg328194.aspx#bkmk_failure`.

See also

- *Setting up an Azure Service Bus endpoint*
- *Consuming messages from an Azure Service Bus*

Consuming messages from an Azure Service Bus

Now that we have written the context to the Azure Service Bus, we need to consume this message. This recipe will focus on writing a console application that continuously listens to incoming messages, pops them off the Azure Service Bus queue, and reads the content of the Dynamics365 `RemoteExecutionContext` included in the message.

Getting ready

Starting with the required assemblies, you'll need the `Microsoft.CrmSdk.CoreAssemblies` as well as `WindowsAzure.ServiceBus` NuGet packages.

You can find the first one by searching for `Dynamics Core Assemblies` in your NuGet manager and the second one by searching for `Azure Service Bus`:

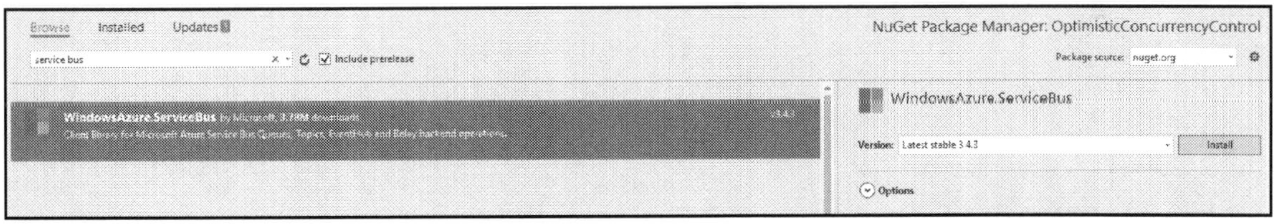

In order to connect to your Azure Service Bus queue, you will need the previously created Service Bus connection string (the RootManageSharedAccessKey connection string, not the queue shared access policy connection string) as well as its queue name.

How to do it...

1. Create a new console application in Visual Studio with a namespace `Packt.Xrm.Azure` (or reuse an existing solution).
2. Create a new class called `EndPointListner` along with its main method.
3. Add the following `using` statements at the top of your class:

```
using Microsoft.Xrm.Sdk;
using Microsoft.ServiceBus.Messaging;
```

4. Add the following code in your main method:

```
var connectionString = "<endpointConnectionString>";
var queueName = "<QueueName>";
var client =
QueueClient.CreateFromConnectionString(connectionString,
queueName);
client.OnMessage(message =>
{
   var result = message.GetBody<RemoteExecutionContext>();
Console.WriteLine(result.PrimaryEntityName);
   Console.WriteLine(result.PrimaryEntityId);
});
Console.WriteLine("Press [Enter] to terminate");
Console.ReadLine();
client.Close();
```

5. Compile your application and run it.
6. Trigger a couple of events in Dynamics 365 that write a message to your queue and watch the console application's output.

How it works...

For an Azure expert or any .NET developer, the code in this recipe is straightforward. We started in step 2 and step 3 by resolving dependency and importing the libraries we will be using: `Microsoft.Xrm.Sdk` for `RemoteExecutionContext` and `Microsoft.ServiceBus` messaging to connect and consume messages from the Azure Service Bus queue.

In step 4, we simply used the connection string and the queue name to connect. We then called `OnMessage`, which is an event-driven method that continuously listens to events triggered by the queue (for example, messages received) and takes a callback method to do something with the message. In our example, we got the message body, which is a .NET binary of type `RemoteExecutionContext` and displayed the primary entity name and GUID from that context.

There's more...

`RemoteExecutionContext` contains significantly more detail than what we consumed in our abridged code. You can retrieve the target entity being updated, pre and post images, as well as details about the execution (user, organization, execution stage, and much more). The sample code from MSDN contains a nice utility method that prints a good summary of what the context contains at `https://msdn.microsoft.com/en-us/library/gg334377.aspx`.

In our code, we used the `OnMessage` method to consume a message from the queue. Alternatively, you can use the `Peek` method to keep the message in the queue while inspecting its content.

You can further enhance the code by implementing a two-way listener that will also return a value to Dynamics 365, as described in the MSDN example: `https://msdn.microsoft.com/en-us/library/gg334438.aspx`. Notice the `TwoWayServiceEndpointPlugin` interface and how the `Execute` method returns a value that is then returned to the producer (Dynamics 365).

See also

- *Setting up an Azure Service Bus endpoint*
- *Building near real-time integration with Azure Service Bus*

Running no code scheduled synchronization using Scribe

Scribe is a third-party solution designed to facilitate the integration between Dynamics 365 and other solutions, or vice versa. Scribe is known for its powerful, no code, point-and-click configurable capabilities.

In this recipe we will demonstrate how to replicate account records on a schedule, from our Dynamics 365 instance to an SQL **platform as a service** (**PaaS**) database instance hosted in Azure using no code.

Getting ready

To get started, you will need a Scribe account; you can set one up for free within minutes to try the solution's capabilities at `https://www.scribesoft.com/`.

Once you have a valid Scribe account, you need to install the Dynamics 365 and SQL connectors (from the Scribe Marketplace) and set up a connection to your Dynamics 365 instance, as well as a connection to a publicly accessible SQL instance that is predefined. You can create new connections by clicking on the + button under **CONNECTIONS** on the dashboard. When setting up your Dynamics 365 connection, make sure you define your instance's discovery URL, not your normal URL (for example `https://disco.crm6.dynamics.com/`). If you are using an SQL instance on Azure, make sure your firewalls are either off or that they white list the Scribe IP addresses (for more details, check out the scribesoft website by navigating to **Resources** | **Scribe Online** and searching for `Whitelisting Requirements`). As usual, you also need the appropriate access to your instances depending on what you are trying to achieve. In our case, we need read access to the Dynamics 365 account and elevated privileges (dbo) on the database as the user will also create the SQL tables from scratch.

How to do it...

1. Log in to your **Scribe** online portal. On the dashboard, click on the + sign. Next, click on the **SOLUTIONS** section and select **Replication**:

2. Enter a name for your solution, `Packt Dynamics 365 to SQL account replication`.
3. Ensure the enabled tick box is selected.

4. Enter a description for your solution, `Scheduled replication of account records between Dynamics 365 and Azure SQL`.
5. Select **Scheduled** under **TRIGGER** and click on **Recurring** under the **SCHEDULING** followed by **Edit**, as follows:

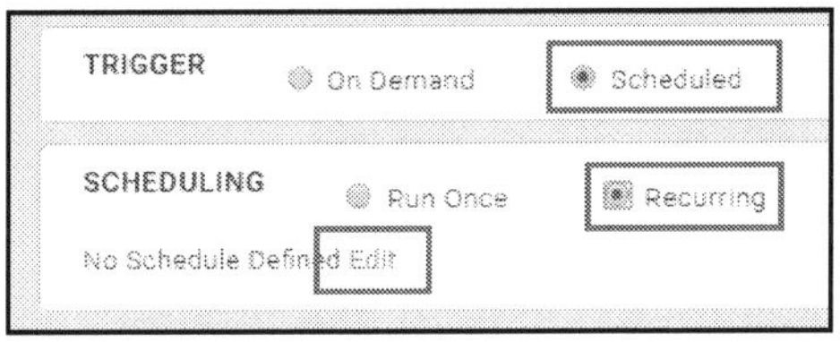

6. Enter a recurring schedule of your choice. In this example we will create a schedule that runs every 30 minutes.
7. Under the **CONNECTIONS** section, select your **Dynamics 365 connection** as the source and your **SQL connection** as your destination.
8. Under **ENTITIES**, select **Selected entities** and click on **Select** to choose **accounts**. Your final solution should look something like this:

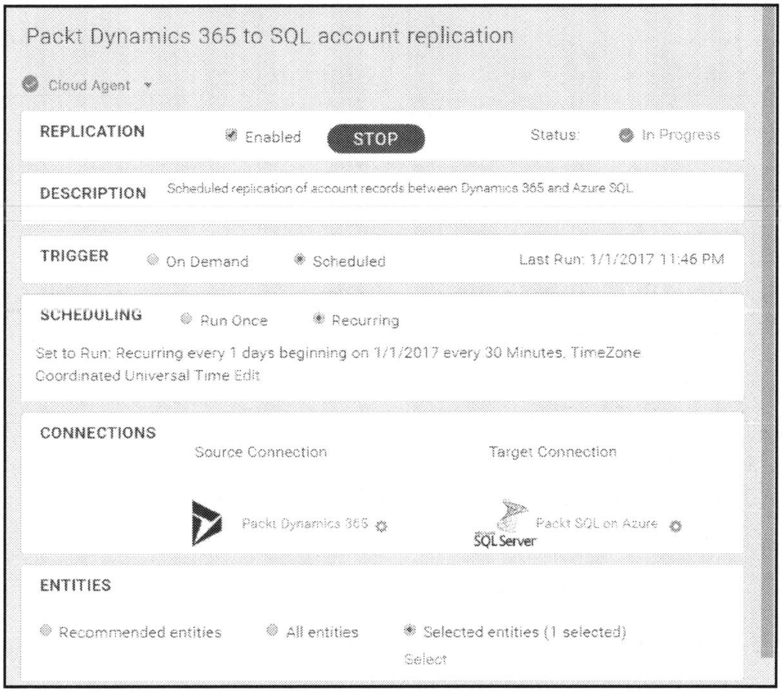

How it works...

In just a few steps, and with no code at all, we created a data replication solution between Dynamics 365 and Azure SQL that runs every 30 minutes.

Behind the scenes, the Scribe cloud agent triggers a synchronization job every 30 minutes and calls the Dynamics 365 API to replicate any new/updated account records with all accessible fields to our SQL instance in Azure. The rest of the mechanism is abstracted for simplicity.

There's more...

This recipe only covers a basic synchronization example. Scribe is capable of much more. Scribe offers point-and-click solutions for more complex examples where data is filtered and transformed before being stored elsewhere. Watch this video for a quick demonstration of the capabilities at `https://www.youtube.com/watch?v=GOdlqRg_CXY&feature=youtu.be`. Scribe also offers a wide range of additional connectors: connectors to SalesForce.com, flat files, Excel, different Dynamics products, and much more. Scribe furthermore offers cloud-based solutions and on-premise solutions. With such feature-rich capabilities, Scribe easily becomes a cost-effective solution to address complex problems that usually take a significant amount of effort to build.

See also

- *Integrating with SSIS using KingswaySoft*
- The *Using the Data Export Service solution for data replication* recipe of `Chapter 9`, *Dynamics 365 Extensions*

Integrating with SSIS using KingswaySoft

SQL Server Integration Services (SSIS) is a great choice when building complex ongoing inter-system integrations or complex one-off data migrations. **KingswaySoft** offers a Microsoft Dynamics 365 Integration product that provides Dynamics 365 specific add-ons to the base SSIS toolset. KingswaySoft add-ons turn complex Dynamics 365 web services integration into high performance, easy-to-use, point-and-click configurable data integration solutions. **Daniel Cai**, Microsoft MVP and a personal inspiration to me becoming a business solutions MVP, is one of the masterminds behind this product.

In this recipe, we will cover a simple scenario, reading the account records from a CSV file and upserting (update or insert if the record is not found) them into Dynamics 365 with a custom-defined primary key. We will also deal with redirecting errors to a separate flat file.

Getting ready

For this recipe, you will need Visual Studio 2015 with **SQL Server Data Tools** (**SSDT**) installed as well as the KingswaySoft Microsoft Dynamics CRM integration software (you can download a fully functional trial for free if you are using it for development purposes and only running your package from within Visual Studio). Although not necessary, you also need some basic SSIS experience to easily follow the recipe.

You will also need the correct privileges in Dynamics 365 to read, create, and update the account records (or any additional privileges you require for your specific scenario).

Finally, you will need two CSV files. One with two columns, `Account Name` and `Phone`, with some sample data. The other is with five columns, `Account Name`, `Phone`, `ErrorCode`, `ErrorColumn`, and `CrmErrorMessage`, with no sample data.

How to do it...

1. Create a new project of type **Integration Services Project** called `Packt.Xrm.SSIS`:

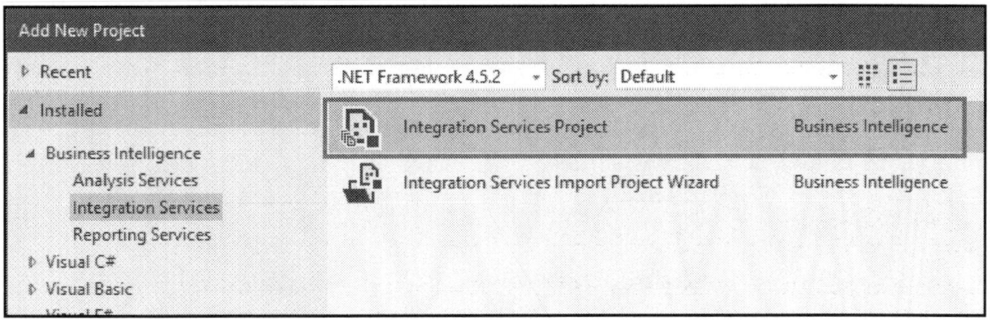

2. Rename the default `dtsx` file to `LoadingAccounts.dtsx`.
3. Add a data flow task and rename it to `Loading Accounts to Dynamics 365`.

4. Right-click on the **Connection Manager** window (usually at the bottom) and select **New Connection** followed by **Flat File**.

5. Enter the following details in **Flat File Connection Manager Editor**:
    - **Connection manager name**: `Account CSV`
    - **File name**: <The location of your accounts file>
    - Click on **OK**

6. Right-click on the **Connection Manager** window again and select **New Connection** followed by **Flat File**.
7. Enter the following details in **Flat File Connection Manager Editor**:
    - **Connection manager name**: `Failure CSV`
    - **File name**: <The location of your failure file>
    - Click on **OK**

8. Right-click on the **Connection Manager** window one last time and select **New Connection** followed by **DynamicsCRM**:

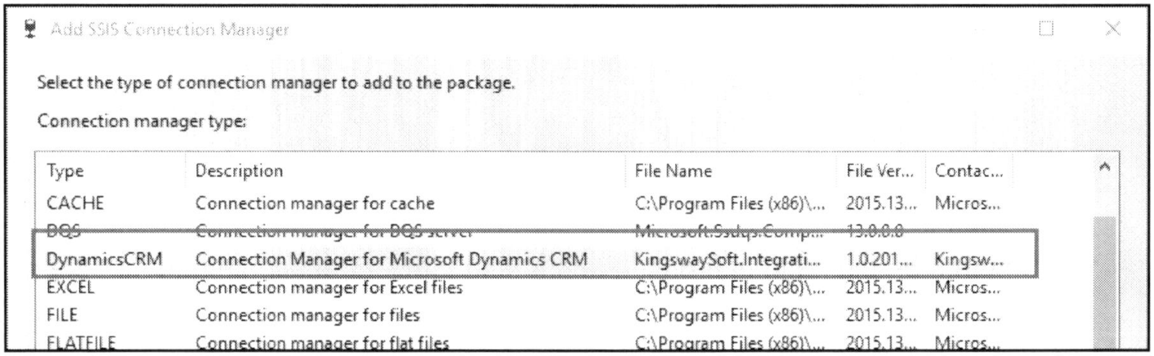

9. Enter your Dynamics 365 details in **CRM Connection Manager Editor**. As an example, take a look at the following:
    - **Authentication Type**: `Online Federation`
    - **CRM Discovery Server**: `https://disco.crm.dynamics.com`
    - Your username and password in the **Authentication** area
    - **Organization**: The organization you are targeting
    - Click on **OK**

10. Right-click on the newly created connection manager and rename it to `Dynamics 365`.

11. Back in your dtsx designer, double-click on **Loading Accounts to Dynamics 365 task**.

12. From your **SSIS Toolbox** (usually the window on the left-hand side) under **Other Sources**, drag and drop **Flat File Source** onto your designer.
13. Double-click on **Flat File Source** and ensure the flat connection manager is Account CSV. Click **OK** when the dialog appears.
14. Right-click on the **Flat File Source** step and rename it to `Account CSV Source`.
15. From the SSIS Toolbox under **Common**, drag and drop **Dynamics CRM Destination** into your designer.
16. Right-click and rename it to `Dynamics 365 Account Destination`.
17. Link `Account CSV Source` normal flow (blue line) to the newly renamed `Dynamics 365 Account Destination`.
18. Double-click on **Dynamics 365 Account Destination**.
19. In **CRM Destination Editor**, enter the following details:
    - **CRM Connection Manager**: `Dynamics 365`
    - **Action**: `Upsert`
    - **Destination Entity**: `account`
    - **Upsert/Update Matching Criteria**: `Manually Specify`
    - **Handling of Multiple Matches**: `Raise an Error`
20. In the columns tab, from the left-hand side map, enter the fields as follows:
    - **Account Name** | **name** (also select the primary key column)
    - **Phone** | **telephone1**
21. In the **Error Handling** tab, on the left-hand side, select the **Redirect rows to error output** option.
22. Click on **OK**.
23. Under **Other Destinations,** drag and drop a **Flat File Destination** task from your toolbox and rename it to `CSV Error Destination`.
24. Wire the error flow (red line) from **Dynamics 365 Account Destination** to the newly created task and click on **OK** after the dialog appears.
25. Double-click on the **CSV Error Destination** task.
26. Ensure **Failure CSV** is selected under **Connection Manager** and **Overwrite data in the file** is selected.
27. Under the **mappings** tab, again on the left-hand side, ensure that the fields are mapped correctly. All names should have a matching counterpart.
28. Click on **OK**.

29. Click on **Start** to launch your package.

    Your final execution will look similar to what is shown in the following figure, with different numbers depending on your records in the CSV file and the records in Dynamics 365:

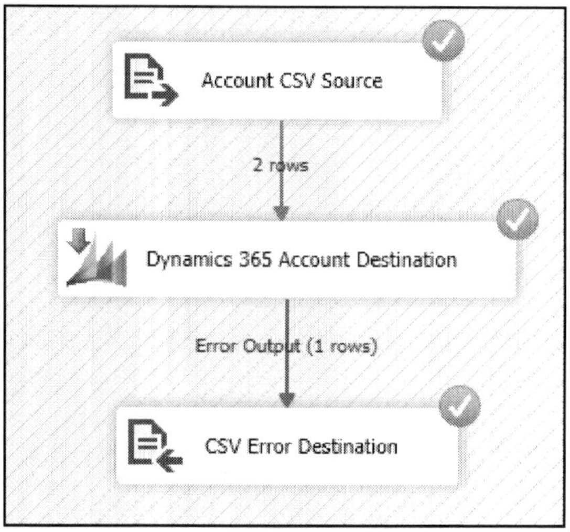

How it works...

From step 2 to step 10, we created the main flow and all the connections that were required. Step 9 specifically might look different depending on whether you are connecting to an online or an on-premise instance. You can find your instance's discovery details in Dynamics 365 by navigating to **Settings** | **Customization** | **Developer Resources**.

In step 19, we created the Dynamics 365 destination task along with the mapping in step 20. The mapping can also be done on lookups. The custom field may be used to resolve the lookup references or, optionally, set items with different resolution options when an item does not exist (for example creating the missing items).

In step 23 through to step 28, we handled the error flow from the Dynamics 365 Account destination task to fill another CSV file with the error details as well as the data that failed. In our example, the error might state `Found multiple records that match the Upsert matching criteria`. It is good practice to handle errors within their own flow, especially with large volumes where you might have several phases to refine your package and rerun the failed records. The error flow may be redirected for a separate SQL data storage location.

There's more...

This abridged recipe might look simple and similar to other Dynamics 365 capabilities, such as the out-of-the-box CSV import or the staged data import; however, we barely scratch the surface of what the KingswaySoft product can do. You can leverage the power of SSIS to define different sources and destinations (databases, OData, and more), handle error flows, and build complex point-and-click packages. Furthermore, the product is one of the few in the market that can process Dynamics 365 audit data in a structured way.

If you want to know more about the product, KingswaySoft's website has some comprehensive documentation as well as some useful video tutorials that can help you get started and understand the product's capabilities.

See also

- The *Staging data imports* recipe of `Chapter 3`, *SDK Enterprise Capabilities*
- *Running no code scheduled synchronization using Scribe*

6
Enhancing Your Code

In this chapter we will cover the following recipes:

- Refactoring your plugin using a three-layer pattern
- Replacing your LINQ data access layer with QueryExpressions
- Logging an error from your customization
- Converting your plugin into a custom workflow activity
- Unit testing your plugin business logic
- Unit testing your plugin with an in-memory context
- Integration testing your plugin end-to-end
- Profiling your plugin
- Building a generic read audit plugin
- Using Cross-Origin Resource Sharing with CRM Online

Introduction

Most customization examples that you will find in books and official articles will mainly focus on the basics to get you started. They seldom delve deeper into how to structure your code for clean code and best practices. Any customization you build--whether using JavaScript, C#, or any other language or framework--should follow best practices. Plugins, for example, can very easily get too large and difficult to maintain if no thought is put into structuring them properly.

In this chapter we will start by refactoring our one class C# plugins into three layers: entry point, business logic, and **data access layer** (**DAL**). We will also introduce design patterns, such as dependency injection, singleton, and factory. Most of the enhancements will leverage fundamental object-oriented paradigms including: inheritance, encapsulation, and polymorphism, among others. A basic understanding of these patterns and paradigms is recommended, but not necessary.

The first recipe is key to the rest of the chapter, as it will enable some new capabilities. Most notably, this includes the ease of unit testing and the ease of swapping classes' implementations with minimum, if any, alterations to the rest of the dependent classes.

We will look at how easy it is to replace a complete DAL implementation in *Replacing your LINQ data access layer with QueryExpressions*, how easy it is to replace our logging class in *Logging error from your customization*, and how easy it is to convert a plugin into a custom workflow activity in *Converting your plugin into a custom workflow activity*, all in this chapter.

From a unit-testing perspective, we will be running a business logic unit test, a live integration test, and an end-to-end plugin test by using an in-memory organization service. Think of in-memory as a fake Dynamics 365 instance built in milliseconds for the purpose of our unit test.

The following simplified sequence diagram highlights some of the layers used in this chapter:

- The first sequence at the top traces the layers traversed when unit testing the business logic. As a true unit test, all dependent layers are either skipped or mocked.
- The second sequence in the middle highlights the live integration test, where the plugin is deployed to Dynamics 365 and triggered through the API to mimic a use case. All layers are invoked and the results are verified back in the live Dynamics 365 instance.

- The last sequence at the bottom traverses all the layers; it bypasses Dynamics 365 and uses an in-memory service context as shown here:

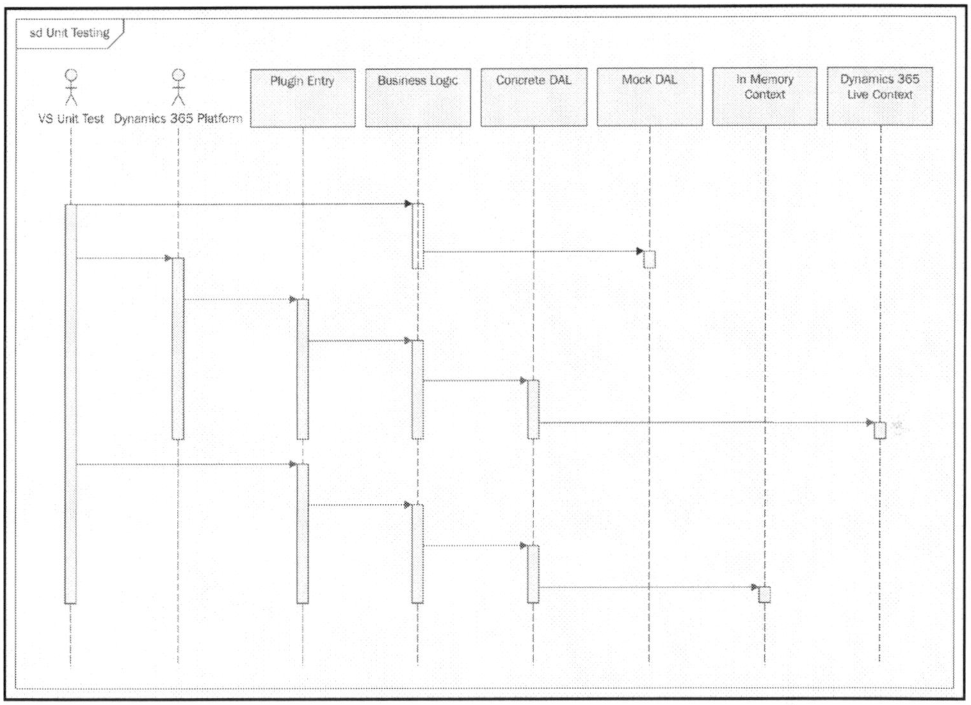

Different combinations are possible because of the multilayered refactoring. Regardless of whether you are building a pure .NET application or a Dynamics 365 extension, best practice and clean code rules apply.

Refactoring your plugin using a three-layer pattern

In previous recipes, we implemented our plugins in the easiest and fastest way to demonstrate specific scenarios. The purpose of this recipe is to enhance the structure of your code and turn it from a one class code behind (spaghetti code where all logic and layers are tangled in one class) to a layered code (lasagna code where each layer is separate and well defined without entanglement). The three layers we will be implementing are the entry layer (the actual plugin), the business logic, and the data access layer. We will also create a few other utility classes to increase reusability.

This recipe will be based on the first plugin we implemented in the *Creating your first plugin* recipe in `Chapter 4`, *Server-Side Extensions*. We will refactor it to use the **inversion of control** (**IoC**) pattern, which will facilitate unit testing. We will be able to easily swap between different DAL implementations and easily convert our core code from a plugin to a workflow or console application.

More specifically, we will extract interfaces for each of the data access layers, along with a base data access class that bundles common methods. A factory class will help resolve concrete classes based on requested interfaces. Separate business logic class will separate the logic from the plugin, and finally a base class for all plugins will contain common logic used by most plugins.

Getting ready

To refactor our existing code, we will base this recipe on the plugin code written in the *Creating your first plugin* recipe in `Chapter 4`, *Server-Side Extensions*. The usage of a compatible Visual Studio IDE is strongly recommended. We will be using Visual Studio 2015. The solution must have the `Microsoft.CrmSdk.CoreAssemblies` NuGet package installed. Optionally, if you are using an organization service context, then you will need the `CrmSvcUtil` early bound classes generated. In this example, we are using the `Pact.Xrm.Entities` namespace for the early bound classes and optionset enums generated in the *Creating early bound entity classes* and *Extending CrmSvcUtil to generate optionsets enum* recipes respectively of `Chapter 3`, *SDK Enterprise Capabilities*.

Alternatively, if you are writing your code from scratch, you can just follow the same patterns for your new plugin.

How to do it...

1. Create a public interface called `IBaseDataAccessLayer` in a folder called `DataAccessLayer`.
2. Add the following `using` statement:

```
using Microsoft.Xrm.Sdk;
```

3. Add the following two signatures:

```
void UpdateEntity(Entity entity);
void Commit();
```

4. Create a public base class called `BaseDataAccessLayer` that implements `IBaseDataAccessLayer` and `IDisposable` in the same folder.
5. Include the following `using` statements:

```
using Microsoft.Xrm.Sdk;
using Packt.Xrm.Entities;
```

6. Remove the organization server and organization proxy from your old plugin and then add a `protected` variable to your abstract class, as follows:

```
protected IOrganizationService OrganizationService;
protected OrganisationServiceContext OrganizationContext;
```

7. Create the following constructor for your class:

```
public BaseDataAccessLayer(IOrganizationService
organizationService)
{
    OrganizationService = organizationService;
    OrganizationContext = new
OrganisationServiceContext(organizationService);
}
```

8. Move the methods highlighted here from your original plugin to the newly created parent class, while ensuring that the organization service context has the correct capitalization. Make sure you refactor those methods as virtual, as per the following code snippet:

```
public virtual void UpdateEntity(Entity entity)
{
    OrganizationContext.UpdateObject(entity);
}
public virtual void Commit()
{
    OrganizationContext.SaveChanges();
}
```

9. Add the `Dispose()` method:

```
public virtual void Dispose()
{
  OrganizationContext.Dispose();
}
```

10. Now that our base class is ready, create a public interface called `IEmailDataAccessLayer` in the same folder that implements `IBaseDataAccessLayer` and `IDisposable`.
11. Add the following `using` statement:

```
using Packt.Xrm.Entities;
```

12. Add the following two signatures:

```
IEnumerable<Email> GetEmails(Guid parentEntityId);
void CloseEmailAsCancelled(Email email);
```

13. Create a public concrete class called `EmailDataAccessLayer` that inherits from `BaseDataAcccessLayer` and implements `IEmailDataAccessLayer`:

```
class EmailDataAccessLayer : BaseDataAccessLayer,
IEmailDataAccessLayer
```

14. Add the following `using` statements:

```
using Packt.Xrm.Entities;
using Microsoft.Crm.Sdk.Messages;
using Microsoft.Xrm.Sdk;
```

15. Add the following constructor to your concrete class:

```
public EmailDataAccessLayer(IOrganizationService
organizationService) : base(organizationService)
{
}
```

16. Move the following methods from your plugin to your concrete class while ensuring that the organization service context has the correct capitalization:

```
public IEnumerable<Email> GetEmails(Guid parentEntityId)
{
    var query = from email in OrganizationContext.EmailSet
        where email.RegardingObjectId.Id == parentEntityId
        &&
        email.StateCode == EmailState.Open
        select new Email
        {
            Id = email.Id,
            Subject = email.Subject
        };
```

```
        return query.ToList();
    }

    public void CloseEmailAsCancelled(Email email)
    {
        email.StateCode = EmailState.Canceled;

        var setStateRequest = new SetStateRequest()
        {
            Status = new
    OptionSetValue((int)email_statuscode.Canceled),
            State = new OptionSetValue((int)EmailState.Canceled),
            EntityMoniker = new
    EntityReference(Email.EntityLogicalName,
                email.Id)
        };
        OrganizationContext.Execute(setStateRequest);
    }
```

17. Create a public interface under the `DataAccessLayer` folder called `ICustomTracingService` that has a one method signature:

```
void Trace(string message, params object[] args);
```

18. Create a public concrete class that implements `ICustomTracingService` called `CrmTracing`.
19. Add the following `using` statements:

```
using Microsoft.Xrm.Sdk;
```

20. Add the following `private` instance variables:

```
private ITracingService _tracingSerivce;
```

21. Add the following constructor:

```
public CrmTracing(ITracingService tracingSerivce)
{
    _tracingSerivce = tracingSerivce;
}
```

22. Implement the following method:

```
public void Trace(string message, params object[] args)
{
    _tracingSerivce.Trace(message, args);
}
```

23. Create a public business logic class called `UpdateEmailLogic` under a `BusinessLogic` folder.

24. Add the following `using` statement:

```
using Packt.Xrm.Extensions.DataAccessLayer;
```

25. Add the following `private` instance variable:

```
private IEmailDataAccessLayer _emailDataAccessLayer;
private ICustomTracingService _tracingService;
```

26. Create a constructor that takes the `IEmailDataAccessLayer` and `ICustomTracingService` parameters, as follows:

```
public UpdateEmailLogic(IEmailDataAccessLayer emailDataAccessLayer,
ICustomTracingService tracingService)
{
    _emailDataAccessLayer = emailDataAccessLayer;
    _tracingService = tracingService;
}
```

27. Create a method called `UpdateAccountEmails(Guid accountId)` with the following implementation:

```
public void UpdateAccountsEmails(Guid accountId)
{
    var emails = _emailDataAccessLayer.GetEmails(accountId);
    int closedEmails = 0;
    int updatedEmails = 0;
    foreach (var email in emails)
    {
        if (string.IsNullOrEmpty(email.Subject))
        {
            _emailDataAccessLayer.CloseEmailAsCancelled(email);
            closedEmails++;
        }
        else
        {
            email.ScheduledStart = DateTime.Today.AddDays(10);
            _emailDataAccessLayer.UpdateEntity(email);
            updatedEmails++;
        }
    }
    _tracingService.Trace("{0} closed emails and {1} updated
emails", closedEmails, updatedEmails);
    _emailDataAccessLayer.Commit();
```

```
}
```

28. Now that the data access layers and their interfaces are created, we can create a public factory class called `DataAccessLayerFactory` under the `DataAccessLayer` folder that implements `IDisposable` and has a reference to `Microsoft.Xrm.Sdk`. The factory class is responsible for resolving interfaces into concrete classes. This helps us avoid hard coding concrete classes and, rather,relies on interfaces in our business logic or plugins.
29. Add the following `private` variables:

```
private IOrganizationService _organisationService;
private IEmailDataAccessLayer _emailDataAccessLayer;
private ICustomTracingService _customTracingService;
private ITracingService _tracingService;
```

30. Create a constructor that takes the organization service and the CRM `ITracingService` as parameters:

```
public DataAccessLayerFactory(IOrganizationService
organisationService, ITracingService tracingService)
{
    _organisationService = organisationService;
    _tracingService = tracingService;
}
```

31. Add the following three methods:

```
public IEmailDataAccessLayer GetEmailDataAccessLayer()
{
    if (_emailDataAccessLayer == null)
        _emailDataAccessLayer = new
EmailDataAccessLayer(_organisationService);
    return _emailDataAccessLayer;
}
public ICustomTracingService GetTracingService()
{
    if (_customTracingService == null)
        _customTracingService = new CrmTracing(_tracingService);
    return _customTracingService;
}
public void Dispose()
{
    if (_emailDataAccessLayer != null)
        _emailDataAccessLayer.Dispose();
}
```

32. Finally, we are ready to refactor the plugin to use the newly refactored structure. Create a public abstract plugin class called `BasePlugin` in a `Plugin` folder that implements `IPlugin`. The abstract plugin holds common routines used in most plugins. With such a base class, we won't have to rewrite the common functionality for each of the plugins.

    ```
    public abstract class BasePlugin : IPlugin
    ```

33. Add the following `using` statements:

    ```
    using Microsoft.Xrm.Sdk;
    using System.ServiceModel;
    using Packt.Xrm.Extensions.DataAccessLayer;
    ```

34. Add the following `protected` variables:

    ```
    protected IOrganizationService OrganizationService;
    protected IPluginExecutionContext PluginContext;
    protected ICustomTracingService CustomTracingService;
    protected Entity Entity;
    protected DataAccessLayerFactory DataAccessLayerFactory;
    ```

35. Add the following `abstract` method and property:

    ```
    public abstract void PostExecute(IServiceProvider serviceProvider);
    public abstract string ExpectedEntityLogicalName { get; }
    ```

36. Remove the local variables from your original plugin and add the organization service as a protected variable.
37. Implement the following `Execute` method:

    ```
    public void Execute(IServiceProvider serviceProvider)
    {
        var tracingService =
    (ITracingService)serviceProvider.GetService(typeof(ITracingService)
    );
        PluginContext =
    (IPluginExecutionContext)serviceProvider.GetService(typeof(IPluginE
    xecutionContext));

        if (!PluginContext.InputParameters.Contains("Target") ||
    !(PluginContext.InputParameters["Target"] is Entity))
            return;

        Entity = (Entity)PluginContext.InputParameters["Target"];
    ```

```
    if (Entity.LogicalName != ExpectedEntityLogicalName)
        return;

    IOrganizationServiceFactory serviceFactory =
(IOrganizationServiceFactory)serviceProvider.GetService(typeof(IOrg
anizationServiceFactory));
    OrganizationService =
serviceFactory.CreateOrganizationService(PluginContext.UserId);

    using (DataAccessLayerFactory = new
DataAccessLayerFactory(OrganizationService, tracingService))
    {
        CustomTracingService =
DataAccessLayerFactory.GetTracingService();
        try
        {
            PostExecute(serviceProvider);
        }
        catch (FaultException<OrganizationServiceFault> ex)
        {
            throw new InvalidPluginExecutionException("An error
occurred in this plug-in.", ex);
        }
        catch (Exception ex)
        {
            CustomTracingService.Trace("Plugin Exception: {0}",
ex.ToString());
            throw;
        }
    }
}
```

38. Move your concrete class in the `Plugin` folder and inherit from `BasePlugin`.
39. Make sure you have the following `using` statements:

```
using Microsoft.Xrm.Sdk;
using Packt.Xrm.Extensions.DataAccessLayer;
using Packt.Xrm.Extensions.BusinessLogic;
```

40. Implement the following `PostExecute` method:

```
public override void PostExecute(IServiceProvider serviceProvider)
{
    var updateEmailLogic = new
UpdateEmailLogic(DataAccessLayerFactory.GetEmailDataAccessLayer(),
CustomTracingService);
    updateEmailLogic.UpdateAccountsEmails(Entity.Id);
}
```

41. Implement the following `ExpectedEntityLogicalName` getter:

```
public override string ExpectedEntityLogicalName { get { return
Account.EntityLogicalName; } }
```

42. Remove all other methods and variables from your `UpdateActivityClass`.

How it works...

In step 1 to step 16, we extracted all the methods related to the DAL into their own hierarchy. We started in step 1 to step 9 by creating a base concrete class along with its interface to give us basic reusable DAL methods, such as `UpdateEntity` (a polymorphic method that accepts any entity) and `Commit`. The base class's constructor instantiates the organization service context as it uses the unit of the work design pattern (as described in the *Creating a LINQ data access layer* recipe of `Chapter 4`, *Server-Side Extensions*). In step 10 to step 16, we created our e-mail-specific concrete DAL along with its interface. The concrete class inherits from the base class, thus including the accessible base class's methods.

From step 17 to step 22, we created a concrete tracing class along with its interface. This specific class simply wraps the CRM tracing service functionality.

S stands for **Single responsibility** in the **SOLID** principle. Having separate DAL classes ensures that each class has a single responsibility.

In step 23 to step 27, we extracted the business logic to call the load and update e-mail methods into a separate business logic class. This class is only dependent on the previous two interfaces created (`IEmailDataAccessLayer` and `ICustomTracingService`) and is unaware that the concrete classes are connected to Dynamics 365.

D stands for **Dependency inversion** in the **SOLID** principle. Our business logic is dependent on interfaces (abstraction), not concrete classes.

In step 28 to step 31, we created a factory class to generate the two concrete classes we created previously, but each method's return type is an interface. The factory uses the singleton pattern to ensure we can reuse classes that are already instantiated. Furthermore, the factory implements `IDisposable` to dispose the DAL classes properly.

In step 32 to step 41, we refactored what is left from the original plugin into an abstract base class and a child class. The base (`BasePlugin`) deals with the most common generic elements of a plugin; it handles extracting the organization service, instantiating the factory class and the tracing service, and handling exceptions by wrapping the plugin execution in a try catch statement.

In step 38 to step 42, we implemented our specific plugin that now inherits from the base plugin. Given that most of the plugin handling details are in the base class, and that the specific work done by the plugin was extracted to the business logic, all we need to do in our concrete class is instantiate the business logic, inject the correct dependencies, and call the correct method on the business logic. Two lines of code in the overridden `PostExecute` method plus one line to override the `ExpectedEntityLogicalName` getter to return the entity's logical name is all that are needed.

Note how we created the majority of the classes as public. This ensures that we can access them from external assemblies to extend them. Feel free to restrict the accessibility as you see fit however; do not expose your classes for the sake of unit testing. Without going too much into a philosophical unit testing debate, Visual Studio allows you to unit test restricted methods if necessary.

O stands for **Open/Close** in the **SOLID** principle: open for extension, but close for alteration.

Our one class plugin has now turned into 10+ classes. The new class diagram now looks like this:

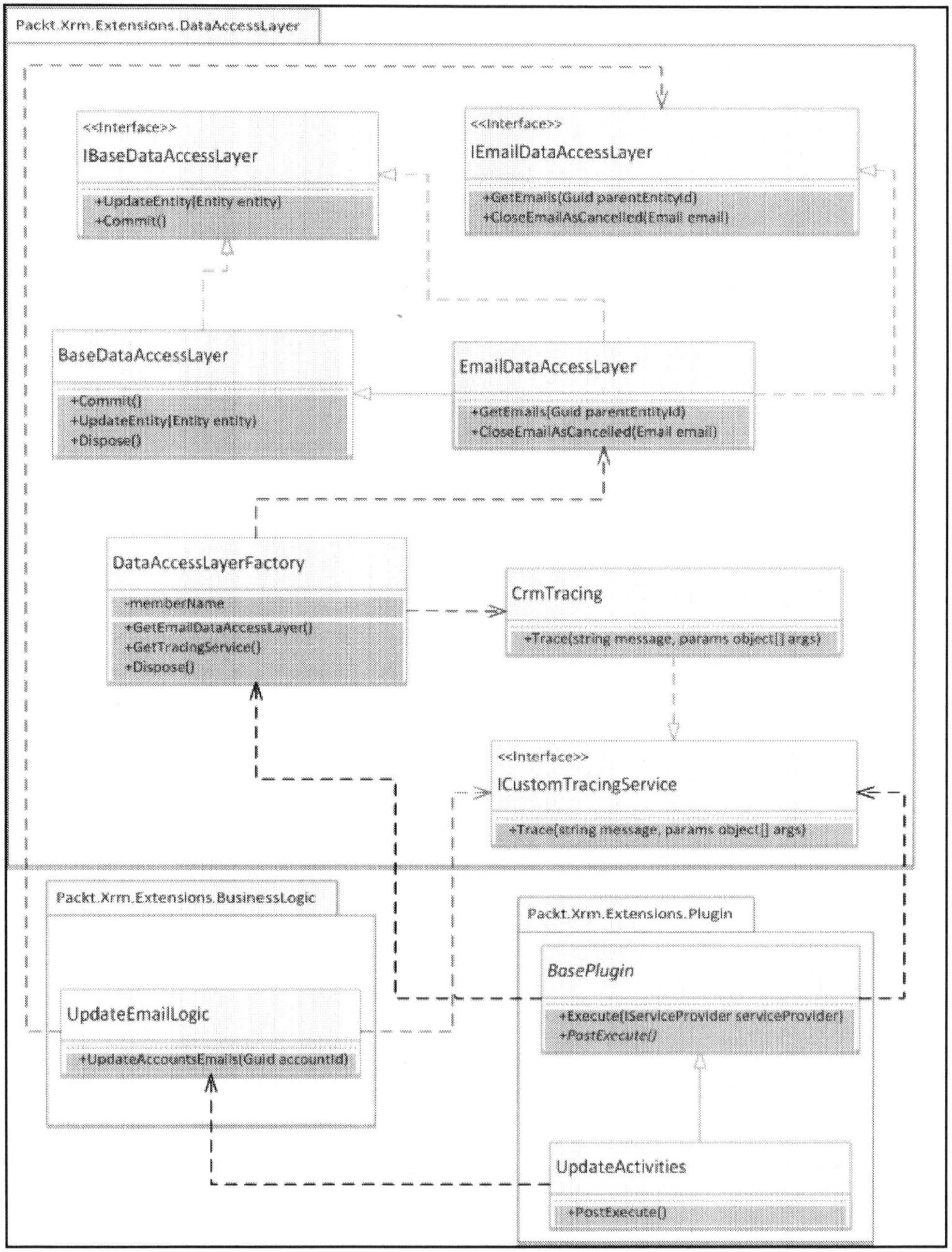

Note how the business logic is only dependent on interfaces (dependency arrows between **BusinessLogic** and **ICustomTracingService** or **IEmailDataAccessLayer**). This is a good example of fundamental object-oriented paradigms at work (encapsulation and polymorphism when injecting mocks or stubs).

> **L** stands for **Liskov substitution** in the SOLID principle. As we will see in the next recipe, we will replace the concrete DAL with a different implementation without altering the correctness of our code.

The abstract base plugin is now only dependent on the factory class and the tracing interface. The concrete plugin is only dependent on the business logic (and also the factory and the tracing interface through its inheritance). The factory is the only class dependent on concrete classes. You can further enhance the factory class to use reflection to load the correct class (configuration-driven instantiation), also rendering it indirectly dependent on the concrete classes.

Why did we complicate our simple one class code? We did that for the sake of better design; the new design follows the SOLID principal. The classes are small and loosely coupled yet cohesive. There is no direct dependency to concrete classes, which means unit testing our business logic is much easier. Given that the actual plugin has been simplified and that it delegates most of the work to the business logic, which enables us to convert our plugin to something else. For example, we can change it to a unit test to test our business logic without using the Dynamics 365 user interface by simply injecting a live Dynamics 365 DAL. Alternatively, we can easily convert a plugin into a custom workflow activity (as described in the *Converting your plugin into a custom workflow activity* recipe later in this chapter).

> TIP
>
> Be pragmatic when refactoring your code. If your project has only a couple of small plugins, this may be an overkill. However, if your instance is heavily customized, then this design ensures consistency in your code, clean unit testable classes, and significant minimization of code duplication through reusability.
>
> Keep in mind that layering introduces abstraction; if you are writing a pre-update plugin that requires a close interaction with pre-images, make sure you deal with the object appropriately between your layers; otherwise, you might lose context details through the abstraction.

There's more...

When extending Dynamics 365, don't be afraid of using industry best practices to enhance your code. Whether you are extending the platform using .NET code, JavaScript, or any other means, code quality rules apply. This recipe covers a basic refactoring example. You can further enhance your code to suit your scenario.

For example, if you have a few plugins that do more or less the same thing with some minor differences (for example, case management automation with different case types), you can create a class hierarchy of business logic with a business layer factory class to choose and instantiate the appropriate class.

> TIP: The Dynamics 365 Developer Toolkit contains a default abstract **PluginBase** that can also be used in lieu of the one mentioned in this recipe.

Another common example is the usage of interfaces for entities. When entities are generated using `CrmSvcUtil`, all classes are created as partial classes (you can create a separate C# partial class to augment these classes). In the *Modeling normalized entities using two different entities* recipe from `Chapter 1`, *No Code Extensions*, we ended up with redundant attributes between the two entity types. If your business logic deals with only the common attributes, you can create a common interface between those entities and rely on polymorphism to pass any of the two to your business logic.

See also

- The *Creating early bound entity classes* recipe of `Chapter 3`, *SDK Enterprise Capabilities*
- The *Creating your first plugin* recipe of `Chapter 4`, *Server-Side Extensions*

Replacing your LINQ data access layer with QueryExpressions

Given that we have refactored our plugin in the previous recipe, we will now demonstrate how easy it is to swap a concrete DAL class with an alternative implementation.

In this recipe, we will replace the LINQ `EmailDataAccessLayer` implementation with a `QueryExpression` implementation. We will also drop the unit of the work design pattern and use `IOrganizationService` instead of `OrganisationServiceContext`.

Getting ready

To implement this recipe, we will need the existing code structure from the previous recipe. If you are starting from scratch, you can follow the code structure from the previous recipe and replace the implementation with your own code.

As with any recipe that deals with C# code, it is strongly recommended that you use a stable version of Visual Studio. In our example, we will be using Visual Studio 2015.

How to do it...

1. Create a new public class called `EmailDataAccessLayerQueryExpression` in the `DataAccessLayer` folder that inherits from `BaseDataAccessLayer` and implements `IEmailDataAccessLayer`:

```
public class EmailDataAccessLayerQueryExpression :
BaseDataAccessLayer, IEmailDataAccessLayer
```

2. Add the following `using` statements to the default ones:

```
using Microsoft.Xrm.Sdk;
using Packt.Xrm.Entities;
using Microsoft.Xrm.Sdk.Query;
using Microsoft.Crm.Sdk.Messages;
```

3. Create a constructor that takes `IOrganizationService` and calls the base constructor:

```
public EmailDataAccessLayerQueryExpression(IOrganizationService
organizationService) : base(organizationService)
```

4. Override the `UpdateEntity` method to use `OrganizationService`:

```
public override void UpdateEntity(Entity entity)
{
    OrganizationService.Update(entity);
}
```

5. Override the `Commit` method to have no implementation:

```
public override void Commit()
{
}
```

6. Implement the `CloseEmailAsCancelled` method to use `OrganizationService`:

```
public void CloseEmailAsCancelled(Email email)
{
    email.StateCode = EmailState.Canceled;

    var setStateRequest = new SetStateRequest()
    {
       Status = new OptionSetValue((int)email_statuscode.Canceled),
       State = new OptionSetValue((int)EmailState.Canceled),
       EntityMoniker = new EntityReference(Email.EntityLogicalName,
          email.Id)
    };
    OrganizationService.Execute(setStateRequest);
}
```

7. Implement the `GetEmails` method to use `QueryExpression`:

```
public IEnumerable<Email> GetEmails(Guid parentEntityId)
{
    var queryExpression = new QueryExpression()
    {
        EntityName = Email.EntityLogicalName,
        ColumnSet = new ColumnSet( "subject"),
        Criteria =
        {
            Filters =
                {
                    new FilterExpression
                    {
                        FilterOperator = LogicalOperator.And,
                        Conditions =
                        {
                            new
ConditionExpression("regardingobjectid", ConditionOperator.Equal,
parentEntityId),
                            new ConditionExpression("statecode",
ConditionOperator.Equal, (int)EmailState.Open)
                        },
                    }
```

```
                }
            }
        };

        var entityCollection =
    OrganizationService.RetrieveMultiple(queryExpression);
        return entityCollection.Entities.Select(e =>
    e.ToEntity<Email>()).ToList();
    }
```

8. Update the `GetEmailDataAccessLayer` method in `DataAccessLayerFactory` to return an instance of the newly created `EmailDataAccessLayerQueryExpression` object:

```
    public IEmailDataAccessLayer GetEmailDataAccessLayer()
    {
        if (_emailDataAccessLayer == null)
            _emailDataAccessLayer = new
    EmailDataAccessLayerQueryExpression(_organisationService);

        return _emailDataAccessLayer;
    }
```

How it works...

We started this recipe by implementing a new class that inherits from the base DAL class and implements the `IEmailDAL` interface.

We implemented the required methods using the alternative design, but we also overrode some of the base class methods that did not quite work with our implementation. More specifically, in step 4, we used `OrganizationService` instead of `OrganizationServiceContext`. In step 5, given that we are not using `OrganizationServiceContext`, there was no need to have an implementation for the `Commit` method. The business logic will still call it, but the call is redundant. Nonetheless, the business logic correctness remains intact.

In step 7, we used the `QueryExpression` class along with `OrganizationService RetrieveMultiple` to retrieve the records we are interested in. Note how we filtered the number of returned columns to the ones we are interested in.

> **TIP:** It is always good practice to limit the number of columns retrieved in order to improve performance. Nonetheless, don't be afraid to return a few more if you want to render your method more reusable.

In step 8, we finally updated our factory class to return an instance of the newly created class.

Note how we didn't change anything in the plugin or the business logic. This is mainly due to the fact that these classes are not coupled with any concrete implementations. The plugin has a layer of separation to the DAL as it only cares about the business logic and the factory class. The business logic is only reliant on the interfaces; it does not care how the classes are implemented as long as they follow the same interface signature. This follows the Liskov substitution principle (**L** in the SOLID principle).

There's more...

The purpose of this recipe is to highlight how easy it is to replace a portion of your code in a few steps without affecting the rest of your application. Although we replaced a concrete implementation with another concrete implementation, this might not be a common scenario. That said, the ability to replace a concrete implementation with a mock or a stub, without altering the integrity of your code, is of high value when you are trying to unit test your application, as we will see in *Unit testing your plugin business logic* later in this chapter.

The replacement doesn't necessarily have to be limited to the data access layers connecting to Dynamics 365; we can also implement substitutions in the plugin input entry level (as demonstrated in this chapter in *Unit testing your plugin with an in-memory context*), at the tracing layer (as demonstrated in the next recipe *Logging error from your customization*), or even the business logic itself.

See also

- *Refactoring your plugin using a three-layer pattern*
- *Logging error from your customization*
- *Unit testing your plugin business logic*

Logging error from your customization

Now that we have refactored our code to allow dependency injection, we can implement a custom login library to log details using a mechanism different from the Dynamics 365 `ITracingService` interface.

In this recipe, we will implement a custom logging library that logs to both the Dynamics 365 `ITracingService` interface as well as a CRM entity, which in turn writes to an Azure Service Bus.

Getting ready

Since we are building on top of an already layered code, we will be reusing the refactored plugin from the first recipe in this chapter, *Refactoring your plugin using a three-layer pattern*. Alternatively, you can start from scratch. If you are building your own plugin, follow the steps from the first recipe to mimic a structure similar to ours.

From an Azure perspective, you will need an existing Azure Service Bus queue, as described in `Chapter 5`, *External Integration, Setting up an Azure Service Bus endpoint*. You will need the plugin registration tool to set up the step that will write to your Azure Service Bus queue.

From a Dynamics 365 perspective, you will need an entity to hold the logs. We created one called `packt_log` that contains a multiple lines text field called `packt_logdetails`. Your user must have created access to this entity. Make sure you also have the correct privileges (**System Customizer** or higher) to deploy and run your plugin successfully.

Finally, similar to previous development recipes, you will need a compatible Visual Studio IDE. We will be using Visual Studio 2015.

How to do it...

1. Under the `DataAccessLayer` folder, create a new public class called `AzureCrmTracing` that implements `ICustomTracingService`.
2. Add the following `using` statements:

```
using Microsoft.Xrm.Sdk;
```

3. Add the following `private` instance variables:

```
IOrganizationService _organizationService;
ITracingService _tracing;
```

4. Add the following constructor:

```
public AzureCrmTracing(IOrganizationService organizationService,
ITracingService tracing)
{
    _organizationService = organizationService;
    _tracing = tracing;
}
```

5. Implement the following method required by the interface:

```
public void Trace(string message, params object[] args)
{
    _tracing.Trace(message, args);

    var entity = new Entity("packt_log");
    entity.Attributes["packt_logdetails"] = string.Format(message,
args);
    _organizationService.Create(entity);
}
```

6. Change the `GetTracingService` method in your `DataAccessLayerFactory` class to return the newly created class:

```
public ICustomTracingService GetTracingService()
{
    if (_customTracingService == null)
        _customTracingService = new
AzureCrmTracing(_organisationService, _tracingService);

    return _customTracingService;
}
```

7. Deploy your updated custom plugin using the plugin registration tool.

8. Using the plugin registration tool again, register a **Create** step named `packt_log` on your Azure endpoint. Make sure **Asynchronous** is selected and leave the rest as default, as shown here:

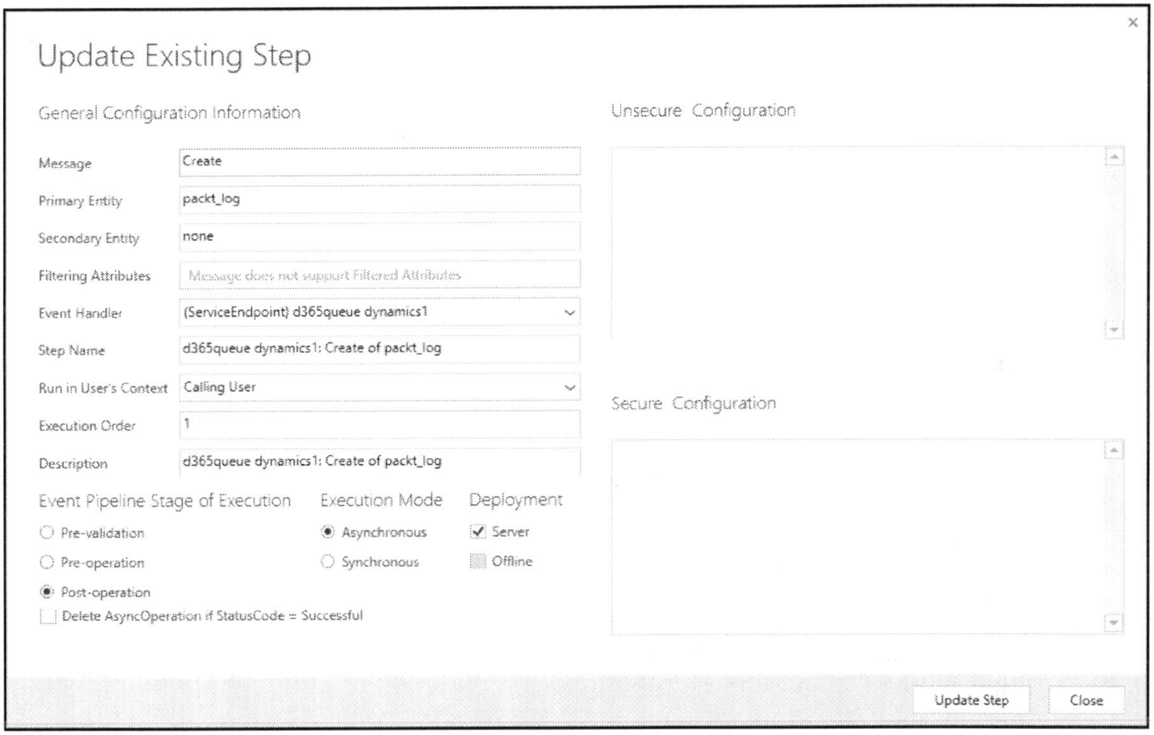

How it works...

The first few steps in this recipe focused on building a new concrete class that implements `ICustomTracingService`. The class's constructor takes both `IOrganizationService` and `ITracingService` as we will be writing to the conventional Dynamics 365 tracing logs, as well as creating a new record in a log entity. The `Trace` method in step 5 does most of the work. We opted to use late binding in this example, but you can also opt for early binding.

In step 6, we reimplemented the `GetTracingService` method in the factory class to return the new tracing class.

In step 7, we deployed our changes to Dynamics 365 (for more details on how to deploy, refer to `Chapter 4`, *Server-Side Extensions, Deploying your customization using the plugin registration tool*).

Finally, in the last step, we registered a new `packt_log` create step to our endpoint, which will write the context to the Azure Service Bus endpoint.

> It is important to note that this technique will have a major performance impact. Creating records synchronously is an expensive operation and can very quickly reach the plugin execution 2 minute timeout limit. Use this in exceptional cases only.

There's more...

We did not cover any steps to consume the messages from the Azure Service Bus in this recipe. The steps to consume the message would be similar to what we described in the *Consuming messages from an Azure Service Bus* recipe of `Chapter 5`, *External Integration*. The log message can be retrieved from the target entity included in the context using the following line:

```
((Entity)result.InputParameters["Target"]).Attributes["packt_logdetails
"]
```

Furthermore, the messages can be reformatted and stored in a Cosmos DB NoSQL database, as described in *Build a generic read audit plugin*.

See also

- The *Consuming messages from an Azure Service Bus* recipe of `Chapter 5`, *External Integration*
- *Building a generic read audit plugin*

Converting your plugin into a custom workflow activity

Now that we have a layered flexible plugin implementation that has loosely coupled components, we will demonstrate how easy it is to reuse the core of our plugin and convert it into a custom workflow activity.

In the first recipe of this chapter, we converted our one class plugin into a three-tiered plugin. The plugin entry point was refactored into two classes: an abstract base plugin class that does most of the work and a specific concrete implementation that instantiates the required business logic, injects the required data access layers, and calls the correct business logic method.

In this recipe we will implement a similar design for a custom workflow activity and reuse the plugin's business logic.

Getting ready

Since we will be reusing an existing plugin and converting it into a custom workflow activity, we will need the refactored plugin from *Refactoring your plugin using a three-layer pattern* in this chapter. Alternatively, you can start writing your own custom workflow activity from scratch; in which case, follow the layering examples from the first recipe in this chapter from step 1 to step 31. Make sure you reference the `Microsoft.CrmSdk.Workflow` NuGet package in your solution. As per most of the custom code recipes, we will be using Visual Studio 2015 to implement the changes.

How to do it...

1. Add a reference to the `Microsoft.CrmSdk.Workflow` NuGet package.
2. Create a new folder in your Visual Studio solution called `CustomWorkflow`.
3. Create a new abstract class called `BaseCustomWorkflow` that inherits from `CodeActivity`:

```
public abstract class BaseCustomWorkflow : CodeActivity
```

4. Add the following `using` statements:

```
using Microsoft.Xrm.Sdk;
using System.ServiceModel;
using Microsoft.Xrm.Sdk.Workflow;
using Packt.Xrm.Extensions.DataAccessLayer;
using System.Activities;
```

5. Add the following `protected` instance variables:

```
protected IOrganizationService OrganizationService;
protected ICustomTracingService CustomTracingService;
protected DataAccessLayerFactory DataAccessLayerFactory;
protected IWorkflowContext WorkflowContext;
```

6. Add the following `abstract` method:

```
public abstract void PostExecute(CodeActivityContext
executionContext);
```

7. Add the following `Execute` method:

```
protected override void Execute(CodeActivityContext
   executionContext)
{
   var serviceFactory =
     executionContext.GetExtension<IOrganizationServiceFactory>();
   var tracingService =
     executionContext.GetExtension<ITracingService>();
   WorkflowContext =
     executionContext.GetExtension<IWorkflowContext>();
   OrganizationService =
serviceFactory.CreateOrganizationService(WorkflowContext.UserId);
    try
    {
      using (DataAccessLayerFactory = new
        DataAccessLayerFactory(OrganizationService,
tracingService))
      {
         CustomTracingService =
           DataAccessLayerFactory.GetTracingService();

            PostExecute(executionContext);
       }
    }
    catch (FaultException<OrganizationServiceFault> ex)
    {
```

```
            throw new InvalidPluginExecutionException("An error occurred
              in the UpdateActivities plug-in.", ex);
        }
        catch (Exception ex)
        {
            CustomTracingService.Trace("FollowupPlugin: {0}",
               ex.ToString());
            throw;
        }
    }
```

8. In the same `CustomWorkflow` folder, create a new public class called `UpdateEmailsWorkflowActivity` that inherits from `BaseCustomWorkflow`.
9. Add the following `using` statements:

```
using System.Activities;
using Microsoft.Xrm.Sdk.Workflow;
using Packt.Xrm.Extensions.BusinessLogic;
```

10. Add the following workflow in the argument:

```
[Input("Account Guid")]
[Default("00000000-0000-0000-0000-000000000000")]
public InArgument<string> AccountGuid { get; set; }
```

11. Add the following `PostExecute` method:

```
public override void PostExecute(CodeActivityContext
  executionContext)
{
    var input = AccountGuid.Get<string>(executionContext);
    var accountId = input ==
      Guid.Empty.ToString().Trim('{').Trim('}') ?
      WorkflowContext.PrimaryEntityId : Guid.Parse(input);
      CustomTracingService.Trace("Input value {0}", input);

    var updateEmailLogic = new
UpdateEmailLogic(DataAccessLayerFactory.GetEmailDataAccessLayer(),
      CustomTracingService);
    updateEmailLogic.UpdateAccountsEmails(accountId);
}
```

How it works...

Although it took us 11 steps to implement this structure, once the class hierarchy is there, it would only take us one step to create a new custom workflow activity. All we need is one class that inherits from `BaseCustomWorkflow` with a few lines of code to reuse the business logic code.

Similar to the *Refactoring your plugin using a three-layer pattern* recipe earlier in this chapter, we refactored our workflow entry into two classes: an abstract class that contains most of the generic reusable workflow routines (`BaseCustomWorkflow` step 3 to step 7) and a concrete specialized class (`UpdateEmailsWorkflowActivity` step 8 to step 11).

Similar to our abstract plugin base class, in step 6, we created a `PostExecute` method to override in our concrete class to which we passed the execution context. This pattern is slightly different from using protected variables. We passed the context as we only expect the scope of the context to be used within the `PostExcute` method. The workflow context is required to extract the input variables, as demonstrated in step 11.

Step 7 looks very similar to our refactored abstract plugin base; we extracted all the reusable common workflow bits into the parent class. The execute method deals with the DAL factory, extracts the common objects from the context, and deals with exception handling. The execute method calls the abstract `PostExecute` method, which is implemented in the concrete class.

Again, our concrete workflow child class looks very similar to our concrete plugin. The only difference is that we had to define an input variable in step 10 and retrieve its value in step 11. The rest of step 11 looks similar to our plugin, where we instantiated the business logic by injecting the concrete DAL from the factory, followed by calling the correct business logic method.

There's more...

The refactoring can be developed a bit more by extracting other useful values from the workflow context and implementing some more reusable functions in the base class. However, this was not necessary for our scenario.

TIP

Follow the **YAGNI** principle: **You aren't gonna need it**. Keep your classes simple and start by only implementing only what you need. If new scenarios appear, add more as required. With simplicity comes ease of readability, which equates to ease of maintenance, improved performance (due to the lack of layering overhead), improved reliability (as you are not introducing potential defects related to the unnecessary code), and your code will be faster and cheaper to implement, among other qualities.
As per the plugin, `Development Toolkit` also includes an abstract workflow base class that can be reused.

Note how we have two ways of extracting the primary entity's GUID in step 11. The first scenario, `WorkflowContext.PrimaryEntityId`, caters for a custom workflow activity. The second (where the input holds the GUID) caters for custom action. Not only did we refactor our plugin into a workflow activity, but we also catered for this activity to be converted into an action (as described in *Creating your first custom action* in `Chapter 4`, *Server-Side Extensions*).

As mentioned in the first recipe of this chapter, we can further change the entry point into a console application that accepts a GUID parameter, effectively turning the code into a portable smoke test executable. We can also integrate the business logic into a unit test (as described in the next recipe, *Unit testing your plugin business logic*).

See also

- *Refactoring your plugin using a three-layer pattern*
- *Unit testing your plugin business logic*
- The *Creating your first custom workflow activity* recipe of `Chapter 4`, *Server-Side Extensions*
- The *Creating your first custom action* recipe of `Chapter 4`, *Server-Side Extensions*

Unit testing your plugin business logic

Another byproduct of refactoring our code is rendering it unit-testing friendly. Separating the layers, especially the data access layer and the plugin entry, means that we now have a true business logic layer that is independent from connections to other systems. We can unit test this business logic as a standalone layer.

In our unit test, we will focus on behavior verification as opposed to state verification.

This unit test will not focus on the state of the records but rather verify that the correct methods were called the expected number of times and with the right parameters. We will follow the **AAA** pattern (**Arrange**, **Act**, **Assert**).

For a state verification unit test, look at the next recipe, *Unit testing your plugin with in-memory context*.

We will unit test the plugin business logic from the first recipe in this chapter. We will mock the `IEmailDataAccessLayer` DAL to return predefined values when the `GetEmails` method is called. We will stub `ICustomTracingService` as we don't really care about what it does. We only need to verify that the business logic calls it correctly and passes the correct parameters.

Getting ready

Since we will be unit testing the business logic of the refactored plugin from the *Refactoring your plugin using a three-layer pattern* recipe from this chapter, we will need the code from that recipe. More specifically, we will need the business logic, the data access layer interfaces, and the generated Dynamics 365 entities (the domain). Our unit test will use the out-of-the-box Visual Studio unit testing capabilities, so you will need a recent stable version of Visual Studio. In this instance, we will be using Visual Studio 2015. For stubbing and mocking, we will be relying on `Moq`, which is a commonly used mocking framework that has been around for a while and receives ongoing support.

Optionally, a certain degree of familiarity with unit testing is recommended to help you follow this recipe.

How to do it...

1. Create a new unit test project under your existing solution called `Packt.Xrm.UnitTest`.
2. Add a reference to the `Moq` NuGet package as well as `Microsoft.CrmSdk.CoreAssemblies`.
3. Add a reference to your existing `Packt.Xrm.Extensions` (refactored) project.
4. Create a new Basic Unit Test class called `EmailUpdateBusinessLogicTest`.

5. Add the following `using` statements:

```
using Packt.Xrm.Extensions.BusinessLogic;
using Packt.Xrm.Extensions.DataAccessLayer;
using Moq;
using Packt.Xrm.Entities;
using Microsoft.Xrm.Sdk;
using System.Collections.Generic;
```

6. Add the following `private` instance variables:

```
private Mock<IEmailDataAccessLayer> _emailDalMock;
private Mock<ICustomTracingService> _tracing;
```

7. Create a private `SetupMocks` method with the following implementation:

```
private void SetupMocks()
{
  _emailDalMock = new Mock<IEmailDataAccessLayer>();
  _emailDalMock.Setup(dal => dal.GetEmails(It.IsAny<Guid>
    ())).Returns(
       new List<Email>() { new Email() { Subject = "sample1"},
       new Email { Subject = "sample2" },
       new Email { Subject = string.Empty }  }
        );
    _tracing = new Mock<ICustomTracingService>();
}
```

8. Create a `TestUpdateEmail` test method with the following implementation:

```
[TestMethod]
public void TestUpdateEmail()
{
    //Arrange
    SetupMocks();

    var businessLogic = new UpdateEmailLogic(_emailDalMock.Object,
_tracing.Object);

    //Act
    businessLogic.UpdateAccountsEmails(Guid.NewGuid());

    //Assert
    _emailDalMock.Verify(dal =>
dal.CloseEmailAsCancelled(It.IsAny<Email>()), Times.Exactly(1));
    _emailDalMock.Verify(dal =>
dal.UpdateEntity(It.IsAny<Entity>()), Times.Exactly(2));
```

```
            _tracing.Verify(trace => trace.Trace("{0} closed emails and {1}
        updated emails", 1, 2), Times.Exactly(1));
        }
```

How it works...

The first few steps of this recipe focused on setting up our unit test class. In step 6, we declared the classes we are mocking as private instance variables. Note how we only used interfaces as we don't really care about their concrete implementations; we focused on their signatures.

In step 7, we defined the stubs and mocks of our data access layer classes. `IEmailDataAccessLayer` gets its `GetEmails` method mocked; given any GUID input, the method returns three e-mails; two with a subject and one without. We then stubbed `ICustomTracingService` to provide us with an empty `Trace` method.

In step 8, we build our unit test. Unit tests are targeted tests. This test only focuses on the `UpdateEmailLogic` method and its behavior. We started by *arranging* our test, by instantiating `UpdateEmailLogic` and injecting the mocked and stubbed classes in its constructor, leveraging the dependency injection pattern we introduced in *Refactoring your plugin using a three-layer pattern* earlier in this chapter. We then *acted* and called the business logic's `UpdateAccountsEmails` with a randomly generated GUID. In the last steps, we *asserted* that the `CloseEmailAsCancelled` stubbed method is called exactly once, and the `UpdateEntity` method is called exactly two times as expected, based on the mock `GetEmails` returned objects. We also verify that the `Trace` method is called once with the correct message parameter.

There's more...

This recipe covers a typical behavioral unit test to make sure that your class's structure is correct. Different schools of thought have different opinions on how to unit test your code. Some might argue that you shouldn't know the internals of your class when unit testing. Without going too much into the broader unit testing debate, this recipe is here to illustrate the refactoring advantages and the structure of your code/unit testing. You can easily build other unit tests to verify your object's states, exception handling, and, as we will see in the next recipe, your data access layer's LINQ queries.

Regarding the choice of `Moq`: as we mentioned in the introduction, `Moq` is an easy-to-use mocking framework that has been around for a long time and is constantly being supported. There are many mocking frameworks out there that you can choose from, including Visual Studio fakes. If you want to know more about the power of `Moq`, visit `https://github.com/Moq/moq4/wiki/Quickstart`.

In this recipe, we touched on mocks and stubs and we also talked about behavioral verification as opposed to state verification. If you want to know more about the types of unit testing, and the different ways in which you can mock/stub your classes, read the timeless Martin Fowler article *Mocks Aren't Stubs* at `https://martinfowler.com/articles/mocksArentStubs.html`.

See also

- *Refactoring your plugin using a three-layer pattern*
- *Unit testing your plugin entry point with an in-memory context*

Unit testing your plugin with an in-memory context

When you are developing a plugin, you would often want to test your customization. If you have an on-premise instance, debugging your code is more or less straight forward. If you have an online instance, you can leverage the new plugin log capabilities or replay your plugin using the plugin registration tool, as described in *Profiling your plugin* later in this chapter.

If you try to integrate test your plugin with a live connection to your Dynamics 365 instance, then you will be penalized with a significant execution time that might quickly eat up the best practice 30 seconds timeframe to run all your unit tests. The best option is to rely on in-memory processing only.

In this recipe, we will unit test our plugin end-to-end as if it was triggered from Dynamics 365. The plugin will not connect to a live Dynamics 365 instance; instead, we will fake an in-memory repository. The unit test will focus on state verification as opposed to behavior verification.

We will use the XrmUnitTest framework (`https://github.com/daryllabar/XrmUnitTest`), created by Microsoft's Business Solutions MVP Daryl LaBar, to help us fake the organization service.

We will start by setting up our in-memory Dynamics 365 mock with testing data. We will then change the state of the record by executing the plugin. Finally, we will retrieve the records from our in-memory repository to assert that the plugin is doing its job.

Getting ready

To get going, we will need the refactored code from the *Refactoring your plugin using a three-layer pattern* recipe earlier in this chapter. This version of our code uses the `CrmTracing` concrete implementation of `ICustomTracingService` and the `EmailDataAccessLayer` concrete implementation of `IEmailDataAccessLayer`. We chose `EmailDataAccessLayer` instead of `EmailDataAccessLayerQueryExpression` since the faking framework will leverage `OrganisationServiceContext` for all CRUD operations and actually execute our LINQ queries through an in-memory context.

As with the previous unit testing recipes, we will be using the out-of-the-box Visual Studio unit testing framework, so you will need a recent version of Visual Studio. In this instance, we used Visual Studio 2015. Furthermore, we will leverage the `Moq` framework to mock the classes we are not interested in. As described in the introduction, we will also utilize the XrmUnitTest framework to fake the organization service.

How to do it...

1. Add a new Basic Unit Test class called `InMemoryEmailUpdateTest.cs` to your unit test project.
2. Add a reference to the following NuGet packages:
    - `Microsoft.CrmSdk.CoreAssemblies`
    - `XrmUnitTest.2016`
    - `Moq`
3. Ensure that you have a reference to the `Packt.Xrm.Extensions` project.

4. Add the following `using` statements:

```
using Packt.Xrm.Extensions.Plugin;
using Moq;
using Microsoft.Xrm.Sdk;
using Packt.Xrm.Entities;
using DLaB.Xrm.LocalCrm;
using DLaB.Xrm.Test;
```

5. Add the following `private` instance variables:

```
private const int NumberOfDaysDifference = 10;
private IServiceProvider _serviceProvider;
private Mock<ITracingService> _tracingMock;
private IOrganizationService _organizationServiceFake;
private Guid _email1Guid;
private Guid _email2Guid;
private Guid _email3Guid;
```

6. Add the following private `SetupMock` method to set up your fakes and mocks:

```
private void SetupMock()
{
    var serviceProviderMock = new Mock<IServiceProvider>();
    _tracingMock = new Mock<ITracingService>();

    _organizationServiceFake = new
LocalCrmDatabaseOrganizationService(LocalCrmDatabaseInfo.Create<Org
anisationServiceContext>());
    var accountGuid = _organizationServiceFake.Create(new Account()
{ Name = "Packt Test" });
    _email1Guid = _organizationServiceFake.Create(new Email() {
Subject = "Mock 1", RegardingObjectId = new
EntityReference(Account.EntityLogicalName, accountGuid) });
    _email2Guid = _organizationServiceFake.Create(new Email() {
Subject = "Mock 2", RegardingObjectId = new
EntityReference(Account.EntityLogicalName, accountGuid) });
    _email3Guid = _organizationServiceFake.Create(new Email() {
Subject = string.Empty, RegardingObjectId = new
EntityReference(Account.EntityLogicalName, accountGuid) });

    var pluginContextMock = new Mock<IPluginExecutionContext>();
    var parameterCollection = new ParameterCollection();
    parameterCollection.Add("Target", new Account() { Id =
accountGuid });
    pluginContextMock.Setup(c =>
c.InputParameters).Returns(parameterCollection);
    var organisationServicefactoryMock = new
```

```
Mock<IOrganizationServiceFactory>();
    organisationServicefactoryMock.Setup(f =>
f.CreateOrganizationService(It.IsAny<Guid>())).Returns(_organizatio
nServiceFake);
    serviceProviderMock.Setup(sp =>
sp.GetService(typeof(ITracingService))).Returns(_tracingMock.Object
);
    serviceProviderMock.Setup(sp =>
sp.GetService(typeof(IPluginExecutionContext))).Returns(pluginConte
xtMock.Object);
    serviceProviderMock.Setup(sp =>
sp.GetService(typeof(IOrganizationServiceFactory))).Returns(organis
ationServicefactoryMock.Object);

    _serviceProvider = serviceProviderMock.Object;
}
```

7. Create the following test method:

```
[TestMethod]
[TestCategory("InMemory")]
public void Fake()
{
   //Arrange
   SetupMock();

   var plugin = new UpdateActivity();
   //Act
   plugin.Execute(_serviceProvider);

   //Assert
   Assert.AreEqual(EmailState.Open,
   _organizationServiceFake.GetEntity(new Id<Email>
   (_email1Guid)).StateCode);
   Assert.AreEqual(DateTime.Now.Date.AddDays
   (NumberOfDaysDifference), _organizationServiceFake.GetEntity
   (new Id<Email>(_email1Guid)).ScheduledStart,
   "Start date not updated correctly for emails with a subject");
   Assert.AreEqual(EmailState.Open,
   _organizationServiceFake.GetEntity(new Id<Email>
   (_email2Guid)).StateCode);
   Assert.AreEqual(DateTime.Now.Date.AddDays
   (NumberOfDaysDifference),
   _organizationServiceFake.GetEntity(new Id<Email>
   (_email2Guid)).ScheduledStart, "Start date not updated
   correctly for emails with a subject");
   Assert.AreEqual(EmailState.Canceled,
   _organizationServiceFake.GetEntity(new Id<Email>
```

```
        (_email3Guid)).StateCode,  "Email without a subject was not
        cancelled");
    }
```

8. Run your unit test in debug mode.

How it works...

Similar to the previous recipe, *Unit testing your plugin business logic*, we started by setting up our unit test class with the correct references.

In step 6, we built our mocks. We mocked `IServiceProvider` to return stubs and mocks for all services we are interested in. More specifically, the organization service is actually an in-memory service generated using the XrmUnitTest framework that leverages the structure from our previously generated class `OrganisationServiceContext` (to generate a context using `CrmSvcUtil`, look at *Creating early bound entity classes* recipe of `Chapter 3`, *SDK Enterprise Capabilities*). The context informs the framework about what schema structure to create in-memory. Any records queried or updated later in our test, needs to be defined in the context. We also populated some data in the fake organization service to use in the business logic. We kept a reference to the e-mail GUIDS to query them during the assert step.

In step 7, we again used the AAA pattern. In the act section, the plugin execution method is called with our prebuilt `IServiceProvider` (mimicking how plugins are called from Dynamics 365). The plugin executes a LINQ query in `EmailDataAccessLayer`,which returns the in-memory records. The plugin also calls and updates the records, which are updated in the in-memory organization service.

Finally, in the assert section, we queried the in-memory organization service and ensured the records' states have been updated as expected.

When we run our unit test in the debug mode, we can intercept every line of our code and inspect the values.

One of the many advantages of using an in-memory organization service is that the object is created at the start of your test and discarded at the end. There is no need to clean up every time you finish testing (unlike when you are connected to a live instance, as described in the next recipe, *Integration testing your plugin end-to-end*).

What we ended up with is a fast, repeatable, independent, disconnected unit test that runs a plugin as a black box and asserts its behavior. Given its disconnected nature, we don't have to deploy our plugin to Dynamics 365 while testing it.

There's more...

XrmUnitTest is a very powerful framework capable of much more than faking an in-memory organization service. Daryl LaBar explains in his video (`https://www.youtube.com/watch?v=dRz1X6pdsk4`) how you can use the framework to switch between an in-memory context and the actual live connection to Dynamics 365, and much more. The framework does have its limitations and LaBar covers a few of them in his video.

Other alternatives to the XrmUnitTest framework are Microsoft's Business Solutions MVP Jordi Montaña's Fake Xrm Easy `https://github.com/jordimontana82/fake-xrm-easy` and out-of-the-box Visual Studio fakes. Note that using Visual Studio fakes doesn't cater for an in-memory context, but rather mocks the results.

This recipe covered end-to-end plugin testing without a Dynamics 365 connection. Alternatively, you can deploy and test your plugin in Dynamics 365 (as described in *Integration testing your plugin end-to-end*). Another option is to simply establish an organization service connection to a live Dynamics 365 (as described in *Connecting to Dynamics 365 from other systems using .NET* from `Chapter 5`, *External Integration*) to inject into a data access layer which you then inject into your business logic. The advantage of the latter option is that you are still debugging the core of your plugin locally (since the entry point has been refactored to only call the business logic) without deploying it to your instance, but with a live Dynamics 365 connection.

See also

- *Refactoring your plugin using a three-layer pattern*
- *Unit testing your plugin business logic*
- *Integration testing your plugin end-to-end*
- *Profiling your plugin*

Integration testing your plugin end-to-end

In this recipe we will write an integration test to verify our plugin correctness. We will replicate the user-driven triggers (usually done through the user interface) using the Dynamics 365 APIs. We will also create the records we are testing, and we change the state of the record. Then, we will verify that the synchronous plugin triggered and executed the expected business logic.

Integration tests like these are valuable when implementing server-side extensions on your Dynamics 365 instance. You will often find yourself changing your plugin, redeploying it, and testing your changes manually. You can automate the last step using the API to streamline the testing part without relying on the web UI.

Getting ready

Here we will run the integration test on the first plugin created in the *Creating your first plugin* recipe in `Chapter 4`, *Server-Side Extensions*. You can also run the test on the refactored plugin described in *Refactoring your plugin using a three-layer pattern* found earlier in this chapter.

The integration test will be written in the form of a unit test, therefore requiring a Visual Studio unit test project. We will leverage the unit test project created in this chapter's *Unit testing your plugin business logic* recipe that uses Visual Studio 2015 and its native unit testing framework.

When running your unit test, make sure your connection string's user has the correct privileges to create and update the necessary records. If you opt to tidy up after the unit test, you will need additional delete privileges. Best practice dictates that you should tidy up the test records, unless you are planning on resetting your environment later.

How to do it...

1. Add a new Basic Unit Test class called `EmailUpdateIntegrationTest.cs` to your unit test project.
2. Add a reference to the `Microsoft.CrmSdk.XrmTooling.CoreAssembly` NuGet package to your solution.
3. Add reference to the `Packt.Xrm.Extensions` project (if not already referenced) and the `System.Configuration` assembly.

4. Add the following `using` statements:

```
using Microsoft.Xrm.Sdk;
using Microsoft.Xrm.Tooling.Connector;
using Packt.Xrm.Entities;
using Microsoft.Xrm.Sdk.Query;
using System.Configuration;
```

5. Add the following `private` instance variables:

```
private IOrganizationService _service;
private Guid? _accountGuid;
private Guid? _email1Guid;
private Guid? _email2Guid;
private Guid? _email3Guid;
private const int NumberOfDaysDifference = 10;
```

6. Add the following `EstablishConnection` method to connect:

```
public void EstablishConnection()
{
    var connectionString =
ConfigurationManager.AppSettings["Dynamics365ConnectionString"];
    var _crmSvc = new CrmServiceClient(connectionString);

    _service = _crmSvc.OrganizationServiceProxy;
}
```

7. Create a `private static` method to create e-mail records:

```
private static Email CreateEmail(Guid accountGuid, string
emailSubject)
{
    return new Email()
    {
        RegardingObjectId = new
EntityReference(Account.EntityLogicalName, accountGuid),
        Subject = emailSubject,
        ScheduledStart = DateTime.Now,
        StateCode = EmailState.Open
    };
}
```

8. Create a `private` method to retrieve e-mails:

```
private Email RetrieveEmail(Guid emailGuid)
{
    return _service.Retrieve(Email.EntityLogicalName, emailGuid,
new ColumnSet("scheduledstart", "statecode")).ToEntity<Email>();
}
```

9. Create a `private` method to create an account with three e-mails attached to it:

```
private void CreateRecords()
{
    var account = new Account()
    {
        Name = "Sample Test"
    };

    _accountGuid = _service.Create(account);

    _email1Guid = _service.Create(CreateEmail(_accountGuid.Value,
"Subject 1"));
    _email2Guid = _service.Create(CreateEmail(_accountGuid.Value,
"Subject 2"));
    _email3Guid = _service.Create(CreateEmail(_accountGuid.Value,
string.Empty));
}
```

10. Create your test method and decorate it with an integration test category and `TestMethod` attributes:

```
[TestMethod]
[TestCategory("Integration")]
public void TestMethod1()
{
    //Arrange
    EstablishConnection();
    CreateRecords();

    //Act
    var account = new Account()
    {
        Id = _accountGuid.Value,
        Name = "Sample Test Updated"
    };
    _service.Update(account);

    //Assert
```

```
    var email1 = RetrieveEmail(_email1Guid.Value);
    Assert.AreEqual(EmailState.Open, email1.StateCode);
    Assert.AreEqual(DateTime.Now.Date.AddDays
(NumberOfDaysDifference).ToUniversalTime(), email1.ScheduledStart,
"Start date not updated correctly for emails with a subject");

    var email2 = RetrieveEmail(_email2Guid.Value);
    Assert.AreEqual(EmailState.Open, email2.StateCode);
    Assert.AreEqual(DateTime.Now.Date.AddDays
(NumberOfDaysDifference).ToUniversalTime(), email2.ScheduledStart,
"Start date not updated correctly for emails with a subject");

    var email3 = RetrieveEmail(_email3Guid.Value);
    Assert.AreEqual(EmailState.Canceled, email3.StateCode, "Email
without a subject was not cancelled");
}
```

How it works...

In the first few steps, we prepared our unit test class for our integration test. We declared the required `using` statements for the Dynamics 365 connection, the query libraries, and a reference to the `CrmSvcUtil` generated classes from our `Packt.Xrm.Extensions` project. We created some private variables to use across the class. In step 6 we instantiated a connection to our Dynamics 365 instance and assigned the organization service proxy to a local variable. We used the same pattern described in *Connecting to Dynamics 365 from other systems using .NET* recipe of `Chapter 5`, *External Integration,* and stored the connection in our unit test `app.config` (don't forget to replace the connection string with your instance's values). Be careful about exposing credentials' details in plain text. Unit tests are typically executed in low risk development environments; nonetheless, you should still follow best practices.

In step 7, we created a method that accepts some parameters to create an e-mail activity associated with an account.

Next we created a method to retrieve the e-mails to inspect them after we have updated the account. To retrieve the records, we are using the organization service `Retrieve` method. The `Retrieve` method takes a column set collection; in our example, we are only interested in the scheduled start date and the record's state. Alternatively, you can also replace the `Retrieve` method with a LINQ query that uses the organization context.

Step 7 and step 8, contain refactored code fragments that are used more than once in our core test method.

> Again, it is expected that you follow best practices when building unit tests. If you find yourself copying and pasting lines of code, consider refactoring them into their own methods.

In step 9, we created a method that will help us with the arrangement of the unit test step. The method will create an account and associate three e-mails to it: two e-mails with a subject and one without a subject. The different e-mails cover the different expected scenarios when updating the account. Refer to the *Create your first plugin* recipe in `Chapter 4`, *Server-Side Extensions*, to understand the business logic behind the plugin we are testing. We retained the newly generated records' GUIDs to reuse in the assert step.

Finally, in step 10, we created the main test method that follows the **AAA** pattern. In the **Arrange** step, we created the account with the three e-mails attached to it. In the **Act** step, we updated the account. In the **Assert** step, we verified that two of the e-mails have an updated start date and that the third e-mail (the one without a subject) is now marked as cancelled. We marked the method with an integration test category attribute. This will help us filter integration tests that traverse the entire stack during ongoing unit tests and only keep them for nightly builds, or hourly rolling builds, due to their long execution time.

There's more...

This scenario showed a simple integration test that ensures that a synchronous plugin is doing its job. Asynchronous customization is harder to test as the time of execution is unknown and difficult to detect. You can introduce a wait condition, but that goes against best practices and is not reliable.

As we described throughout the recipe, clean code best practices also apply to unit tests. In this particular example we are only implementing one test. If you are planning on implementing several integration test classes, consider refactoring the code into class hierarchies. For example, create an abstract class that handles the Dynamics 365 connection and includes some reusable methods along with class structures to implement in child classes. At the end of the day, unit tests are C# classes and they will have to be reviewed, maintained, refactored, and updated over time.

One item that has been omitted from this recipe is the test's final tidying up. Best practice dictates deleting any record created specifically for the test. To clean up, you'll have to write a method decorated with a `ClassCleanup` attribute that will delete the created records. The GUID private variables have been initialized as nullable on purpose: in case the unit test fails at any stage, some of the GUIDs might remain null. Your cleanup method will check any non-null GUIDs and delete their corresponding records.

See also

- The *Creating your first plugin* recipe of `Chapter 4`, *Server-Side Extensions*
- The *Connecting to Dynamics 365 from other systems using .NET* recipe of `Chapter 5`, *External Integration*
- *Unit testing your plugin business logic*

Profiling your plugin

In this recipe we will demonstrate how to capture a plugin execution context from an online execution and replay it locally using the plugin registration tool so that we can debug from Visual Studio.

Getting ready

Given that we will be debugging an existing customization, you will need an already registered plugin in your Dynamics 365 instance, along with its corresponding plugin step. In our example, we will be using the first plugin created in this book from the *Creating your first plugin* recipe in `Chapter 4`, *Server-Side Extensions*.

You will also need a compatible version of Visual Studio. Additionally, you will need your plugin code to attach your IDE to the plugin registration tool process and debug the execution.

Most of the work will be done from the plugin registration tool. You can find the tool under the Dynamics 365 SDK `<SDK Folder>\Tools\PluginRegistration` folder. In order to push your changes to Dynamics 365, you will need a **System Customizer** role or a higher.

A basic understanding of Visual Studio debugging is recommended but not mandatory in order to easily follow the recipe.

How to do it...

1. Log in to your instance using the plugin registration tool and click on **Install Profiler**. Wait until you get the **Profiler Installed Successfully** dialog:

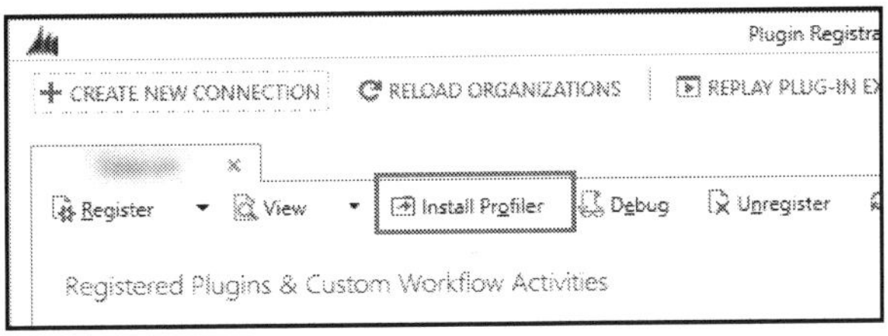

2. Locate your already registered plugin step under **Registered Plugins & Custom Workflow Activities**. Select it and click on **Start Profiling**:

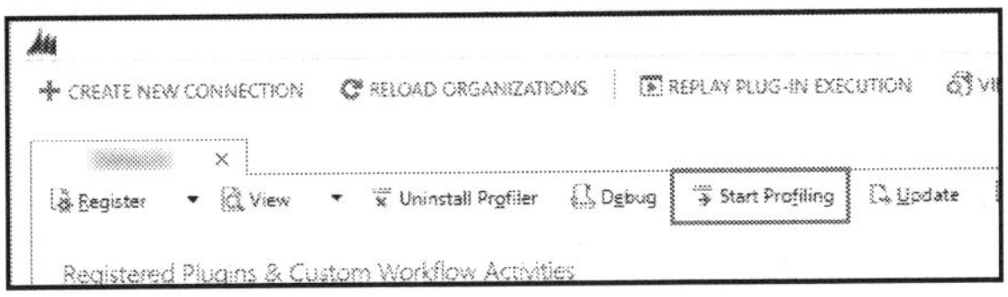

3. Ensure that `Exception` is selected in step 1. Leave the rest as default:

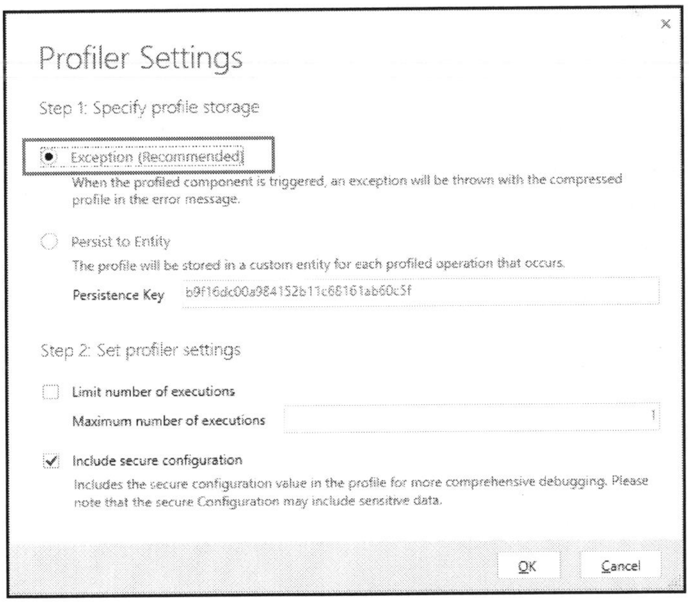

4. Back in Dynamics 365, run the action that triggers your plugin from the user interface and click on **Download Log File** from the exception dialog to download **ErrorDetails.txt**:

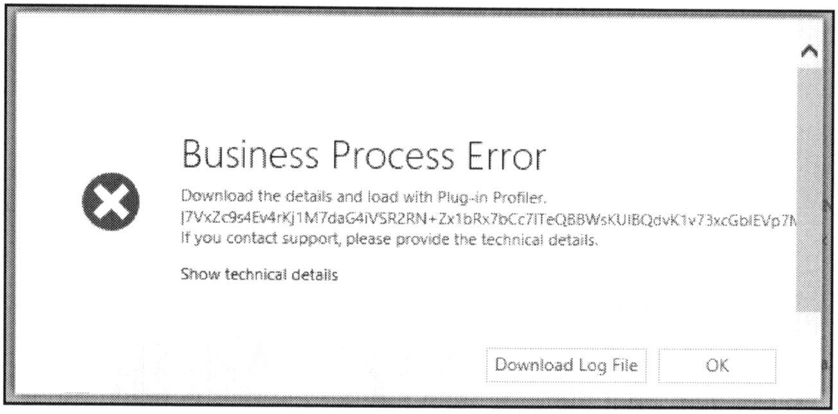

5. In Visual Studio, click on **Attach to Process...** from the **Debug** menu:

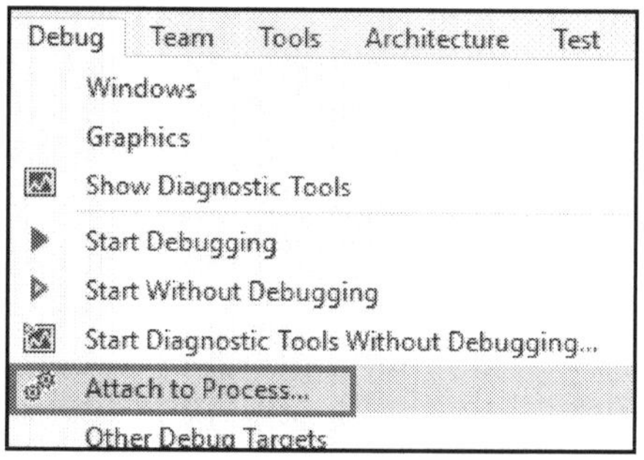

6. From the **Attach to Process** dialog, select **PluginRegistration.exe** and click on **Attach**:

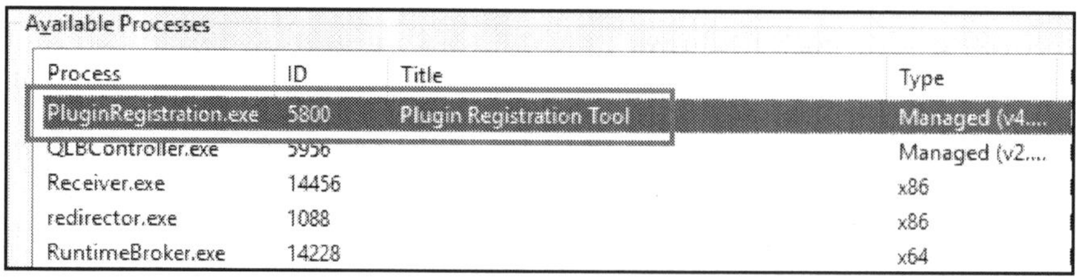

7. Back in your **Plugin Registration** tool, click on **Debug**:

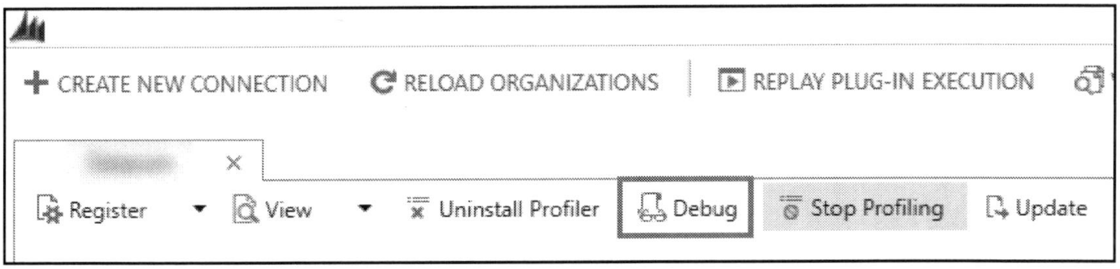

8. Enter the following details in the **Replay Plug-in Execution** dialog:
    - **Profile**: The path to the downloaded `ErrorDetails.txt`
    - **Assembly Location**: The path to the `Packt.Xrm.Extensions.dll` plugin assembly
    - **Plugin**: The plugin name as `Packt.Xrm.Extensions.Plugin.UpdateActivity`
9. Click on **Start Execution** and Visual Studio will start breaking at the breakpoints.
10. Once completed, don't forget to select your plugin step and click on **Stop Profiling**:

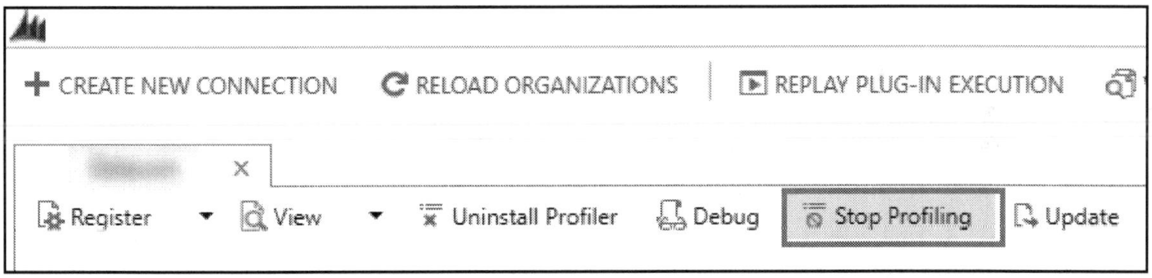

How it works...

In step 1, we started by installing the profile into our Dynamics 365 instance (for details on how to connect, check the *Deploying your customization using the plugin registration tool* recipe in `Chapter 3`, *SDK Enterprise Capabilities*). Behind the scenes, this will install a managed solution with the **Plug-in Profile** entity, the **PluginProfiler.Plugins** plugin, as well as some **Web Resources** and a **Site Map** extension:

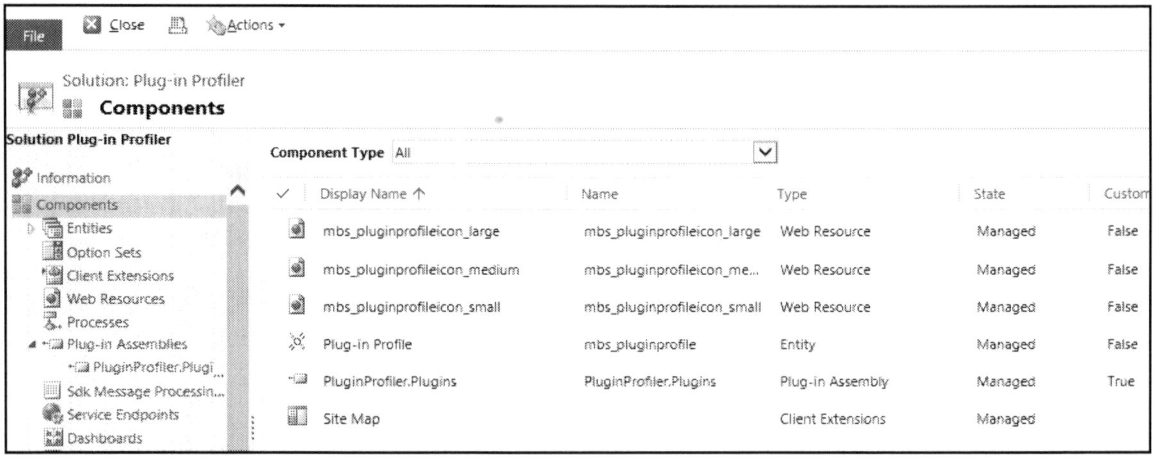

In step 2 and step 3, we enabled an existing plugin step for profiling and set up the profiling configuration. The dialog in step 3 is self-explanatory. We opted for the default option of throwing an exception when the plugin being profiled runs; however, you can opt to persist the profile in a Dynamics 365 entity (**Plug-in Profile** that shipped with the **Plug-in Profiler** managed solution). You can also limit the number of times the plugin profiler triggers.

Next, in step 4, we triggered the plugin being profiled and we were prompted with an exception that contains an encoded execution profile.

In step 5 and step 6, we attached Visual Studio to the Plugin Registration tool process.

In step 7 to step 9, we passed in the details of the plugin to execute, associated it with the profile we got from our Dynamics 365 instance, and started executing the plugin locally. Behind the scenes, the plugin registration tool loads the plugin assembly and executes the plugin by passing the context as if it was executing within Dynamics 365; however, it will run locally. In fact, the replayed plugin will still connect to your Dynamics 365 live instance to execute the rest of the plugin.

Finally, in step 10, we ensured that the profiler has been disabled in order to ensure no further exceptions are returned when we try to execute the plugin in Dynamics 365 again.

You can automatically turn off profiling by limiting the number of profiled executions while setting up your profiler.

There's more...

Not only does this technique give us step-by-step debugging capabilities, but we can also assess our customization's performance. Newer versions of Visual Studio can calculate the time lapse between method calls, which might give you pointers on where a performance bottleneck is. However, the results might be misleading when debugging due to Visual Studio's manual interaction overhead and latency connecting to Dynamics 365 (the code is executing locally but still connects to a Dynamics 365 instance). If you would like to learn more about how to use the plugin profiler for performance analysis, read this MSDN article at: `https://msdn.microsoft.com/en-us/library/hh372952.aspx`.

The **Plug-in Traces** log area in the plugin registration tool also produces some interesting output, which includes the overall execution duration and any Dynamics 365 tracing messages, as shown here:

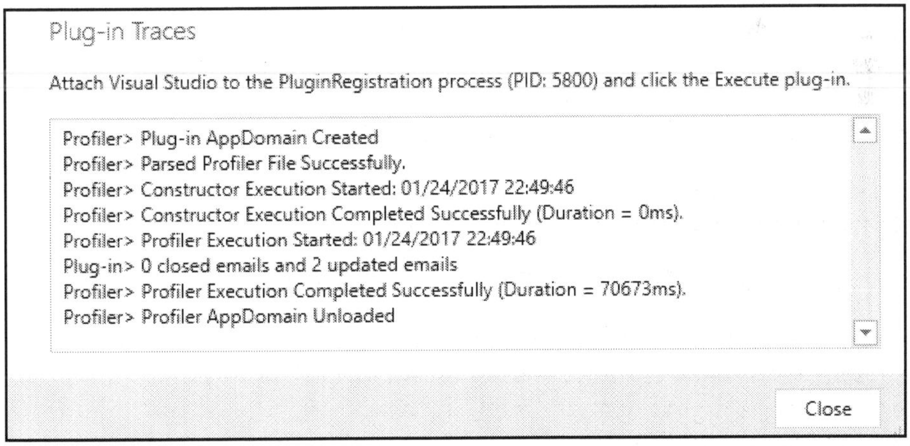

See also

- The *Deploying your customization using the plugin registration tool* recipe of `Chapter 4`, *Server-Side Extensions*
- The *Debugging your plugin in Dynamics 365 on-premise* recipe of `Chapter 4`, *Server-Side Extensions*

Build a generic read audit plugin

In the *Setting up an Azure Service Bus endpoint* recipe earlier in this chapter, we used built-in plugin capabilities to write a plugin context to an Azure Service Bus queue when a specific event is triggered (update of a specific field).

We can also use this same capability to also trigger an event when records are read, effectively creating a read audit notification/log.

In this recipe we will configure a read plugin step to write its context to an Azure Service Bus queue. We'll then create a listener that will gather the user GUID, the entity name and the entity GUID of the record read, and store those values in a NoSQL Azure Cosmos DB (previously known as Document DB) database in the JSON format:

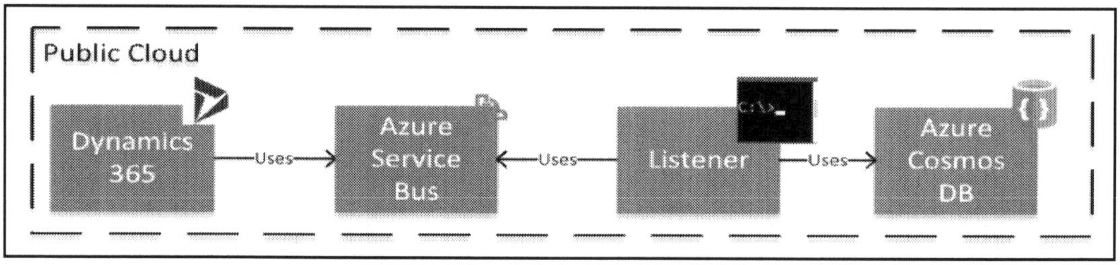

Getting ready

You will need an Azure Service Bus endpoint registered in Dynamics 365 as set out in the *Setting up an Azure Service Bus endpoint* recipe earlier in this chapter. You will also need an Azure user able to create a Cosmos DB instance and a corresponding collection. The following are the steps to create a Cosmos DB instance:

1. Log in to your new Azure portal and navigate to **+** | **Database** | **Cosmos DB**:

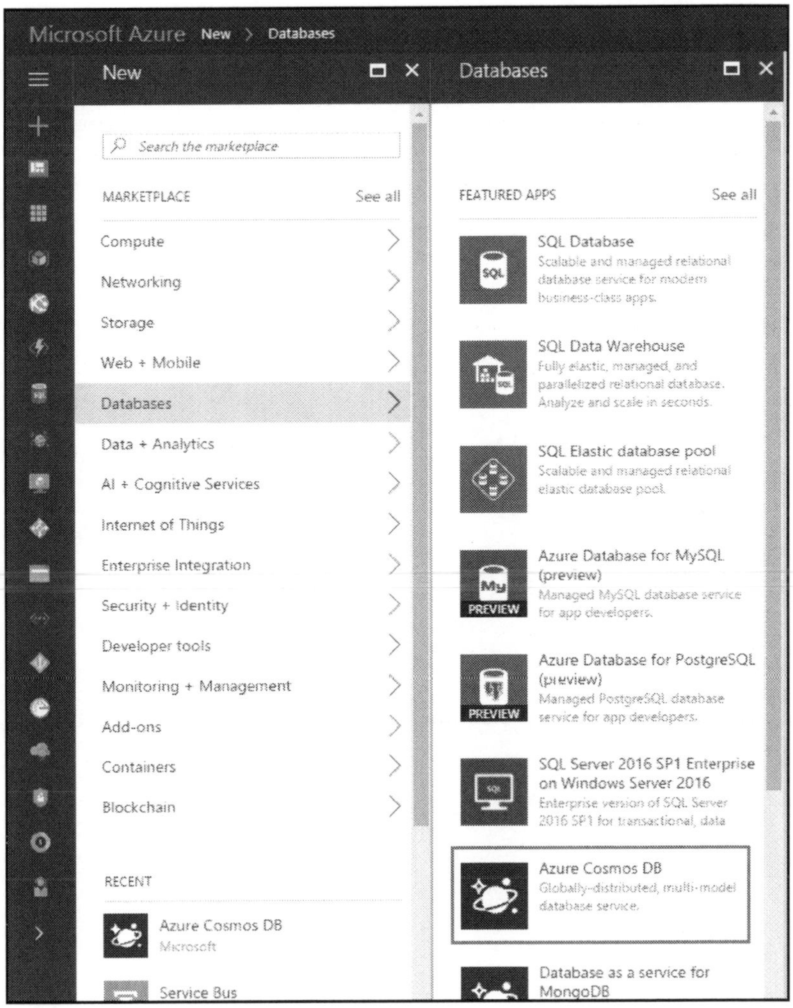

2. In the NoSQL form, enter an ID (for example, `packtlog365`) and ensure **NoSQL API** is set to **DocumentDB** and then click on **Create** after filling the rest of the mandatory fields.
3. Once created, navigate to your NoSQL resource and navigate to **Overview** | **+ Add Collection**.
4. Enter the `Audit` value in the **Collection Id** field and enter `Dynamics365` as the **Database** name:

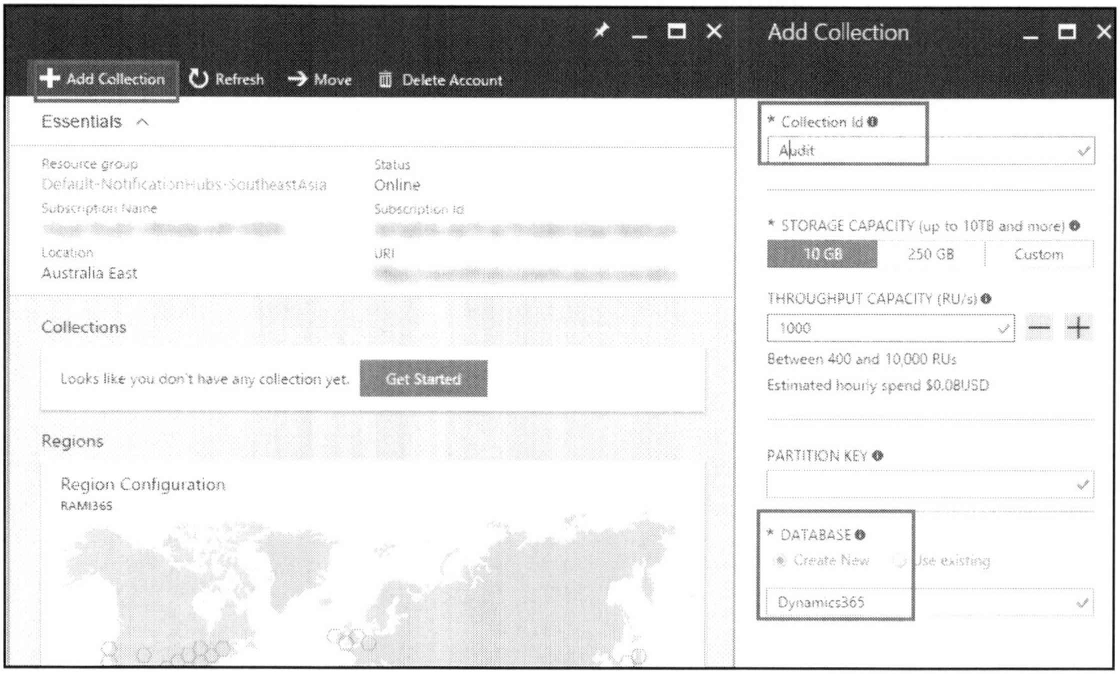

5. Once created, navigate back to your initial NoSQL and select **Keys** and copy `URI` as well as `Primary Key` from the **Read-write Keys** tab.

From a Dynamics 365 perspective, you will need the usual system customer or higher security role to register the read plugin steps. For testing purposes, you will need read access to the entity in question. In our example, we will use the accounts entity.

How to do it...

1. Using the plugin registration tool, register the following steps on your Azure Service Bus endpoint:
    - **Message**: `Retrieve`
    - **Primary Entity**: `account`
    - **Execution Mode**: `Asynchronous`
    - Click on **Register New Step**

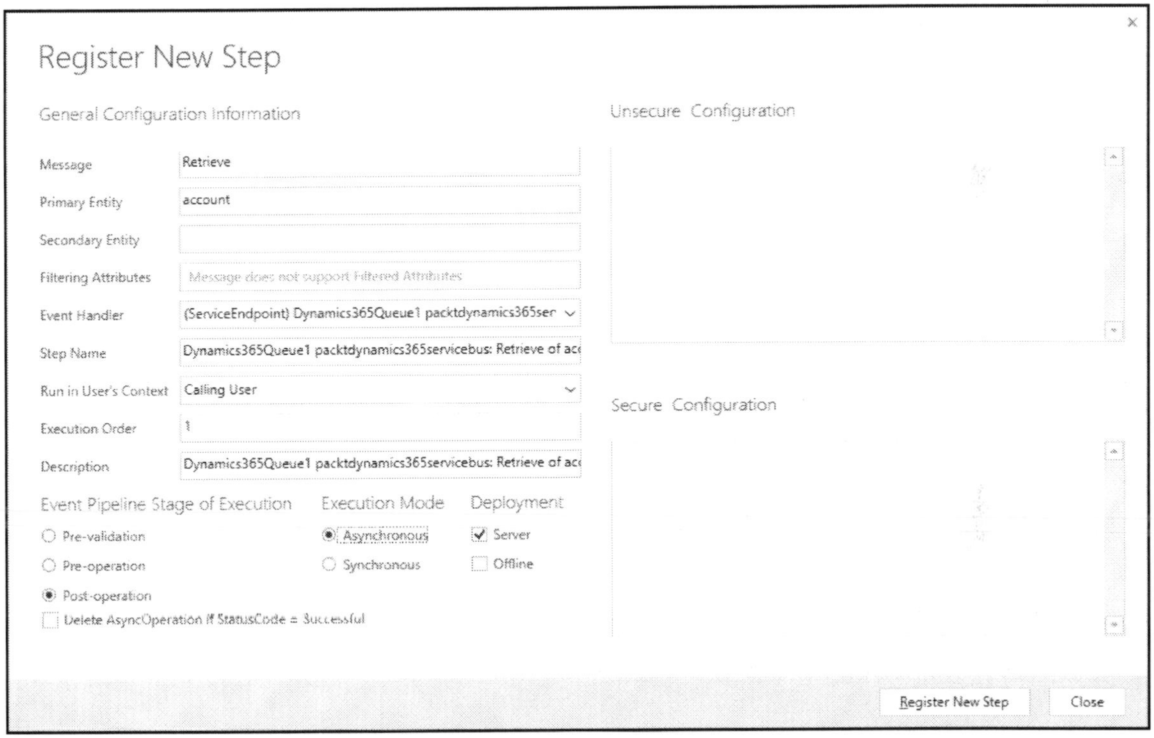

2. In Visual Studio, create a new console application called `Packt.Xrm.ReadAudit`.
3. Add the following four NuGet packages:
    - `Microsoft.Azure.DocumentDB`
    - `Windows.Azure.ServiceBus`
    - `Newtonsoft.JSON`
    - `Microsoft.CrmSdk.CoreAssemblies`

4. Add the following `using` statements:

```
using Microsoft.Azure.Documents.Client;
using Microsoft.ServiceBus.Messaging;
using Newtonsoft.Json.Linq;
using Microsoft.Xrm.Sdk;
```

5. Add the following `private constant` variables:

```
private const string endpointUri =
"https://.documents.azure.com:443/";
private const string primaryKey = "<Your Primary Key>";
private const string databaseName = "Dynamics365";
private const string collectionName = "Audit";
private const string connectionString =
"Endpoint=sb://.servicebus.windows.net/;
SharedAccessKeyName=CrmQueue;SharedAccessKey=;EntityPath= ";
private const string queueName = "dynamics365queue";
private static DocumentClient docClient;
```

6. Add the following code in your main method:

```
var client =
QueueClient.CreateFromConnectionString(connectionString,
queueName);
docClient = new DocumentClient(new Uri(endpointUri), primaryKey);
 var dbUri = UriFactory.CreateDocumentCollectionUri(databaseName,
collectionName);

client.OnMessage(message =>
{
    var result = message.GetBody<RemoteExecutionContext>();
    var readLog = $"{{userId:'{
      result.InitiatingUserId}',entity:'{
      result.PrimaryEntityName}',entityId:'{
      result.PrimaryEntityId}'}}";
    var parsedReadLog = JObject.Parse(readLog);
    docClient.CreateDocumentAsync(dbUri, parsedReadLog).Wait();
}
);
Console.WriteLine("Press [Enter] to terminate");
Console.ReadLine();
client.Close();
```

7. Run your console application.
8. Retrieve an account record in Dynamics 365.
9. Query your Cosmos DB in Azure for new entries.

How it works...

First, we attached a step to our Azure Service Bus endpoint that triggers when a record is retrieved. The event is triggered when a record is opened through the user interface, or when the record is retrieved using the Dynamics 365 SDK, or even when using the web API. This leverages the built-in Dynamics 365 Azure-aware plugin to write the plugin's context to the Azure endpoint.

In step 2 to step 5, we created a console application that consumes the execution context from the queue and stores the details in a NoSQL database.

Make sure you replace the values in step 5 with your specific ones. The first four parameters are `endpointUri`, `primaryKey`, `databaseName`, and `collectionName` related to your Cosmos DB instance (for guidance on where to get the values, read the *Getting ready* section of this recipe). `ConnectionString` is related to your Azure Service Bus queue's connection string (the *Consuming messages from an Azure Service Bus* recipe in `Chapter 5`, *External Integration*, describes how to get the connection string).

This abridged recipe does not cover exception handling; it is at your discretion to enhance the consumer's code to deal with exceptions.

As we saw in the *Consuming messages from an Azure Service Bus* recipe earlier in this chapter, the `OnMessage` method listens to the queue's events (triggered when the message is queued) and calls a delegate method to execute some logic. In our case, it sends a JSON-formatted message with the read details to a Cosmos DB database.

The remote execution context contains details about who made the call, details about the query, as well as the returned result set (attribute values). For example, if the record name is included, you can retrieve it using the following:

```
((Entity)result.OutputParameters.FirstOrDefault().Value).Attributes["name"]
```

One thing to note: when we are writing the message back to Cosmos DB, we are using an asynchronous method synchronously; best practice would dictate that you turn your method asynchronously as well. For simplicity, we've opted to use `Wait()` instead.

There's more...

This recipe covered the retrieve step. You can also use `RetrieveMultiple` to cover searches and view auditing, however, `RetrieveMultiple` will contain a different structure.

The code is using the Azure Service Bus pattern (as described in the *Setting up an Azure Service endpoint* recipe of `Chapter 5`, *External Integration*) to send the read audit trail details to a system outside of Dynamics 365. This is due to the limitation introduced when running a plugin code in sandbox mode, which restricts the usage of some libraries (in our example, `Microsoft.Azure.Documents.Client`). An alternative design might leverage a custom entity within Dynamics 365 to hold read logs as described earlier in this chapter.

Our service bus consumer relays the data to a Cosmos DB database. We chose this NoSQL database for its ease of use, flexibility, reliability, and scalability. NoSQL database gives us the power of storing fragments with different structures. For example, a read audit might only include the user GUID, the entity type, and the GUID of a record, whereas an exception log might also include a stack trace. If you want to know more about Cosmos DB, visit `https://azure.microsoft.com/en-us/services/cosmos-db/`.

Alternatively, you can choose other databases, such as MongoDB, or even a structured relational database such as Microsoft SQL.

See also

- The *Consuming messages from an Azure Service Bus* recipe of `Chapter 5`, *External Integration*
- *Logging error from your customization*

Using Cross-Origin Resource Sharing with CRM Online

Using the Dynamics 365 web API within Dynamics 365 web resources is straightforward. We previously covered a web API in a few recipes; (*Querying 365 data using the Web API endpoint* and *Building custom UI using Angular* recipes of `Chapter 2`, *Client-Side Extensions*, and *Connecting to Dynamics 365 from other systems OData (Java)* recipes of `Chapter 5`, *External Integration*); however, accessing the web API from the client side on a different web application is a bit more challenging.

If you simply create a request using `XMLHttpRequest` from a locally hosted web application to the web API, you will receive the following error:

```
No 'Access-Control-Allow-Origin' header is present on the requested
resource. Origin 'http://localhost' is therefore not allowed access.
The response had HTTP status code 401.
```

An unauthorized 401 exception is returned due to missing authentication details. In this recipe, we will build a single-page HTML application (SPA) with some JavaScript to call the web API and retrieve the top two accounts ordered by name. We will also use the `ADAL.js` Microsoft library to help us with the Azure AD authentication.

Getting ready

In order to get your Azure AD authentication working, you will first need to set up your web application in Azure AD. The process is similar to what we described in `Chapter 5`, *External Integration, Connecting to Dynamics 365 from other systems OData (Java)* except for the following steps:

1. When creating the application, **Application Type** has to be `Web app / API`:

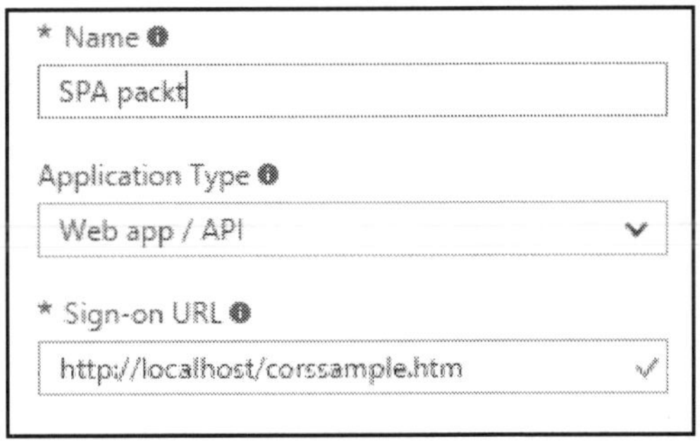

2. Once created, you will have to update the application manifest. From the same page where you can view your newly created application details, there is a **Manifest** edit button at the top:

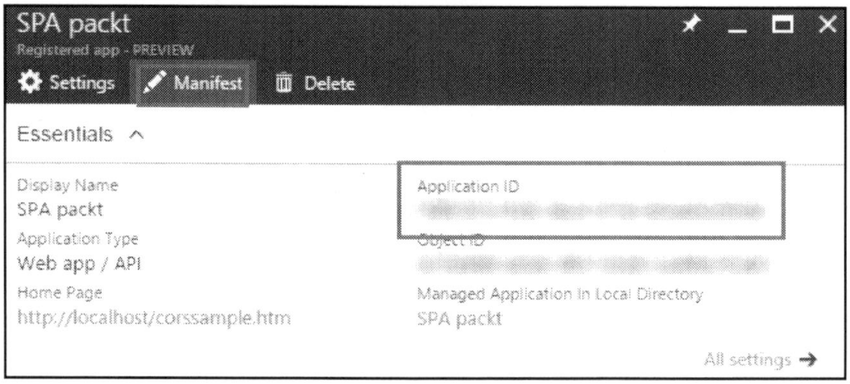

3. Click on **Manifest** and update the content to state:

```
"oauth2AllowImplicitFlow": true
```

4. Then, upload **Manifest** back by clicking on the **Upload** button at the top:

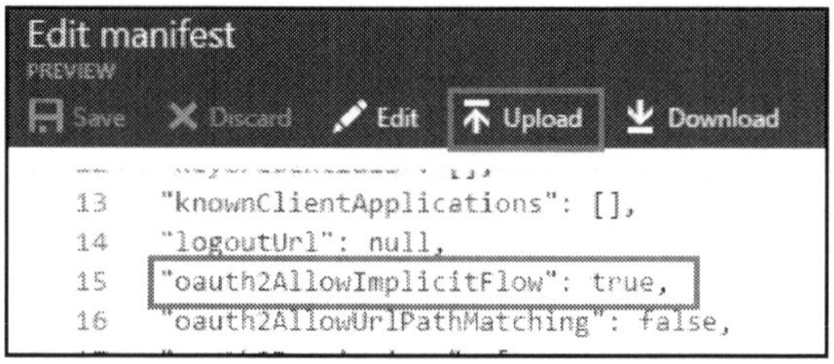

Don't forget to set the correct permissions and optionally, click on the **Grant Permission** button at the top of the **Required Permissions** summary screen in order to avoid having the users accept the delegated permissions. In this scenario, however, it is preferable to omit this step.

From the preceding step, you will need to retrieve the generated **Application ID**. You can get it from your registered application essentials summary page, as highlighted in the previous picture.

From the Dynamics 365 side, the user that you will use to get access to your instance needs read access to account records.

Finally, you will need a location to host your HTML, such as an instance of IIS.

How to do it...

1. Start by creating a `connect.js` JavaScript file with the following code:

```
var organizationURI = "https://.crm6.dynamics.com";
var tenant = ".onmicrosoft.com";
var clientId = " 00000000-0000-0000-0000-000000000000";
var pageUrl = "http://localhost/corssample.htm";

var endpoints = {
    orgUri: organizationURI
};

window.config = {
    tenant: tenant,
    clientId: clientId,
    postLogoutRedirectUri: pageUrl,
    endpoints: endpoints,
    cacheLocation: 'localStorage',
};

var user, authContext, message, errorMessage ;

document.onreadystatechange = function () {
  if (document.readyState == "complete") {
    authenticate();
  }
}

function authenticate() {
    authContext = new AuthenticationContext(config);

var isCallback = authContext.isCallback(window.location.hash);
    if (isCallback) {
        authContext.handleWindowCallback();
    }
    var loginError = authContext.getLoginError();
    if (isCallback && !loginError) {
        window.location =
authContext._getItem(authContext.CONSTANTS.STORAGE.LOGIN_REQUEST);
    }
    else {
        //TODO handle error
```

```
    }
    user = authContext.getCachedUser();
}

function login() {
    authContext.login();
}
function getAccounts() {
    authContext.acquireToken(organizationURI, retrieveAccounts)
}

function retrieveAccounts(error, token) {
    if (error || !token) {
        //TODO handle error
        return;
    }
    var req = new XMLHttpRequest()
    req.open("GET", encodeURI(organizationURI +
"/api/data/v8.2/accounts?$top=2&$select=name&$orderby=name"),
true);
    req.setRequestHeader("Authorization", "Bearer " + token);
    req.setRequestHeader("Content-Type", "application/json;
charset=utf-8");
    req.setRequestHeader("OData-MaxVersion", "4.0");
    req.setRequestHeader("OData-Version", "4.0");
    req.onreadystatechange = function () {
        if (this.readyState == 4) {
            req.onreadystatechange = null;
            if (this.status == 200) {
                var accounts = JSON.parse(this.response);
                document.getElementById("list").innerHTML = "<ol>";
                for (index = 0; index < accounts["value"].length;
++index) {
                    document.getElementById("list").innerHTML +=
"<li>" + accounts["value"][index].name + "</li>";
                }
                document.getElementById("list").innerHTML +=
"</ol>";
            }
            else {
                //TODO handle error
            }
        }
    };
    req.send();
}
```

2. Then create a simple HTML page called `corssample.htm` with the following code:

```
<!DOCTYPE html>
<html>
<body>
    <p id="list">Start</p>
    <script
src="https://secure.aadcdn.microsoftonline-p.com/lib/1.0.13/js/adal
.min.js"></script>
    <script type="text/javascript" src="connect.js"></script>
    <button onclick="login()">Login</button>
    <button onclick="getAccounts()">Get top 2 accounts</button>
</body>
</html>
```

3. Host your application on a local IIS instance on port 80.
4. Navigate to `http://localhost/corssample.htm` using a chrome browser.
5. Click on the **login** button and follow the authentication steps.
6. After logging in, click on the **Get top 2 accounts** button.

How it works...

We started in step 1 by creating our `connect.js` JavaScript library. The first four lines represent variables that are specific to your implementation. The organization URI is your Dynamics 365 organization URI. The tenant is your active directory domain. The client ID is the same as your application ID that you retrieved earlier in this recipe. Finally, the page URL represents your custom application's URL. The URL will look different in each of your SDLC environments.

Also, in step 1, we created our HTML: a simple page with a JavaScript library reference and two buttons. One calls the login function the other calls the `getAcounts` function.

The authenticate function is first called on the page load event. It manages the authentication and ensures that you have an authentication context object (used later).

The `login` function is called when the login button is pressed. The `login` function then calls the `authContext login` function. The login function is encapsulated in the ADAL library and takes care of redirecting the user to the Microsoft Azure AD authentication page and ensuring that the user is authenticated.

Finally, `getAccount` wraps the `retrieveAccount` method in an `acquireToken` function from the ADAL library that first checks whether the user has a valid token and then calls the callback function that actually retrieves the account records.

The `retrieveAccount` function calls the usual `XMLHttpRequest` that we have used in previous recipes, except that we also populate an authorization header with a token passed from the `acquireToken` function. The call back method of `XMLHttpRequest` parses the JSON response and populates the list in the HTML page.

> What we built is a wrapper around the call that checks whether a token is issued and is not expired before proceeding; otherwise, it will redirect to the login page if required.

In the last four steps, we deployed our page into a local IIS instance and tested it.

There's more...

This abridged example is a simplified version of the one described in the MSDN article found at `https://msdn.microsoft.com/en-us/library/mt595797.aspx`.

The pattern of registering an app to access the web API is the same when using the Web API outside of your Dynamics 365 instance. We also covered a Java client example in the *Connecting to Dynamics CRM from other systems OData (Java)* recipe of `Chapter 5`, *External Integration*.

Microsoft also provides many variations of the ADAL libraries for different languages and frameworks at `https://github.com/AzureAD/`. You will find versions for Angular.js, Python, Android, and Objective C, among others.

See also

- The *Querying 365 data using the Web API endpoint* recipe of `Chapter 2`, *Client-Side Extensions*
- The *Building custom UI using AngularJS* recipe of `Chapter 2`, *Client-Side Extensions*
- The *Connecting to Dynamics 365 from other systems OData (Java)* recipe of `Chapter 5`, *External Integration*

7
Security

In this chapter, we will cover the following recipes:

- Building cumulative security roles
- Configuring business unit hierarchies
- Configuring access based on hierarchical positions
- Configuring and assigning field-level security
- Setting up teams and sharing
- Setting up Access Teams
- Encrypting data at rest to meet the FIPS 140-2 standard
- Managing your Dynamics 365 online SQL TDE encryption key

Introduction

Dynamics 365 is a robust platform with a proven track record spanning more than 10 years. The most attractive attributes of the product are all the features you get straight out of the box. Most of these features are complex and time consuming to implement if they were to be written from scratch on a bespoke application. The security model is at the top of the list of great features.

The security model in Dynamics 365 is comprehensive and capable of addressing a wide range of security requirements. From coarse grain access to instances using Office 365 security groups, to simple CRUD privileges, to field-level security, the authorization model has evolved over the years to cater for more granularity.

It is paramount to have a solid grasp of the fundamental security building blocks offered by the product. This will help you make educated decisions when modeling security. At the core of the Dynamics 365 security controls are **security roles**. The security roles provide per entity granular privileges based on record ownership. Privileges can also be set at different levels, as described here:

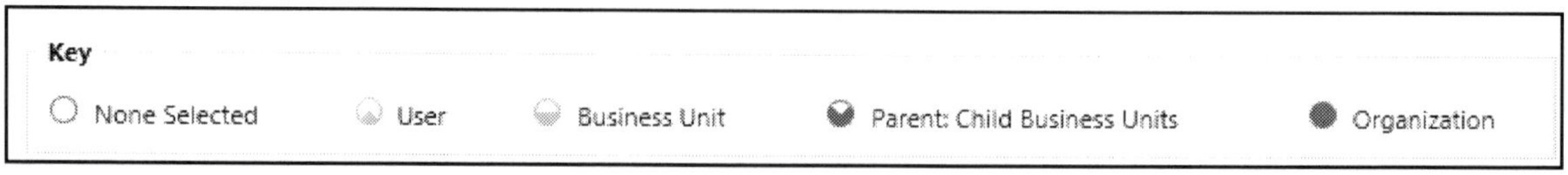

- **None**: No access
- **User**: Only the owner has the privilege (user or team)
- **Business Unit**: The user has the privilege to all records (of that entity) owned by users or teams at the same business unit
- **Parent: Child Business Unit**: Users have the privilege to all records (of that entity) owned by users or teams at their business unit and all child business units
- **Organization**: The user has the privilege to all records (of that entity)

It is important to note that not all entities follow this level of ownership. For example, some can be owned by business units (users, equipment), and others are owned by an organization (this can be configured when creating custom entities). The following screenshot shows how you can define the ownership level when creating a custom entity:

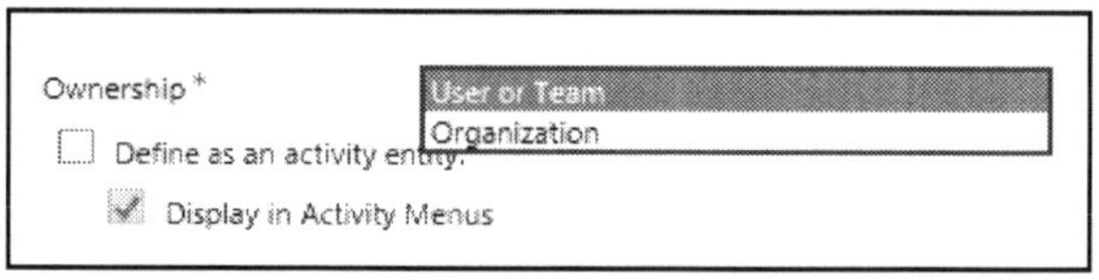

Note that security roles are cumulative. As you assign additional roles to a user with additional privileges, the final set of privileges is the sum of all privileges combined.

In addition to security roles, Dynamics 365 offers team sharing, ad-hoc sharing, field-level security, and Access Teams. We will cover most of these in this chapter.

Each security modeling technique has implications on flexibility and performance. For more details on scalability, read the white paper *Scalable Security Modeling with Microsoft Dynamics CRM 2015* at `https://technet.microsoft.com/en-us/library/dn683914(v=crm.7).aspx`.

Building cumulative security roles

The Dynamics 365 authorization mechanism is comprehensive and flexible. One of its greatest features is its capability to provide users with cumulative privileges as more security roles are added.

In this recipe we will build three cumulative roles: a base role that every user logging in through the web user interface must have, a read role, and a write role. The union of all three roles will enable users to read/write account and contact entities.

Getting ready

As per most recipes in this chapter, a `Packt` solution to store your configuration is recommended but not mandatory. You will also need the correct privileges to configure the security roles. Typically, a System Administrator role is used to configure security roles, as the role includes all the necessary privileges required to 'transfer' those privileges into a role. However, the main security privilege required is CRUD to security roles located under **Business Management** | **Entity** in security roles.

TIP

If you are assigning security roles to other users, you need the same privileges as that role (or higher) to be able to transfer them. You cannot assign someone a privilege unless you've got it yourself. Typically, a user with System Administrator privileges deals with security roles.

How to do it...

1. Navigate to **Settings** | **Security** | **Security Roles**.
2. Create a new role called `Base UI User`.
3. Assign the security role to your root Business Unit.
4. In the **Core Records** tab, add the following privileges:

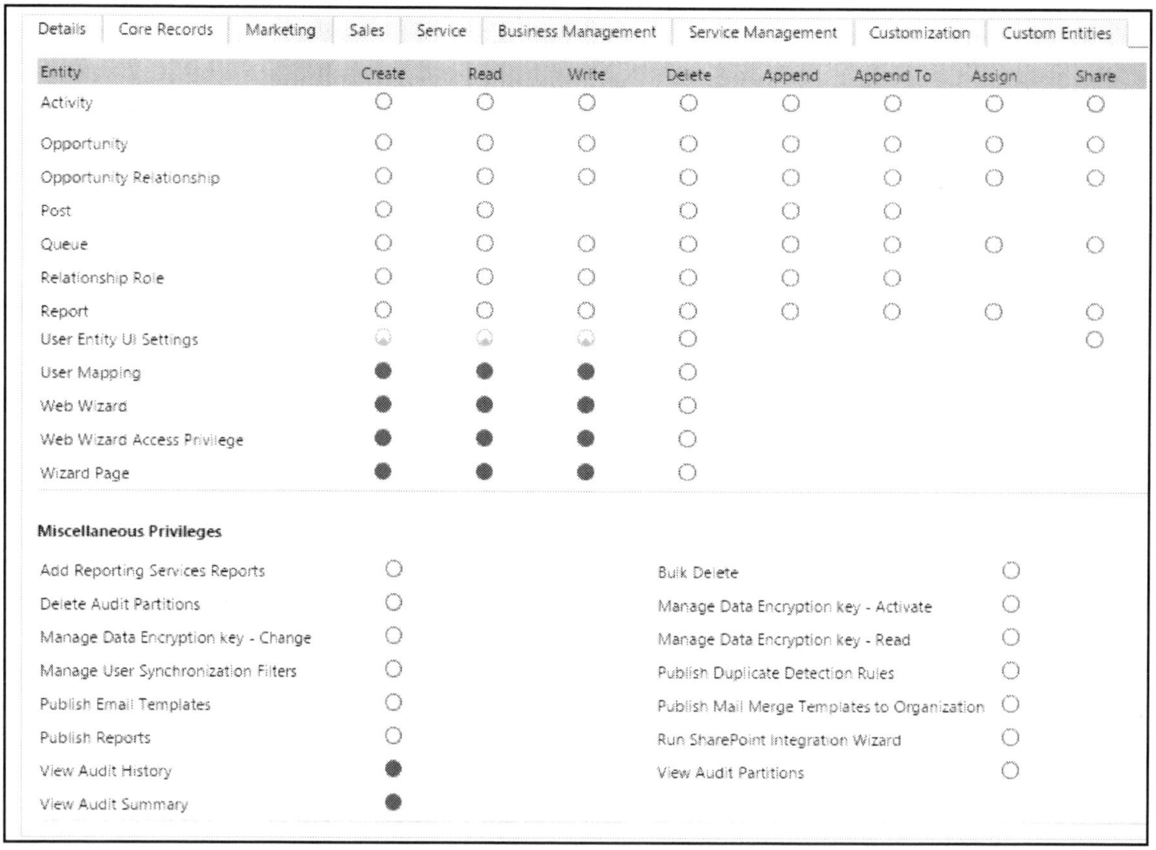

5. Under the **Business Management** tab, add the following privileges:

6. Under the **Customization** tab, add the following privileges:

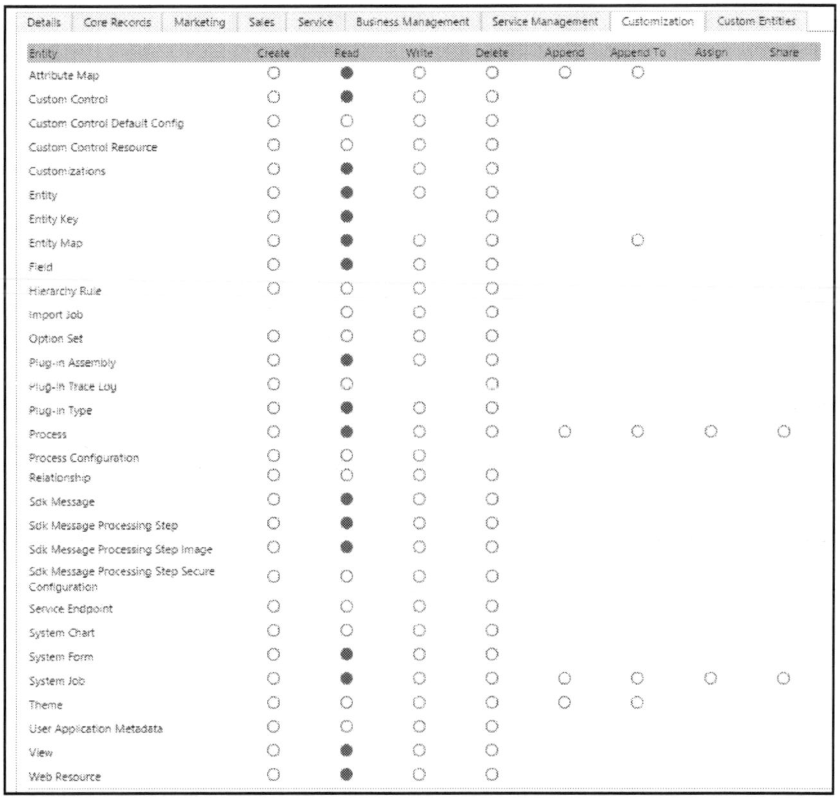

7. Create a new security role called `Read` assigned to the root business unit with the following read privileges to the account and contact entities under the **Core Records** tab:

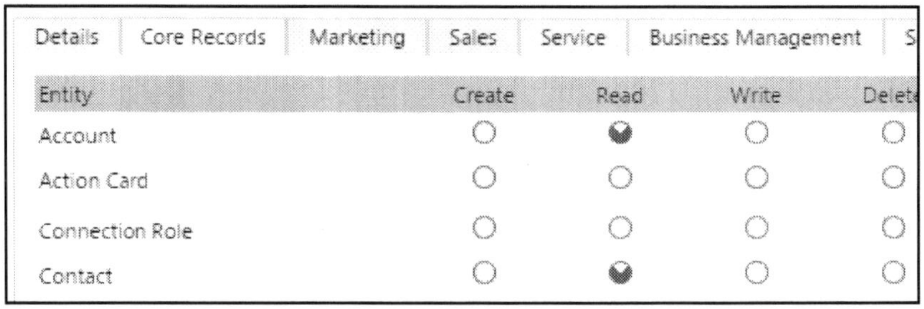

8. Create a new security role called `Write` assigned to the root business unit with the following write privileges to the account and contact entities under the **Core Records** tab:

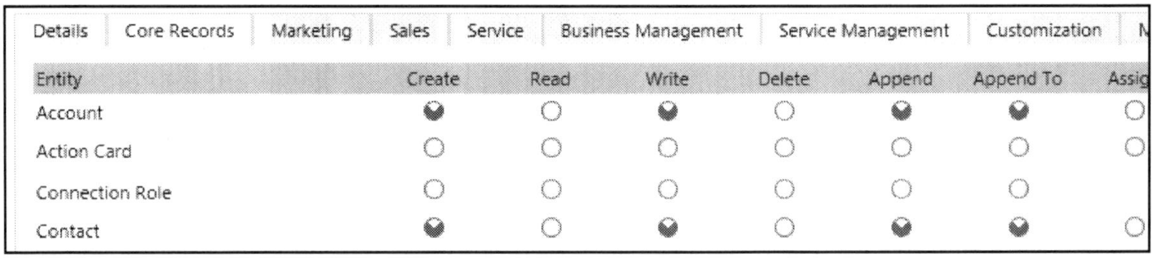

How it works...

We started by creating a base role that gives users basic access to the platform. The base role, for example, gives users read access to business units, entities' schema, SDK messages, system forms, and so on. This role by itself does not give you access to anything else in the system, just blank access.

We then created a role to read accounts and contacts and finished off by creating a role that gives full write access to the accounts and contacts. Note how we left off **Assign** and **Share**, as these are special privileges that can be forked into their own security role.

The union of all three roles will give a user all privileges required to access the system and read/write to accounts and contacts:

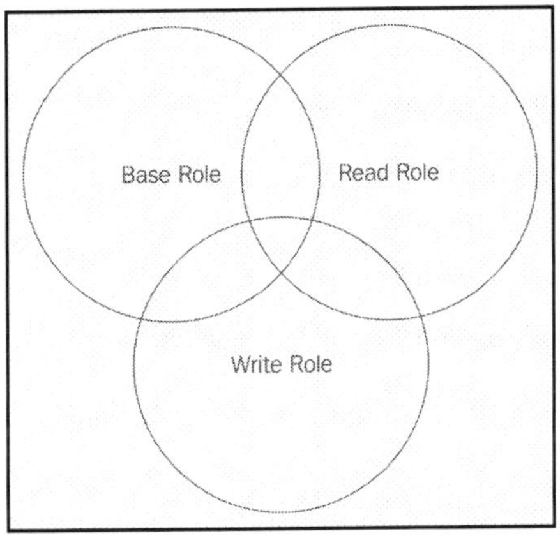

We provided the privileges at a **Parent: Child Business Units** level. However, this can be done at any other level depending on your requirements. Refer to the introduction of this chapter to understand the different levels and some of their respective scenarios.

We assigned all the security roles to the root business unit. Roles created at a parent business unit level are inherited by all children business units.

Furthermore, to package security roles in a solution, they have to be defined at the root business unit level. As a rule of thumb, it's always best practice to define security roles at the topmost business unit.

There's more...

Security roles in Dynamics 365 give you a range of options to address complex security requirements. In the next recipe, we will deal with how business unit hierarchies can be used in conjunction with the security roles we just created.

See also

- *Configuring business unit hierarchies*

Configuring business unit hierarchies

The business unit hierarchy feature is one of the most powerful authorization features in Dynamics 365 that was developed in the product's early days. Business unit hierarchies give you flexibility. If you were to implement such a mechanism in a bespoke application, it would take a lot of time and effort and would probably not match Dynamics 365's stability. The security capabilities of Dynamics 365 in general are a very appealing reason to choose the product as a **commercial off-the-shelve** (**COTS**) solution.

In this recipe we will scratch the surface of business units' hierarchies. We will implement two child business units as depicted in the following screenshot. We will then implement a new (global read) security role on top of the two previously created ones.

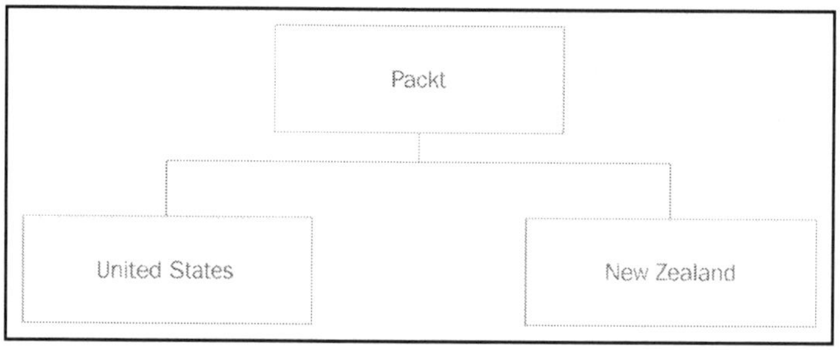

Getting ready

In order to create business units, you will need `Create` right on the **Business Unit** entity located under **Business Management** | **Entity** | **Business Unit** in security roles.

As mentioned in this recipe's introduction, we will be leveraging the existing security roles from the first recipe.

How to do it...

1. Navigate to **Settings** | **Security** | **Business Units**.
2. Click on **New** and create a `United States` business unit with `Packt` as the parent.
3. Click on **Save and New** and create another business unit called `New Zealand` with `Packt` as the parent then click on **Save and Close**.
4. Navigate to **Settings** | **Security** | **Business Units**.

5. Open the previously created `Read` role and navigate to **Actions** | **Copy Role** and give it the name `Read Global`.
6. Update the `Read Global` role to allow `Read` at the organization level, as shown here:

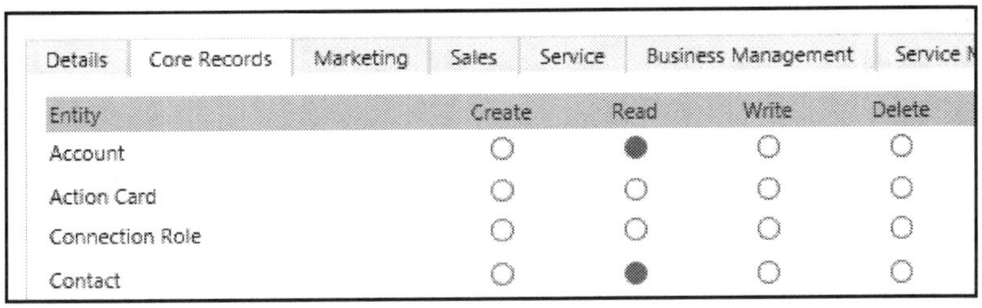

7. Reassign the role to the `United States` business unit by navigating back to the **Details** tab and changing the value in the **Business Unit** field.
8. Test your new roles by assigning users to the different business units.

How it works...

In step 1 to step 3, we created the business unit hierarchy and, in step 5 and step 6, we created a global security role to give users read access to all **Accounts** and **Contacts**.

Security roles are based on ownership. If a record belongs to a user from a sibling business unit, the reused security role from the previous recipe won't give you any access to it. However, the **global read** security role will give you `read` access.

The global read was created at a child business unit level; therefore, only users belonging to that child business unit will be able to get assigned the security role.

The security roles and business units can work in a range of combinations. For instance, if a user belongs to the Packt business unit, then the `Parent: Child Business Unit` read role allows the user to read across the entire organization because the user is at the root level. However, if the user belongs to a child business unit, then they can only read records owned by users at their level (or below).

When you assign a user to a new business unit, the user loses all its security roles. Beware when reassigning administrators (or your own user) to new business units.

There's more ...

For a deeper understanding of the Dynamics 365 security modeling techniques and performance implications, read the white paper *Scalable Security Modeling with Microsoft Dynamics CRM 2015* at `https://technet.microsoft.com/en-us/library/dn683914(v=crm.7).aspx`.

See also

- *Building cumulative security roles*

Configuring access based on hierarchical positions

As of Dynamics CRM 2015, users that belong to certain hierarchies may be able to access their direct reports' records without the need for sharing.

Hierarchy works using either **Manager Hierarchy** (based on the user's manager hierarchy) or **Position Hierarchy**. In this recipe we will focus on the latter.

Getting ready

To configure security hierarchies, you will need a **System Customizer** or higher security role. More specifically, when changing or assigning positions, you will require the **Assign a position to a system user** and **Change hierarchy security settings** privileges. Both these privileges are available by navigating to **Business Management** | **Miscellaneous Privileges**.

How to do it...

1. Navigate to **Settings** | **Security** | **Hierarchy Security**.
2. In the **Hierarchy Security** form, enter the following:
    - Tick **Enable Hierarchy Modeling**
    - Select **Custom Position Hierarchy**
    - Set **Hierarchy Depth** as `3`
    - The **Hierarchy Security** dialog will look as per this screenshot:

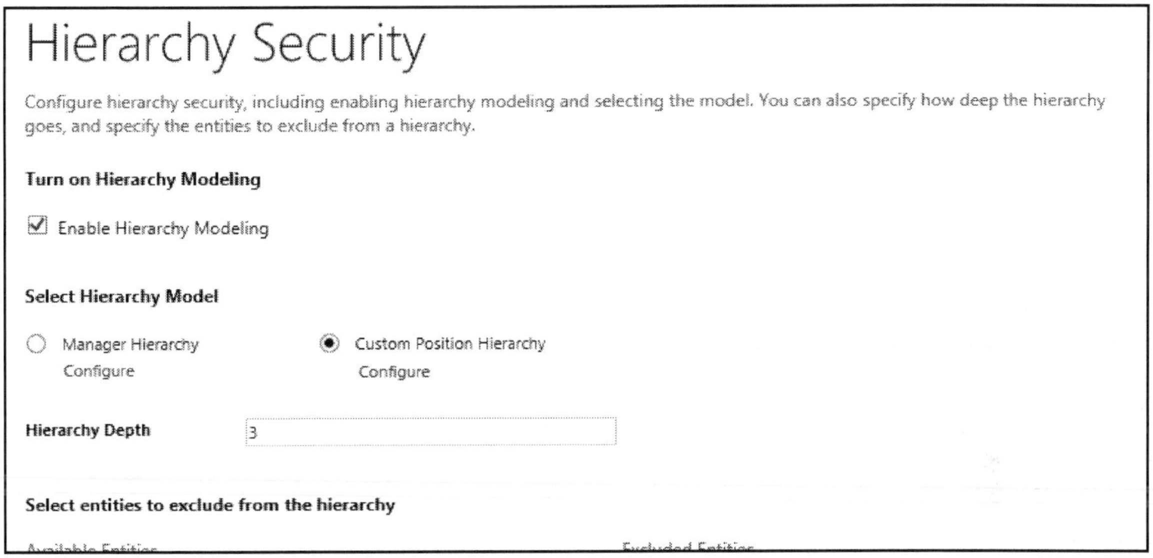

3. Click on **Configure** under **Custom Position Hierarchy**.
4. Click on **New** and create a position called `Lead` and then click on **Save**.
5. Click on **New** and create a position called `Developer` and then select `Lead` as **Parent Position** and click on **Save and Close**.
6. Back in **Hierarchy Security**, click on **Save and Close**.
7. Navigate to **Settings** | **Security** | **Users**.

8. Click on the ellipsis (**...**) in the ribbon and select **Change Position** to assign your users new positions as per the following screenshot:

How it works...

We started in step 2, by enabling hierarchy modeling and we chose **Custom Position Hierarchy**. You can only choose one or the other, not both.

We then created a position hierarchy in step 4 and step 5 and we assigned some positions in step 8.

If `Developer` now owns a record, that record will be accessible by users that have the `Lead` position. Rather than sharing, the position hierarchy will take care of rendering the records accessible. No additional configuration or manual actions are required.

> Note that you will need to at least give the user read access to the entity to be able to view the shared records (even if `Lead` won't have access by default).

There's more...

Similar to position hierarchy, you can also use Manager Hierarchy. In this case, you need to populate the manager field for each user by navigating to **Summary** | **Organization Information** | **Manager** on the user form.

If you want to visualize the position hierarchy or the user's hierarchy graphically, click on the little hierarchy icon on the left-hand side of the users or positions. The following two screenshots highlight the visualization icon position and an example hierarchical visualization:

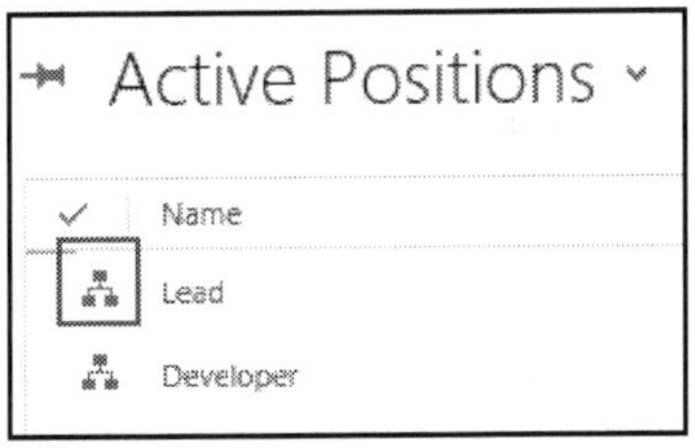

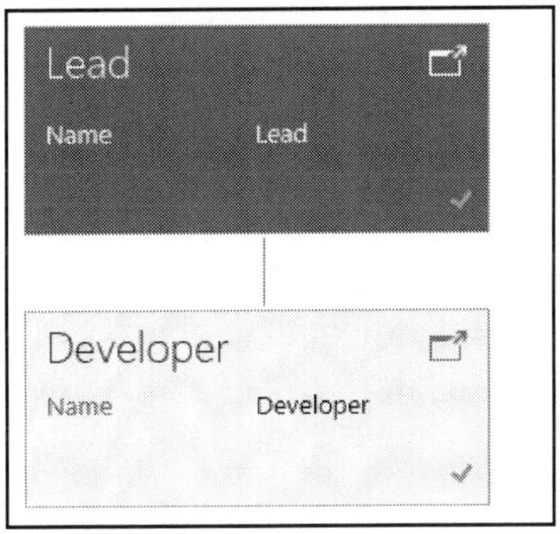

See also

- *Configuring business unit hierarchies*
- *Setting up teams and sharing*
- *Setting up Access Teams*

Configuring and assigning field-level security

For a long time, field-level security was a top ask from Dynamics CRM users. During Dynamics CRM 4.0 era, many attempted to implement field-level security based on roles. However, most of the customization was limited to the frontend web interface that rendered the solution somewhat insecure. Some third-party add-ons had more comprehensive solutions until the feature was introduced in Dynamics CRM 2011.

In this recipe, we will enable the e-mail address on the contact entity for field security, and then we will create a read profile to allow users associated with it to be able to read the attribute.

Getting ready

As per the previous security configuration, we will need a `Packt` solution to contain our changes. From a security privilege perspective, you will need a System Administrator to create and update the profiles.

How to do it...

1. Navigate to **Settings** | **Solutions** | **Packt** | **Entities** | **Contact** | **Fields**.
2. Double-click on **emailaddress1** and select **Enable** for **Field Security** and then click on **Save and Close**. The field might not be on the first page of attributes, but rather on a subsequent one:

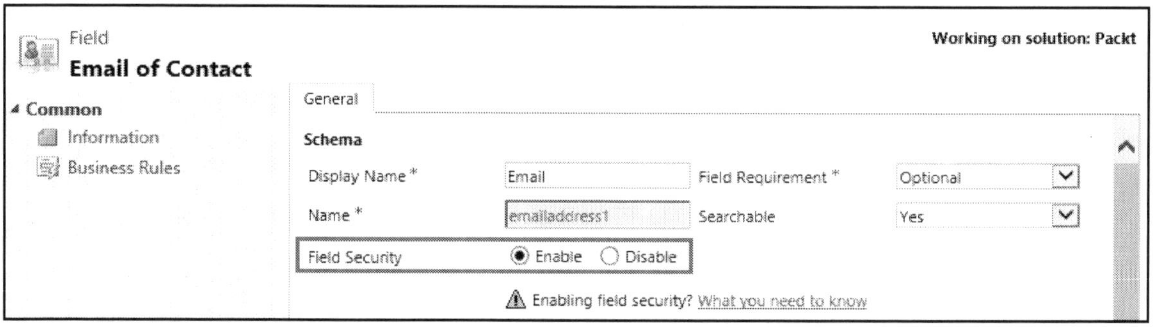

3. Click on **Publish All Customizations**.
4. Back in your solution, click on **Field Security Profiles** and then click on **New**.
5. Enter the `Packt` security profile under **Name** and click on the **Save** button.
6. Under **Field Permissions** from the left-hand side navigation, double-click on **emailaddress1** and in the dialog, select **Allow Read** as `Yes`, and then click on **OK**:

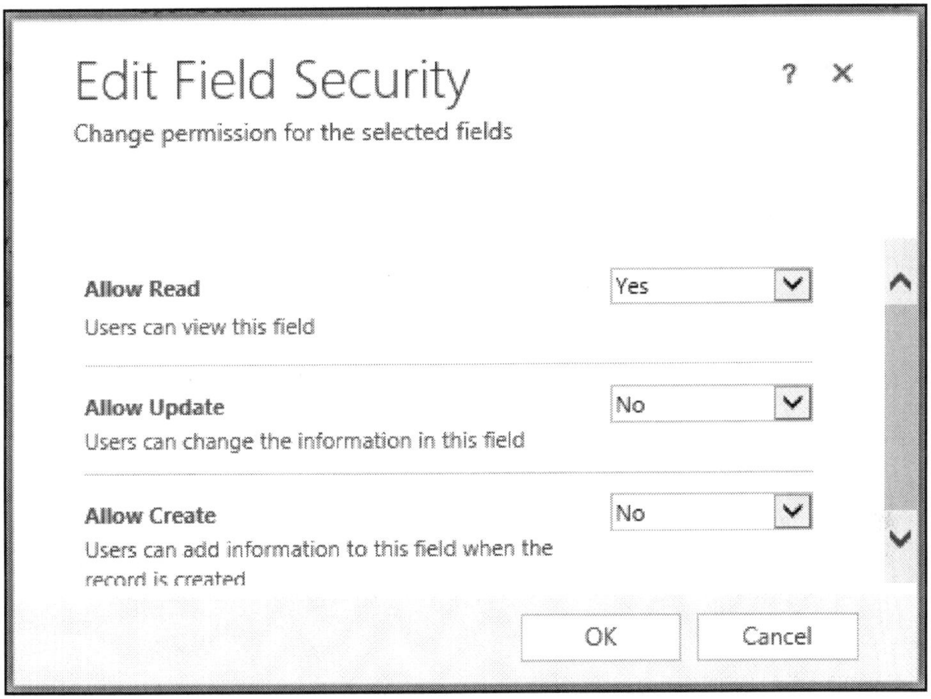

7. Select **Users** from the left-hand side navigation and click on **Add**, select a user of your choice, and then click on **Select** and **Add**.
8. Click on **Save and Close**.

How it works...

In step 2, we defined the specific attribute as being field-security-enabled. In step 4 to step 8, we defined a security profile; we defined what access the profiles enable in step 6, and we added `Users/Teams` that are part of this security profile.

In this particular example, we enabled a `Read` privilege; however, we can also define `Create` and `Update` privileges.

Behind the scenes, the user is granted access to that specific field and will be able to read the value behind it.

Field-level security applies to all layers, including the SDK, the web API, and reports.

Field-level security cannot be applied to attributes that are part of an alternate key combination.

Note that if a user does not have read access to a field, the user will still be able to see the field itself in the web interface but the value will be replaced by dots.

There's more...

Similar to security roles, security profiles are cumulative. You can create a separate read-only and a separate update-only profile and a user that has both will be able to read and update the attribute.

See also

- *Building cumulative security roles*

Setting up teams and sharing

Another great security feature in Dynamics 365 is team ownership. Team ownership greatly enhances complex sharing scenarios across different business units.

As discussed previously in this chapter, the Dynamics 365 security model is driven by record ownership and business unit structure. In the *Configuring business unit hierarchies* recipe earlier in this chapter, we discussed how users belonging to different business units, and with different security roles, will have access to different records with different levels of privileges. In this recipe we will demonstrate how a user who usually doesn't have full privileges to a record can easily get correct access by becoming a member of a team with the correct security role.

Leveraging the security model created in this chapter's *Configuring business unit hierarchies*, we will extend the example to include a team belonging to the `United States` business unit and with the global security role to show how team membership increases the privileges a user has. This diagram highlights the business unit structure as well as the user membership and access:

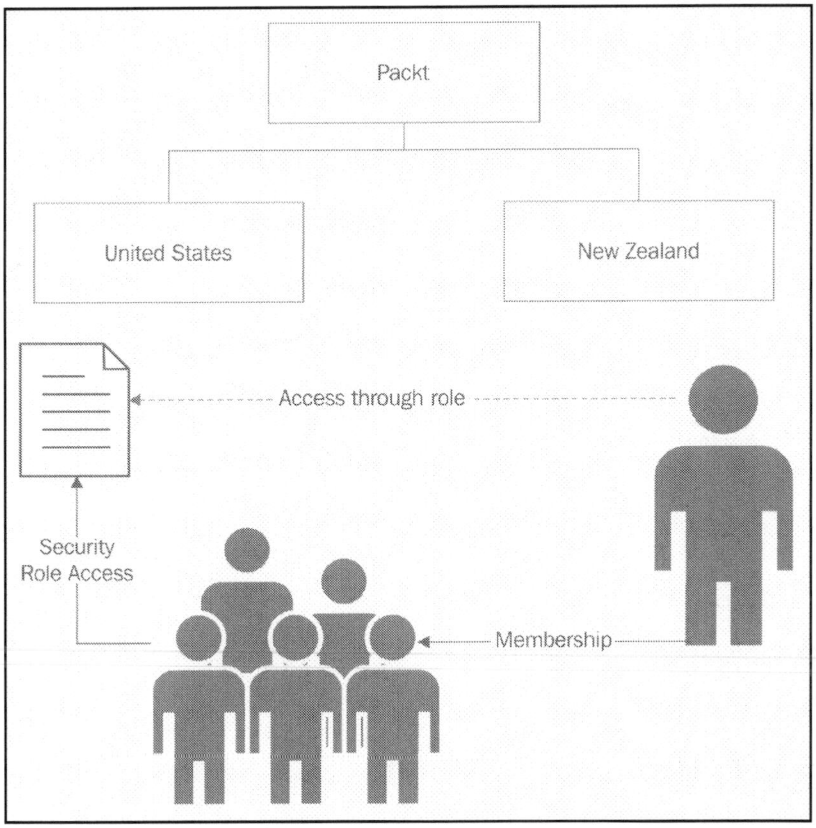

Getting ready

For this recipe, you will need the business unit structure and the security roles created in the *Configuring business unit hierarchies* recipe from this chapter.

To assign someone to a team, you will need to have the **Team**'s **Append To** privileges located under **Business Management** | **Entity** | **Team** in security roles. Furthermore, you will need to have equivalent or higher privileges than the security roles offered by the team.

How to do it...

1. Navigate to **Settings** | **Security** | **Teams**.
2. Click on **New** and create a team with the following details:
    - **Team Name**: `Global Team`
    - **Business Unit**: `Unites States`
    - **Administrator**: `<yourself>`
    - Click on **Save**
3. Click on **MANAGE ROLES**, select `Global Read`, and click on **OK**:

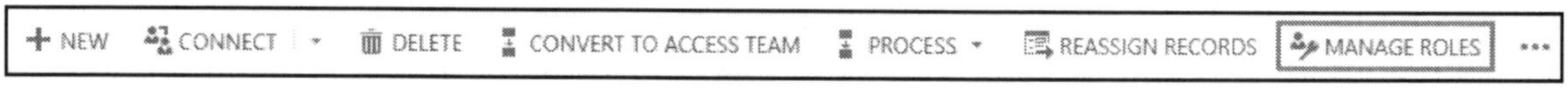

4. Add a user that belongs to the `New Zealand` business unit with the (limited) `Read` security role to the newly created team by clicking on the **+** button and searching for the user:

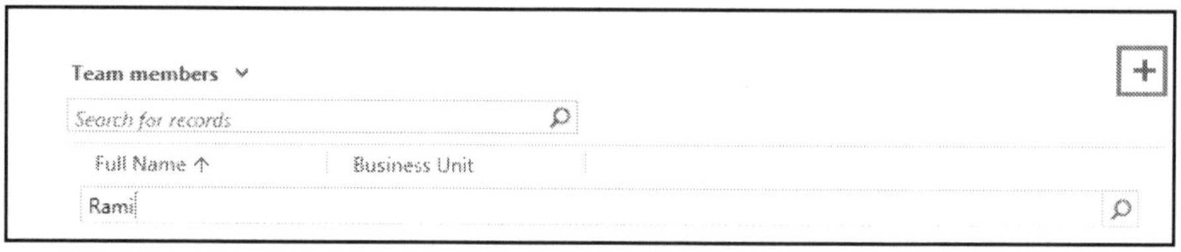

How it works...

As discussed in this chapter, Dynamics 365 uses the cumulative of all possible privileges a user has in order to define their full set of privileges. In other terms, your privileges are the sum of what you have, as opposed to what a security role does not provide you.

In this recipe, we created a team with elevated privileges and assigned a user to the team.

> TIP: You don't have to always create new teams. Each business units will have its own teams created by default.

The user then inherits the elevated privileges and will appear as part of the team's business unit.

There's more...

This recipe described one way of using the team to elevate a user's privileges. This is a common practice when users often require greater privileges temporarily. Creating a team with elevated privileges and adding and removing users from that team is an easy way to manage temporary privileges.

> **TIP**: Keep in mind that every time you change the security roles of a user (including changing teams) the security principles cache in Dynamics 365 is flushed which might cause a performance overhead.

Another way of leveraging the power of teams is for ownership. When a record privilege is set at the user level (as per the screenshot), the record can be the owner by a user or a team. When owned by a team, all users that are part of that team will have the same privileges to the record:

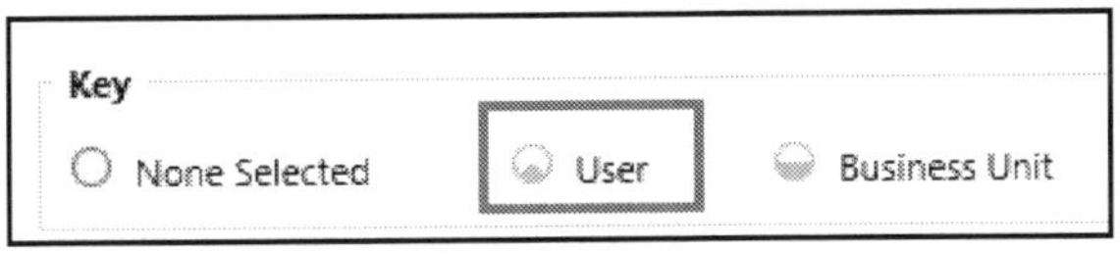

The same access applies when a record is owned at a Business Unit level that the user does not have access to. The record becomes available when the user becomes a member of a team in that Business Unit.

See also

- *Building cumulative security roles*
- *Configuring business unit hierarchies*

Setting up Access Teams

Access Teams are a relatively new addition to Dynamics 365. The feature was introduced in Dynamics CRM 2013 as a solution for large-scale sharing.

Access Teams enable security on a per-record basis and is easier to manage and control than record sharing. Furthermore, Access Teams can be manipulated using the SDK, making it a good candidate for security extensions to deal with complex security requirements.

Here we will focus on manually populated Access Teams where we define a template for an entity. The team is automatically created by Dynamics 365 for each record of that type when a user is manually added. We'll create the template for `Accounts`.

Getting ready

To create an Access Team template, the entity in question needs to be enabled for **Access Teams**. By default, the **Access Teams** feature is not enabled. To enable it, navigate to your customization area: **Settings** | **Solutions** | **Packt** | Entities | **Account**. In the general details of the entity (in our case, **Account**), select **Access Teams** located under the **Communication & Collaboration** header as shown here:

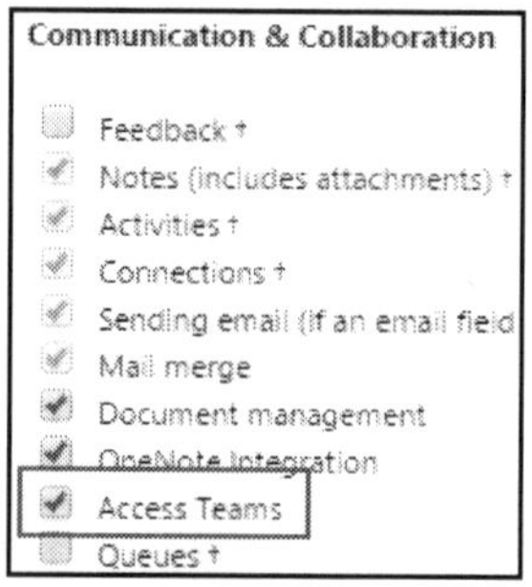

Note that the default number of entities that can be enabled for team access is five. The setting may be changed by updating the `MaxEntitiesEnabledForAutoCreatedAccessTeams` deployment value.

In order to set up an Access Team template, you require a minimum set of privileges on the team entity (`Create`, `Read`, `Assign`, `Assign To`).

The team entity privilege can be found under **Business Management** | **Entities** in security roles.

To manually add users to Access Teams, you need the shareprivileges on the record in question. This is similar to sharing records except that it is managed through the Access Team. If you add the users to the Access Team using `AddMembersToTeamRequest`, then you will need write privileges on the team entity.

In order to inherit the security privileges of a team access, you need at least the equivalent privileges to the entity type set at the user level in one of your security roles.

How to do it...

1. Navigate to **Settings** | **Security** | **Access Team Templates**.
2. Click on **New** and create a new team template with the following details:
   - **Name**: `Account Write`
   - **Entity**: `Account`
   - **Access Rights**: Tick on **Write**
   - Click on **Save & Close**
3. Navigate to the **Account** form by going to **Settings** | **Solutions** | **Packt** | **Account** | **Forms** and open the **Account Main** form.
4. Insert a subgrid where suitable with the following details; then click on **OK**:
   - **Name**: `Write_Team`
   - **Label**: `Write Access Team Users`
   - Navigate to **Data Source** | **Records** and select **All Record Types**
   - **Entity**: `Users`
   - **Default View**: `Associated Record Team Members`
   - **Team Template**: `Account Write`
5. Click on **Save and Close** and then click on **Publish All Customizations**.
6. Navigate to an account's record and add a user (that does not have access to that record) to the account's `Write Access Team`.

How it works...

We started by creating the Access Team template to give any user in the team write access to the specific record.

Note how the list does not include a `Create` right. `Create` is handled by security roles. Once created, security roles' authorization handles default privileges. Access Teams come in to set privileges to a specific record.

If you cannot see the entity you are after in step 2, chances are it is not access-team-enabled. Read the *Getting ready* section of this recipe for details on how to enable an entity for Access Team.

In step 2 to step 5, we added the specific Access Team subgrid to the form to easily manipulate who is part of the list. Finally, in step 6, we added a user to the Access Team, giving them special access to a specific record that they would not have access to otherwise.

The Access Team is only created when the first user is added to the team. The access team is deleted when the last user is removed from the team.

Access Teams are relatively faster and more scalable than Owner Teams. Access Teams do not have security roles associated with them, rendering them faster to query given the simpler structure.

Entities can contain one or more Access Teams based on Access Team templates. When users join an Access Team, they inherit the privileges associated with that team regardless of their current privileges. Access Teams are also cumulative like security roles.

One thing to keep in mind is that the privilege is only applied to the one record. All related records will still follow the default security roles. Extra customization can propagate the user's membership to additional Access Teams belonging to related records. Furthermore, security role hierarchies (**User**, **Organization**, **Parent: Child Business Unit**), are irrelevant as Access Teams are not driven by ownership.

One more thing to be aware of is that team access templates are not solution-aware. They are treated as data and need to be transported using a different mechanism between SDLC environments.

There's more...

Access is designed for scale. The white paper *Scalable Security Modeling with Microsoft Dynamics CRM 2015* at `https://technet.microsoft.com/en-us/library/dn683914(v=crm.7).aspx` highlights design considerations given different scenarios. The paper highlights that Access Teams are the preferred mechanism when users have in excess of a thousand team membership.

For a functionality comparison between Access Teams and Owner Teams, read the MSDN article at `https://msdn.microsoft.com/en-us/library/dn481569.aspx`.

See also

- *Setting up teams and sharing*

Encrypting data at rest to meet the FIPS 140-2 standard

Dynamics 365 has the capability of encrypting data at rest (with a customer-controlled key) for some attributes in order to comply with the FIPS 140-2 standard. Dynamics 365 online has data encryption enabled by default.

It is recommended that you change the default encryption key when you first create your online instance.

Dynamics 365 online has all its data encrypted at rest using SQL TDE as stated in `https://technet.microsoft.com/en-us/library/jj134930.aspx#BKMK_Securing`:
All instances of Dynamics 365 (online) use Microsoft SQL Server Transparent Data Encryption (TDE) to perform real-time encryption of data when written to disk, also known as encryption at rest.

In this recipe, we will demonstrate how to enable encryption in an on-premise Dynamics 365 implementation.

Note that once encryption is switched on, it cannot be disabled.

Getting ready

The user enabling the encryption must be a System Administrator and must be part of the `PrivUserGroup` Active Directory security group created during the Dynamics 365 installation. Additionally, your deployment must be configured to use HTTPS. If your deployment doesn't, you will have to change the **MSCRM_CONFIG** | **DeploymentProperties** | **DisableSSLCheckForEncryption** | **BitColumn** - a practice that is not recommended.

How to do it...

1. Navigate to **Settings** | **Data Management** | **Data Encryption**.
2. In the **Data Encryption** dialog, enter an encryption key under **Activate Encryption Key** and click on **Activate** as the following screenshot shows:

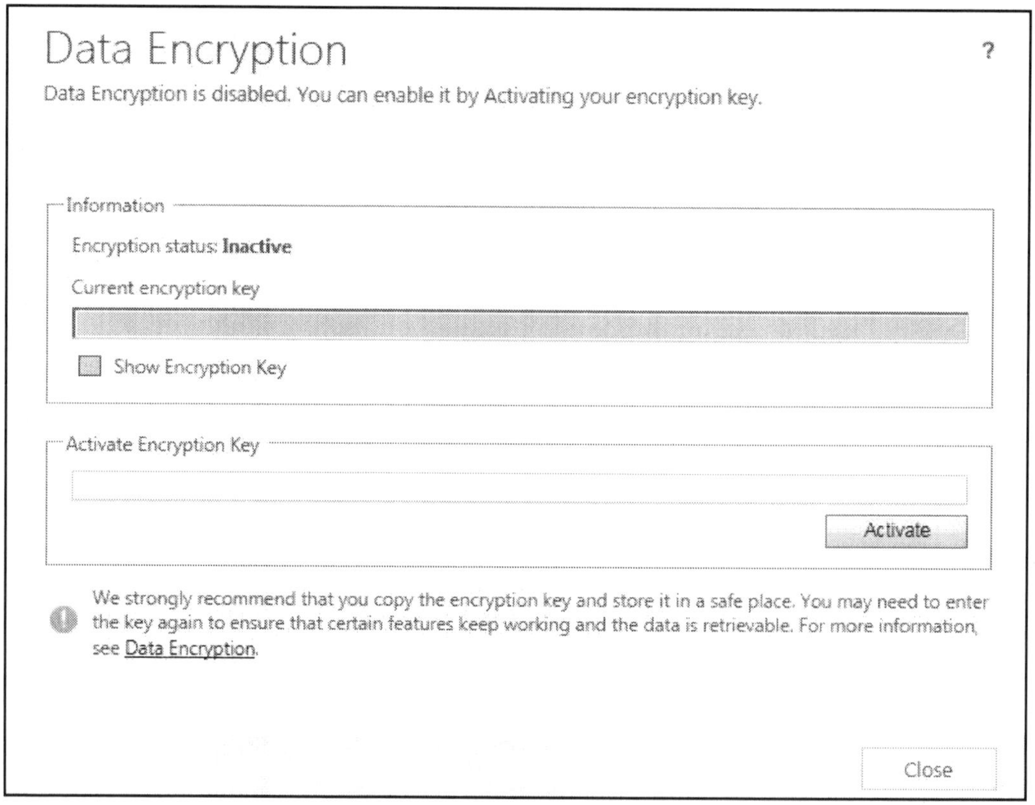

How it works...

Behind the scenes, Dynamics 365 leverages SQL Server cell level encryption to encrypt the following attributes:

Entity	**Attribute**
EmailServerProfile	EmailServerProfile
IncomingPassword	IncomingPassword
EmailServerProfile	EmailServerProfile
OutgoingPassword	OutgoingPassword
Mailbox	Mailbox

Unfortunately, at the time of writing this, there is no way to encrypt fields other than the ones highlighted in the preceding table.

There's more...

In terms of best practice, it is a good idea to back up your encryption key somewhere safe.

If you want to know more about encryption, read the MSDN articles at `https://technet.microsoft.com/library/dn531199(v=crm.7).aspx` and `https://msdn.microsoft.com/en-nz/library/dn481562.aspx`.

Dynamics 365 on-premise also supports SQL Server **transparent data encryption** (**TDE**).

TIP

Note that TDE-enabled databases will suffer from an approximate 10% performance penalty as stated in the Dynamics 365 implementation guide.

See also

- *Managing your Dynamics 365 online SQL TDE encryption key*

Managing your Dynamics 365 online SQL TDE encryption key

In Early 2017 Microsoft announced that all new Dynamics 365 instances will be encrypted at the SQL Server level using **Transparent Data Encryption** (**TDE**) as described in `https://technet.microsoft.com/en-us/library/jj134930.aspx#BKMK_Securing`. Shortly after the announcement Microsoft enabled a feature to allow its customers to control the TDE key through the *Dynamics 365 Administration Centre*. By default, the key will be defined by Microsoft until an administrator changes it.

Getting ready

In order to change the key, you will need an instance of Dynamics 365 with a Plan 1 or Plan 2 subscription (sandbox or production). You also need a user with either Office 365 Dynamics service administrator (or higher, such as global administrator) or with the Dynamics 365 System Administrator security role.

How to do it...

1. Login to your Office 365 tenancy by navigating to https://portal.office.com.
2. Click on the **Admin** tile.
3. From the left navigation bar navigate to **Admin Centers** | **Dynamics 365**.
4. In the **Dynamics 365 Administration Center** navigate to the **INSTANCES** tab; then click the instance to update, followed by **EDIT** in the right dialog.

5. In the **edit instance** page under **data encryption settings,** click on the **manage key** button as shown here:

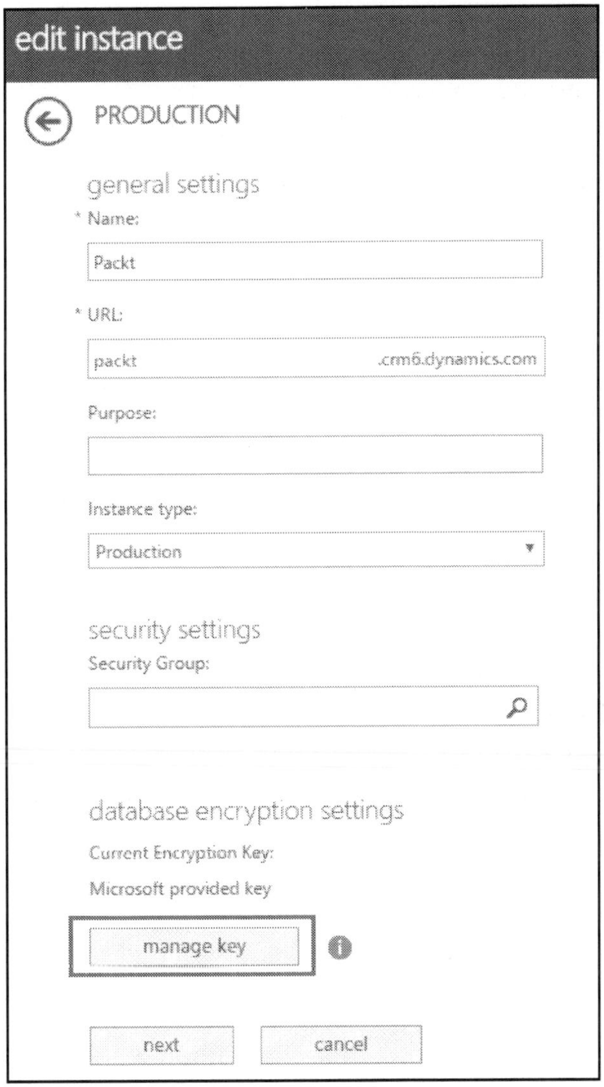

6. Click **ok** in the **Are you sure you want to manage your encryption key** dialog.
7. In the **manage your database encryption key** click on **new** as shown in this screenshot:

8. Enter your encryption key password in the **download your new encryption key** dialog; then click on **OK,** as shown here:

9. In the **Are you sure you want to change your encryption key** dialog click on **yes**.
10. Your new encryption key will automatically download. The key has a `.pfx` extension.

How it works...

In step 1 to step 5, we navigated to the location where we can manage the encryption key.

In step 6 to step 9, we created a new key, protected it with a password, and confirmed that we want to change the key.

Finally, in step 10 we downloaded the key.

Make sure you backup your key in a secure location as Microsoft will not have access to the key or to the encrypted data anymore.

By following these 10 steps you will have encrypted your data at rest with a key that you manage. Any existing or newly created data will be encrypted from then onward.

It is important to understand the risks associated with encryption keys. A malicious administrator can potentially render an instance unusable by encrypting it, locking it, and deleting the encryption key. Luckily the encryption takes 72 hours to complete giving you a window to roll back before any damage is caused. For more details read the TechNet article at `https://technet.microsoft.com/en-us/library/mt492471.aspx#KM_risk`.

There's more...

This recipe covered steps to create a new key from within the Dynamics 365 Administration Center; however, you can create your own PFX or BYOK key and import it. For more details read the *About BYOK* section in the TechNet article at `https://technet.microsoft.com/en-us/library/mt492471.aspx#KM_details`.

Reverting to a Microsoft managed key

If you want to revert your decision to a Microsoft managed encryption key, you can always go back to the **manage your database encryption key** dialog and clicking on the **revert** button.

See Also

- *Encrypting data at rest to meet the FIPS 140-2 standard*

8
DevOps

In this chapter, we will cover the following recipes:

- Exporting Dynamics 365 solutions using PowerShell
- Deploying solutions using PowerShell
- Building a solution hierarchy
- Patching a solution
- Staging a solution
- Using SolutionPackager to save solutions in source control
- Packaging your solution with configuration data using PackageDeployer
- Triggering builds on solution version increments
- Integrating your deployment cycles with Octopus Deploy

Introduction

DevOps has been a buzz word for quite a few years now. Many platforms have embraced the discipline and integrated it within their development life cycle. Over the years, Dynamics CRM/365 followed the trend and kept the platform modern and up to date. The introductions of solutions in CRM 2011, the introduction of the SolutionPackager and PackageDeployer, and the `Microsoft.Xrm.Data.PowerShell` extensions are all examples of baby steps to support the DevOps story. Some of these tools were spawned out of the necessity to support new features (for example, `AppSource`) with Microsoft repurposing some of its own tools for generic reuse by the public.

The recipes in this chapter will cover a few DevOps fundamentals, such as solution exports and imports, bundling configuration data with solutions, source control integration, and deployment orchestration. Stitched together, you will end up with a strong DevOps story to tell.

The following diagram depicts a development life cycle with the steps described in this chapter:

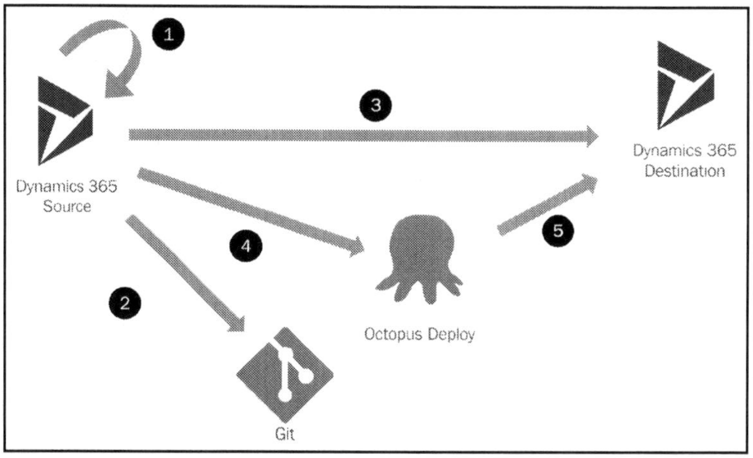

Each of the steps numbered in the preceding diagram corresponds to one or more recipes in this chapter:

1. Building solution hierarchies and incrementing versions.
2. Using SolutionPackager to save solutions in source control.
3. Patching a solution, staging a solution, and deploying a solution using PowerShell.
4. Exporting Dynamics 365 solutions using PowerShell.
5. Integrating your deployment cycles with Octopus Deploy.

Exporting Dynamics 365 solutions using PowerShell

Ever wondered whether you can write a script to automatically export a solution from one instance of Dynamics 365 and import it into another instance? The answer is yes; all you need is `Microsoft.Xrm.Data.PowerShell`.

The `Microsoft.Xrm.Data.PowerShell` extensions are created and maintained by the Microsoft staff. The two main contributors are Kenichiro Nakamura from Microsoft Japan and Sean McNellis from Microsoft corporate US. The extensions are wrappers around the Dynamics 365 SDK capabilities to enhance the platform's PowerShell scripting capabilities.

In this recipe, we will learn how to script a solution export from Dynamics 365 into the filesystem. This recipe is the foundation for later automation, discussed in this chapter to integrate with source control, to import solutions, and more.

Getting ready

As described in the introduction, the `Microsoft.Xrm.Data.PowerShell` extensions are required to run the script, which require PowerShell x64 version 4.0 or above.

Here are the steps for the installation:

1. Download the latest version in the ZIP file format from the GitHub repository at `https://github.com/seanmcne/Microsoft.Xrm.Data.PowerShell/releases/`. At the time of writing, the latest version for Dynamics 365 is 2.5.

2. Once downloaded, right-click on the ZIP file and tick the **unblock** checkbox, as shown in following screenshot:

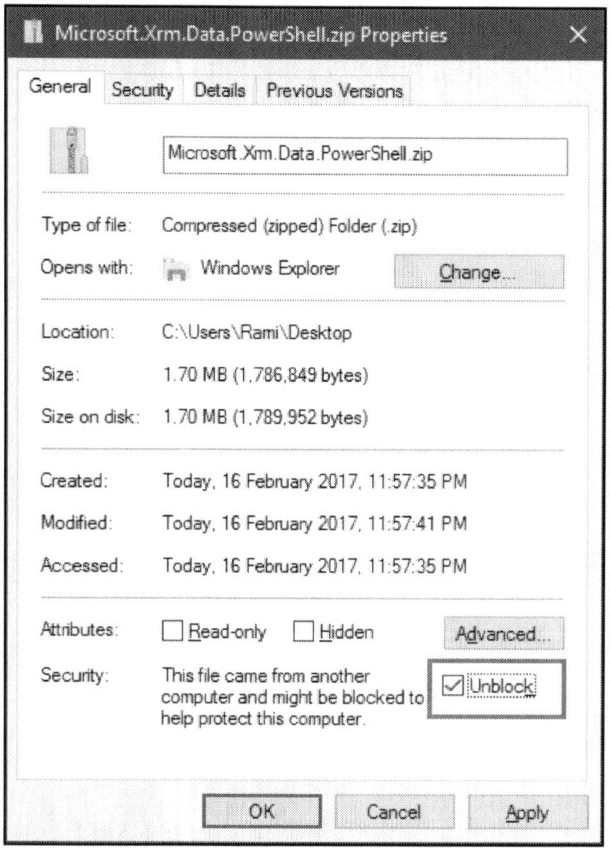

3. Extract the compressed files into `%WINDIR%\System32\WindowsPowerShell\v1.0\Modules\Microsoft.Xrm.Data.PowerShell`.
4. Launch a PowerShell console and import the newly downloaded module by running the following command:

```
Import-Module Microsoft.Xrm.Data.Powershell
```

...And now you will be ready to start.

If you receive an error stating `Import-Module: Could not load file or assembly`, you most likely forgot to unblock the downloaded assemblies, as mentioned in step 2 above.

Note that if you are running a script, ensure that you have script execution permissions by running a `Set-ExecutionPolicy` command, for example, `Set-ExecutionPolicy RemoteSigned`. Alternatively, you'll need to pass the `-ExecutionPolicy Bypass` each time you run a script.

The latest installation instructions can be found at `https://github.com/seanmcne/Microsoft.Xrm.Data.PowerShell`.

Dynamics 365 prerequisites

You will also need the correct **System Customizer** or higher security roles to export solutions from Dynamics 365.

We are also assuming that you have a solution in your Dynamics 365 instance called `Packt`.

How to do it...

1. Run the `Connect-CrmOnlineDiscovery -InteractiveMode` command and follow the familiar prompt to connect.
2. Run the following command:

```
Export-CrmSolution Packt
```

How it works...

In the first step, we established a connection to our Dynamics 365 instance using the familiar interactive login dialog we have seen in other chapters.

We then issued the command to export the solution called `Packt`. The command will export the solution in the unmanaged mode.

There's more...

In this recipe, we used the `-InteractiveMode` switch to connect to Dynamics 365. This method requires human intervention to enter the connection details. Alternatively, you can use `Get-CrmConnection` and pass the connection details to automate that step, as described later in this chapter in *Triggering builds on solution version increments* and *Integrating your deployment cycles with Octopus Deploy*.

`Export-CrmSolution` has a collection of switches and extra parameters you can leverage. For example, you can give your ZIP file a different name, specify a different export path, specify which version of Dynamics 365 you are targeting using the `TargetVersion` (8.0, 8.1, 8.2), export the solution as managed by adding the `-Managed` parameter, and so on. For more information on the `Export-CrmSolution` parameters, run the `Get-Help Export-CrmSolution -Detailed` command.

> With every release of Dynamics CRM\365, Microsoft publishes a solution compatibility matrix to understand which destination instance versions are compatible with which source solutions' instance version. Check the MSDN article for details at `https://msdn.microsoft.com/en-us/library/gg334576.aspx#BKMK_VersionCompat`.

You can run the `Get-Command *crm*` command to see all the possible commands provided by the extensions. If you need further details or would like to know more about how to use a command, run the `Get-Help <commandname>` command.

See also

- *Deploying solutions using PowerShell*
- *Using SolutionPackager to save solutions in source control*
- *Triggering builds on solution version increments*
- *Integrating your deployment cycles with Octopus Deploy*

Deploying solutions using PowerShell

Similar to the export capabilities, the `Microsoft.Xrm.Data.PowerShell` commands also offer solution import capabilities using `Import-CrmSolution`.

This recipe will cover the PowerShell commands to import a solution into Dynamics 365.

Getting ready

Similar to the previous recipe, you will need to install the `Microsoft.Xrm.Data.PowerShell` module. Check the previous recipe for details on how to install and the prerequisites.

From a Dynamics 365 perspective, you will need the **System Customizer** or **System Administrator** role to import solutions into your instance.

Obviously, we'll need a solution to import. In this instance, we'll use a managed version of the solution exported in the previous recipe.

How to do it...

1. Run the `Connect-CrmOnlineDiscovery -InteractiveMode` command and follow the prompt to connect.
2. Run the following command:

```
Import-CrmSolution -SolutionFilePath Packt_managed_0_0_0_1.zip -
PublishChanges
```

How it works...

As in the previous recipe, in step 1, we connected to a Dynamics 365 instance. In step 2, we ran the command to import the previously exported manage solution. The -`PublishChanges` switch instructs the command to publish all changes after the solution is imported.

There's more...

As per most of the module's command, `Import-CrmSolution` has a range of additional parameters that can be used. Among them are `ActivatePlugIns`, which ensures that all plugins included in the solution are activated, and `OverwriteUnManagedCustomizations`, which overrides previously imported unmanaged customizations. For more details, run `Get-Help Import-CrmSolution -Detailed`.

> When an import fails, it fails silently. Make sure you always increment your solution number before exporting in order to easily identify whether the latest version was imported successfully to your destination instance. You can achieve that by simply running the `Set-CrmSolutionVersionNumber` command. Version increments are also useful to allow you to track changes overtime.

By coupling `Export-CrmSolution` and `Import-CrmSolution`, you can create a script that would promote a Dynamics 365 solution from one environment to another. This is a baby step toward **continuous integration** (**CI**) DevOps automation.

See also

- *Exporting Dynamics 365 solutions using PowerShell*
- *Triggering builds on solution version increments*
- *Integrating your deployment cycles with Octopus Deploy*

Building a solution hierarchy

The introduction of solutions in Dynamics CRM 2011 significantly simplified promoting your configuration and customization from one SDLC environment to another.

Solutions can be used to create hierarchies of dependent solutions, each containing a subset of your components. Separating solutions simplifies deployments by turning large-scale deployments into a collection of smaller deployments.

In `Chapter 2`, *Client-Side Extensions*, we created a JavaScript concurrency library that we bundled within the `Packt` solution. We then hooked the library with the `OnLoad` event on the contact form. Recognizing that the concurrency library can be leveraged and reused in other entities, or even other implementations, it is wise to separate it into its own solution. The `Packt Common` solution created in this recipe will house any reusable common libraries or customization to easily transport them between implementations without worrying about any components that are dependent on them.

Getting ready

For this recipe, you will require the base `Packt` solution used in `Chapter 2`, *Client-Side Extensions*, as well as the JavaScript concurrency library customization and the entity dependent on that library. Alternatively, you can build your own solutions and customization and bundle them in a similar way.

From a security perspective, as with most solution-related recipes, you will need at least a **System Customizer** role.

How to do it...

1. Navigate to **Settings** | **Solutions**.
2. Click on **New** and create a new solution with the following details:
    - **Display Name**: `Packt Common`
    - **Publisher**: `Packt`
    - **Version**: `0.0.0.1`
    - Click on the **Save** button
3. Click on **Web Resources** on the left-hand side navigation and then click on the **Add Existing** button.
4. Find and select the concurrency JavaScript `packt_/js/concurrency.js` and click on **OK**.
5. Click on **Save and Close**.
6. Navigate back to your original `Packt` solution and remove the concurrency JavaScript library from it.

How it works...

In this simple recipe, we barely scratched the surface of solution hierarchies by separating a common library, and the entities dependent on it, into two separate solutions, as highlighted in this diagram:

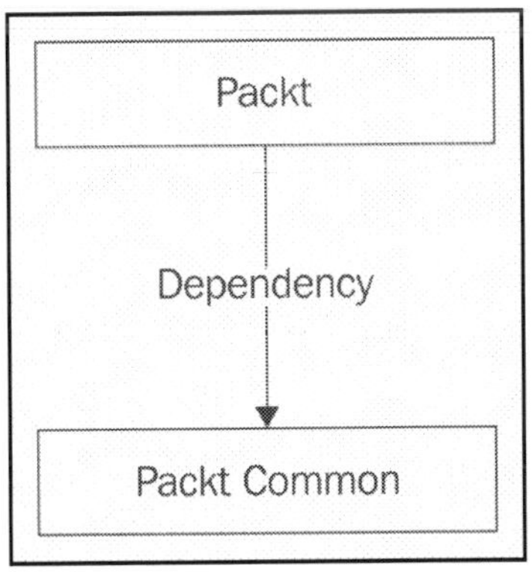

When deploying the solutions into a new environment, you must deploy the `Packt Common` solution first, as the `Packt` solution has a dependency on its components. Subsequently, the `Packt` solution can be deployed without any refreshes to the `Packt Common` solution, if not required. Conversely, you can deploy an update to your common library without re-releasing any of the entities.

There's more...

Other typical practices include separating security roles, reports, and workflows into their own separate solutions. This provides you the necessary modularity when you redeploy your solutions.

An alternative to solution hierarchies is solution patching. You can still keep everything in one solution and apply small solution patches that include the bare minimum required when deploying. This mitigates the risk of large deployments but might introduce solution upgrade complexities.

> TIP: Be careful when cherry-picking what needs to be packaged in your patch and ensure you are not missing anything out.

See also

- *Patching a solution*

Patching a solution

Up until Dynamics CRM 2015, releasing a solution was a big task. Before solutions (CRM 4.0 era and before), System Customizers had to pick and choose what to promote to the next environments. Most included all customizations to avoid leaving anything behind. Solutions were introduced in CRM 2011 and have been improved over the years. Most notably, with CRM 2016, the concept of patching was introduced. Instead of releasing your entire solution, which might introduce a risk to your deployment, you can now narrow a release to the minimum required. Your patch, for example, might include an updated view, additional fields, or an updated form.

In this recipe, we will patch our `Packt` base solution and include an updated field along with an updated form.

Getting ready

In order to patch a solution, you will need the base `Packt` solution (or equivalent) already set up in your environment. The `Packt` solution has been used throughout the book; however, you can simply create a new solution of your choice.

How to do it...

1. Navigate to **Settings** | **Solutions**.
2. Click on the **Packt** solution and click on the **Clone a Patch** button:

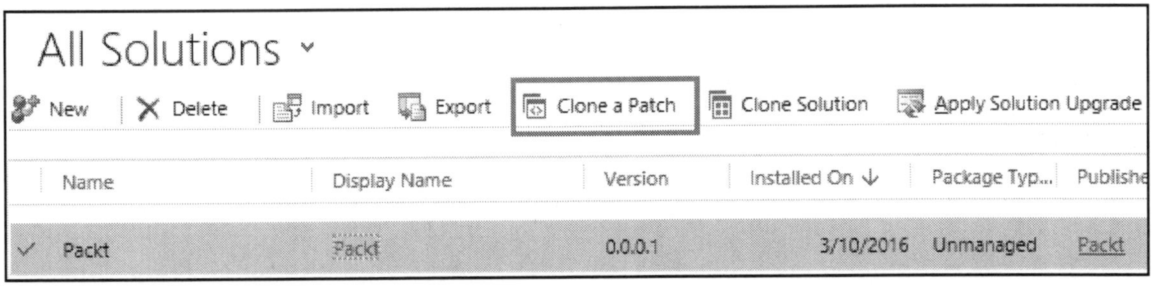

3. In the **Clone a Patch** dialog, keep the values as they are in the default and click on **Save**.
4. Open the newly created patch and click on **Add Existing**.
5. Select **Account** from **Solution components**, and then click on **OK**.
6. From the **Account** entity, select a view that was not present in the `Packt` base solution and click on **Finish**.
7. Click on **Save and Close**.

How it works...

We started in the first few steps by selecting our base solution and creating a patch for it. Note how, in step 3, Dynamics 365 automatically incremented the minor version number. When we open the newly created solution in step 4, you will notice that the patch does not contain any components. The whole point of a patch is to only add a few items to your solution.

TIP: If you are after the complete base solution with alterations instead of an empty solution with minor additions, consider using a `Clone` solution.

In step 4 to step 6, we chose the items to add and saved the patch. The patch is now ready to be exported and deployed into another environment.

There's more...

For more details on patching scenarios, read the MSDN article at `https://msdn.microsoft.com/en-us/library/mt593040.aspx`.

Once your solution is patched, the original solution cannot be altered until the patch is merged back. To enable the solution again, select the base solution and click on the **Clone Solution** button from the ribbon. For more details, read the following section of the same MSDN article at `https://msdn.microsoft.com/en-us/library/mt593040.aspx#Anchor_4`.

See also

- *Building a solution hierarchy*

Staging a solution

The capability to stage managed solutions was introduced in Dynamics CRM 2016. One of the problems addressed by staging is deleting components bundled in a managed solution.

In the past, to delete managed solution components, you had to introduce a holding solution (holding solutions are intermediary solutions that look like the final solution (with the deleted components) but they keep the schema (and the data) intact). The original solution was then deleted, and then the updated managed solution was reimported, followed by the holding solution removal.

The steps were cumbersome but unavoidable. The introduction of staging allows you to resolve the same problem addressed by two steps: stage and upgrade.

This recipe focuses on the steps required to stage a solution followed by its upgrade.

Getting ready

First, you must have an existing managed solution installed on your instance.

> TIP: Staging solutions only works on managed solutions.

When you try to import a newer version, the import wizard will prompt you for a staging option. In this example, we will start with the `Packt` managed solution V0.0.0.1, and then try to install V0.0.0.2. The latter version will have some components removed.

From a security perspective, we will require a **System Customizer** role or higher in order to import solutions.

How to do it...

1. Navigate to **Settings** | **Solutions**.
2. Click on **Import** and select your updated solution and then click on **Next**.
3. In the **Solution Information** dialog, click on **Next**.

4. In the **Import Options** dialog, tick the **Stage for upgrade** checkbox and click on **Import**:

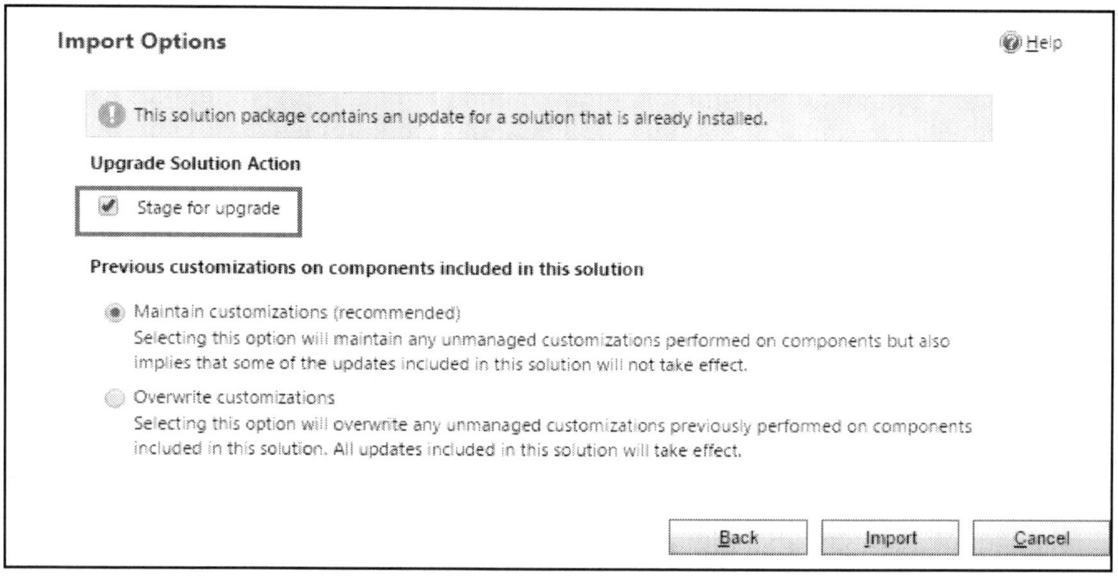

5. Once the import is complete, you can click on **Apply Solution Upgrade** from the import prompt:

6. Alternatively to step 5, you can navigate to the list of solutions, select your old solution, and click on **Apply Solution Upgrade**:

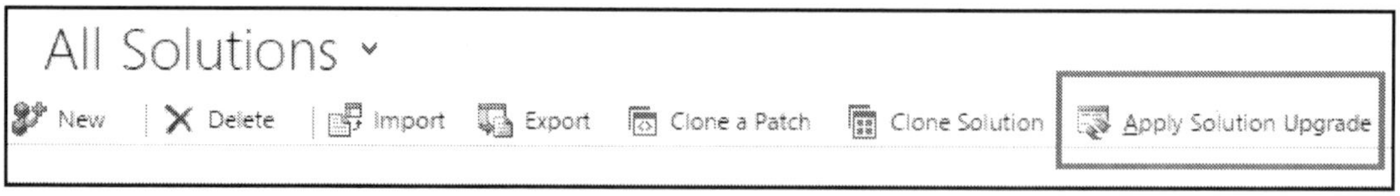

How it works...

The steps to stage and upgrade a managed solution are simple. All you have to do is tick the box when importing a newer version (step 4). Once the solution is imported successfully, you can upgrade it as set out in step 5 and step 6.

Behind the scenes, the solution upgrade takes care of deleting removed attributes without affecting the remaining data/schema and, most importantly, without complaining about the missing components.

See also

- *Patching a solution*

Using SolutionPackager to save solutions in source control

In this recipe, we will focus on storing a fragmented Dynamics 365 solution in the source control. More specifically, we will be using **SolutionPackager** to extract a Dynamics 365 solution into a folder that is Git initialized. We will then export an updated solution that had some components removed and demonstrate how the items will be removed from source control.

SolutionPackager is a utility introduced with Dynamics CRM 2013. It allows you to explode a Dynamics CRM\365 solution into small fragments. SolutionPackager also allows you to implode the extracted files back into a zipped solution file.

We primarily chose Git as it is becoming the mainstream distributed version control system, as well as for its ease of use. Git will recognize filesystem changes without the need to check-out files. We will use a local repository without connecting or pushing to a remote repository.

Getting ready

Given that we will be using Git, you will need to download a Git client. In our instance, we are using the command-line Git for Windows which can be downloaded from `https://git-scm.com/downloads`.

If you have a fresh Git install,consider doing a first-time setup. For example, you can set your user name and email by running the following commands:

```
git config --global user.name "Rami Mounla"
git config --global user.email  rami@packt.com
```

For more details about first-time setups, read the following article:

https://git-scm.com/book/en/v2/Getting-Started-First-Time-Git-Setup.

We will also extract the solution in a directory called `Solution` that needs to be a Git repository (initialized). You can initialize a folder by typing the `git init` command.

We will also need two Dynamics 365 solutions. One that has all components called `Packt365_0_0_0_15.zip`, and one that has fewer components called `Packt365_0_0_0_16.zip`. In our example, we will have one solution with the account entity with a view and a form and the other (V0.0.0.16) with only a form.

To extract the solution, we will need the Dynamics 365 SDK. The `SolutionPackager` executable is available under the `<SDK Folder>\Bin` folder. Copy `SolutionPackager.exe` to a parent folder relative to a `TempSolution` folder and the `Solution` folder to simplify the commands execution.

How to do it...

1. Execute the following commands from the command line in the `Solution` and `TempSolution` parent directory:

```
SolutionPackager.exe /action:Extract /zipfile:Packt365_0_0_0_15.zip
/folder:.\TempSolution
robocopy .\TempSolution .\Solution /e /purge /move /xd .git
cd Solution
git add .
git status .
git commit -m "First commit, full solution"
cd..
SolutionPackager.exe /action:Extract /zipfile:Packt365_0_0_0_16.zip
/folder:.\TempSolution
robocopy .\TempSolution .\Solution /e /purge /move /xd .git
cd Solution
git add .
git status .
git commit -m "Second commit, removed component"
```

How it works...

In step 1, we called `SolutionPackager` with the `/action:Extract` and `/folder:.\TempSolution` parameters to explode the solution to the `TempSolution` folder.

> If we didn't use a staging folder, SolutionPackager would have deleted all the files in the destination folder that are missing from the extracted solution, including the `.git` folder.

The `robocopy` command in step 2 moved all the files from the `TempSolution` folder to the Git repository directory Solution. The `/purge` option ensured all files missing from the source were deleted in the destination, while `/xd` ensured the `.git` folder was ignored (in order to avoid deleting your git repository details). The `/e` option ensured all files were moved recursively, including folders and subfolders.

In step 3, we staged all the changes to be committed. The status from step 4 should look like what is shown in the following figure if this is the first time the files are being committed:

```
C:\temp\Solution>git status
On branch master

Initial commit

Changes to be committed:
  (use "git rm --cached <file>..." to unstage)

        new file:   Entities/Account/Entity.xml
        new file:   Entities/Account/FormXml/main/{8448b78f-8f42-454e-8e2a-f8196b0419af}.xml
        new file:   Entities/Account/RibbonDiff.xml
        new file:   Entities/Account/SavedQueries/{00000000-0000-0000-00aa-000010001002}.xml
        new file:   Other/Customizations.xml
        new file:   Other/Relationships.xml
        new file:   Other/Solution.xml


C:\temp\Solution>
```

In step 5, we committed the changes locally.

In step 6, we repeated the same process with the updated solution that has fewer elements. The status in step 7 will highlight the fragment changes and the deleted items, as the following screenshot shows:

Finally, in step 8, we commited the latest changes.

There're more...

In this recipe, we covered an integration example with a Git repository. Another popular repository is **Microsoft Team Foundation Server**, **TFS** (also know as **Visual Studio Team Services**, **VSTS**). TFS requires a more elaborate script that compares files and checks out/in the files using the `tf` command.

The PowerShell script's pseudo code will look similar to the following steps:

- Using `tf.exe undo /recursive` undo any pending changes recursively
- Using `tf.exe get /recursive` get the latest version from TFS
- Using `tf.exe checkout /recursive` checkout all existing solution files within the solution folder
- Using `Get-CrmConnection` connect to Dynamics 365
- Using `Export-CrmSolution` export the solution
- Using `SolutionPackager.exe` extract solution to solution folder
- Using `tf.exe add` add the files that need to be checked in
- Using `tf.exe undo` undo checkout to files that need to be deleted
- Using `tf.exe delete` mark files to be deleted
- Using `tf.exe checkin /recursive` check-in all your changes

In his blog `https://waelhamze.wordpress.com` Wael Hamze, Dynamics 365 ALM enthusiast, explains different techniques to integrate your Dynamics 365 with TFS including a sample script of the preceding pseudocode. He even built his own open source CI/CD Dynamics CRM/365 framework, located at `https://github.com/WaelHamze/xrm-ci-framework`.

See also

- *Integrating your deployment cycles with Octopus Deploy*

Packaging your solution with configuration data using PackageDeployer

The PackageDeployer executable was introduced with the Dynamics CRM 2013 SDK.

PackageDeployer allows us to import one or more solutions to Dynamics 365 and can bundle configuration data, as well as custom code execution, all in one augmented package.

The easiest way to create a new package is to use the integrated Visual Studio Dynamics 365 Package solution template (demonstrated in this recipe). At the core of the process is an XML file that contains all the deployment directives.

> The PackageDeployer solution has some significance in the Dynamics 365 ecosystem. In `Chapter 9`, *Dynamics 365 Extensions*, we will cover Dynamics 365 AppSource applications. Behind the scenes, all AppSource deployments actually use the PackageDeployer code base to get deployed into your Dynamics 365 instance.

We will cover how to install a solution along with some reference data using PackageDeployer in this recipe.

Getting ready

To get going, you will need a solution, a Dynamics 365 instance, the SDK, and Visual Studio.

Dynamics 365 instance

Other than the usual **System Customizer** or higher privileges required to deploy a solution to your target instance, you will need a solution to deploy, along with some reference data to import.

Dynamics 365 SDK

Download the Dynamics 365 SDK. The Package Deployer is located at <SDK Folder>\Tools\PackageDeployer.

Visual Studio

You will need a compatible version of Visual Studio (2012, 2013, or 2015). In this example, we will use 2015. You also need the CRM SDK template, which you can download from http://go.microsoft.com/fwlink/p/?LinkId=400925. The CRM SDK template contains Dynamics 365 Visual Studio templates, including the one required for Package Deployer.

Files

In this recipe, we will reuse the Packt solution created in Chapter 2, *Client-Side Extensions*, as well as an account CSV file.

The Package Deployer is not meant to deal with large data migration; it is designed to import small amounts of records meant for configuration or as reference data. However, for simplicity in this recipe, we chose the accounts entity with only two records.

We will export the solution as managed and name it Packt_0_0_0_1_managed.zip.

The account CSV file will be called AccountsRecords.csv and will have the following details:

```
Account Name,Email
Packt 365,packt365@test.com
Packt 366,packt366@test.com
```

It is recommended that you have an XML mapping file to map the CSV columns to entity attributes in Dynamics 365. However, for simplicity, we omitted the mapping file in favor of default field names that will be automatically mapped to the corresponding entity attributes.

How to do it...

1. In Visual Studio, navigate to **File** | **New** | **Project...**
2. Create a new package of type **CRM Package** by navigating to **Visual C#** | **CRM SDK Templates** | **CRM Package**. Give it the name `PacktPackageDeployment`, shown as follows:

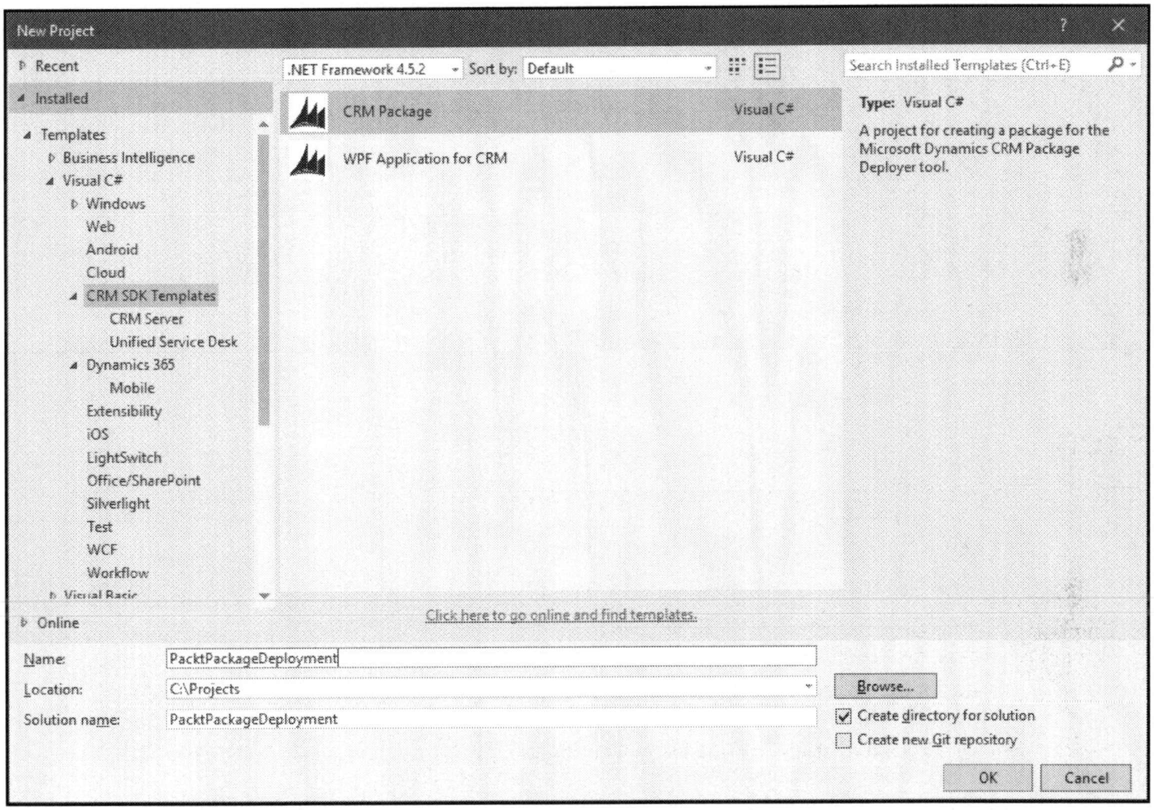

3. Add the exported managed solution Packt ZIP `Packt_0_0_0_1_managed.zip` to **PkgFolder**.
4. Add `AccountRecords.csv` to **PkgFolder**.

5. Ensure that all added files are always copied to the output folder. Right-click on each file, click on **properties**, and select **Copy always** under **Copy to Output Directory,** as highlighted in this screenshot:

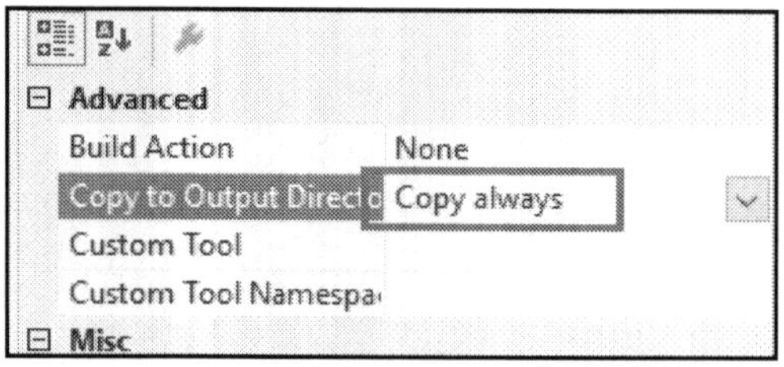

6. Update `ImportConfig.xml` with the following details:

```
<?xml version="1.0" encoding="utf-16"?>
<configdatastorage
xmlns:xsi="http://www.w3.org/2001/XMLSchema-instance"
xmlns:xsd="http://www.w3.org/2001/XMLSchema"
                  installsampledata="false"
                  waitforsampledatatoinstall="true"
                  agentdesktopzipfile=""
                  agentdesktopexename=""
                  crmmigdataimportfile="">
  <solutions>
    <configsolutionfile
solutionpackagefilename="Packt_0_0_0_1_managed.zip"
                       overwriteunmanagedcustomizations="true"
                       publishworkflowsandactivateplugins="true"/>
  </solutions>
  <filestoimport>
    <configimportfile filename="AccountRecords.csv"
                  filetype="CSV"
                  associatedmap=""
                  importtoentity="account"
                  datadelimiter=""
                  fielddelimiter="comma"
                  enableduplicatedetection="true"
                  isfirstrowheader="true"
                  isrecordownerateam="false"
                  owneruser=""
                  waitforimporttocomplete="false"/>
  </filestoimport>
  <filesmapstoimport>
  </filesmapstoimport>
</configdatastorage>
```

7. Compile your solution.
8. Copy `PkgFolder` with all its content from the solution output folder to the same folder as `PackageDeployer.exe <SDK>\Tools\PackageDeployer`.
9. Copy `PacktPackageDeployment.dll` from your output folder to the same folder from the previous step.
10. Run `PackageDeployer.exe` and follow the familiar login prompt.
11. Follow the prompts by clicking on **Next** until you reach the final page. Click on **Finish** to end the process.

How it works...

In the first 5 steps, we built the Visual Studio solution that contains all the files required to deploy our Dynamics 365 package. In step 5 specifically, we ensured that the added ZIP and CSV files are copied to the output folder after compilation, otherwise, files would be omitted. In step 6, we edited the `ImportConfig.xml` file to contain all the directives that will help the solution deployer import the correct files with the correct mapping. Our version is a simplified starting point; all we are doing is importing one solution and one CSV file called `AccountRecords.csv` that contains account records. We did not even specify a mapping file, as the CSV file contains the default attribute names that will allow automatic mapping. Most of the tags and attributes from `ImportConfig.xml` are self-explanatory. Nonetheless, the complete documentation is available at `https://msdn.microsoft.com/en-us/library/dn688182.aspx`.

In step 7, we compiled the solution, and in step 8 and step 9, we copied the relevant outputs to the `PackageDeployer` folder. We then launched PackageDeployer and followed the prompts. In step 11, the Package Deployer automatically picked up the files and deployed them to the designated instance that we logged-in to.

You can only deploy one package at a time; however, if more than one package are available, you will be prompted to select which one you are after:

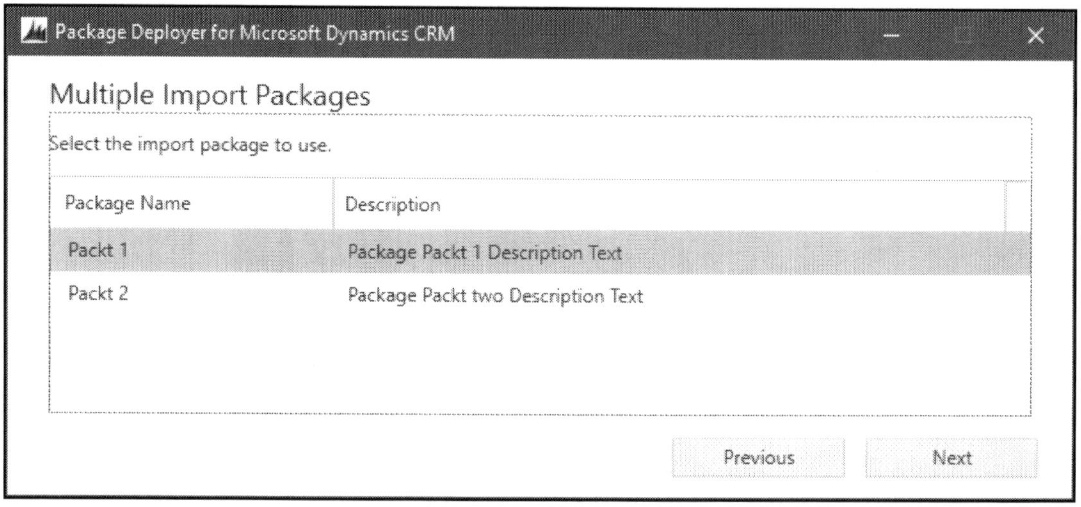

If you receive an error stating **No import packages were found. Exiting the program...**, chances are you did not copy the compiled DLL.

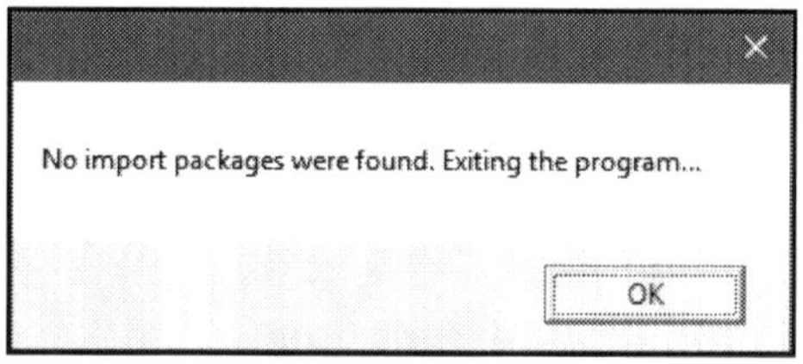

There's more...

In this recipe, we barely scratched the surface of the PackageDeployer tool. The Package Deployer is similar to the PowerShell `Import-CrmSolution` cmdlet and the bulk data import combined together with additional features and a user interface. The tool has a vast variety of options. For example, it can display a start and end HTML page, it can import reference data compressed in a ZIP file, it can upgrade solutions, and it can even import different language packs. Furthermore, the Package Deployer allows the execution of custom code along with your deployment to execute some automation logic during the deployment. For more details, refer to `https://msdn.microsoft.com/en-us/library/dn688182.aspx`.

Last but not least, PackageDeployer can also be triggered from PowerShell scripts. For more details, read the TechNet article at `https://technet.microsoft.com/en-us/library/dn647420.aspx`.

See also

- *Deploying solutions using PowerShell*

Triggering builds on solution version increments

In this recipe, we will implement a polling application that monitors a solution for version updates. When a version is updated, the script will automatically download the updated solution.

There are at least a couple of ways in which we can monitor the solution version update: either using the C# SDK libraries or using PowerShell. In either case, we can poll Dynamics 365 and monitor a particular solution to check whether it has been updated. Unfortunately, Dynamics 365 solutions do not support plugins or workflows which rules out an event-driven design.

This recipe will focus on the PowerShell option and will use Windows scheduling services to trigger the script on a predefined interval.

Getting ready

In order to monitor a solution, we will need a Dynamics 365 development environment containing a solution that we can update. In this recipe, we will use the `Packt` solution created in earlier chapters.

This recipe will focus on the PowerShell option to monitor the solution. This option is dependent on the `Microsoft.Xrm.Data.PowerShell` add-on to work. Refer to the first recipe in this book for details on how to install the add-on.

From a security perspective, a **System Customizer** or higher role is required as we will be updating the Dynamics 365 solution version.

How to do it...

1. Create a new PowerShell script in the `c:\Temp` folder called `SolutionMonitor.ps1`.
2. Copy the following code to your script:

```
param (
    [string]$solutionShortName = "Packt",
    [string]$versionFileName = "C:\temp\version.txt",
    [string]$username = "@.onmicrosoft.com",
    [string]$password = "",
    [string]$exportLocation = "C:\temp",
    [string]$instance = "https://.crm.dynamics.com",
    [string]$organisation = ""
)
Import-Module Microsoft.Xrm.Data.Powershell

$securePassword = ConvertTo-SecureString $password -AsPlainText -
Force
$credentials = New-Object System.Management.Automation.PSCredential
($username, $securePassword)

$connection = Get-CrmConnection -Credential $credentials -ServerUrl
$instance -OrganizationName $organisation

$solution = Get-CrmRecords -EntityLogicalName solution -
FilterAttribute uniquename -FilterOperator "eq" -FilterValue
$solutionShortName -Fields friendlyname,version -conn $connection

If ($solution.Count -ne 1) {
    Write-Error "The number of retuned solutions is not correct.
Expected 1, returned $($solution.Count)"
    exit 1
}

$latestVersion = $solution.CrmRecords[0].version
$oldVersion = Get-Content $versionFileName

if($latestVersion -eq $oldVersion){
    Write-Host "Latest version matched previous version.
Terminating script."
    exit 0
}

Export-CrmSolution $solutionShortName $exportLocation -conn
$connection
```

```
$latestVersion > $versionFileName
```

3. Launch **Windows Task Scheduler**.
4. Right-click on **Task Scheduler (Local)** and click on **Create Task...** with the following details:
    - Under the **General** tab: **Name** as `Dynamics 365 Packt Solution Export`
    - Under the **Trigger** tab: Click on **New**
    - Under **Settings**, select **Daily**.
    - In **Advanced settings**, tick **Repeat task every** and select **1 hour**.
    - Under the **Actions** tab, click on **New**
    - In **Action**, select **Start a program**
    - In **Program/script**, type `Powershell.exe`
    - In **Add arguments (optional)**, type `-ExecutionPolicy Bypass C:\Temp\SolutionManager.ps1`

How it works...

At the core of this recipe is the PowerShell script that we created in step 2. The script connects to a Dynamics 365 instance of your choice using `Get-CrmConnection`, checks the version of a specific solution, and compares it to a version stored in a local file. If the version has not changed, the script exits with a value of 0 (success). If the version is different, the script then downloads the solution to a local folder and adjusts the version number in the local file to match the new one.

> TIP: Don't forget to replace the default input arguments with your correct values or to pass the correct values at runtime.

The script can definitely be improved to follow best practices. For example, it is considered bad practice to pass your credentials in plain text when using the `Get-CrmConnection -Credential` parameter.

> TIP: Consider using the `Import-Clixml` cmdlet instead, at `https://msdn.microsoft.com/en-us/powershell/reference/5.1/microsoft.powershell.utility/import-clixml`.

The script can also be refactored into smaller functions to maximize reusability.

Nonetheless, this recipe is not focused on PowerShell best practices, but rather automation capabilities.

In step 4, we created a new Windows scheduled task to call the script every hour.

There's more...

If you want to minimize your server footprint, you can opt to use Azure PowerShell with its own scheduling capabilities at `https://docs.microsoft.com/en-us/azure/scheduler/scheduler-powershell-reference`.

Alternatively, you can opt to recreate the same logic in C# using the Dynamics 365 SDK and store the latest version in a small database. You can then embed the logic in the web API call that can be hosted on an Azure App Service, as we did in `Chapter 5`, *External Integration*. You can then use an Azure Scheduler to call that logic on an interval, as described in *Running Azure scheduled tasks* of the same chapter.

This recipe is yet another baby step toward building a complete CI/CD pipeline.

See also

- *Integrating your deployment cycles with Octopus Deploy*
- *Using SolutionPackager to save solutions in source control*

Integrating your deployment cycles with Octopus Deploy

When releasing a large enterprise application deployment, orchestration and automation are very important. Given that modern deployment tools accept PowerShell scripting and Dynamics 365's ability to be deployed using PowerShell scripts, the platform becomes a good candidate for deployment automation.

In this recipe, we will leverage what we've learned in previous recipes on PowerShell deployments and integrate the capabilities with a deployment tool. More specifically, we will be using Octopus Deploy to promote a solution to an instance of Dynamics 365.

Getting ready

To get started, you need to set up Octopus Deploy and address some of the Dynamics 365 prerequisites.

Octopus Deploy

Given that this recipe relies on Octopus Deploy, we will need an accessible instance with enough privileges to create and configure a deployment project. For details on how to install Octopus Deploy, follow the steps in `https://octopus.com/docs/installation`. The Octopus server, or one of its tentacles, needs access to your Dynamics 365 instance. The tool should also be aware of your different SDLC environments. In this specific example, we will be deploying to a development instance.

Given that this recipe will focus on deployment rather than build automation, we expect the Dynamics 365 solution to already be uploaded to the deployment server. For that, we will need the Octopus Deploy command in tool to push the artifact to the server. The components can be downloaded from `https://octopus.com/downloads`.

To push the artifact to Octopus Deploy you will need the API key. The key can be retrieved by navigating to **User** | **Profile** | **API Keys in** Octopus Deploy:

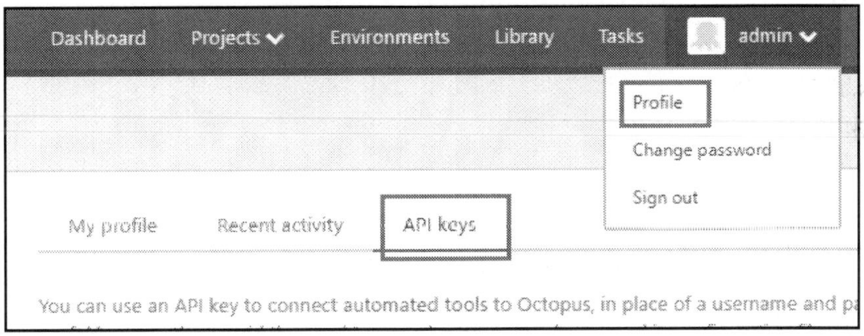

Dynamics 365

From a Dynamics 365 perspective, we will need an exported solution (`Packt_managed.zip`) ready to be promoted to the next environment. We will also need a destination instance and a user with the correct privileges to deploy the solution (**System Customizer** or higher). The script that deploys your solution depends on the `Microsoft.Xrm.Data.Powershell` extensions. You will need to have them installed on the server that will be running the deployment (Octopus server or tentacle server). Refer to the first recipe in this chapter for installation details.

How to do it...

1. Log in to your Octopus Deploy instance and navigate to **Projects** | **All**.
2. On the **Projects** page, click on **Add project** and create a project with the name `Dynamics 365`.
3. Click on the **Save** button.
4. In the `Dynamics 365` project page, click on **Process** on the left-hand side navigation and then click on **Add step**.
5. Hover over **Run a Script** and click on **Add step**.
6. On the **Step details** page, add the following details:
    - **Step name**: `Deploy Dynamics 365 Solution`
    - **Run on**: `Octopus Sever`
    - **Script source**: `Script file inside a package`
    - **Package feed**: `Octopus Server (built-in)`
    - **Package Id**: `Packt`
    - **Script file name**: `ImportDynamics365Solution.ps1`
    - **Script parameters**: `-username #{username} -password #{password} -instance #{instance} -organisation #{organization}`
    - Click on **Save**

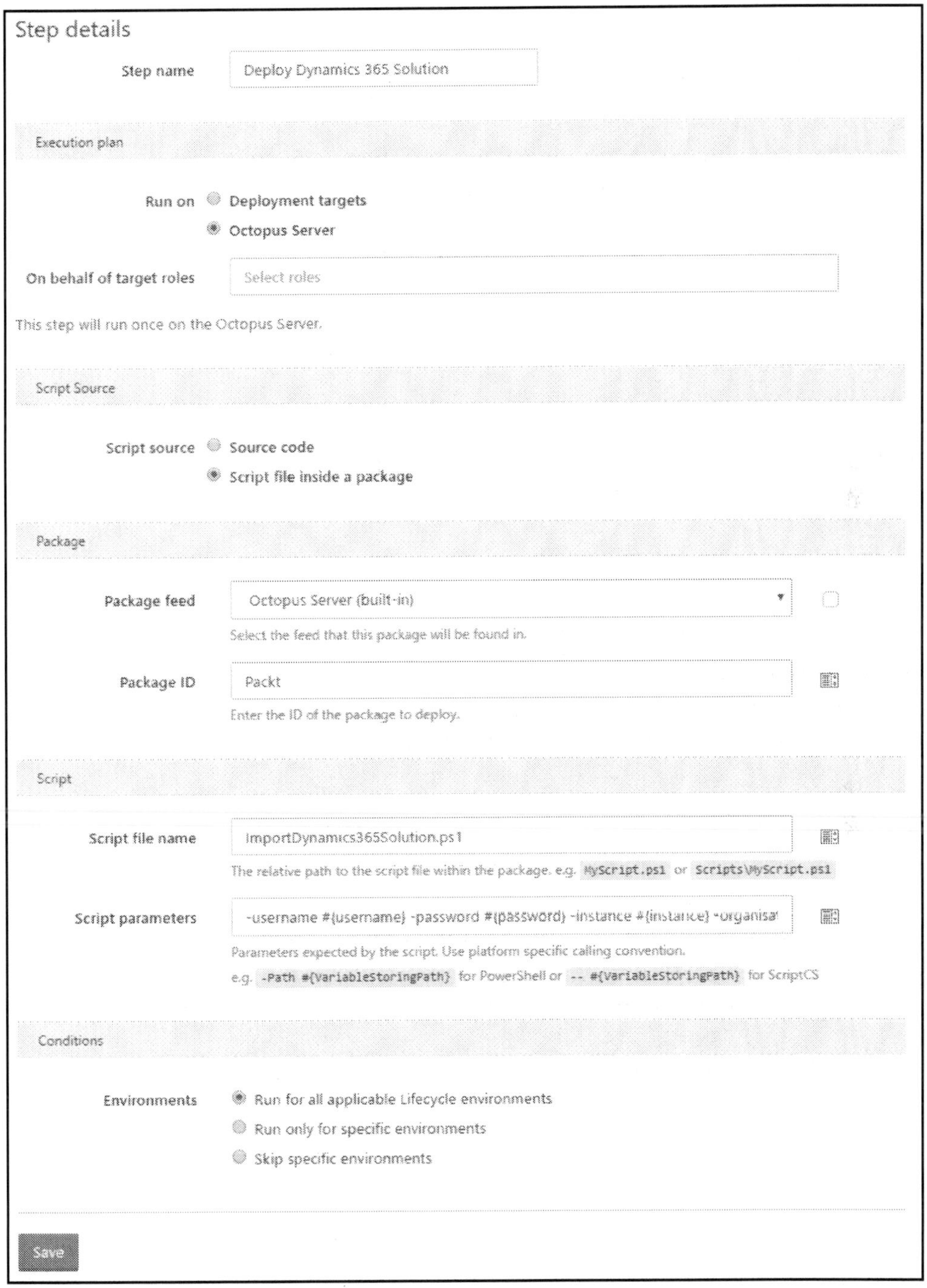
Step details
Step name
Deploy Dynamics 365 Solution
Execution plan
Run on
Deployment targets
Octopus Server
On behalf of target roles
Select roles
This step will run once on the Octopus Server.
Script Source
Script source
Source code
Script file inside a package
Package
Package feed
Octopus Server (built-in)
Select the feed that this package will be found in.
Package ID
Packt
Enter the ID of the package to deploy.
Script
Script file name
ImportDynamics365Solution.ps1
The relative path to the script file within the package. e.g. MyScript.ps1 or Scripts\MyScript.ps1
Script parameters
-username #{username} -password #{password} -instance #{instance} -organisa
Parameters expected by the script. Use platform specific calling convention.
e.g. -Path #{VariableStoringPath} for PowerShell or -- #{VariableStoringPath} for ScriptCS
Conditions
Environments
Run for all applicable Lifecycle environments
Run only for specific environments
Skip specific environments
Save

7. Back in your Dynamics 365 project, click on **Variables** from the left-hand side navigation, create the following variables with their corresponding values and set the scope to `Development`:
    - Instance
    - Organization
    - Username
8. Create a password variable, click on the value field, click on **Show editor**, and enter the following details:
    - **Choose a variable type**: `Sensitive`
    - In the **Value** pane, enter your password
    - Click on **Apply**

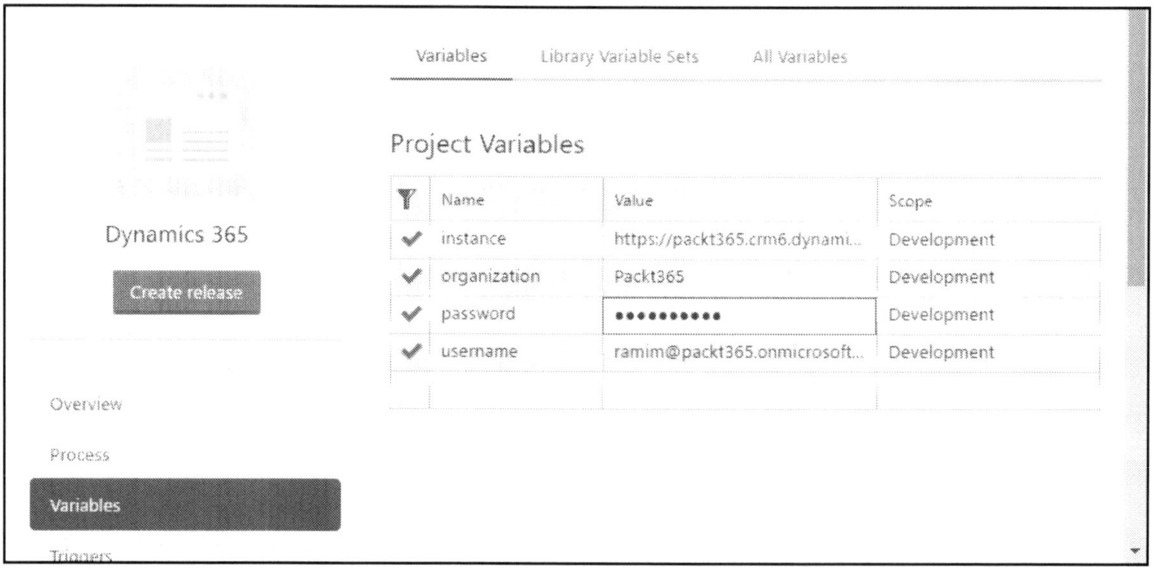

9. Back in your filesystem, create a PowerShell script called `ImportDynamics365Solution.ps1` with the following code:

```
param (
    [string]$username,
    [string]$password,
    [string]$instance,
    [string]$organisation
)
Import-Module Microsoft.Xrm.Data.Powershell
```

```
$securePassword = ConvertTo-SecureString $password -AsPlainText -
Force
$credentials = New-Object System.Management.Automation.PSCredential
($username, $securePassword)

$connection = Get-CrmConnection -Credential $credentials -ServerUrl
$instance -OrganizationName $organisation

Import-CrmSolution -SolutionFilePath Packt_managed.zip -conn
$connection -PublishChanges
```

10. Package `ImportDynamics365Solution.ps1` and `Packt_managed.zip` into one ZIP file called `Packt.0.0.0.1.zip`.
11. Upload your artifact (newly created ZIP file) to Octopus Deploy using the `octo` command line:

```
octo push -server=<octopus server URL> --package=Packt.0.0.0.1.zip
-apiKey=<api key>
```

12. Back in Octopus, click on your Dynamics 365 project and then click on **Create release**.
13. Select the artifact version you just uploaded (version 0.0.0.1) from the list of packages and click on **Save**.
14. On the **Release** page, click on **Deploy to Development**.
15. On the Development deployment page, click on **Deploy now** and monitor the progress.

How it works...

In step 1 to step 6, we defined our deployment process, which essentially contains one PowerShell script to deploy the solution. We defined the package name in step 6.5. Octopus Deploy is clever enough to identify the package name suffixed by a version number. We also defined a set of variables that were passed to the script in step 6.7 and we set them up in step 7 and step 8. We defined the scope of the variables as Development.

> TIP: We can define the same variable names with different values for a different scope to cover our different SDLC environment (test, system integration test, user acceptance, preproduction, production).

Note how we created the password variable as sensitive in step 8. This will ensure passwords are protected and only visible to people with the right privileges. The password will be passed to the script unencrypted.

In step 9, we created our script which accepts the four parameters that we previously defined. The script is similar to the one we created in the *Deploying your solution with PowerShell* recipe earlier in this chapter.

In step 10, we zipped our package, and in step 11 we pushed it to the Octopus Deploy server. Make sure you replace the API key with the correct value, as described in the *Getting ready* section.

In the last four steps, we released to our Dynamics 365 development instance uisng the latest uploaded artifact.

There's more...

This is just the tip of the iceberg of what this tool can do. The deployments can be greatly enhanced to include a full deployment, including data, multiple solutions, configuration, and build server integration. For simplicity, we selected the PowerShell script within our artifact; alternatively, you can create the script separately within Octopus Deploy in order to avoid repackaging the same script over and over again.

Furthermore, given that the import PowerShell cmdlet fails silently, you can enhance your import script by checking whether the correct version on the destination server matches the artifact's version.

See also

- *Deploying solutions using PowerShell*

9

Dynamics 365 Extensions

In this chapter, we will cover the following recipes:

- Dynamics 365 applications
- Dynamics 365 Common Data Services
- Building a Dynamics 365 PowerApp
- Using Flow to move data between CDS and Dynamics 365
- Installing a solution from AppSource
- Using the Data Export Service solution for data replication
- Building Power BI dashboards from CRM data

Introduction

Over the years, Dynamics CRM has evolved from a standalone application to a platform with a strong supporting ecosystem. Many extensions have been introduced to enhance the platform's versatility, but also to extend its integration patterns. In this chapter, we will cover **Dynamics 365 apps**, **AppSource**, **PowerApps**, **Flow**, **Common Data Services** (**CDS**), and **Power BI**.

In particular, the PowerApp, Common Data Services, and Flow are a collection of synergetic products that allow integration between different Office 365 and/or non-Microsoft platforms. Custom point and click mobile apps can be created in minutes that write to the Common Data Services, which triggers a Flow automation, which in turn writes to Dynamics 365, as shown in the following diagram:

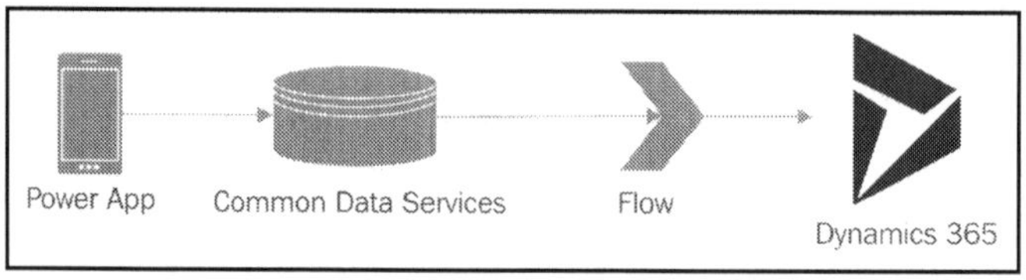

Dynamics 365 applications

Less is more. One of the most powerful UI design principles is to only make available to users the absolute minimum required for them to do their work. French author Antoine de Saint-Exupery summed it up beautifully when he wrote: *Perfection is achieved, not when there is nothing more to add, but when there is nothing left to take away*.

Dynamic 365 recently introduced the concept of apps. Apps are nothing but a presentation layer on top of our existing base Dynamics 365 instance. Apps are like a lens that allow a user group to view an instance in a way that makes sense to them. They allow you to simplify the default view into exactly what your user group needs. It is about removing the clutter and the noise that distracts users and affects their experience.

Typically, apps are used when you've got two different business units in an organization that require access to the same data in an instance, but use the data slightly differently. You can design forms and views that only expose the relevant attributes to each unit, while ignoring the rest. Additionally, you can secure your data using conventional security roles and Dynamics 365 business unit structure, as described in `Chapter 7`, *Security*.

In this recipe, we will create a simple app called `Packt`, which is accessible using the `<Organization URL>/Apps/Packt` URL. Only one entity will be exposed in the `Packt` app through the site map navigation: `contacts`.

Getting ready

In order to create an app, you will need to be a System Customizer or higher on a Dynamics 365 instance.

How to do it...

1. Navigate to **Settings** | **My Apps**, as shown in the following screenshot:

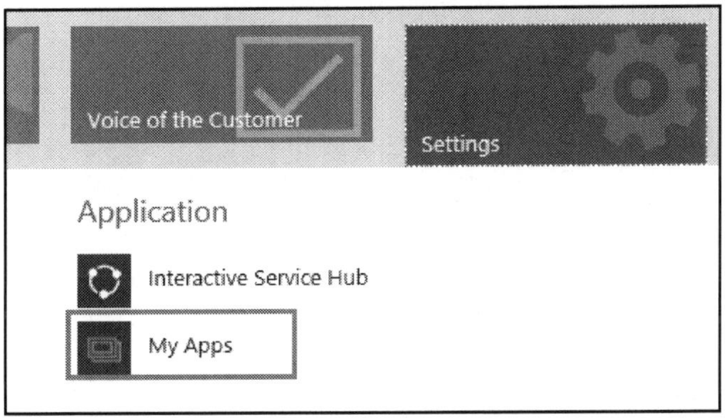

   Alternatively, if the title does not appear, you can can navigate to **Settings** | **Solutions** | **Packts** | **Apps**.

2. Click on **CREATE APP** in the top-right corner.
3. Type `Packt` in the **Name** field and click on **Done** in the top-right corner, as shown here:

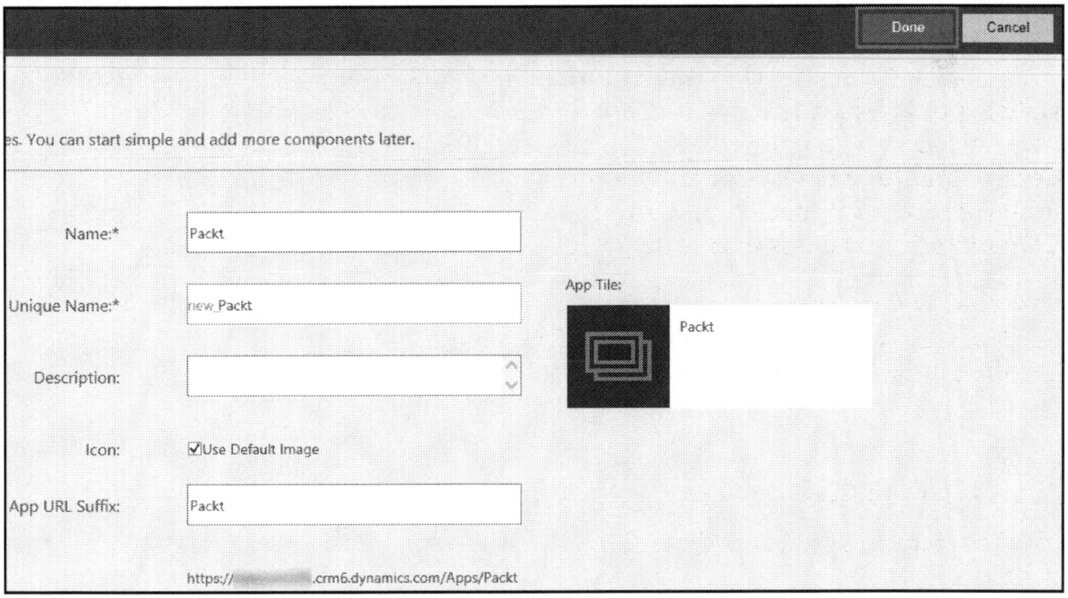

4. In the **App Designer** screen, click on the blue arrow to configure **Site Map**:

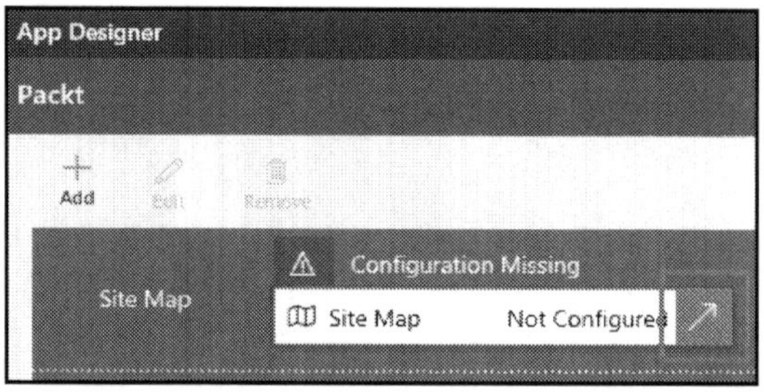

5. Click on the **New Area** tile and enter the name `Packt Area`.
6. Click on **New Group** and enter `Packt Group`.
7. Click on **New Sub Area** and enter the following details, followed by clicking on **Save And Close** in the top-right corner:
   - **Type**: Select `Entity`
   - **Entity**: Enter `Contact`
   - **Title**: Type `Individual`

8. Click on **Save And Close** in the top-left corner.
9. Back on the **App Designer** page, click on **Save**.
10. Click on **Publish**.

How it works...

Creating a Dynamics 365 app is very simple yet, very powerful. In this recipe, we used point-and-click configuration to create our app.

In step 1, we navigated to **My Apps**, which is located under the **Application** group. We created a new app called Packt in step 2 and step 3. The app URL suffix will dictate the URL you can use to access your app. Make sure you choose a meaningful suffix to make it easier to access and recognize. Both the URL and the unique name need to be unique; otherwise, you will be prompted with a validation error.

In step 4 to step 7, we defined the site map with only one entity: `contacts`. In step 5, we defined a high-level **Area** called `Packt Area`. In step 6, we defined the **Group** called `Packt Group` under that area. In step 7, we added a **Sub Area** as a link to the contacts entity. Notice how we renamed the tile to `individuals`.

> If you rename a tile linked to an entity, consider renaming the entity to ensure consistency. This includes the entity's messages, view, forms, and relationships to the entity. Otherwise, the name used in the navigation will differ from the rest of the application (for example in advanced find).

In the last three steps, we saved and published the app to make it accessible to users.

> TIP: If your sitemap changes are not reflected after you publish them, you might be using an unsupported language. Consider temporarily changing to English U.S. while authoring the site map.

As explained in the introduction, an app adds a presentation layer on top of your default application to provide your end users with an enhanced simplified user experience. In our example, we are assuming that the users will only be using the contact entity. Although the app filters the entities from the site map, the rest is still accessible through other means, such as advanced find. If users have access to more than one app, they will realize that their personal settings and their roles/access will be the same across different apps.

Multiple app users will be able to select the different apps by clicking on the chevron next to the Dynamics 365 top-left logo (or custom logo if the instance is themed):

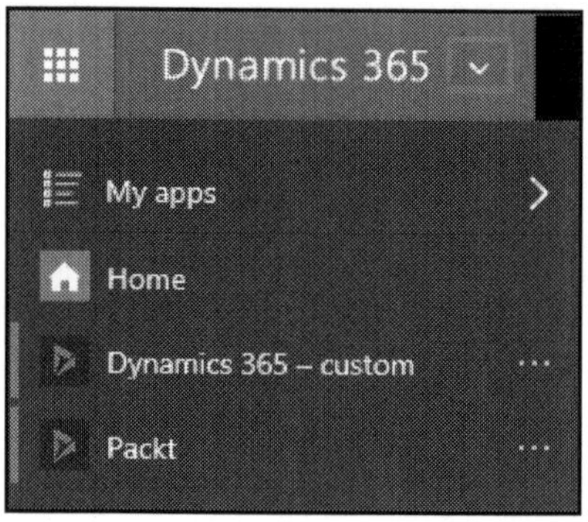

There's more...

As per most other recipes, we have barely delved into what Dynamics 365 apps can do.

In step 7, for example, you've got the option to include dashboards, entities, web resources, and URLs. In the advanced section at the bottom, you can also introduce additional properties, such as specific language displays, and conditions on when the tile will appear based on client type, SKUs, and so forth.

At the app level, there are other useful restrictions that you can introduce. Among them are limitations on what views are available within the app, as well as limits to forms, charts, and business process flows. Furthermore, and one of the most import features of apps, is the capability to limit who has access to the app based on their security roles. To do so, navigate to **My Apps**, click on the ellipsis in your app tile, and select **Manage Roles**:

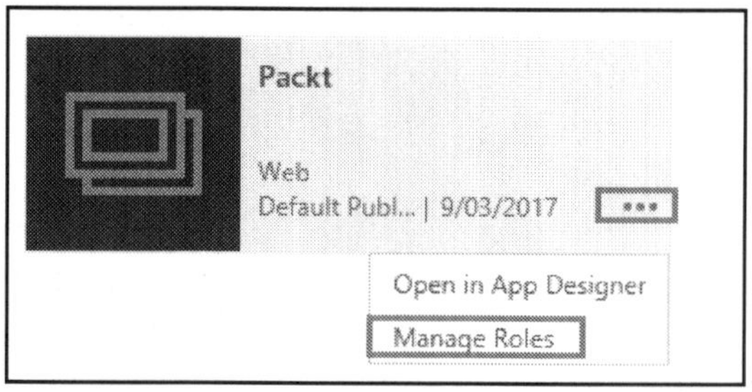

In the **Manage App - Packt** dialogue, select **Give access only to these roles**, followed by the roles you want to have access to your app:

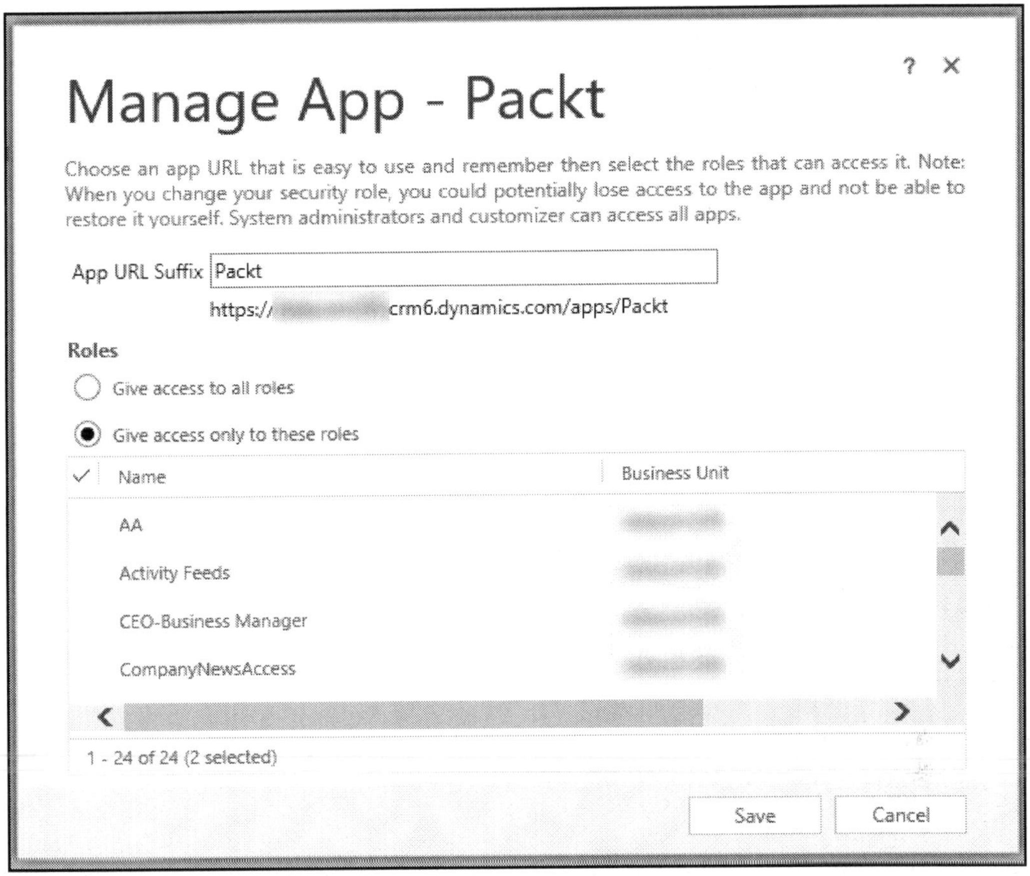

As an alternative to Dynamics 365 apps, you can opt for a PowerApp option, which also provides users with an even simpler solution targeted for mobile devices.

Limitations

Keep in mind that the Dynamics 365 (online) limitations still apply at the platform level. For example, if you are connecting to SharePoint, by default, all your apps will hook into the SharePoint structure. Also, any limits on the number of "resources" also apply at the platform level, for example, number of entities, access teams, workflows, and active business process flow per entity.

Another limitation is related to the underlying schema. Attributes will have the same display names across the different apps. You will be faced with challenges when the different user groups want different display names for attributes in common. Furthermore, not all entities support multiple forms. Appointments being one of them. Default views, search views, and associated views are in common as well.

See also

- *Building a Dynamics 365 PowerApp*

Dynamics 365 Common Data Services

TheC**common Data Service** (**CDS**) is a great addition to the Office 365 ecosystem. It offers an Azure-based, easy-to-use data modeling service that can store data securely to be shared across a wide range of applications.

You will notice that the default data model shipped with the service has many similarities to the Dynamics 365 applications (CRM and operations). Even the vocabulary used to describe the model is similar to Dynamics 365 (entities, attributes, lookups, picklists) as well as the current limitations (1:N relationships are allowed, but at the time of writing, you cannot create 1:1 relationships).

In this recipe, we will extend the default data model that comes with the Common Data Services to include a feedback entity. The entity will hold one text field for the description, one picklist for the sentiment, and one lookup to the contact entity. This recipe is the foundation for the next two recipes that will use PowerApps and Flow to move the data from a PowerApp to Dynamics 365 through the CDS.

Getting ready

In order to use the CDS, you will need a license and the correct permissions that allow you to use the service. For more details on this, read the following article, as the services come in different versions with different sets of features:

`https://powerapps.microsoft.com/en-us/pricing/`

To modify your data model, you will need a CDS environment and a database already created. In order to get a database up and running, follow these steps:

1. Log in to your Office 365 portal and click on the **PowerApps** icon.
2. Click on **Entities** on the left-hand navigation and click on **Create database**.
3. In the following dialog, click on **Create new environment:**

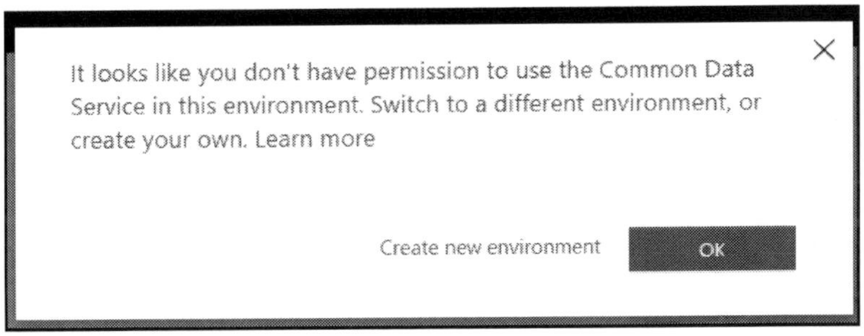

Enter the subsequent information:

- **Environment name**: `Packt CDS`
- **Region**: your preferred region
- Click on **Create environment**

4. Once your environment is created, click on **Create database**.
5. In **Create a database for this environment**, select **Give all users access** and click on **Create database**.

In the preceding steps, we effectively created an environment called `Packt CDS`. You can create an additional SDLC environment by navigating to **Settings** (cog at the top right) | **Admin center**.

How to do it...

1. Log in to your Office 365 portal and click on the **PowerApps** icon.
2. On the left-hand navigation, click on **Entities**, followed by **+ New entity** in the top-right corner.

3. In the new dialogue, enter the following details:

    - **Name**: `Feedback`
    - **Display name**: `Feedback`
    - **Description**: `Feedback entity to contain positive and negative customer feedback`
    - Click on **Next**:

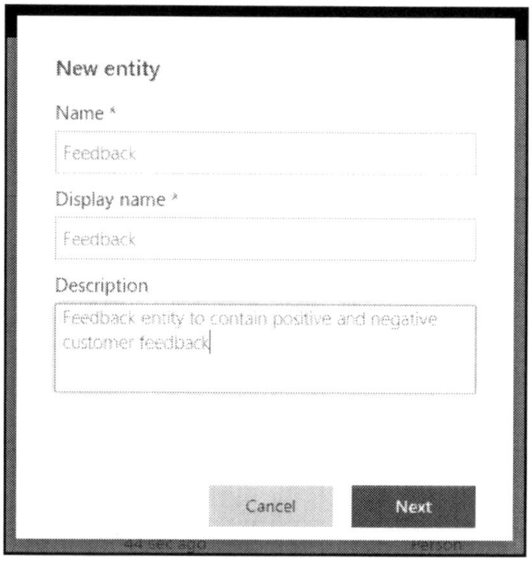

4. In the **Feedback** entity, create new fields by clicking on the **+ Add field** field in the top-right corner with the following details:

DISPLAY NAME	NAME	TYPE
Feedback content	FeedbackContent	Multiline Text
Sentiment	Sentiment	Picklist All/Positive/Negative/Zero

The feedback page should look like the following screenshot:

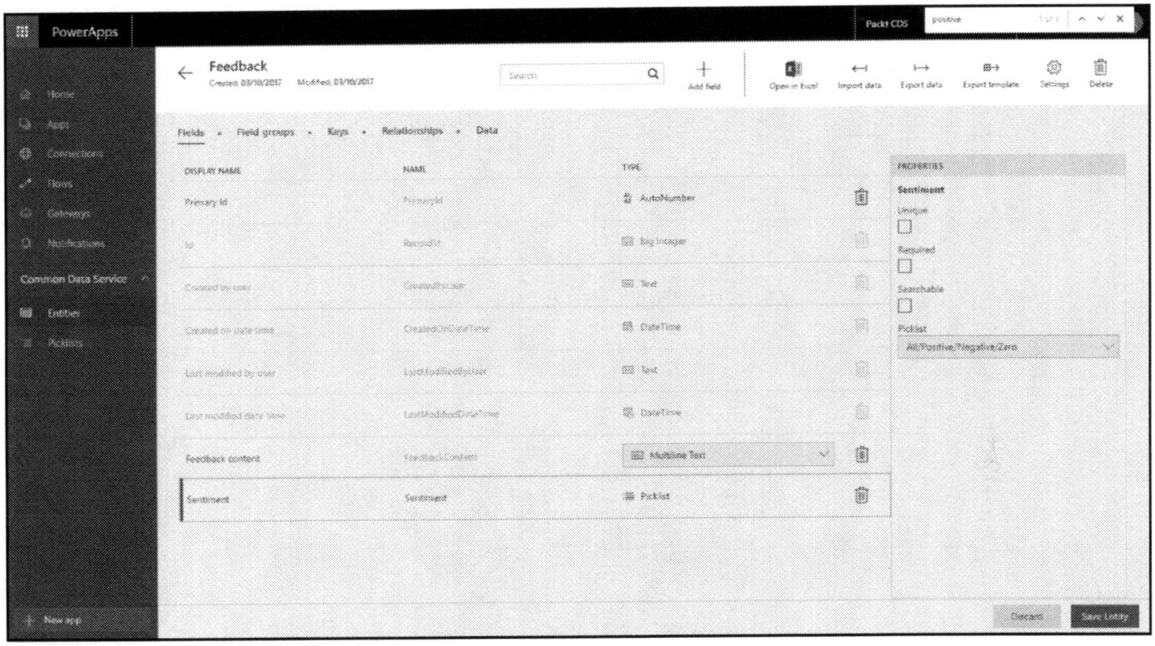

5. Click on the **Relationships** tab and then click on **New relationship** at the top. Enter the following details:
    - **RELATED ENTITY**: `Contact`
    - **DISPLAY NAME**: `Customer`
    - **NAME**: `Customer`
    - **DESCRIPTION**: `Customer providing feedback`
    - Click on **Save** Entity, as shown in the following screenshot:

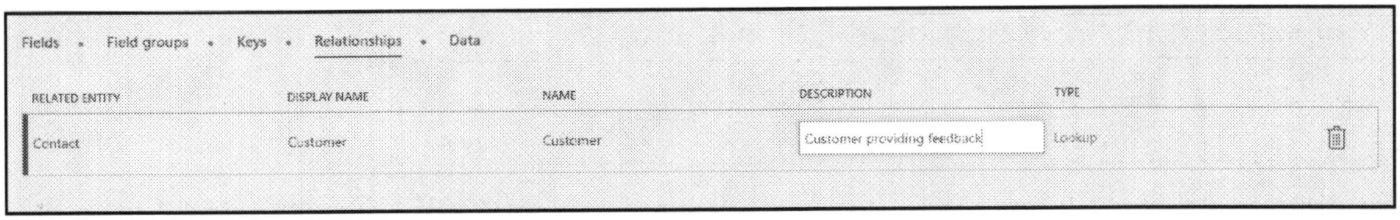

How it works...

With modern data modeling tools, building a data model has become a point and click exercise. As we demonstrated in this recipe, we created a new entity, along with a set of attributes, by simply clicking on the **+ new** buttons and entering the details we are after; no need to worry about the underlying infrastructure and databases.

In step 3, we created a new entity called `Feedback`. Notice how, by default, every entity will include four fields that cannot be deleted: `Created by user`, `Created on date time`, `Last modified user`, and `Last modified date time`, as well as a `Primary ID` field that can be altered. In step 4 and step 5, we created additional attributes. In step 4, we created simple attributes, of which, one is a picklist (dropdown) of an existing picklist type (All/Positive/Negative/Zero). You can create your own picklist by clicking on **Picklists** on the left navigation, as shown in the following screenshot:

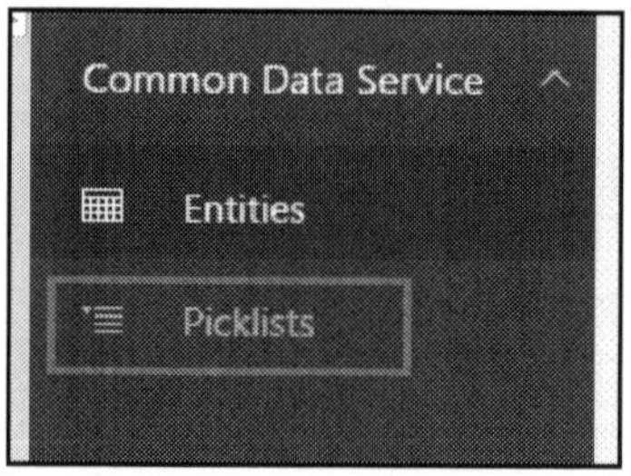

There are other data types that you can choose from, each with their own validation and behavior: Email, Number, and Website URL are a few among others.

For more information on data types, refer to the following article:

`https://docs.microsoft.com/en-us/common-data-service/entity-reference/field-data-types`

For each newly created attribute, you can select whether the field is to be unique, required, or searchable.

In step 4, we created a lookup; a relationship to another entity effectively creating a 1:N relationship.

As of the writing of this book, the CDS does not support N:N or 1:1 relationships.

There's more...

The vanilla Common Data Services already contain a set of default entities that look very similar to some of the entities available in the Dynamics 365 ecosystem. Account, Contacts, Case, Lead, and Opportunity are familiar ones that we can find in the Dynamics 365 Sales module.

> TIP: As a rule of thumb, if you require entities that look similar to the default ones, reuse the entities rather than creating new ones from scratch.

Strong security is one of the main selling points of the CDS. You can secure your data model by navigating to **Settings** | **Admin Center** (also accessible from `https://admin.powerapps.com`), selecting an **Environment**, and creating **User roles** and **Permission sets**, as shown:

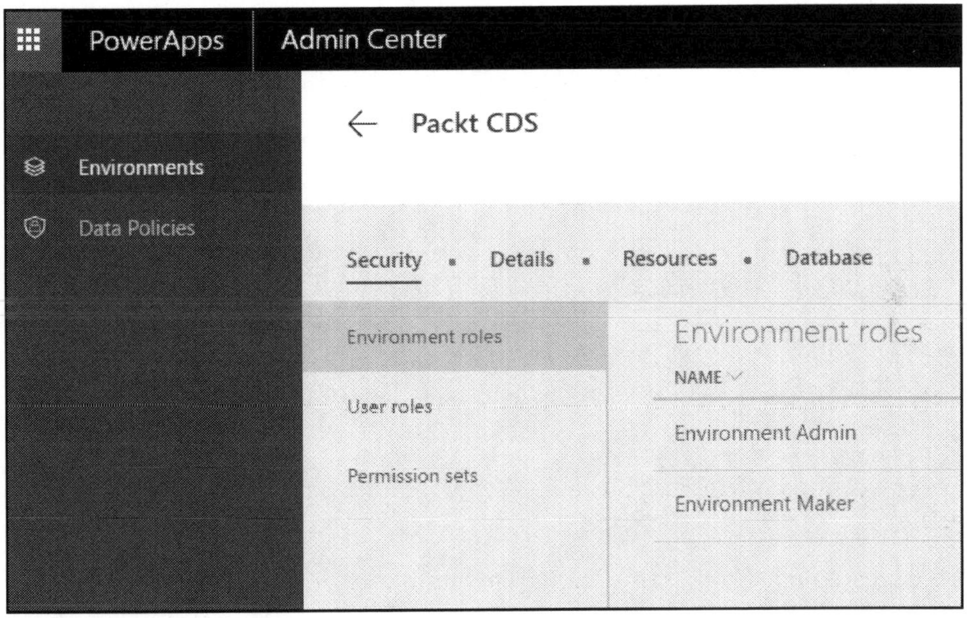

For more information about security, read the following article at `https://docs.microsoft.com/en-us/common-data-service/entity-reference/security-model`.

See also

- *Using Flow to move data between CDS and Dynamics 365*
- *Building a Dynamics 365 PowerApp*

Building a Dynamics 365 PowerApp

In this recipe, we will create a PowerApp application that collects and writes feedback to the feedback entity previously created in the CDS. We can connect straight to Dynamics 365 instead of CDS, however, we want to demonstrate how to use the middle layer to communicate between platforms.

Getting ready

As per the previous recipe, you will need a license that includes PowerApp capabilities. PowerApps are included in Dynamics 365 Enterprise Edition Plan 1 (or higher) or can be purchased independently.

From a CDS perspective, you will need an existing environment with a database containing the `Feedback` entity, as created in the previous recipe. Alternatively, you can use the same pattern with a different entity of your choice. Make sure you have the correct privileges (Read/Create in our example) for the entity you are manipulating.

How to do it...

1. Log in to your Office 365 portal and click on the **PowerApps** icon highlighted as follows:

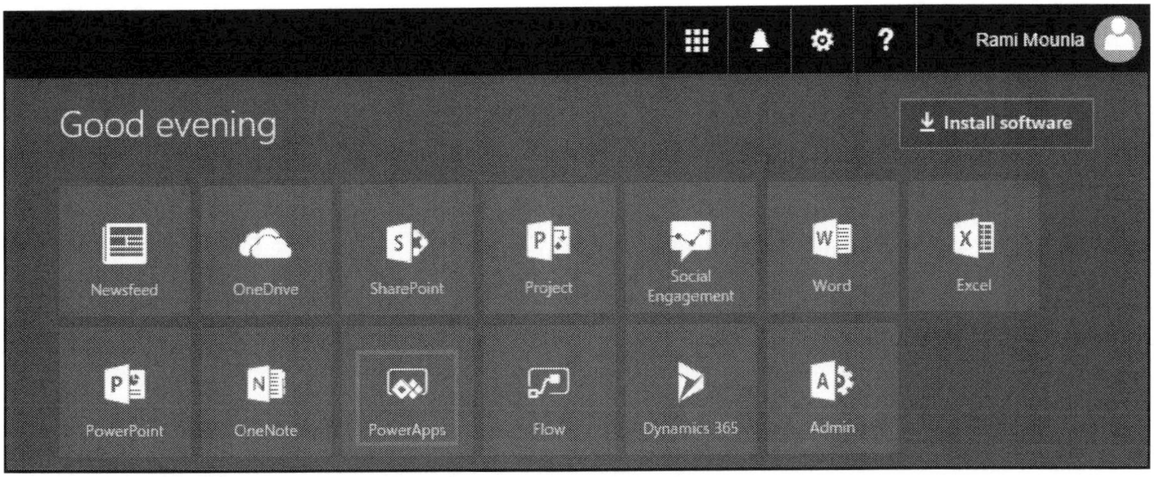

2. From the left navigation, click on **Apps,** followed by **+ New app** in the bottom-left corner, as shown in following screenshot:

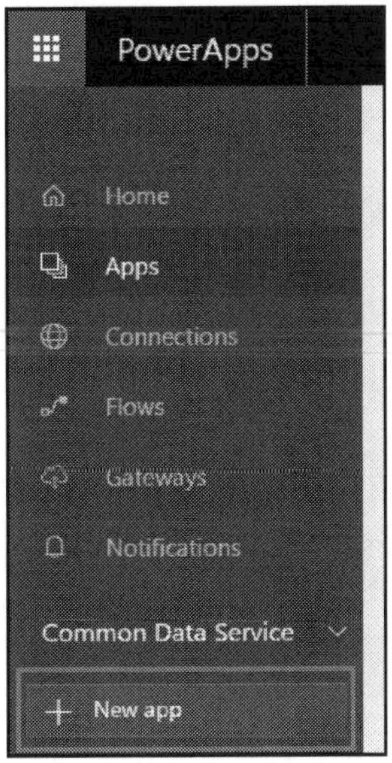

3. In the **Create an app in Packt CDS** screen, select **Blank app** | **Phone layout**.
4. In PowerApp Studio, click on **Data sources** | **Add data source** from the right dialog. Select the **Common Data Services** model.
5. Tick the checkbox next to **Feedback** and click on **Connect**.
6. From the insert tab, click on **New screen** and rename it to `Create Feedback` by clicking on the name tag in the **Content** tab. Ensure that the data source is set to `Feedback`, as shown in following screenshot:

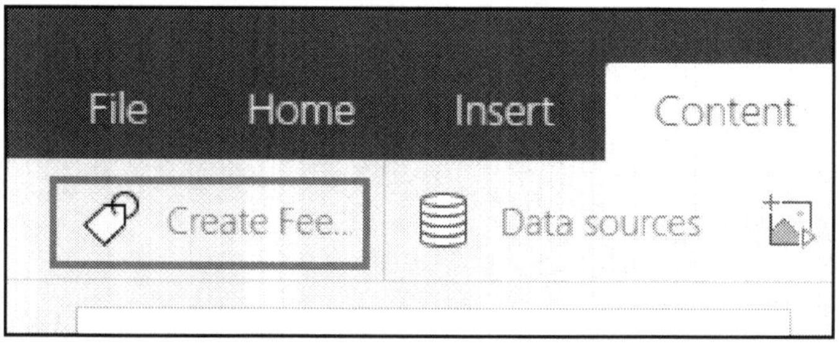

7. In the new screen, insert a form called `Form1` by clicking on **Forms** | **Edit** from the **Insert** tab.
8. Set the data source on the newly created form to your **CDS** | **Feedback** and click on **Connect**.
9. From the list of fields, unhide the following fields in order to ensure that they are properly placed on the form:
    - `Customer`
    - `Sentiment`
    - `FeedbackContent` (set the `FeedbackContent` data card to `Edit Multiline Text`).
10. Click on the screen and, from the **Insert** tab, insert a **Cancel** icon and a **Check** icon with the respective actions:
    - `ResetForm(Form1);Back()`
    - `SubmitForm(Form1);Back()`

Your screen layout should now look something like this:

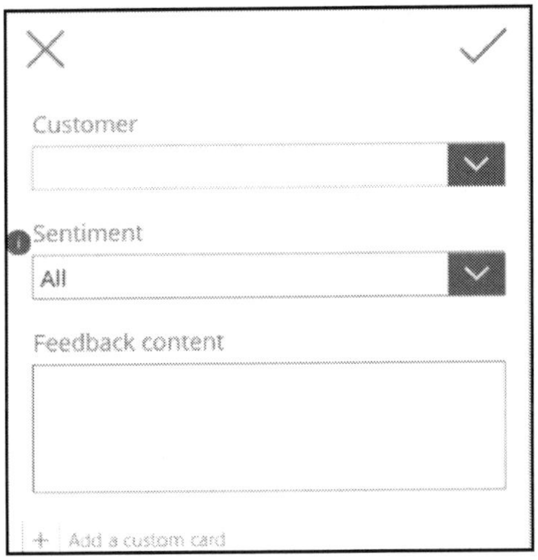

11. Navigate back to your first screen (Screen1).
12. From the **Insert** tab, click on **Text box**. Enter the `Feedback` text.
13. From the **Insert** tab, again, insert a **Text gallery Vertical** control and maximize it to cover the entire space under the title text.
14. Select the newly added control, and under **Options** | **Content**, click on the **datasource** icon and select **Feedback**, as shown here:

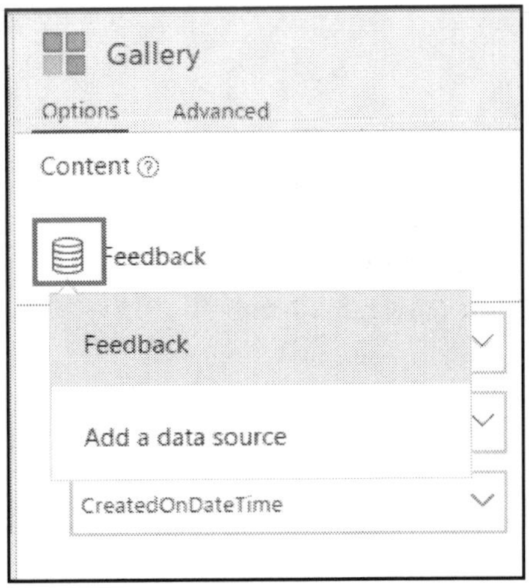

15. Back in the gallery control, ensure that the three displayed fields have the following fields. Order the fields as per the next screenshot:
    - `ThisItem.Sentiment`
    - `ThisItem.CreatedOnDateTime`
    - `ThisItem.FeedbackContent`
16. From the insert tab, insert a **+ Add** icon, as shown here:

17. Click on the newly created icon and add the following `OnSelect` Action:

```
NewForm(Form1);Navigate('Create Feedback', ScreenTransition.Fade)
```

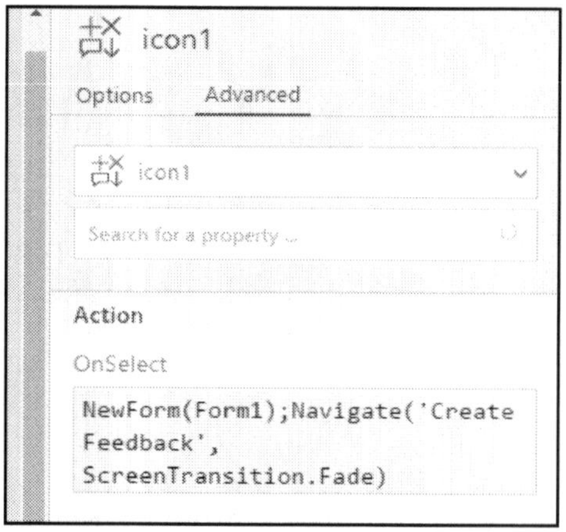

18. From the **File** menu, save your app as `FeedbackApp`.

How it works...

In the first 3 steps, we created a new blank mobile app. Although, we can start from a data source which leverages existing templates and already built screens, we opted instead to start from scratch to demonstrate each step required to connect.

In step 4 and step 5, we set our data source to the feedback entity in the Common Data Service.

Step 6 to step 10 focused on the "edit" screen. We inserted an edit form connected to the `Feedback` entity (steps 7 and 8) and added some of the fields in step 9. In step 10, we added two buttons to save and go back or submit and go back. Note how we reset the form using `ResetForm(Form1)` when clicking the cancel button. If we don't reset the form the user may navigate back to the screen and see old data.

Step 11 to step 17 focused on the "view" screen. In step 13 and step 14, we created the gallery control that will display all feedback items. In step 15, we defined which fields to display for each item. In step 16 and step 17, we created a button to navigate to the new page. Note how we first instantiated the form by calling `NewForm(Form1)`, otherwise nothing will appear on the screen. In step 18, we saved the app. You can choose to save it on a local drive or push it to the cloud.

There's more...

PowerApps have much more to offer. In this recipe, we focused on creating and displaying feedback. We did not look into validation, formatting, editing existing feedback, and the rest of the goodness that PowerApps offer:

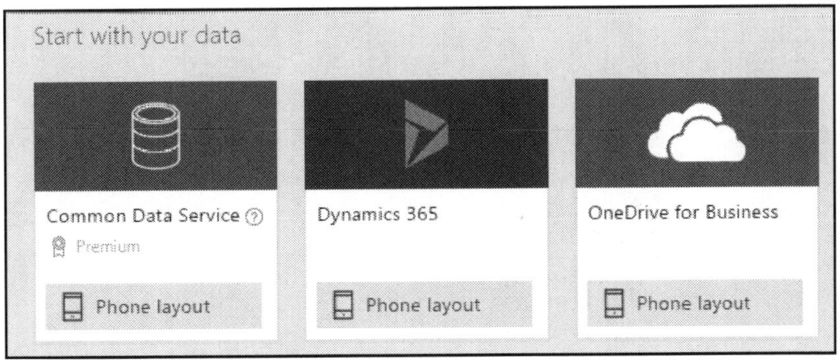

PowerApps have a wide range of default templates that can be reused. The screenshot preceding shows a select sample. For example, you can create an app starting from an entity in CDS. The app will start with most of the screens from this recipe already implemented and ready to be used. We opted to start with a blank canvas to highlight and explain all the steps required to create a custom app.

To run the app using a modern phone, download the PowerApps app and log in using your Office 365 credentials. Once logged in, you'll see your app ready to be used.

See also

- *Using Flow to move data between CDS and Dynamics 365*
- *Dynamics 365 Common Data Services*

Using Flow to move data between CDS and Dynamics 365

Now that we have created a feedback entity in our Common Data Services and have a PowerApp application that populates data into our entity, we will need a mechanism to transport the data from one platform to the other. Flow will help us replicate that data.

In this recipe, we will automate the creation of a new feedback record in Dynamics 365 when a feedback record is created in CDS.

Getting ready

Given that we're moving feedback data from one CDS to Dynamics 365, we will need the feedback entity created in both platforms. The Dynamics 365 entity does not have to exactly match the CDS one; however, some degree of attribute compatibility is required. For example, the sentiment can be a picklist in the CDS, but in Dynamics 365, it may be a text field.

In addition to the platform's schema, you will need the correct license to be able to create and use a Flow process. Flow can be purchased independently or bundled with Dynamics 365 Plan 1 or higher. Finally, the user used to create a record in Dynamics 365 must have created privileges on the Feedback entity in Dynamics 365.

How to do it...

1. Log in to your Office 365 portal and click on the **Flow** icon.
2. Make sure that in the top-right corner, you are connected to the correct environment, **Packt CDS**, in our example:

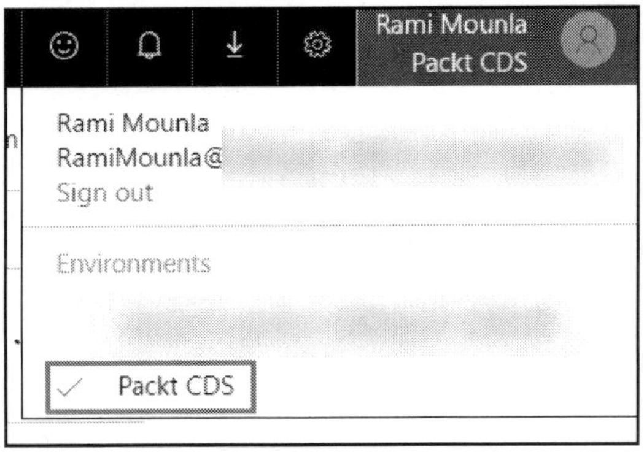

3. Click on the **My flows** tab, followed by **Create from blank**.
4. In the **Search all services and triggers field**, search for `Common Data Services` and select **Common Data Services - When a record is created,** as shown here:

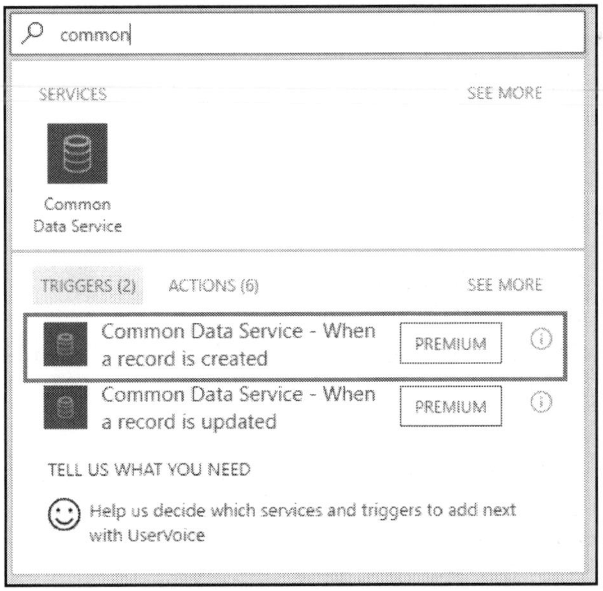

5. On the next screen, select your database and entity name. In our example, the values are `default | feedback`.
6. Click on **+ New step | Add an action** and search for **Dynamics 365 - Create a new record**. Enter the correct Dynamics 365 instance you would like to connect to and select Feedbacks (custom created entity) under **Entity Name**:

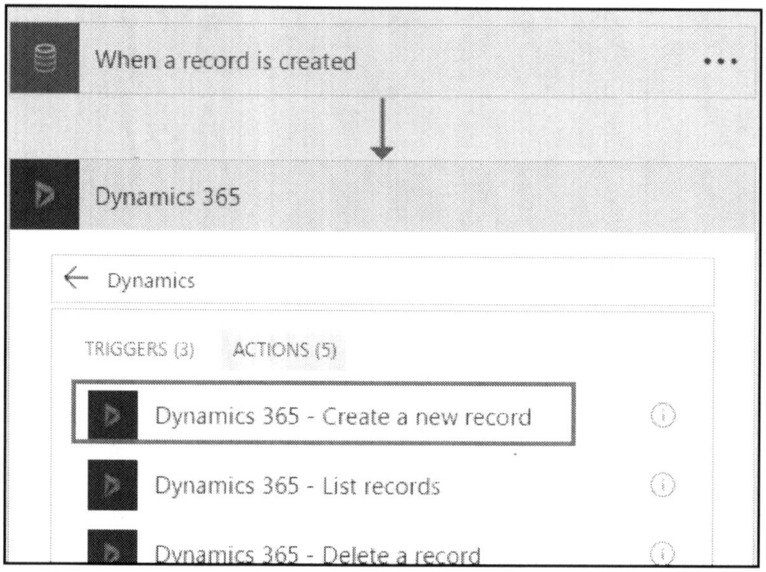

7. Click on **Show advanced options** and enter the following mapping, as shown:
    - **Name:** `Customer Full name and Sentiment`
    - **Sentiment**: `Sentiment`
    - **Feedback Content**: `Feedback content`
    - **Customer**: `Customer Full name`

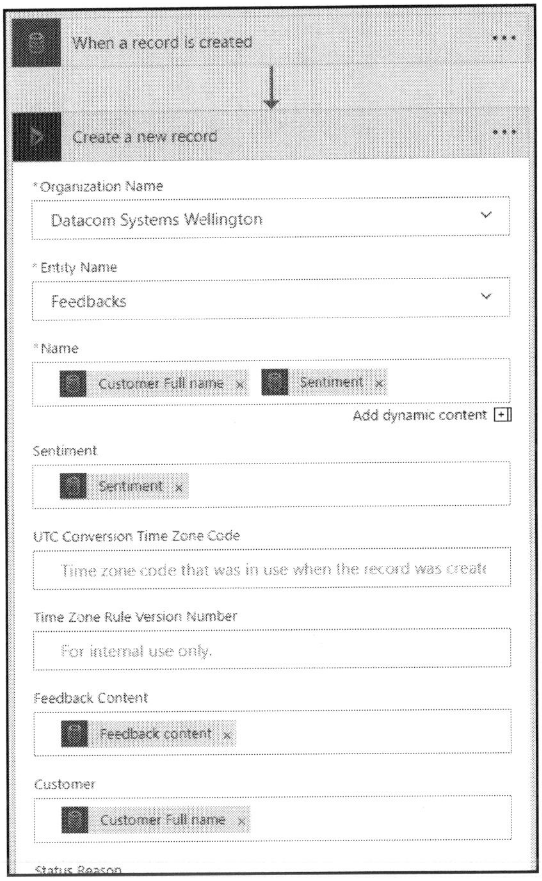

8. Click on the **Create flow** button at the top of the screen:

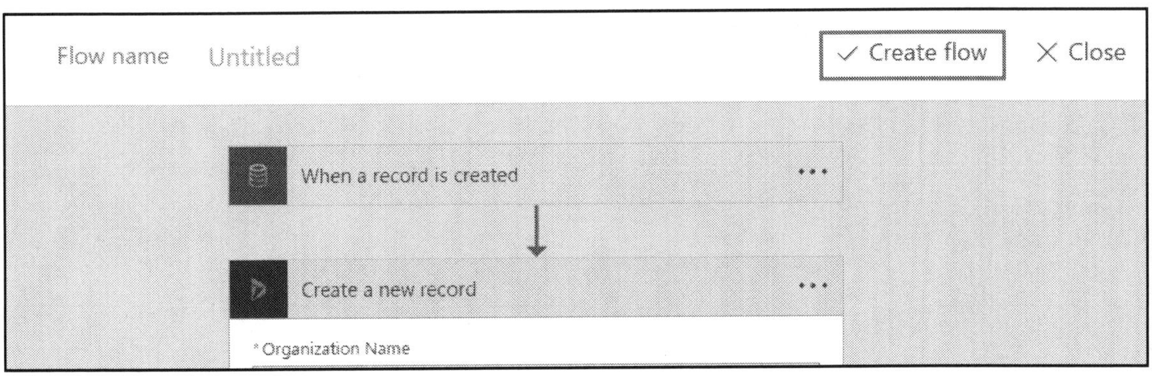

How it works...

Flow comes with a wide range of preexisting templates that you can start with. We decided to start from scratch to demonstrate how easy it is to create a flow of data between CDS and Dynamics 365 even without the templates.

In step 1 to step 3, we ensured that we had the correct environment and created a blank Flow.

In step 4 and step 5, we defined the event that will trigger the flow: on creation of a feedback record in CDS.

In step 6 and step 7, we defined the step to create a corresponding record in Dynamics 365. We first defined a connection to a Dynamics 365 instance in step 6 followed by the field mapping in step 7. As described in the introduction, the data types don't have to necessarily match; as long as they are compatible, you shouldn't have any issues.

There's more...

This is but an introduction to what Flow can do. It can connect to a wide range of platforms, from simple Excel spreadsheets to non-Microsoft platforms such as `https://www.salesforce.com`. Default templates can also facilitate integration by configuring and fine-tuning reusable Flows.

In this recipe, we implemented a simple one-step flow that replicates data between two platforms. Flow can deal with multi-step processes as well as conditional branching.

For more details about Flow, check the guided learning portal at `https://flow.microsoft.com/en-us/guided-learning/` and the video enabled comprehensive documentation at `https://flow.microsoft.com/en-us/documentation/getting-started/`.

If you are after some more control over your integration, consider using Azure Logic Apps at `https://azure.microsoft.com/en-us/services/logic-apps/`.

Execution monitoring

If you would like to monitor your Flow process, you can navigate to the **My Flows** tab and click on the **i** icon next to your process name:

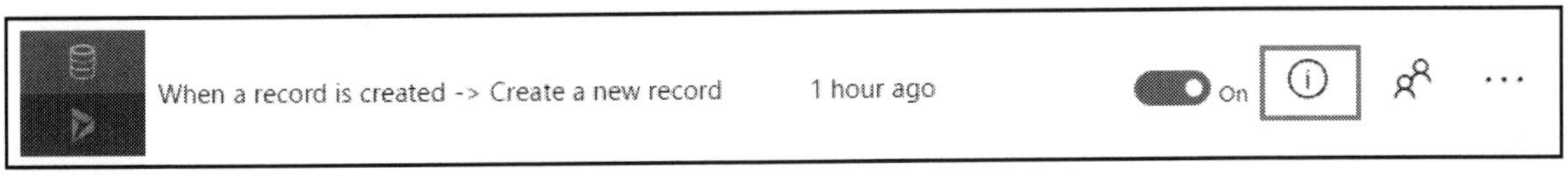

You can further click on each executed instance and visualize a map of the steps that succeeded or failed. The execution result will look something like this:

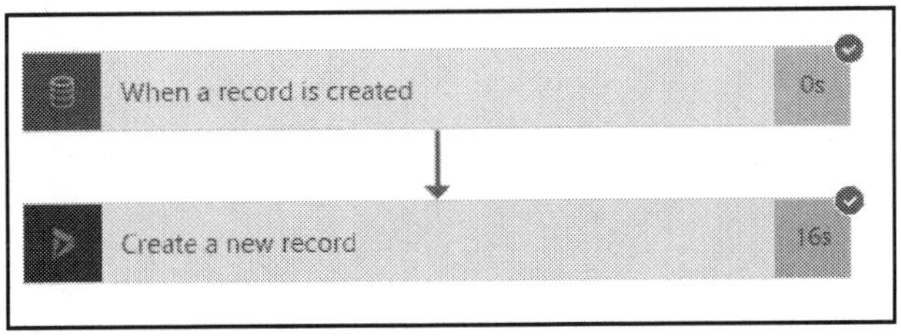

See also

- *Dynamics 365 Common Data Services*
- *Building a Dynamics 365 PowerApp*

Installing a solution from AppSource

Following the modern trend, each platform nowadays has a market place: Dynamics 365 is no exception. AppSource is the Dynamics 365 market place that supersedes Pinpoint.

AppSource is full of useful add-ons that can easily be installed onto your Dynamics 365 instance as well as other platforms.

In this recipe, we will demonstrate how to install the Data Export Services solution (required for the next recipe) from AppSource.

Getting ready

In order to install the add-on, you will need administrative rights on your Office 365 instance. Currently, this is only possible via a *Global administrator* role or Office 365's *Dynamics 365 service administrator*.

How to do it...

1. Navigate to **Settings** | **Dynamics Marketplace** under the **Customization** group.
2. In the AppSource dialog, search for `data export`.
3. Select the `Microsoft Dynamics 365 - Data Export Service` solution and click on **Get it now** as shown in the following screenshot:

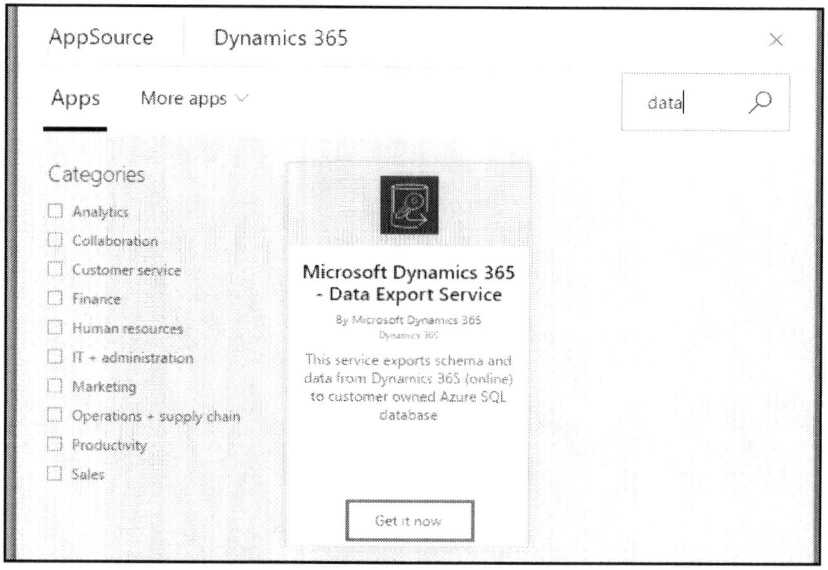

4. In the next dialog, tick the tick box and click on **Continue**.
5. In the next dialog, select the instance you want to deploy to, tick the **terms and conditions** tick boxes, and click on **Agree**.

6. You will then be redirected to **Dynamics 365 Administration Centre** (following screenshot) with the new solution marked as **Installation pending**:

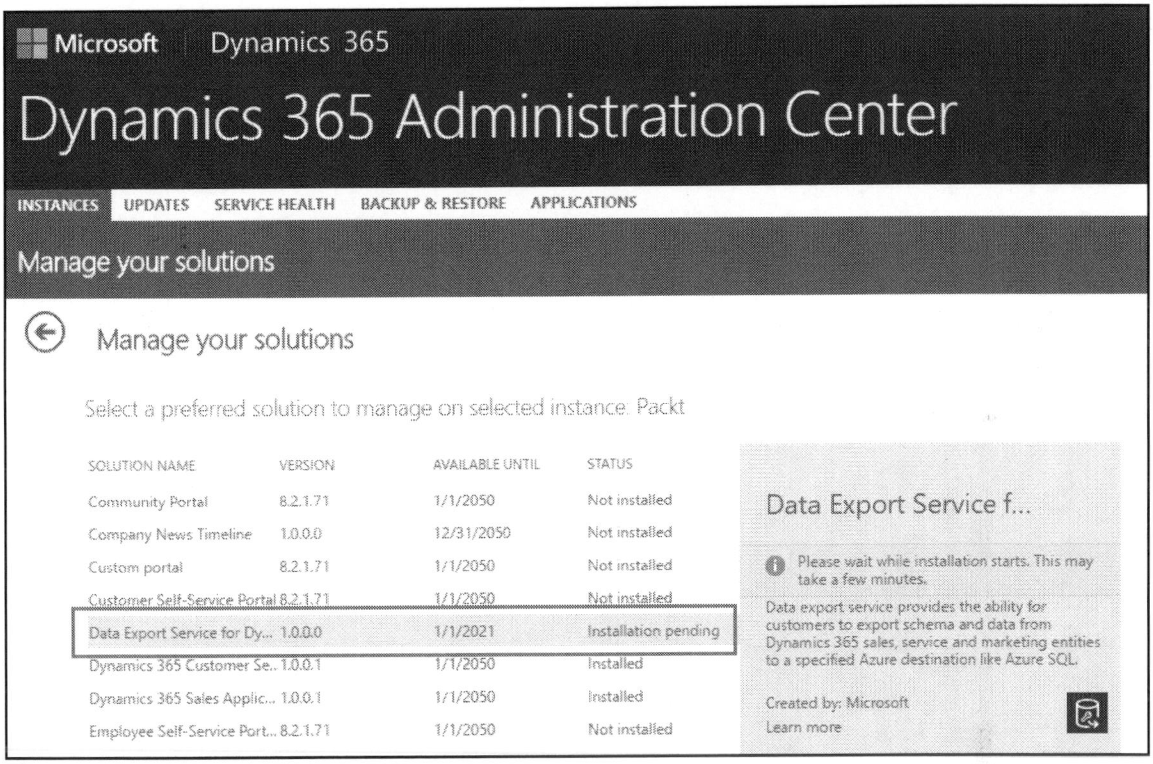

7. When the status changes to installed, navigate back to Dynamics 365, refresh your browser and you will see the new icon appear, as shown in the following screenshot:

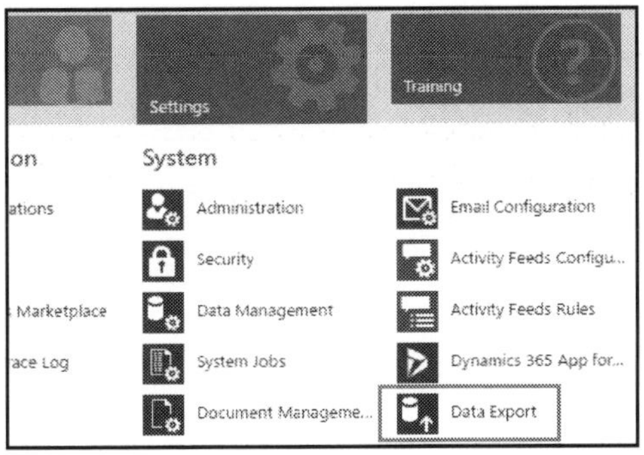

How it works...

Installing an AppSource app is straightforward. It is as easy as searching for it (step 1 to step 3--notice how you can filter by different categories), agreeing on the terms and conditions, then selecting your instance and installing it (step 4 and step 5). The new solution will appear in your instance (step 6 and step 7). No further configuration is required. Although, some more complex apps might require a certain level of configuration before you can start using them efficiently.

Note that if you navigate to `https://appsource.microsoft.com/`, you will also find applications targeted for Cloud Solutions, Office 365, and Power BI.

Behind the scenes, AppSource uses PackageDeployer (described in `Chapter 8`, *DevOps*) to deploy the package--another reason to use PackageDeployer. It deploys the Dynamics 365 solutions, imports the reference data, and executes any custom code required to get the solution up and running.

There's more...

Dynamics 365 AppSource applications currently come in the following three flavors:

- Utilities/solutions installed straight to your instance with no external dependencies
- Solutions that are complemented by an external website, offered as a self-provisioned SaaS
- Solutions that are complemented by an external website but require the vendor's intervention to install an end-to-end functioning product

All apps must provide a free trial option, as dictated by the review guidelines.

If you are planning on submitting an application to AppSource, you'll have to demonstrate that your solution follows a high level of quality. Currently, Microsoft goes through a very rigorous set of inspections for each app submitted. First, the app must meet the review guidelines published in the following PDF at `https://smp-cdn-prod.azureedge.net/documents/AppsourceGuidelines/Microsoft%20AppSource%20app%20review%20guidelines.pdf`. The code is then reviewed to ensure that best practices are followed, including a security review.

Functional testing is not Microsoft's responsibility; however, if they do find serious bugs, they will reject your package.

Microsoft may contact you to ensure that you are willing to support the application on all current Dynamics 365/Online versions (not all subscriptions would be using the latest version) and that you are willing to upgrade your app as new versions of Dynamics 365 are released. All these gates are there to ensure that AppSource hosts high quality supported solutions that will safely work on your current Dynamics 365 instance, as well as future versions.

See also

- The *Packaging your solution with configuration data using PackageDeployer* recipe of `Chapter 8`, *DevOps*

Using the Data Export Service solution for data replication

The **Data Export Service for Dynamics 365** is a relatively new solution introduced for the purpose of replicating data from Dynamics 365 to a publicly accessible SQL server. The integration is a point and click solution that does not require any code. The replication is useful for data analytics, business intelligence reporting, machine learning, and intensive read operations.

The Dynamics 365 Data Export Service is a free of charge add-on.

In this recipe, we will replicate the account entity from Dynamics 365 to an SQL PaaS database on Azure.

Getting ready

Other than installing the Data Export Service for Dynamics 365 as described in the previous recipe, there are quite a few prerequisites required to get the solution up and running:

Office \ Azure tenancy

You must have your Office 365 tenancy associated with your Azure tenancy, as the *Data Export Service for Microsoft Dynamics 365* enterprise application residing within that tenancy will be granted access to the Key Vault containing your connection string.

SQL database

You will need to have a publicly accessible Microsoft SQL Azure instance (PaaS or hosted on Azure Virtual Machines). The easiest option is to create a SQL PaaS instance similar to the one mentioned in the *Running no code scheduled synchronization using Scribe* recipe of `Chapter 5`, *External Integration*. Ensure the firewall rules are either turned off or that the Data Export Service IP addresses are whitelisted. The IP address depends on your geographical location. The different addresses are listed in this article `https://technet.microsoft.com/en-us/library/mt744592.aspx#Anchor_15`. It is also recommended that you enable the **Allow access to Azure services** option.

Key Vault

You will also need to create a connection string to our SQL instance that will be stored in an **Azure Key Vault**. The Key Vault will be granted read permission to our Dynamics 365 application. In order to achieve this, your Dynamics 365 Azure tenancy must be the same as the one holding the Key Vault.

The Data Export Service solution contains a script that can help with the key generation. The script is accessible in Dynamics 365 by navigating to **Settings** | **Data Export** | **+NEW** | **i** (next to **Key Vault URL**):

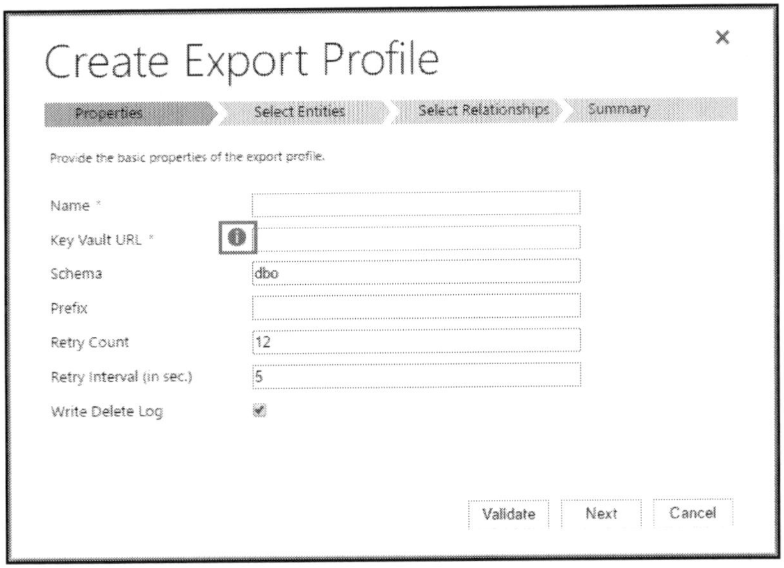

The script requires the following inputs:

- `$subscriptionId`: Your Azure subscription GUID that will contain the Key Vault. Accessible from the Azure diagnostics (as described in `Chapter 5`, *External Integration, Connecting to Dynamics 365 from other systems using OData (Java)* under subscriptions, as show in this screenshot:

```
"subscriptions": {
  "subscriptions": [
    {
      "subscriptionName": "Free Trial",
      "subscriptionID": "[illegible]",
      "status": "Enabled",
      "subscriptionPolicies": {
        "locationPlacementId": "PublicAndAustralia_2014-09-01",
        "quotaId": "FreeTrial_2014-09-01",
        "spendingLimit": "On"
      },
      "requireRdfe": true,
      "authorizationSource": "Legacy"
    }
  ]
},
```

- `$keyvaultName`: A name of your choice for the Key Vault (3 to 24 characters)
- `$secretName`: A secret name of your choice
- `$resourceGroupName`: Your Azure Resource Group that will hold the Key Vault
- `$location`: The geographical location of your Resource Group
- `$connectionString`: Your SQL PaaS connection string.
- `$organizationIdList`: You Dynamics 365 organization GUID accessible from the **Developer Resources** by navigating to **Settings** | **Customization** | **Developer Resources** as shown here:

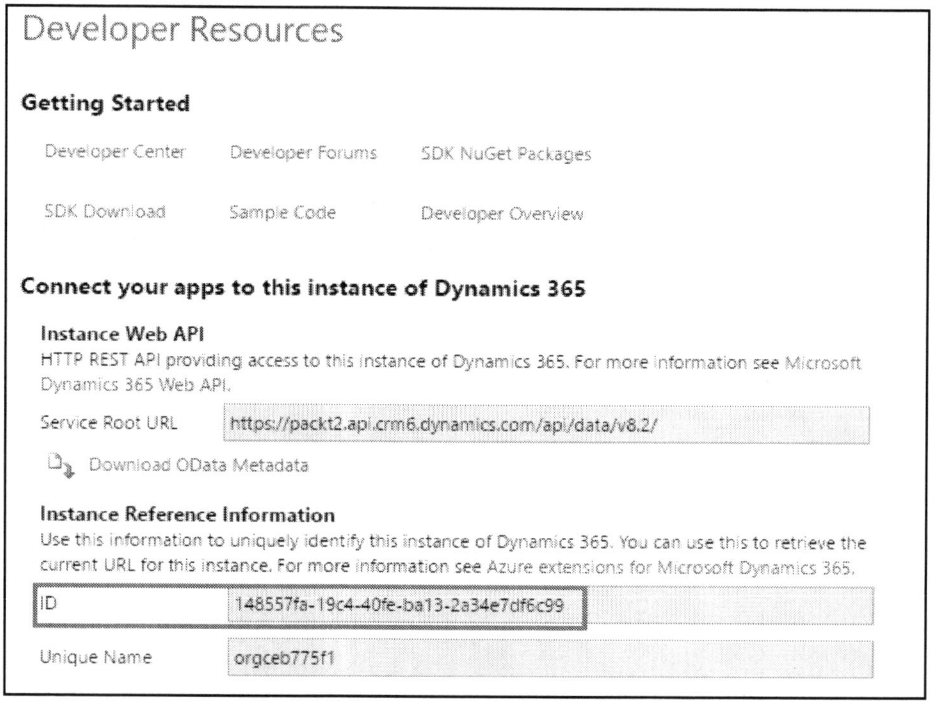

- `$tenantId`: Your Azure AD tenancy GUID. Read `Chapter 5`, *External Integration, Connecting to Dynamics 365 from other systems using OData (Java)* for details on how to retrieve your tenancy AAD GUID.

To execute the script, you will require the *AzureRM* and *Azure* Modules pre-installed. To load them, run the following command in PowerShell 5 or above:

```
Install-Module AzureRM
Install-Module Azure
```

If executed successfully, the script must not return any errors and should return the Key Vault URL at the end.

Change tracking on custom entities

From a Dynamics 365 perspective, any entity that needs to be replicated must have **Change Tracking** enabled. Out of the box entities are enabled by default. Custom entities can be enabled by navigating to the relevant Entity Definition page of your entity and ticking the **Change Tracking** checkbox. Furthermore, to create a profile you will require the System Administrator role.

How to do it...

1. Navigate to **Settings** | **Data Export** and click on **+ New**.
2. Enter the following values in the **Properties** stage of the **Create Export Profile** dialog and keep the rest as default, as shown as follows:
    - **Name**: `Packt replication`
    - **Key Vault URL**: <the Key Vault URL generated in the *Getting ready* section>

- **Prefix**: `packt`

3. Click on **Validate** (this is optional) then **Next**.
4. In the **Select Entities** stage, select the entities to replicate and click on **Next**. In this example, we selected **Account**.
5. Click on **Next** in the **Select Relationships** stage.
6. Review your changes in the **Summary** stage and click on **Create & Activate**.

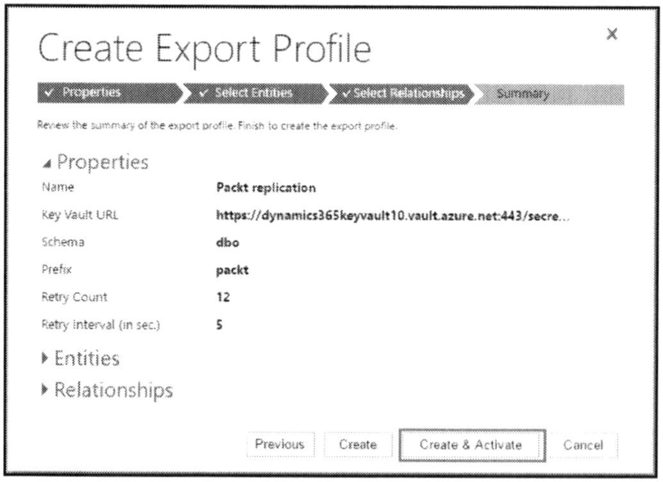

How it works...

In 6 easy steps, we created a data replication of an entire Dynamics 365 entity into a SQL server.

In step 2, we entered the necessary details to connect to our SQL database using the Azure Key Vault generated in the *Getting ready* section.

In step 3, we selected the required entities to be replicated, and the rest was just following the wizard steps.

Behind the scenes, the data export service synchronizes the entire table behind the selected entity, followed by delta increments as the records get updated in Dynamics 365 (thus the need for the custom entities to be Change Tracking enabled). The service uses a combination of *Azure Service Fabric, Azure Service Bus, Azure Blob Storage,* and *Azure SQL*. For more details read the TechNet article at `https://technet.microsoft.com/en-us/library/mt744592.aspx#Anchor_17`.

There's more

In this recipe, we replicated an entity, but you can also select relationships to be replicated in step 5. Only many-to-many (M:N) relationships will be selectable as the others are considered a table or lookup replication.

The add-on also allows for error handling and resynchronization, as described in this article `https://technet.microsoft.com/en-us/library/mt744592.aspx#resolve_issues`.

Additionally, the Data Export Services provide an API interface to be managed programmatically as defined in: `https://msdn.microsoft.com/en-us/library/mt788315.aspx#Anchor_1`.

For more detail on the Data Export Service for Dynamics 365, read the following MSDN article at `https://msdn.microsoft.com/en-us/library/mt788315.aspx` as well as the following TechNet article at `https://technet.microsoft.com/library/a70feedc-12b9-4a2d-baf0-f489cdcc177d`.

See also

- The *Running no code scheduled synchronization using Scribe* recipe of `Chapter 5`, *External Integration*.

Building Power BI dashboards from CRM data

Dynamics 365 offers a wide range of reporting capabilities. View, charts, SSRS reports, and Word and Excel templates are the usual options. The out-of-the-box reporting capabilities are great when reporting on Dynamics 365 data; however, if you need richer analytics that span across multiple platforms, Power BI is your solution.

In this recipe, we will create a simple pie chart that displays accounts' cities filtered by the state of **Washington** (**WA**) to demonstrate how to integrate a Dynamics 365 centric Power BI report into your Dynamics 365 dashboard. Our only data source will be Dynamics 365.

Getting ready

In order to embed Power BI charts into your Dynamics 365 instance, you'll need to enable the capability first. To do so, navigate to **Settings** | **Administration** | **System Settings** and click on the **Reporting** tab. Then select, **Yes** next to **Allow Power BI visualization embedding**, as shown in the following screenshot:

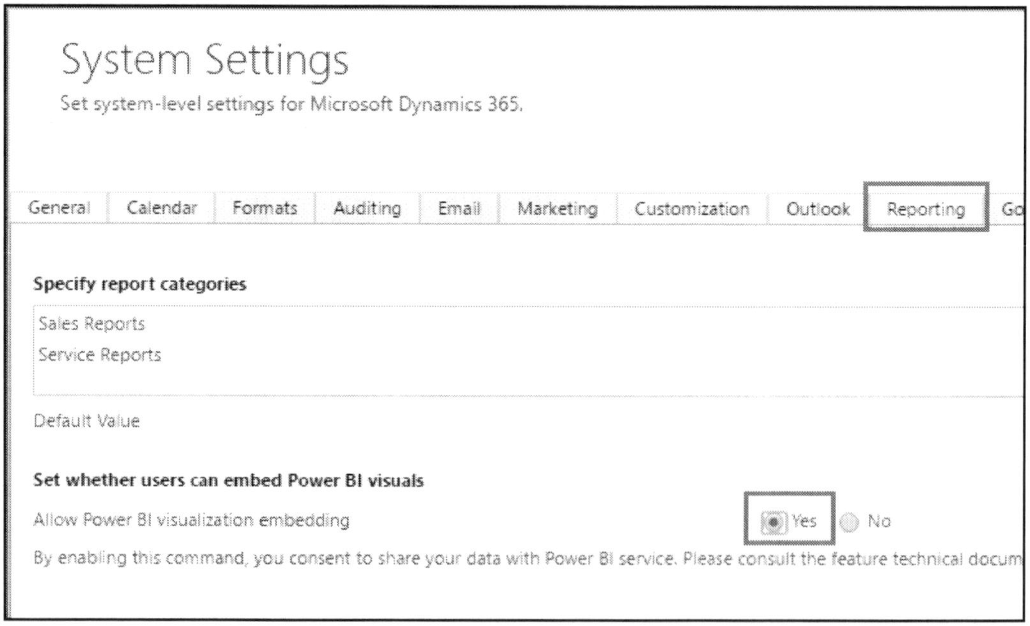

Given that this recipe focuses on the Power BI Desktop edition, you will need to download and install Power BI Desktop. You can download the 64-bit version from `https://go.microsoft.com/fwlink/?LinkId=521662&clcid=0x409`.

You will also need to make sure you sign in to `https://powerbi.microsoft.com` using your Dynamics 365 account. This will ensure that a license (even if free) is allocated to your account.

Given that the Power BI report will be using the latest OData V4 endpoint, the user impersonated to connect to your Dynamics 365 instance will require OData access as well as read rights to the entities queried. In this example: `Accounts`.

How to do it...

1. Start Power BI Desktop.
2. Log in using your Dynamics 365 account by clicking on the **Sign in** button in the top-right corner:

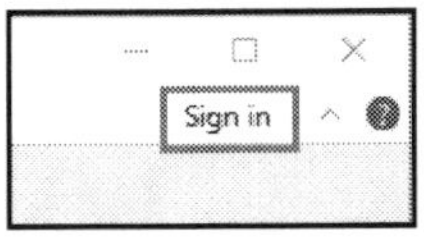

3. Click on the **Get Data** icon under the **External Data** grouping and, in the dialog, search for `Dynamics 365` and click on **Connect**, shown as follows:

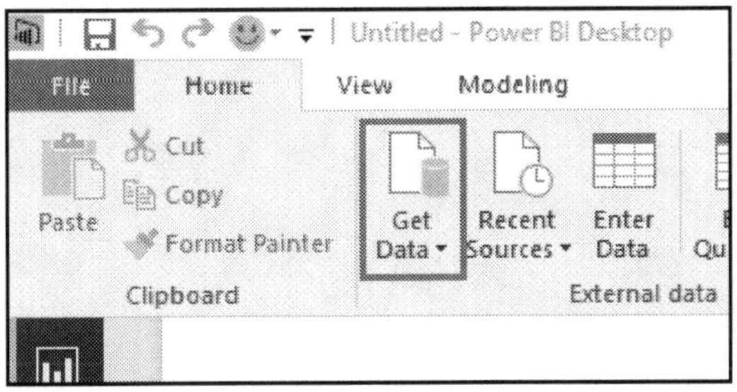

4. Enter your organization OData Endpoint, following the format `https://<organization url>/api/data/v8.2`, as shown in the following screenshot:

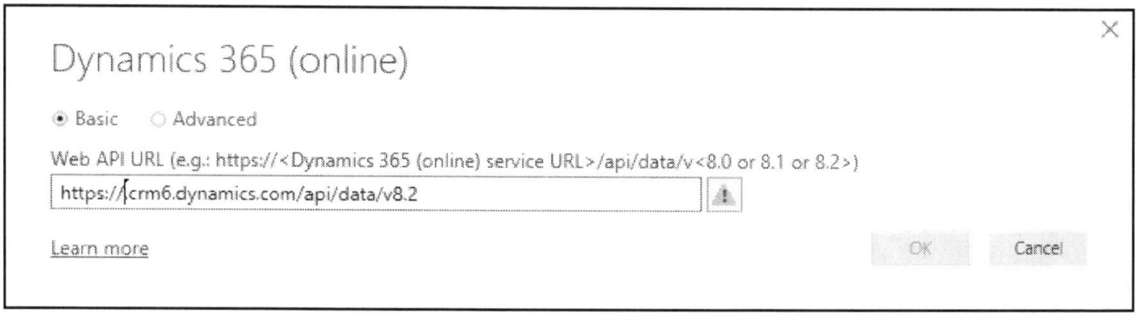

Now, select **Organizational account** to enter the credentials to log in:

5. Next, you will be prompted with the **Navigator** screen. Search for the entity you are after and tick the box next to it, then click on **Edit**. In our example, we will choose accounts, as shown here:

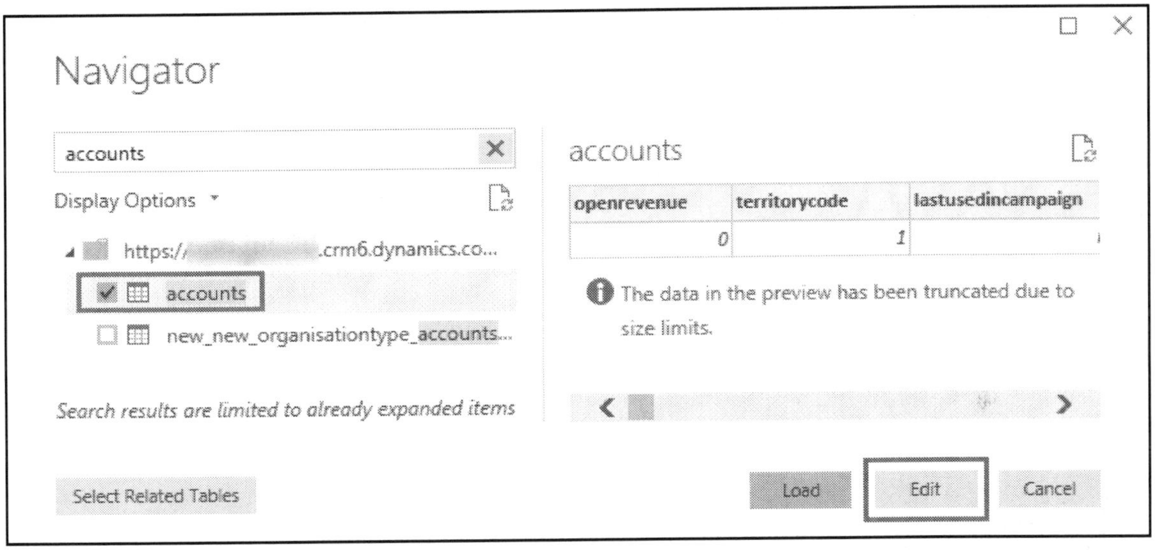

6. In your Query Editor, click on **Choose Columns** and select the following columns only then click on **OK**:
    - `name`
    - `address1_stateprovince`
    - `address1_city`

7. Select the dropdown next to **address1_stateprovince** and filter the content to only show WA values, as per this screenshot:

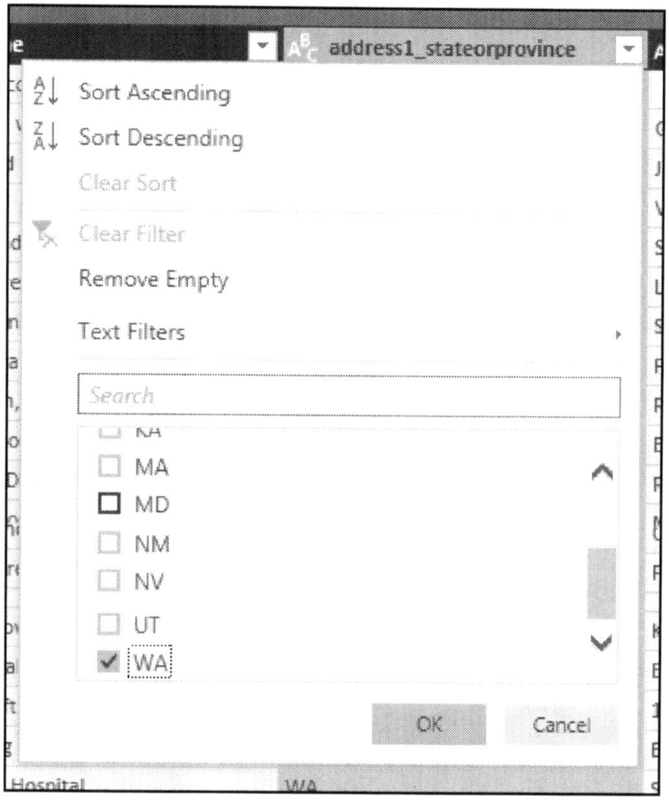

8. Click on **Close & Apply**.

9. In Page1 of your report edit, click on the pie chart icon in the **Visualizations** window and drag and drop **address1_city** from the **Fields** window to both the **Details** and **Values** fields, as shown in the following screenshot:

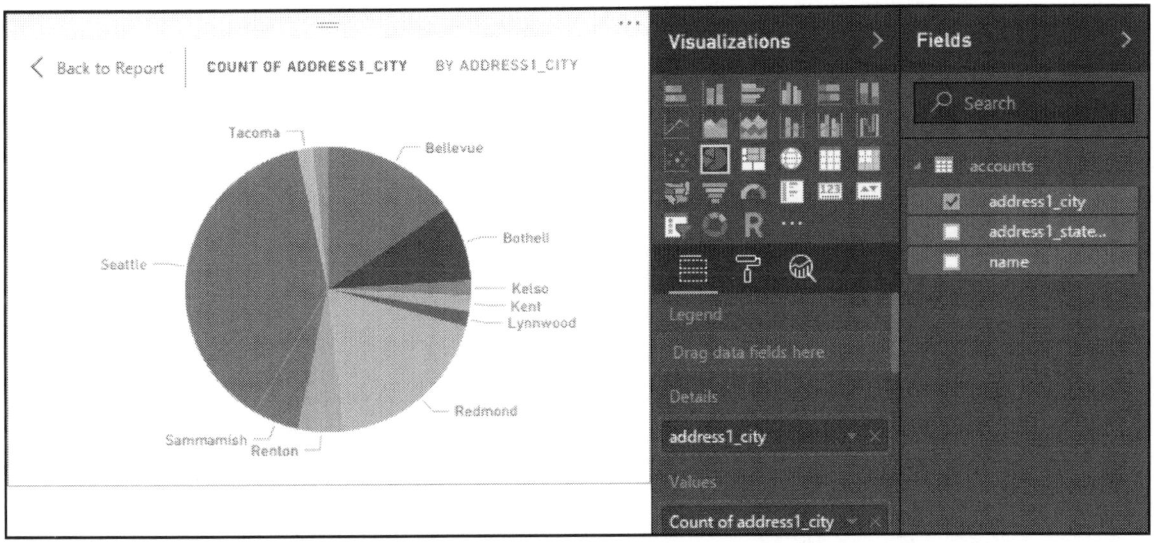

10. Click on the **Publish** button located in the **Home** ribbon under the **Share** grou, as shown here:

You will be prompted to save your file. Call it `Accounts Pie Chart By City.pbix` and click on **Save**.

11. Once the publishing is successful, click on **Open 'Accounts Pie Chart By City.pbix' in Power BI** to navigate to Power BI online, as shown in the following screenshot:

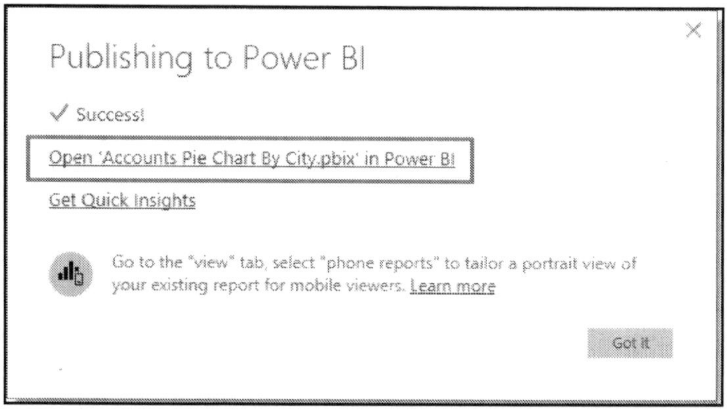

12. On the report page, select the chart and click on the pin at the top of the screen. In **Pin to dashboard**, select **New dashboard** and enter `Packt Dashboard`, then click on **Pin**.
13. Navigate to your newly created dashboard by clicking on `Packt Dashboard` under **Workspace** | **Dashboards** on the left-hand navigation. Select the ellipsis (...) on your chart, click on the edit icon, and change the title to `Account Pie Chart by City in WA`. Click on **Apply**.
14. Back in Dynamics 365, navigate to a Dashboard area, such as **Sales** | **Dashboards**, and click on **New** and select a layout of your choice.
15. Click on the Power BI icon in one of the empty tiles, as shown here:

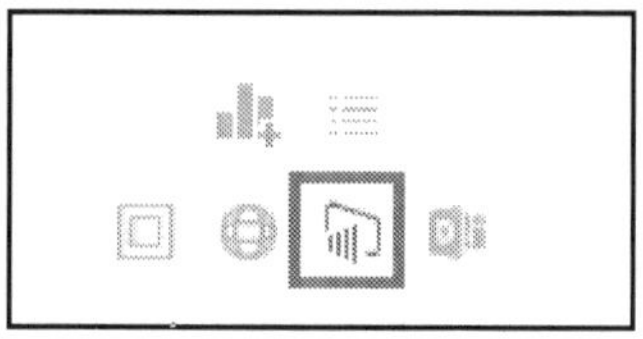

16. From the drop down, select the name of your Power BI Dashboard (`Packt Dashboard`) and the name of your chart (`Account Pie Chart by City in WA`), then click on **OK**, as shown in the following screenshot:

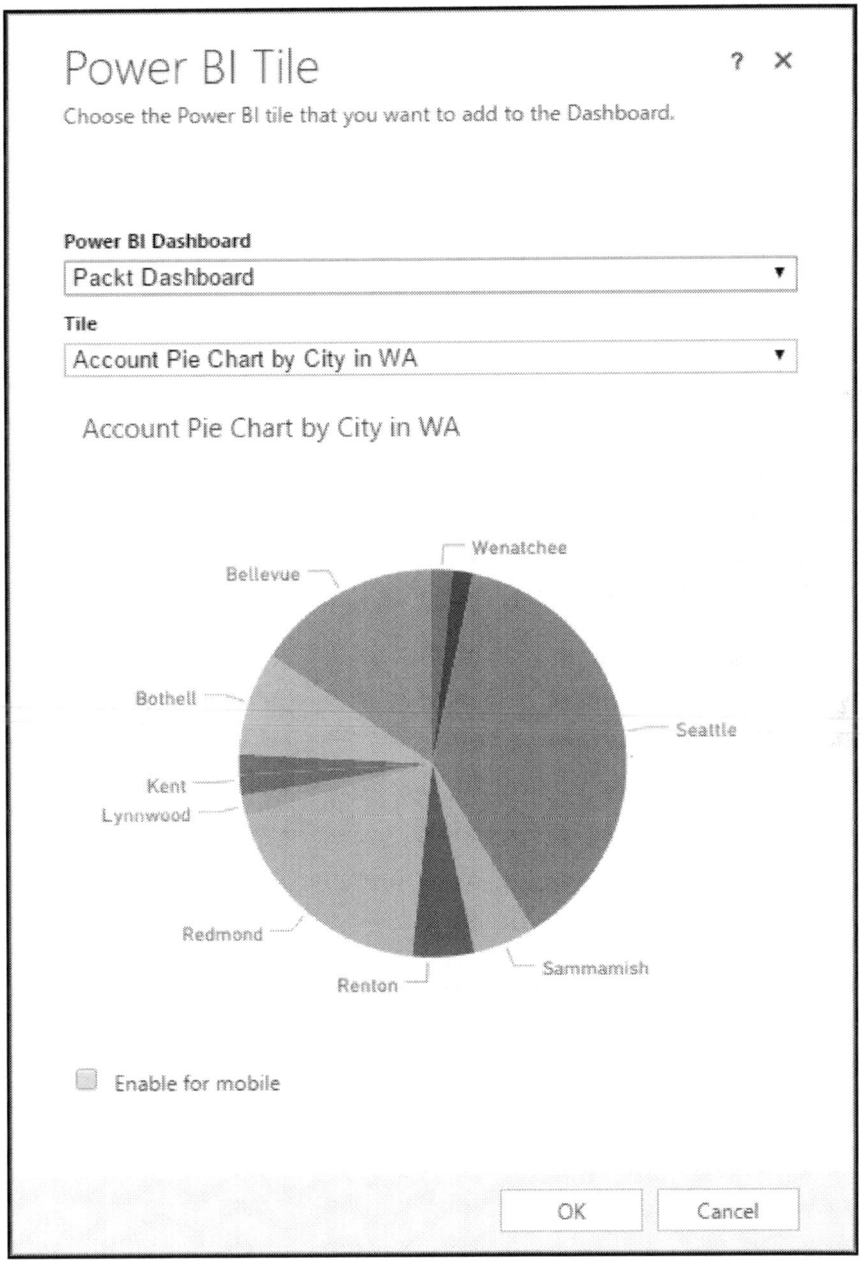

17. Click on **Save** and give your dashboard a name.

How it works...

In the first two steps, we launched Power BI and signed in using our Dynamics 365 account to establish a link to the platform which ensures that the published reports are hosted correctly and accessible by Dynamics 365.

In step 3 to step 8, we defined our data source and the entity/data we will be using. We entered our Dynamics 365 organization URL. Yours might look slightly different. If in doubt, you will get the correct value under **Settings** | **Customizations** | **Developer Resources** | **Instance Web API**. We then selected the correct entity, the correct columns, and the filtering criteria to report on in step 5, step 6, and step 7 respectively.

In step 9, we built our pie chart by dragging and dropping the `address1_city` attribute into the correct chart sections (details and values). We kept the legend empty for simplicity and then published to Power BI in step 10.

In Power BI, online, we ensured that the chart is positioned on a newly created easy-to-find dashboard in step 12 and step 13.

Finally, in step 14 to step 17, we created a Dynamics 365 dashboard that hosts the Power BI chart. Given that we are using the same account in Power BI Desktop, Power BI online, and Dynamics 365, our chart will seamlessly appear as we move from one platform to another.

There's more...

Once again, we touched on what this powerful platform can do. This recipe is not focused on the capabilities of Power BI, but rather integrating Power BI with Dynamics 365. In fact, the chart could just as easily have been created using out-of-the-box Dynamics 365 capabilities.

From a licensing perspective, Power BI comes in two flavors: a free limited version and a pro version. For more details about pricing and capabilities, refer to the following article at `https://powerbi.microsoft.com/en-us/pricing/`.

A
Architectural Views

With a career that spans across development and architecture, I was keen to include a chapter about architecture in this book. Given that it doesn't fit the cookbook format, I settled for an additional appendix.

In the typical solution architecture documentation fashion, I will highlight the different architectural viewpoints relevant to different stakeholders during a Dynamics 365 implementation. Most of the solution architecture document content is driven from requirements. Given that the appendix is for a generic solution, it will focus on out-of-the-box capabilities that were covered in this book.

In this chapter, I will cover the following views:

- **Business view**: Describes the different business capabilities of a Dynamics 365 platform
- **Logical view**: A sample logical representation of Dynamics 365 components
- **Deployment view**: Focuses on DevOps and deployment capabilities of the Dynamics 365 platform

As an architect, I am also responsible for addressing **non-functional requirements** (**NFRs**). Dynamics 365 covers the majority of the NFRs out-of-the-box, with extension options to expand the capabilities, as discussed later in the appendix.

Given Microsoft's recent cloud-first strategy, the rest of this chapter will focus on Dynamics 365 online SaaS offered by Microsoft. As such, the Physical View has been dropped as it would only make sense if the solution has specific Azure-hosted components, which is beyond the scope of this book.

Business view

Dynamics 365 is converting its offering into a set of modularized components that can be deployed to a base platform. Currently this includes **Sales**, **Customer Service**, **Project Service Automation** (**PSA**), and **Field Services** (**FS**) modules that can be purchased separately. Over time, even the core customer module could potentially be offered as a separate component.

The following diagram highlights some of the out-of-the-box Dynamics 365 Business capabilities, as well as some of the available extensions:

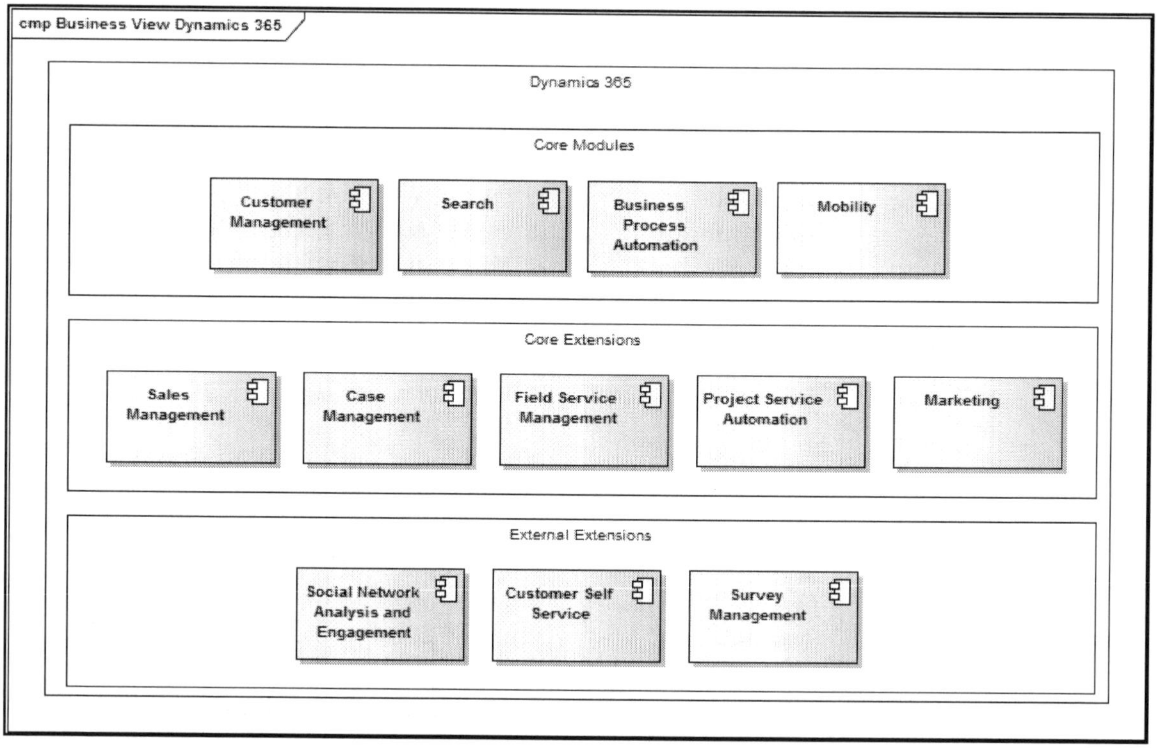

Customer management

Customer management is one of the core components catered for by Dynamics 365. The customer management module was even core to the first Microsoft CRM release; it represents the *C* in CRM. This screenshot highlights the Sales module navigation that provides most of the customer management capabilities:

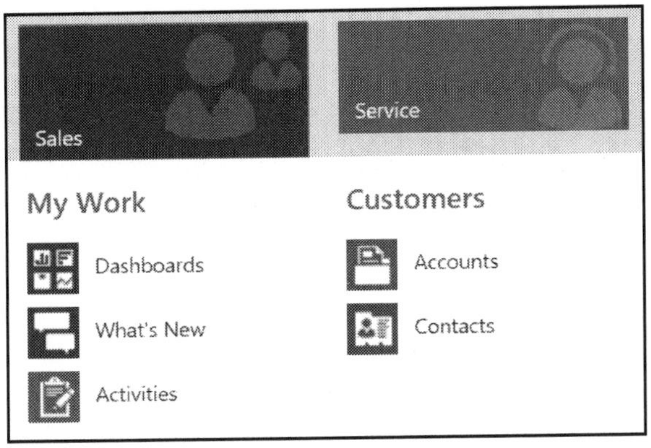

Customer management offers out-of-the-box, fully-configured account and contact entities, along with their relationships. Furthermore, the customer module offers a range of interactions (activities) that can be associated with accounts, contacts, or Dynamics 365 users. Activities can be any of the following: e-mails, letters, phone calls, faxes, or appointments. Custom activity types can also be configured to fill any gap not provided with out-of-the-box types. Historical and future activity views give you a 360 visualization of all interactions that have been had, or ones to be had with a customer. Activities are also used for internal staff collaboration.

Search

Dynamics 365 currently offers three different kinds of search capabilities, with a fourth option recently announced; these are as follows:

- **Quick global search**: Keyword search across multiple entities
- **Entity quick search**: Keyword search targeted at one entity
- **Advanced Find**: Targeted entity search using a point and click query building user interface
- **Custom Search (future)**: Microsoft recently announced search extensions using third-party search engines

Sales management

The sales module is also one of the long-standing modules introduced during the early days of CRM. As the name would suggest, the sales module is focused on the sales pipeline. It offers the capability of recording leads, opportunities, sales, products, pricelists, invoices, purchase history, KPIs, and goals. Over the years, the out-of-the-box reporting capabilities improved to paint a comprehensive picture of the sales pipeline segmented per salesperson per month as shown here:

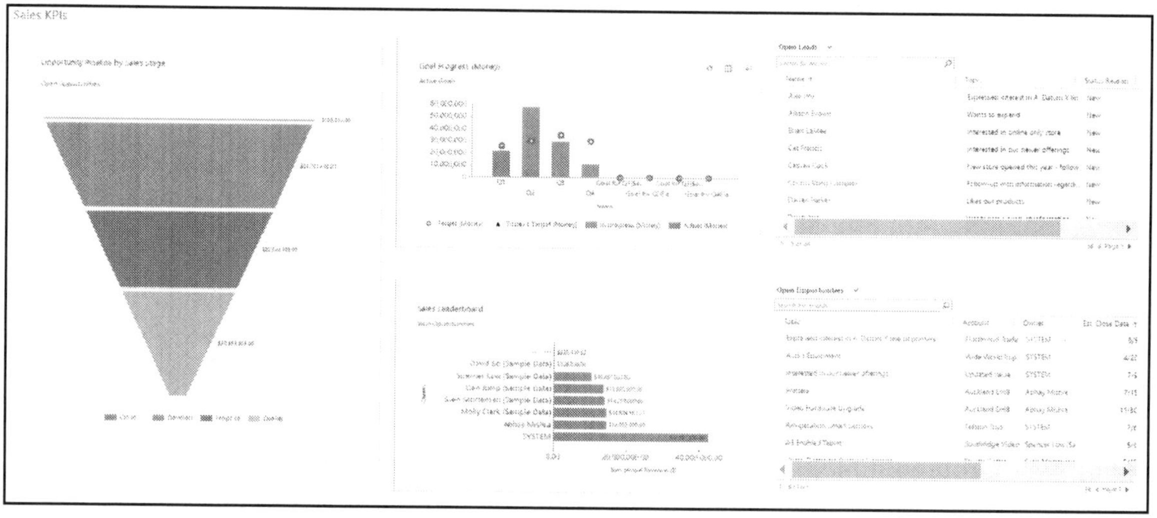

Case management

The Customer Service Module complements the sales modules, but is also a good standalone module that provides case management capabilities. Customer service is centered on creating a case and tracking its progress until completion. Case management, as well as other capabilities, can be guided by a business process flow that easily progresses a case by following a series of sequential steps. This ensures that all required information is recorded and that the correct process is adhered to:

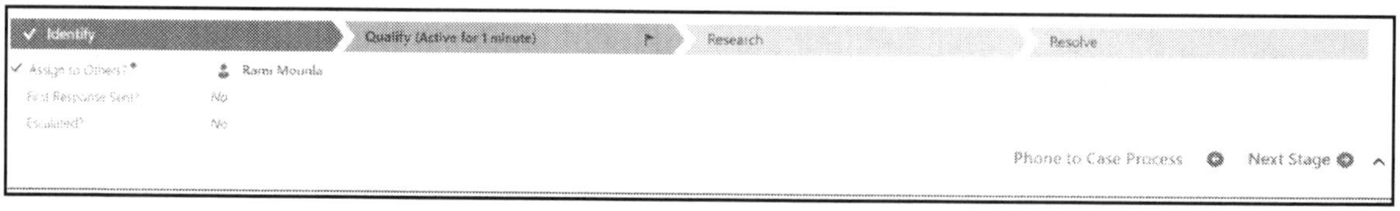

Note that a business process flow can also span across multiple entities.

Knowledge-based articles

The **knowledge-based** (**KB**) capability is usually also referenced within the customer service module. KB offers a repository of searchable, formatted knowledge articles to record solutions to previously encountered problems.

Field servicemanagement

Another good module that complements the sales module is Field Services. It allows the vendor to improve their sales end-to-end processes by offering scheduled maintenance or ad-hoc repair services.

Furthermore, this rich module includes resource management (capabilities management, automated scheduling optimization), GIS mapping, and even machine learning to suggest preemptive maintenance plans.

The Field Service module is a good candidate for integration with Azure IoT to monitor machinery and automatically dispatch maintenance jobs.

Customer self service

Dynamics 365 portals offer self-service portal capabilities which enables external customers to monitor and interact with records in Dynamics 365. The portal offers a secure way to surface the data using a modern web interface.

Marketing

The marketing module offers comprehensive end-to-end campaign management capabilities to initiate, plan, execute, and follow up on campaigns. The marketing module also provides out-of-the-box reporting to track campaign budgets, as well as customer responses/uptakes.

More recently, Microsoft partnered with Adobe and is planning on releasing a revamped marketing module based on the existing Dynamics module, as well as Adobe's powerful marketing suite.

Mobility

System of engagement (a story from the Dynamics CRM 2013 era) enables users to install Dynamics CRM/365 on their mobile devices so they can engage with customers whilst on the move. Mobile capabilities are available across a range of devices, and mobile devices can also work offline. Dynamics 365 follows the build-once-deploy-everywhere philosophy where the forms are designed once, with the final result rendering appropriately on each device based on the form factor. This screenshot highlights the different rendering types:

Business process automation

Workflows and business rule automation empowers non-technical users to automate business processes using a point-and-click user interface. This method is the preferred automation extension technique over code customization. The preference is due to its implementation simplicity and upgradability, which ultimately equates to cheaper implementation costs.

Project automation

Project Service Automation provides project management automation, starting from securing an opportunity, all the way to delivering a project. Planning, estimation, contracts, resource management, budget tracking, and invoicing are among the features provided by the module.

Survey management

The voice of the customer add-on provides easy-to-build (within Dynamics 365), rich control-enabled internal and external surveys. Survey responses can also be tracked and reported/analyzed. This specific module has a separate **Software as a Service** (**SaaS**) component that hosts the surveys accessible by the public. The surveys generated in Dynamics 365 are pushed to the survey portal and the results are synchronized back to Dynamics 365 periodically.

Social Network analysis and engagement

Microsoft Social Engagement (**MSE**) provides rich capabilities for monitoring and analyzing social media networks (Twitter, Facebook, news feeds, and many more). Sentiments, trends, and interests can be reported on and analyzed with the possibility to engage in conversations and convert microblogs to leads. MSE uses machine learning behind the scenes to understand sentiments.

Logical view

The following diagram depicts a logical view of a sample Dynamics 365 solution with some enabled add-ons and integration points:

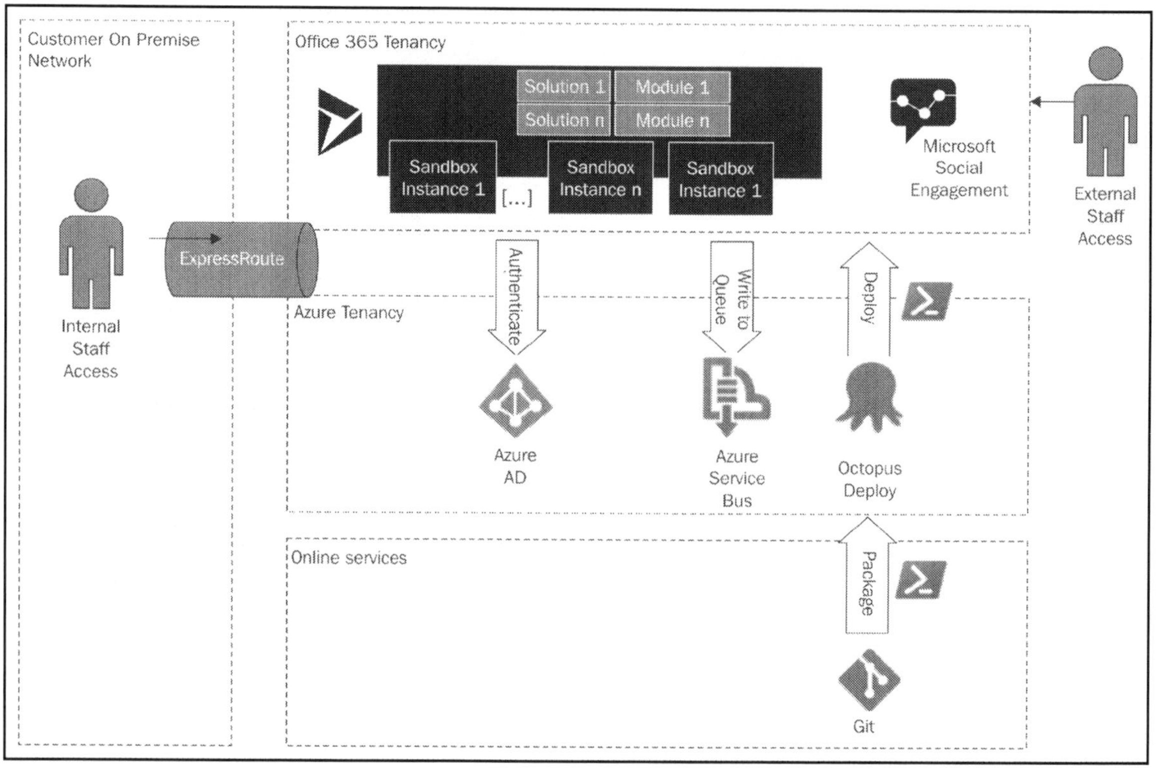

The preceding diagram highlights network/tenancy boundaries, internal and external access routes to the platforms, integration points (authentication through Azure AD, messaging through to Azure Service Bus), and deployment options.

From a Dynamics 365 perspective, it highlights solutions and modules (capabilities) installed on the instances, sandbox and production instances, and add-on SaaS solutions such as MSE.

Deployment view

The Dynamics CRM/365 DevOps story has improved with time. Microsoft kept the platform up-to-date by introducing scripting libraries to improve automation, which makes continuous delivery and continuous integration possible.

`Chapter 8`, *DevOps*, focuses on DevOps in general, including scripting and integration with deployment orchestration tools.

Manual

Over the years, manual deployments through the UI were the most common way of deploying Dynamics CRM solutions; this is still the preferred method for smaller solutions and standalone Dynamics 365 implementations that do not require integration with other products.

The process is simple. A System Customizer or System Administrator can upload a Dynamics 365 solution (ZIP file) to a new environment using the solution import user interface, as follows:

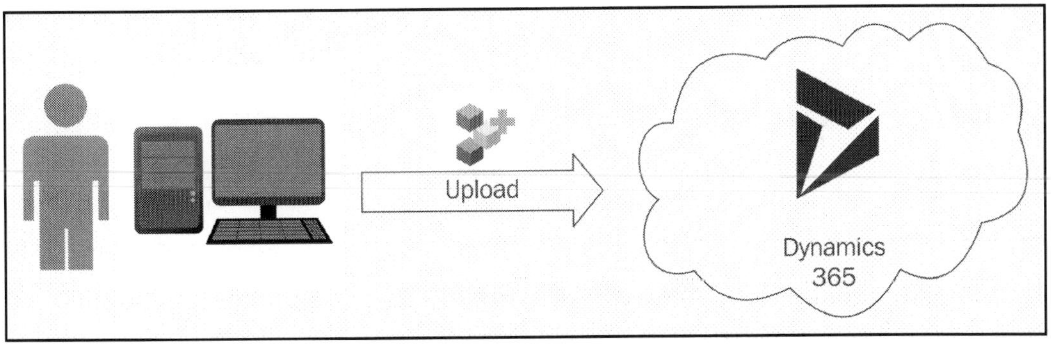

Automation

The introduction of the `Microsoft.Xrm.Data.PowerShell` module helped automate integration and solution deployments to Dynamics 365. The module enables CI/CD possibilities, as well as integration with deployment orchestration products such as Octopus deploy. The .NET Dynamics 365 SDK also offers deployment capabilities, which is the basis of the PowerShell module. Here is a sample continuous integration pipeline:

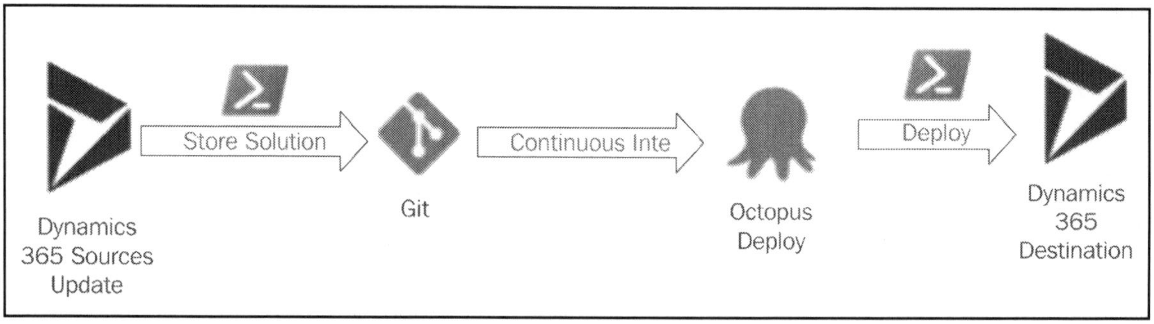

Furthermore, automated releases can be triggered when a solution changes in a Dynamics 365 source environment with minimum to no human intervention.

Non-functional requirements

When writing solution architecture documents, some common NFRs are always referenced. The following select few NFR qualities descriptions demonstrate how to address/answer the NFRs for a standard Dynamics 365 online platform.

Availability

Microsoft Dynamics 365 offers a financially backed 99.9% uptime SLA, as described in the following article:

`http://go.microsoft.com/fwlink/?LinkID=196557&clcid=0x409`

High availability is achievable through geo-redundancy, as described later in the *Data redundancy* section.

Only one site is primary at any one time. Upon a disaster, the secondary site takes over. From an enduser's perspective, the switch is seamless and automatic.

More recently, Microsoft announced multi-site read capabilities to improve performance using load balancing.

Reliability

Coupled with the 99.9% uptime SLA, Microsoft provides a wide range of internal monitoring capability to ensure that the platform is running reliably. This includes the following:

- Data redundancy
- Database monitoring
- Preventative maintenance
- Server monitoring
- Public and data center network monitoring
- Routine DR exercises

Most of the preceding features are covered in the Microsoft Dynamics CRM online Service Description located at:
`https://www.microsoft.com/en-us/download/confirmation.aspx?id=30185`.

Recoverability

Recoverability is achievable through data redundancy, disaster recovery, and backup and restore functionality.

Data redundancy

Dynamics 365 data is replicated four times. The original copy and a real-time replica are kept on the primary site. Two additional near real-time replicas are located in a secondary site within the same geo-location. Microsoft also holds copies out-site of your geo for extreme measures.

Some data processing might also be stored in other geo-locations, depending on the services used. Not all SaaS offerings are available in all geographical data centers, for example, machine learning is available in limited locations. Visit this site to understand feature availability across the different geographical centers:

`https://azure.microsoft.com/en-us/regions/services/`

Disaster recovery

Disaster recovery (**DR**) is exercised on a planned (frequent monthly/quarterly service updates) and unplanned (unforeseen outage) basis. Planned DR exercise results are not shared with the public, but submitted to an auditor for compliance. DR is transparent to endusers and solutions implemented using managed .NET code. For unmanaged code, a small routine is required to ensure that the solution falls back to the correct DR URL as described in the following article:

`https://msdn.microsoft.com/en-us/library/hh771583.aspx`

The Dynamics 365/CRM Online service continuity program ensures that the platform is up and running, and that outages are kept to a minimum. For further details about service continuity, read the following TechNet article:

`https://technet.microsoft.com/pt-pt/library/jj134081(v=crm.7).aspx#BKMK_CRM_Online_Svc_Continuity.`

Backups

Automated backups take place every day and can also be done on-demand. Backups are kept for three days before they are automatically destroyed. Backups can only be restored on sandbox instances (as a safety precaution).

Microsoft recently announced some enhancements to its Dynamics 365 backup capabilities where users can download offline copies or store backups into an Azure storage.

Security

The security NFR is covered by a few of the platform's capabilities as described in this section.

Data encryption in transit and at rest

Dynamics CRM/365 in transit data has always been encrypted when using the online SaaS offering. The platform currently uses the HTTPS protocol with **Transport Layer Security** (**TLS**) 1.2 encryption.

Recently, Microsoft announced that data at rest is also encrypted using TDE (`https://technet.microsoft.com/en-us/library/jj134930.aspx`).

> *"All instances of Dynamics 365 (online) use Microsoft SQL Server Transparent Data Encryption (TDE) to perform real-time encryption of data when written to disk, also known as encryption at rest"*

Read the *Managing your Dynamics 365 online SQL TDE encryption key* recipe of `Chapter 7`, *Security*, for instructions on how to change the key.

Online backups are encrypted for FIPS compliance and are stored in secured off-site vaults.

Authentication

Authentication for Dynamics 365 online is usually done using Azure AD (standalone or synchronized with on-premise Active Directory).

Authorization

Authorization can be done at several levels of granularity as follows:

- **Office security groups**: Authorizes users at the instance level. Office security groups can be synchronized with local Active Directory security groups
- **Security roles**: Authorizes access at the entity/business unit level
- **Access teams**: Authorizes access at the record level
- **Field level security profiles**: Secures access at the field level

More details about authorization can be found in `Chapter 7`, *Security*.

Compliance certificates

To address security concerns, Microsoft ensures that its data centers are accredited. Microsoft publishes all the compliance certificates its data centers hold. The following link highlights some Dynamics 365 compliance offerings:

`https://www.microsoft.com/en-us/trustcenter/cloudservices/dynamics365#compliance`

Auditability

Out-of-the-box Dynamics 365 provides audit trail capabilities to all entities that have been configured to log their activities.

Audit trails can record create, update, and delete activities; however, they do not record read logs. Read logs can be custom implemented using retrieve and retrieve multiple plugin messages, as described in `Chapter 6`, *Enhancing Your Code*.

> Auditing, in general, is resource intensive and will have an impact on performance, especially for on-premise installations. Furthermore, auditing requires a significant amount of extra space to store the history logs.

Audit trail logs are partitioned into three month blocks and can be deleted once the three months have lapsed.

Performance

Microsoft employs a number of techniques at different levels of the platform to ensure that performance is adequate for all of its customers.

Microsoft infrastructure

Microsoft uses scale groups to handle variable platform load--Scale pods are collections of servers that fulfill all the needs of a Dynamics 365 instance. Each scale pod has a different performance capability. As a tenant's load increases, the Dynamics 365 instances are automatically (and seamlessly) transferred to a more performant scale group to deal with the load. This mechanism also ensures that other tenants sharing the same scale group remain unaffected. The following screenshot illustrates a virtual representation of scale groups and their capabilities as highlighted in `https://microsoftaucrm.wordpress.com/category/microsoft-crm-cloud/`:

Hard limitations

As highlighted throughout this book, Microsoft imposes hard limits (timeouts) on process run times. The limits are there to keep the platform resources unhogged and performance under control.

Azure ExpressRoute

In 2015, Microsoft announced the compatibility of Dynamics 365 with Azure ExpressRoute. ExpressRoute provides a direct network connection between your organization (or through your ISP) to the Microsoft data centers. Connections like this enhance reliability and speed, decrease latency, and increase security. The following diagram illustrates a sample ExpressRoute set of capabilities:

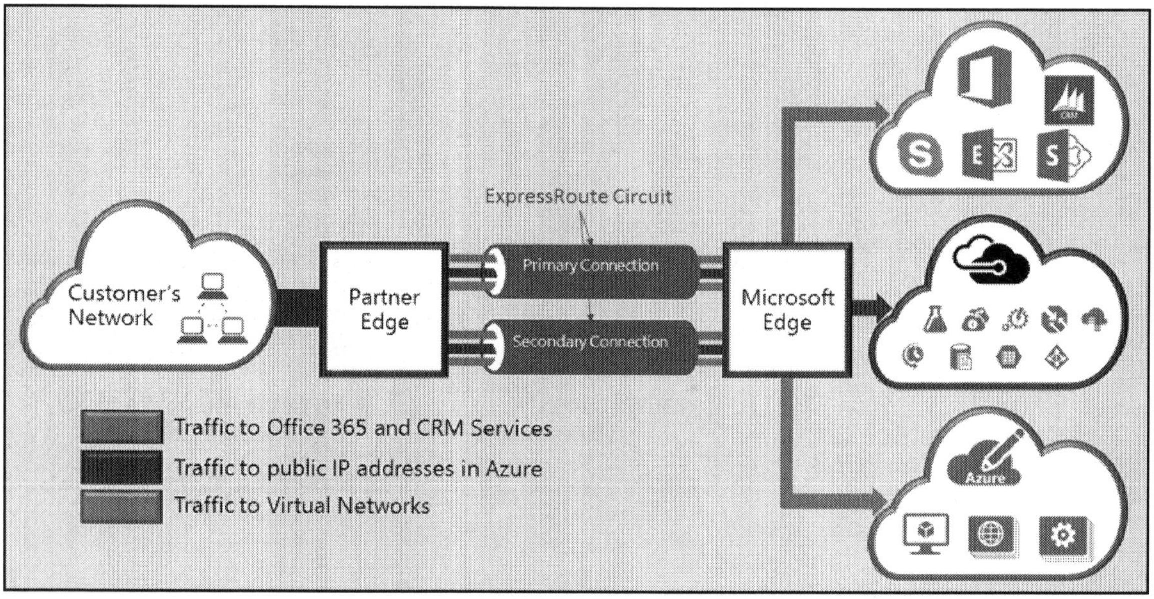

User interface enhancements

Microsoft introduced revamped forms in Dynamics CRM 2015 update 1. The new forms improve loading performance by up to 300%. The enhanced rendering engine keeps the loading time to a minimum, regardless of the number of fields displayed on the form:

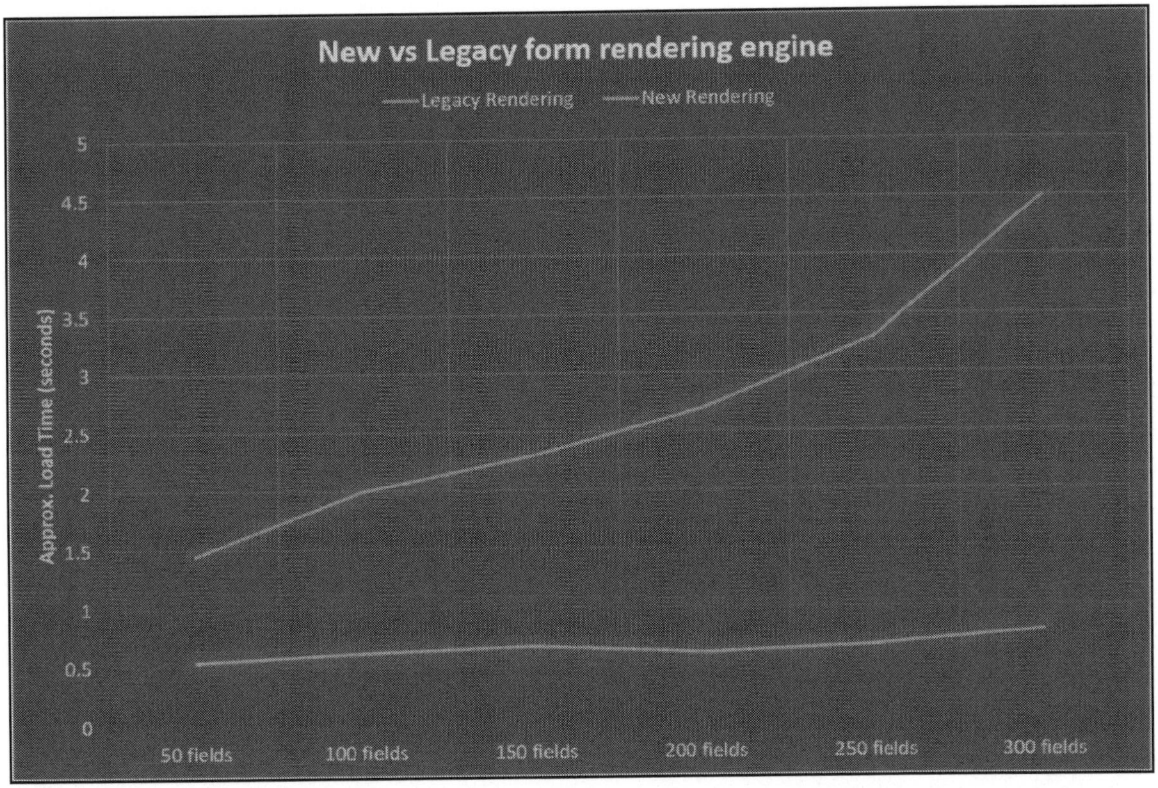

Further details can be found at `https://blogs.msdn.microsoft.com/crm/2015/04/29/microsoft-dynamics-crm-online-2015-update-1-new-form-rendering-engine/`.

Scalability

Dynamics 365 is capable of serving tens of thousands of concurrent users. As described in the previous section, scale pods provide an elasticity capability to deal with increased demand.

Interoperability

In `Chapter 5`, *External Integration*, we described all the different integration patterns and capabilities. The following list highlights some of Dynamics 365's interoperability options:

Web services

Dynamics 365 can easily be integrated with by using its out-of-the-box Web API RESTful services, along with OData v4.0 or the deprecated SOAP web services. Integration using web services is platform agnostic.

Plugins and workflows

Plugins and workflows are also good candidates for interoperability. Triggered Dynamics 365 events can be coupled with integration processes and other platforms. Plugins and workflows can run both synchronously and asynchronously.

Client-side integration

As described in `Chapter 2`, *Client-Side Extensions*, the client-side API provides full JavaScript capabilities. Integration with other systems on the frontend is a possibility, especially when coupled with other frameworks, such as Angular JS.

Integration tools

There are a few Microsoft and third-party tools that can also help in the integration with other platforms. Among them are: Scribe for data replication; KingswaySoft for SSIS packages; Microsoft Flow for business user integration; Dynamics 365 Data Export Service for data replication, and Azure Enterprise Service Bus and Microsoft Azure Logical apps for developed integrations.

Flexibility

This section describes how configuration and customization extensions enhance the platform's flexibility.

Configuration

Out-of-the-box, the platform provides a wide range of fit-for-purpose capabilities that require little to no configuration. However, acknowledging that there is no silver bullet, the platform is extendable using a point-and-click user interface to achieve the following:

- Schema and relationship configuration
- UI forms configuration
- Views, charts, dashboard, and report configuration
- Workflow automation and business rules configuration

Client-side extensions

Where configuration reaches its limitations, several other options are available. From the client-side, custom build web resources may include the following:

- JavaScript
- CSS
- HTML
- XML

Custom .NET code for server-side extensions

Custom plugins and workflow activities can be implemented using the .NET framework and the Dynamics 365 SDK. .NET extensions are typically used for service-side extensions.

Custom reporting

Custom reports can be implemented using **SQL Server Reporting Services** (**SSRS**) or PowerBI (see `Chapter 9`, *Dynamics 365 Extensions*).

Portability

Dynamics 365 is built using the .NET framework and a Microsoft SQL server backend. The platform is hosted on Windows servers and can be provisioned as Software or a Service, or deployed on-premise.

Dynamics 365 online database backups may be requested from Microsoft by logging a support call. This may simplify moving an online instance to on-premise, however, the move is not as trivial as restoring a database backup. The shift typically involves data migration exercises. Conversely, Microsoft is working hard to make the shift from on-premise to online as easy as a push of a button.

Reusability

Most of the Dynamics 365 extensions are built in a way to promote reusability.

Dynamics 365 common solutions can bundle reusable configuration and customization (schema, client-side, or server-side extensions) across different instances. Building reusable solutions is described in `Chapter 8`, *DevOps*. Furthermore, the Dynamics marketplace AppSource has hundreds of reusable Dynamics 365 solutions that can be installed on your online instance to enrich your platform's capability.

Deploy-ability

Solutions are at the core of Dynamics 365's deployment capabilities. They can be prompted from one environment to another. Furthermore, platform updates ensure a stable and secure environment.

Solution deployments

As described earlier in this chapter, Dynamics 365 solutions can be deployed manually using the Dynamics 365 user interface or automatically using PowerShell scripts or the .NET Dynamics 365 SDK. Deployments do not require a platform outage as they do not require shutdown/restart of the platform.

Rollbacks

Some solutions (managed) may be rolled back (although, sometimes dependencies might restrict which solutions can be uninstalled). Scheduled or on-demand backups can also be used as restore points to rollback a deployment.

Upgrades

Major upgrades to the platform are typically done every six months. Platform administrators have the ability to schedule an upgrade through the interface (opt-in). Upgrades can be delayed, but not indefinitely. Upgrades typically require an outage of thirty minutes to two hours within a twelve-hour window.

Manageability

Dynamics 365 can be managed from different locations, each with a different purpose and a different set of capabilities.

Through Office 365, administrators can do the following:

- Check the health of the platform
- View usage reports
- View upcoming scheduled maintenance messages
- On-board and off-board users
- Allocate or upgrade/downgrade licenses
- Submit a service request ticket to Microsoft
- Purchase additional Dynamics 365 instances or modules

Through the Dynamics 365 Admin Center within Office 365, administrators can do the following:

- View space usage
- Schedule upgrades
- Take ad-hoc backups
- Restore backups to sandboxes
- Reset instances to their vanilla state
- Convert production instances into sandboxes and vice-versa

Through Dynamics 365's Administration, area administrators can do the following:

- Manage user security roles
- Disable users
- Manage instance-wide settings
- Manage data (for example, imports)
- Customize and configure the platform
- Create custom business apps
- Check an instance usage using Organization Insight

B
Dynamics 365

Microsoft CRM was first released in 2003. Throughout the years, the platform has seen a significant number of enhancements to its rich offerings, as well as numerous modernization efforts. The platform saw a change in focus from system of records (relationships) to system of engagements (mobility) to now system of intelligence (machine learning and Cortana Intelligence). More than a decade later, Microsoft Dynamics 365 was announced bringing with it the most significant set of changes to the Dynamics suite of products.

A few notable changes introduced in Dynamics 365 worth discussing in this appendix are: rebranding, new capabilities, and licensing changes.

Rebranding

For the first time since its introduction under the Dynamics umbrella more than a decade ago, the platform has a completely redesigned new logo and a rebrand to Dynamics 365. The change marked a departure from its pure CRM roots to the new modularized structure that also bundled the Dynamics ERP products into one offering.

Modularity

Dynamics 365 was marketed as a set of modular components that can be purchased individually or as part of a plan.

At its new launch, the product offered sales, customer service, field service, project automation, marketing, and operations (previously known as Dynamics AX) modules as part of its enterprise edition. Module's business capabilities were discussed in Appendix A. Additionally, a **small to medium business** (**SMB**) edition was introduced, which offers a similar bundle with less modules, limited capabilities, and a finance module instead of the operations one (previously known as Dynamics NAV).

In addition to the Dynamics module mentioned earlier, Microsoft also offers PowerApps and Flow as add-ons to the platform. PowerApps provides easy-to-build mobile extensions to the platform that integrate straight with Dynamics 365 or through the **Common Data Services** (**CDS**) using Flow (we covered integration recipes in `Chapter 9`, *Dynamics 365 Extensions*).

Looking at the bigger Microsoft ecosystem, Dynamics 365 is marked as a good candidate to integrate with Azure IoT, Cortana Intelligence, Power BI, SharePoint, and many other platforms. Vertical solutions and add-ons can also be installed from the Dynamics marketplace AppSource (also covered in `Chapter 9`, *Dynamics 365 Extensions*). The following diagram highlights the different components of an end-to-end Dynamics 365 solution:

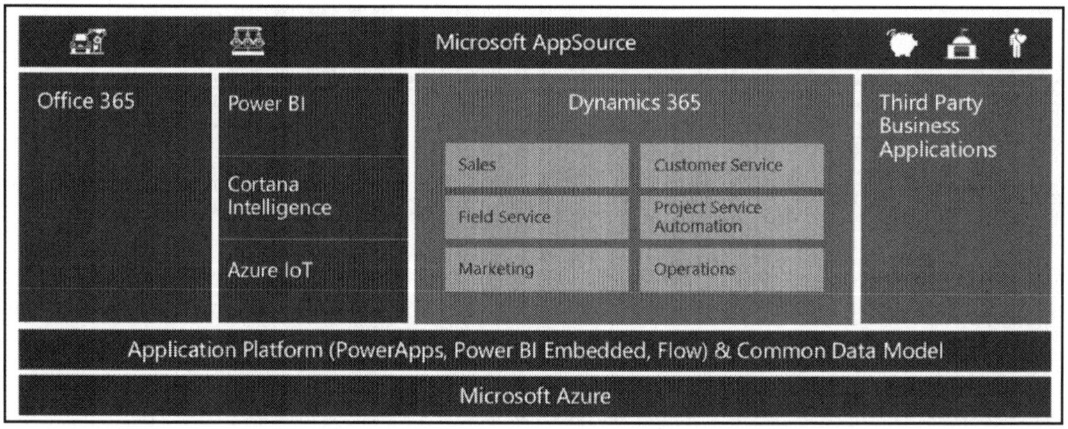

Licensing

From a licensing perspective, Dynamics 365 saw a departure from the familiar essential, basic, professional, and enterprises licenses to a team member, application-based, or plan-based licensing model.

Device licensing is also available for scenarios where multiple users access Dynamics 365 through a shared device. Volume discounts can also be applied to organizations that purchase a large number of licenses.

Team member licenses are equivalent to essential licenses in previous Dynamics CRM versions. Team member licenses only offer read-write to account, contact, custom entities, and a few other supporting capabilities. However, most of the remaining out-of-the-box entities can only be accessed in read-only mode.

The following extract from the licensing guide highlights the different access types based on the different license types:

	Team Members	Sales	Customer Service	Field Service	Project Service Automation	Plan 1
All Dynamics 365 Enterprise edition Data	○	○	○	○	○	○
Dynamics 365 for Operations functionality: Record Time & Expense; create requisitions; manage budgets; approval of Operations time, expense & invoices; edit & respond to inquiries for: quality control, service orders	●	●	●	●	●	●
Accounts and Contacts, Activities & Notes	●	●	●	●	●	●
Knowledge Management, Interactive Service Hub	●	●	●	●	●	●
Record Time & Expense, Manage personal information, Apply for projects	●	●	●	●	●	●
Custom entities	●[1]	●[1]	●[1]	●[1]	●[1]	●[1]
Dual Use Rights for equivalent Dynamics 365 CAL (if exists)	●	●	●	●	●	●
Run workflows & On-demand processes	●[2]	●[2]	●[2]	●[2]	●[2]	●
Microsoft Project Online Essentials, Gamification Fan & Spectator rights	●	●	●	●	●	●
Portal Only: Self-Serve Case Submission & Chat initiation as supportee (not agent)	●[3]	●[3]	●[3]	●[3]	●[3]	●[3]
Portal Only, Non-Employee Only: Update Work Orders, Create & Update Opportunities	●[3]	●[3]	●[3]	●[3]	●[3]	●[3]
User reports, dashboards, and charts	●	●	●	●	●	●
Configure system reports, system charts, system dashboards	×	○	○	○	○	●
Leads, Opportunities, goals, contracts, quotes, orders, invoices, competitors	○	●	○	○	○	●
Sales Campaigns, quick campaigns, marketing lists, prices lists, product lists	○	●	○	○	○	●
Unified Service Desk	○	●	●	○	○	●
Full Case Management, Services, resources, work hours, facility, equipment, articles	○	○	●	○	○	●
Work Orders, Schedule & Dispatch with Schedule Board, Service Agreements, Field Service Invoices & Purchase Orders, Customer Assets, Inventory, Repairs & Returns	○	○	○	●	○	●
Projects, Project Expenses & Estimates, Resource Availability View & Schedule Management, Project Price Lists/Contracts/Invoices, Approve Project Transactions, Microsoft Project Online Premium	○	○	○	○	●	●
PowerApps	○[4]	○[4]	○[4]	○[4]	○[4]	●
Microsoft Social Engagement, Voice of Customer, Mobile Offline, Gamification Player & Admin	×	●	●	●	●	●
Create workflows, bulk data import, and customizations across entities included in Application	×	○	○	○	○	●

● Full Access Rights ○ READ only/Limited access rights ✖ No access rights

Whereas this screenshot highlights the different types of usages based on different licenses:

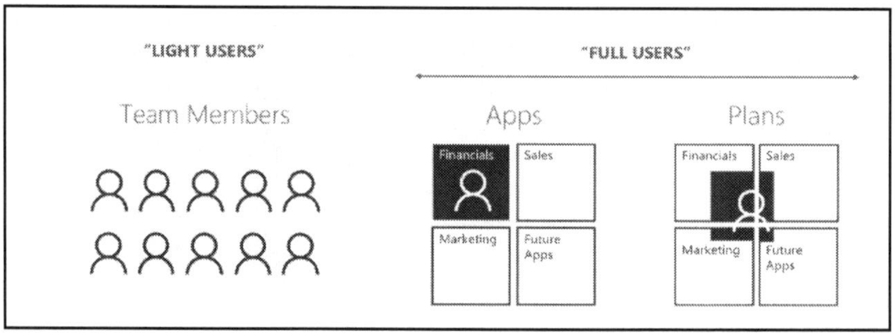

The application-specific licenses grant access to one or more modules. This license is the cheaper option for users that are primarily interested in one module. However, if users are interested in more than one module, then Plan 1 or Plan 2 licenses are the more economical options. A Plan gives you the license to use a collection of modules, as highlighted in the following screenshot. The Plan 2 license includes all of Plan 1's offering plus operations:

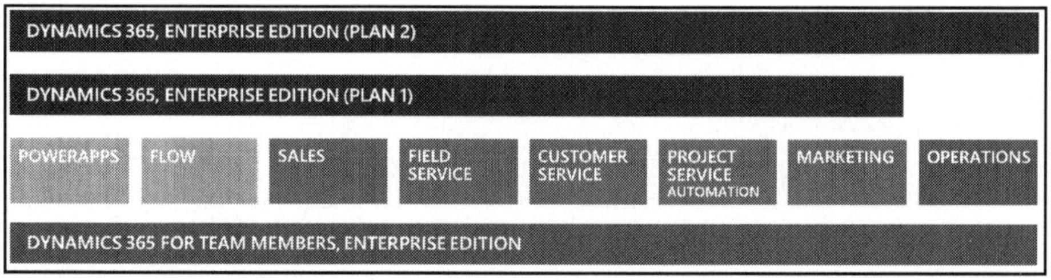

TIP

Different license types can be mixed between users within one Office 365 tenancy. Volume discounts can also be applied to organizations that purchase a large number of licenses.

Instances

Dynamics 365 instances were also revamped. Specifically, sandbox instances, which were once equal in capabilities to their production counterparts, are now classified into tiers 1 to 5. Tier 1 sandboxes are the cheapest basic instance with limited scalability, whereas tier 5 are the most expensive ones that mirror production instances and are capable of withstanding large load tests.

Storage

At the time of writing, a base Dynamics 365 package includes 5 GB of storage. Every additional 20 licenses offer an additional 5 GB of storage for your instances. Currently, there is a technical limitation of a maximum 5 TB of total storage.

> Dynamics 365 (Plan 1) and Dynamics 365 for Operations storage are counted separately.

Further reading

- To learn more about the enterprise offering, read the Dynamics 365 enterprise edition licensing guide at:
  `http://download.microsoft.com/documents/en-us/dynamics/pricing/Dynamics_365_Enterprise_edition_Licensing_Guide.pdf`
- For further information about the SMB edition, read the Dynamics 365 Business edition licensing guide at:
  `http://download.microsoft.com/documents/en-us/dynamics/Dynamics%20365%20Business%20edition%20Licensing%20Guide.pdf`

Dynamics 365 Add-ons

In addition to the core modules described in appendix A, Dynamics 365 offers a range of add-ons. The following Dynamics 365 Administration Center screenshot demonstrates a sample solution management page:

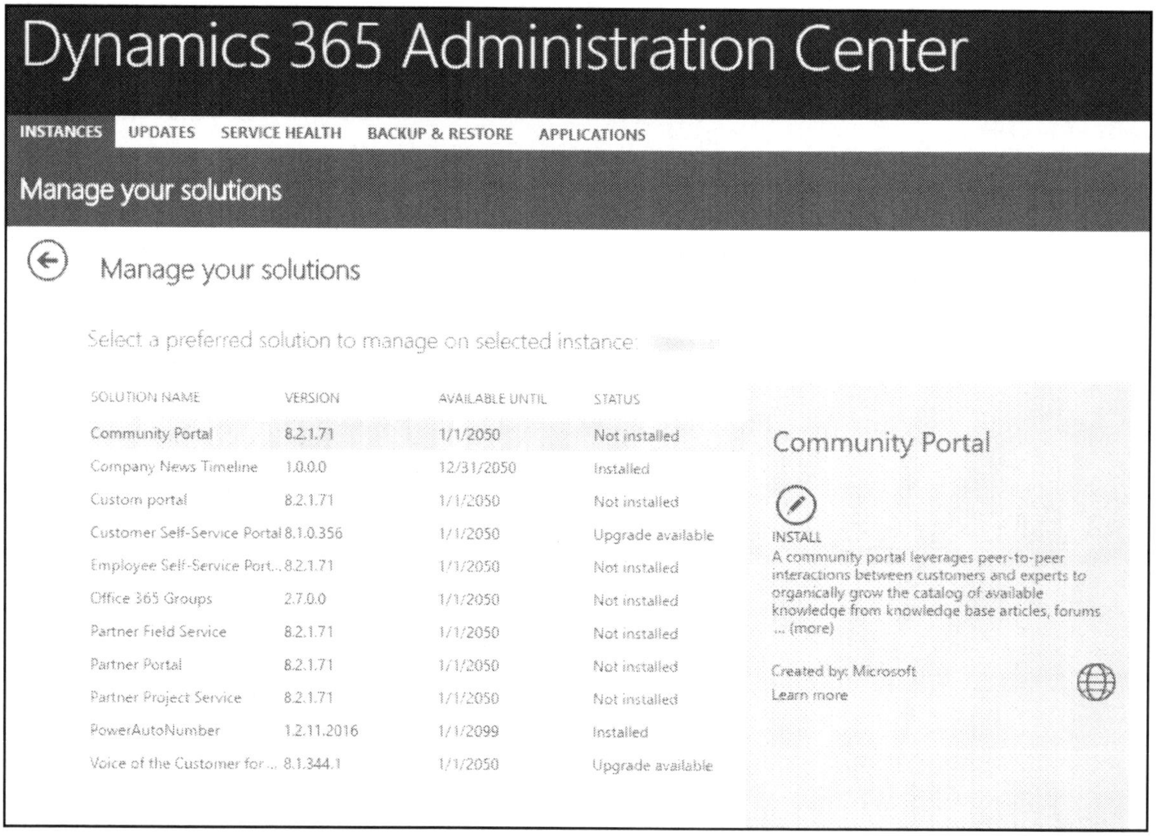

Some can be installed from the Dynamics 365 Administration Center by navigating to **INSTANCES** | **<Your Instance's Solutions>**, while others are available in the Dynamics marketplace, AppSource (`https://appsource.microsoft.com/en-us/`). Microsoft solutions are usually available through the administration center, whereas third-party solutions are hosted on AppSource. The following screenshot shows a sample selection of add-ons available on AppSource:

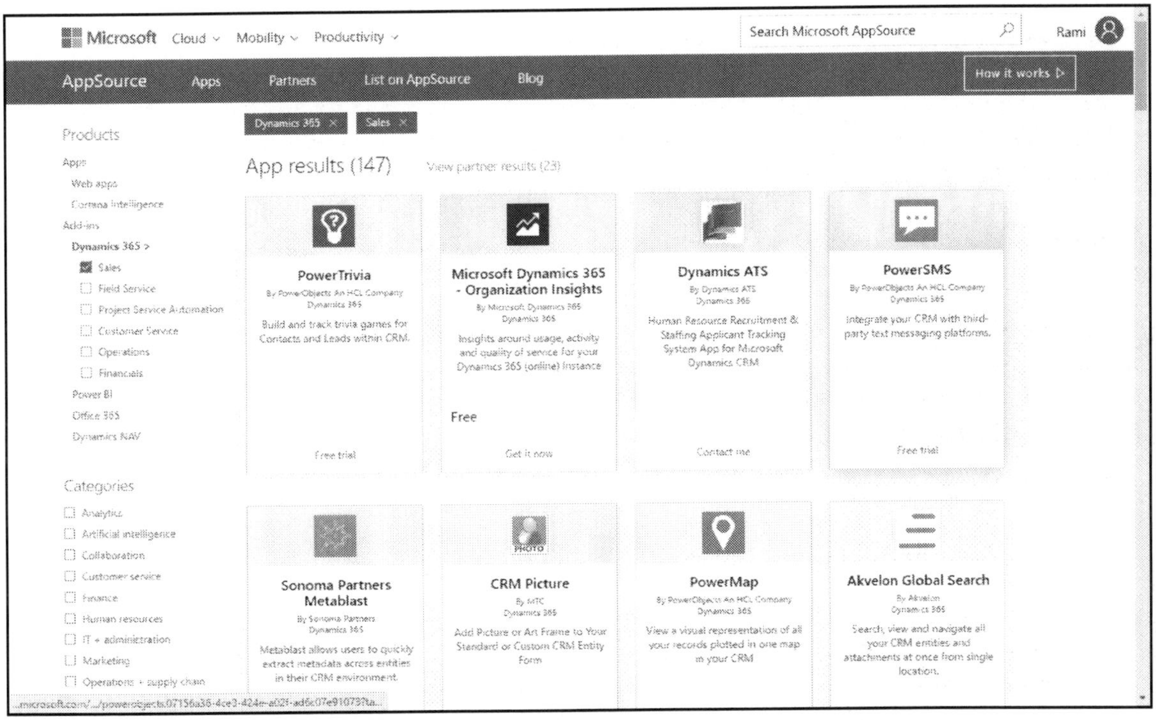

There are hundreds of additional add-ons available for the platform. Some are free, while others require a license. The most notable ones are:

- Data Export Services
- Microsoft Social Engagement
- Organization Insight
- Portals
- Voice of the Customer
- Gamification

Conclusion

Microsoft Dynamics 365 is a mature product that has a proven track record in the market world-wide. It is among the leaders in its magic quadrant. Due to its completeness, its rich set of comprehensive features, and continuous support from the Microsoft product team (with strong endorsement from Microsoft's CEO, Satya Nadella and direction from Microsoft Executive Vice President Scott Guthrie), the platform receives a lot of attention and is a breeze to work with.

Every year, as part of my MVP privileges, I get to meet the Dynamics 365 product team at Microsoft in Redmond, Washington. With no exception, every team member is energetic and enthusiastic about the product; they are eager to improve on it and to listen to any issues the MVPs and the community have.

Throughout this book, we have covered a wide scope of topics from no-code configuration, to hefty code customization. We also touched on the security capabilities of the platform, DevOps, and some of the more recent changes to Dynamics 365. Although only lightly touching on some of the topics to demonstrate the broad range of capabilities, this book is aimed at encouraging newcomers as well as seasoned Dynamics 365 users to broaden their skills and understanding of the platform and to encourage best practices when implementing large-scale solutions.

Hope you enjoyed it!

Index

E

K

L

M

N

O

T

U

V

W

X

Y

23536664R00255

Printed in Great Britain
by Amazon